GEORGE

GEORGE

A biography of
VISCOUNT TONYPANDY

Edwin H. Robertson

Marshall Pickering
An Imprint of HarperCollins*Publishers*

Marshall Pickering is an Imprint of
HarperCollins*Religious*
Part of HarperCollins*Publishers*
77–85 Fulham Palace Road, London w6 8jb

First published in Great Britain
in 1992 by Marshall Pickering

1 3 5 7 9 10 8 6 4 2

Copyright © 1992 Edwin H. Robertson

The Author asserts the moral right to be
identified as the author of this work

A catalogue record for this book is
available from the British Library

ISBN 0 551 02704 5

Photoset in Linotron Ehrhardt by
Rowland Phototypesetting Ltd
Bury St Edmunds, Suffolk

Printed and bound in Great Britain by
HarperCollinsManufacturing Glasgow

To Mam

CONTENTS

ILLUSTRATIONS

All photographs are taken from the personal collection of Lord Tonypandy

ACKNOWLEDGEMENTS

It would not have been possible to write this biography of so rich a character as the Rt Hon. George Thomas, Viscount Tonypandy, without the help of a large number of people. This has been generously given.

First of all, the subject himself of this book, George—and, as he says "even the children still call me George"—has been an invaluable help. He has taken a great interest in the writing at every stage of the book, and he has given me his expert advice on aspects of life which were quite new to me. He has commented freely on the drafts that I have shown to him, adding new material, but never trying to influence my judgements. This is not a book by Tonypandy. We already have his Memoirs. Without his hospitable help this would have been a duller book and the writing of it much less pleasant.

Two libraries have also been of great help and the staff of both have been kind, efficient and tolerant: The National Library of Wales, where Tonypandy deposited the greater part of his correspondence, and the Library of the Royal Institute of International Affairs in Chatham House. I am grateful to the staff of both.

Several people have allowed me to quote from their letters and I am particularly grateful to the Rt Hon. Lord Hailsham of St Marylebone for allowing me to quote at length from his letters to George at the time of Hailsham's bereavement.

There are many other people with whom I have talked, and government departments which have yielded up papers. Throughout I have been amazed at the readiness with which people have responded with helpful suggestions and information about a man whom almost everybody seems to like.

My thanks also to the publishers, and in particular to Christine Whitell, who has nursed this manuscript through many stages, as though she were bringing up a child. Her enthusiasm for the book has greatly helped in the more arduous parts of the work and her comments have proved very perceptive. I think it is a better book for what she has done.

Vera Phillips has taken on the heavy and detailed task of putting the book through her word processor and has endured a myriad of changes. Her encouragement and wise comments have added to the clarity of the writing. I am most grateful to her.

EDWIN ROBERTSON

PREFACE

On 29th January 1989, George Thomas, the Viscount Tonypandy, celebrated his eightieth birthday in grand style. Where else could it be but in Cardiff, where he had been for fourteen years a teacher and which he represented as one of its Members of Parliament through all his years in the House of Commons. There was a gala concert in the splendid St David's Hall, and a birthday party, but it was in typical George Thomas style. He asked for birthday presents, not for himself, but for the children. He is not married, but gives his love and support to the thousands of children who are cared for by the National Children's Home. On that special day, George invited guests to share his birthday by sending a card with a donation for the NCH, or by buying a ticket for the star-studded concert. The star who stole the show was George himself. He had postponed his treatment for cancer at St Thomas's Hospital until he had celebrated his birthday. The highlight of the show was the moment when Nerys Hughes led him by the hand to the stage, where he thanked his audience for gifts of £20,000 for the National Children's Home, of which he was then chairman. It was a celebration weekend, with a civic banquet at Cardiff Castle on the Saturday evening, morning service at Victoria Park Methodist Church on the Sunday, then this fabulous birthday concert on the Sunday evening. Next day, he was on parade again at the Princess of Wales Hospital, Bridgend, in support of their scanner appeal fund. Then back at once to St Thomas's Hospital, London, for the delayed treatment of his cancerous growth.

The *South Wales Echo* summed up that weekend under the headline "A Grandpa for all the Children . . .", with words that caught the spirit of this incomparable weekend:

> It was like a long, glorious weekend with Grandpa. Love and mischief, old stories, old friends, humour and heartache, pride and sadness, all rolled into the one magnificent liquorice all-sort, which is George Thomas, Viscount Tonypandy.

Once out of hospital, the celebrations went on, but he was a sick man. London's Guildhall was the scene for a glittering banquet given by the National Children's Home for their best friend and chairman on 3rd May. It was attended by the highest in the land, who honoured this miner's son who had achieved so much in a long life of service to his country. He rose to the occasion magnificently, although without a trace of arrogance; but ravaged by illness, he collapsed before the evening was ended. The television news cameras reflected both his fortitude and weakness, probing deeply in close-up.

Shortly after that evening I was due to see him at his home at Cardiff, and I wondered if that meeting would ever take place.

A few weeks later, when he was out of hospital and had recuperated in Cyprus, my Editor, Christine Whitell, and I called on him in Cardiff. He was as alert as a kitten. His enthusiasm grew with each memory recalled, each story told. He was planning a trip across Wales to Aberystwyth, where he had sent all his official papers. "I'll meet you at Cardiff station and drive you there," he said. I was not at all sure, but came the day and he was not allowing anyone else to drive. Wherever he went they knew him. The garage attendant was "my son", and he never failed to thank everyone for a service done. He was the soul of courtesy. He, who could talk straight to princes, put the ordinary person completely at ease—more, made him or her feel not ordinary at all, but unique and special. As we checked in at the hotel, they brought out the VIP visitors' book. He signed, "Tonypandy". Christine and I must have looked enquiringly, because at once, with his winning smile, he commented, "They expect it here. In the Rhondda Valley, I'm George."

At the National Library of Wales we saw the files of papers neatly arranged in sixty-two boxes labelled "Tonypandy". There was enough material there to furnish a series of volumes, for this man has lived many lives. But he was not in those boxes. There was a life which was truly George, and that life I was learning. His humour is irrepressible: "We're chapel," he said, as we came into the hotel lobby. "We have to have separate rooms." From that moment it was a procession of instant friends. People came to him who had only the slightest or even no reason for being noticed and he greeted them like life-long friends. Where there had been a real connection, he remembered it in seconds. Having packed us off to bed shortly after ten, because we had had a very busy day, he came back to join an impromptu concert in the hotel bar and to hear the pianist play "Cwm Rhondda" just for him. His stories never ended. All Wales seemed to be his near relatives, and the youngest would get special attention. A young student leaving the library was squashed into our taxi and before we returned to our hotel, George knew all about him and appeared to be about to adopt him! Next morning, I knew that this book could only have one title, "*George*".

The conviction grew when we drove back next day across the hills of mid-Wales and lingered in the Rhondda Valley. In Aberystwyth, he was treated like a lord, but in the Rhondda, he was King—a people's king, who had titles for others, but not for them. To them he was their "George".

We entered a pub at Treherbert at the upper end of the Valley and George did not have to announce himself. They would not bow the knee to a king, these men of the Rhondda, but they fell over themselves to take George's hand. He loved them all, and even the homely food served was received as though it were the best that Paris could provide. He was at home amidst the framed sepia pictures of early days in the Valley, or models of a mineshaft, amidst men—and one woman—who were tough and servants to no one. "No speeches here," they cried out to George, but with affection. Even the young men playing billiards put down their cues and edged to the door to greet him as he left.

We drove on down the Valley to Tonypandy. He basked in the recognition by his people. At every street corner we stopped to hear someone, and usually a crowd, thank God that he was looking so well and then recall some distant triumph or tragedy in which George had played a part. The history of the past sixty years of Tonypandy—the place where once they heard the sound of the turning wheel from which the town is named—came alive with every step. Tonypandy is written on his heart. It had to be the name of his viscountcy.

We drove on to Cardiff where he had once taught and later successfully stood for Parliament. His seat was always safe. We came back to his bungalow, which he had acquired for his mother and called by her maiden name, "Tilbury". His mother pervades the house still. She was and is the greatest influence in his life. His faith and his political convictions stem from her and from her remarkable father, John Tilbury.

CHAPTER ONE

◆◇◆

The Rhondda Valley

THOMAS GEORGE THOMAS was born in Port Talbot in the January of 1909, and his younger brother, Ivor, towards the end of the same year in nearby Cwmavon during a disastrous period in the life of the family. The older children had all been born in Tonypandy: Ada May in 1902, Dolly, 1904; Emrys, 1906. The whole family was back in the Rhondda by 1910 and it was there that they grew up. Tonypandy, like Penygraig and Trealaw, where for a time they also lived, lies in the mid-Rhondda twenty miles to the north-west of Cardiff. The valley ends abruptly in Blaenrhondda. The head of the valley rises to form part of the foothills of the magnificent Brecon Beacons, whose wild and untamed beauty contrasts loudly with the ravaged loveliness of the industrialized valleys below. They were a family of the Rhondda Valley, and George was strongly influenced by it. When he was eighty, he could say that half of his life had been spent in the Rhondda and half in Cardiff, but he was most strongly marked by the nature of the Rhondda Valley, its physical landscape, its communities and its chapels. When asked, in later life, for his recipe for long life, he replied, "Methodist faith and Co-op food." These he acquired among the mining communities of the Rhondda.

The Physical Nature of the Valley

There is an aching memory in the hearts of the people of the Valley, a yearning for natural beauty, which in its darkest days found expression in poetry and song. The phrase, "How green was my Valley", resonates in the mind like a Methodist hymn. Few people respect poets as the Welsh do. When he was a schoolboy going for the first day to Tonypandy Grammar School, George Thomas learnt this lesson in a way that he never forgot. Passing a road sweeper, he

I

saw the older boys take off their hats to him as they walked by. The new boy followed suit, but asked, "Why do we take off our caps for him? He's the road sweeper." The reply shamed him: "He won the chair for poetry at the National Eisteddfod. He is a great man." It summarized the Welsh character at the time and evoked the memory of the Valley's natural dignity before the coal smudged its face and shaved the luxurious growth from its hills.

Forty years before George was born, visitors to the Valley wrote of its "singular beauty" and "the emerald greenness of its meadows". In 1803, Benjamin Meakin described his surprise at finding so rich a valley far beyond his expectation as he travelled in South Wales: "The contrast of the meadows, rich and verdant, with mountains the most wild and romantic surrounding them on every side, is in the highest degree picturesque." Yet it was no Garden of Eden, softly nurturing its people. It was untameably wild. The densely wooded valley had to be cleared and food earned from the soil by the sweat of the brow. Even visitors who were entranced by the beauty found food scarce and life rough and harsh. "Oatmeal bread, with a relish of miserable cheese; and the beer where they have any is worse than none", wrote one traveller. Despite its physical beauty, the Rhondda was poor, its people dependent upon good harvests, with little reserve for the bad years.

The Effect of Coal Mining

A new source of wealth lay beneath the beauty of the luxuriant Valley. Coal had been known for a very long time, but it was extracted on a small scale, like petty pilfering from the gardens of Mother Nature. Coal, however, was eventually to reshape the Valley and its people, all but suffocating their natural love for poetry, music and beauty. The Eisteddfod bard who swept the roads of Tonypandy was a symbol for the entire Valley. Everywhere necessity threatened to silence the song of the soul. The parable of the road sweeper was not lost on George. The narrow, steep-sided valleys formed small, close-knit communities, often running into one another but fiercely jealous of their local independence. The exploitation of the coal in the valleys by landowners who were not of their number led to a shared poverty in which there was warmth, friendliness, pride and fierce passion. Whether they spoke English or Welsh, the people honoured their language and used it with richness and pride. Poverty did not make them mean, but equal. They had no time for class divisions and honoured people only for what they were or what they could do— love or write poetry, or sing, or trace with skill the generations of their ancestors. These things which they honoured had nothing to do with wealth, except the wealth of the human spirit. They came away from the hell of life "down the pit" singing in part-song. They challenged the ugliness of coal with the beauty of their voices which echoed the once green Valley of their memory. Yet every mother wanted to rescue her boy from the pit. This gave to the women of Wales that passion for education which they instilled into their sons, seeking to fill the colleges of Oxford rather than the nameless graves of victims of pit disasters.

The Gradual Change

The fires of the Industrial Revolution demanded coal, and under the rich verdure of the valleys of South Wales lay seams of the finest coal in the world. In the middle of the nineteenth century, Aberdare, Merthyr and Neath were "developed" but, for a while, the Rhondda remained "untameably wild". The forests and rivers were full of fish, game and wild life. George's grandfather—his earliest hero—would tell of how a squirrel could travel from the source of the river to Pontypridd, tree by tree without touching the ground. There was charcoal burning and the occasional outcrop of industry, mills and wheels. There were crops, however precarious, of oats, corn and barley. But the poverty of the Valley brought the people together in their need and they talked of new prosperity coming to the neighbouring valleys with the mining of coal. That prosperity would scarcely touch them, but would create huge wealth for the landowners and those who owned the equipment to extract the coal. None the less, some crumbs might fall to them from the rich man's table. They did not resist the coming of the mines.

South Wales knew enough already about ambitious landowners, who during the period before the mining development bought up the land and leased it out for farming or building. With a ninety-nine year lease, many felt safe with the houses they bought. George was to realize the insecurity of this much later. His first political campaign, after being elected MP for Cardiff, was in support of a Leasehold

Reform Bill. The grandchildren of those who had bought ninety-nine year leaseholds found themselves evicted in old age, and with huge bills for putting the vacated properties in order. Most of the Rhondda farms and estates came into the hands of absentee landlords, who bought the land cheap with an eye to rising values: the Marquis of Bute, who owned a considerable part of Cardiff; the Earl of Dunraven; Crawshay Bailey of Merthyr; and the de Winton family of Brecon. The management of community affairs was, of course, left in more local hands. These local managers were the lesser squires of the valleys: families like Hywel Llewelyn of Tyndraw, William Morgan of Maendy and Thomas Edwards of Tynewydd. These lesser squires were nearer to the people and understood the grinding pressure of poverty. They were yeoman farmers themselves and knew the vagaries of climate and crops. Many were compassionate and much loved. They were important in the Rhondda.

There was a close social structure below them, but it was nothing like as rigid as in England. There were tenant farmers who were respectable, but often poor. Craftsmen, such as wool manufacturers, smiths and masons, had their place in the structure and beneath them were the labourers, servants and apprentices. Everyday contact in the life of these isolated communities brought them to understand one another. Particularly in times of great poverty, when crops had failed, or prices had fallen, there was a rallying of the community.

Charles Preece prefaces his story of Mother Shepherd, a remarkable Salvation Army worker in the Valley, with an account of protests in the 1840s. These protests were by Chartists against injustice and poverty. They were supported by people of all social strata. The first chapter of his book, *Woman of the Valley*, describes the occasion when Bennie, a sturdy man of thirty-three, literate and in good standing, was called to support the demonstration against the authorities. His wife tried to dissuade him, saying it was no business of his, he was not affected by the poverty, but he insisted: 'The military are holding our missionary Henry Vincent and some of our men prisoner in Westgate prison. John Frost who used to be Mayor of Newport, Justice of the Peace, no less, has called us out to show our strength.'

In times of crisis the community closed ranks. The Rhondda Valley came more slowly to the experience of protest. It had been something of a backwater for most of its history, disturbed from time to time by events and disasters from outside—wars, plagues, industrial disputes such as the Chartists raised, or economic changes that lowered the price of what they had to sell and at the same time put up the price of what they had to buy. But these were temporary disturbances which their forefathers had endured since the fourteenth century.

The Quickening Pace of Change

The last and most disruptive of these periodic interruptions to the ordered life of the Rhondda came with the development of the coal industry. Its effect can best be demonstrated by the increase in population, mostly by immigration from other parts of Wales and from England and Ireland. Cwm Rhondda had a population of about 500 in the seventeenth century, and even by 1851 it had risen to only 951. Within the next ten years it trebled to more than three thousand. By the end of the nineteenth century, a few years before George was born, the population of Cwm Rhondda was 113,715. Slowly, the face of the Valley altered. In the mid-nineteenth century the Rhondda was still a rural valley with small pits in Trealaw and Tonypandy. It was in 1855 that the change came with the sinking of the first deep steam-coal pit in Cwm Saerbryn. After that there was no hope of saving the rural aspect of the Rhondda. By 1874, Thomas Nicholas was lamenting the loss of a lovely valley:

> A new spirit has entered the Rhondda Valley, which cannot afford room for other rubbish than its own. Deep pits, tall chimneys, whistling engines, long drawn out villages, with teeming multitudes of men, women and children, white by nature, but black from coal, are now the visible objects; and it is hard to believe that this vale was once the Gem of Glamorgan.

This was the Rhondda Valley to which George Thomas's grandfather came in 1872. He came, a distinguished Methodist class leader, from Petersfield in Hampshire, where he had known the prejudice and discrimination of the Established Church against Dissenters. He came with his wife and family to make a better living in the growing industrial area, and he succeeded. He turned his attention to building and became a building contractor.

Only a few years later, conditions in the Rhondda were vividly described in letters from the Salvation Army who, operating from London, wanted to send a young woman officer to conduct meetings there. In contrast to Aberdare, where the Army had been working, the Rhondda was described as

> one of the blackest hells in South Wales. Drunkenness, wife-beating, debauchery, gambling and cock-fighting . . . The devil and the drink sellers have it all their own way with the poor colliers . . . People say that it's not safe to go out at night unless you are prepared to fight your way along the road. There's just a narrow street at the bottom of the Valley.

The Rhondda was building a reputation for violence and drunkenness, 'men and women tearing at each other like wild beasts'. The Salvation Army had not actually set foot in the Rhondda by then, but knew its reputation. The root of the trouble was not the original Rhondda families, formed by the beauty of the Valley, but the multitude who had swamped the original inhabitants, and the conditions in which they were forced to live and work. How true the reputation was, it is difficult to say. But there is no doubt that life was rough in all the mining villages, and the rapid change with the influx of so many different people was bound to bring chaos. There is nothing strange about this to those of us who have lived in parts of London or any other deprived urban area. The Church of England report, *Faith in the City*, in the 1980s was among many that ascribed the causes of violence in housing estates to the influx of different kinds of people into an area and the crowded and insanitary conditions in which they were forced to live.

The Chapels

It was a pit disaster in the Dinas Colliery in 1879 that brought the Salvation Army in to do what it could for the forty-six widows and 130 children left fatherless by this tragedy.

The Salvation Army and the Quakers did great emergency work in the Rhondda Valley, but it was the chapels, more than any other influence, that ultimately made the Valley what it became. The Rhondda was now a settlement area, with the memory of the past continuing in the minds of very few. The hills were already scarred, and people scarcely believed that much-repeated story of the squirrel hopping from branch to branch the length of the Valley.

The Christian Church in Wales has a continuous history, owing nothing to Rome, but everything to the Celtic Christian tradition.

Long before Pope Gregory sent Augustine to convert the Anglo-Saxons, the Celtic Church sent three bishops to the Council of Arles in AD 313. In England, the Britons were conquered by the Romans, but in Wales they remained free. Neither appear to have made any attempt to convert the invaders, but eventually the Church of England embraced Wales too. This union changed the character of the Welsh Christians, who came more and more under English control. The Church tended to support the landowners and mine owners. It played an important part in shaping the character of rural Rhondda, but by the time coal came the influence of the Church was in decline among the people. The rebels, who were prepared to fight for justice, often found the Church on the side of law and order, advocating not only "peaceful" demonstrations, but often no demonstrations at all. The homilies frequently urged the people to be content with their lot, accepting the position in which God had placed them—"the rich man in his castle, the poor man at his gate".

There were political agitators, usually lumped together under the name of Chartists, and they were often quite prepared to resort to violence. Clashes with the police and sometimes with the army were frequent. The Church set its face against the Chartists. A revolutionary movement was ready to take over, but the good sense of the people of the Valley reacted against both the violent rebels and the reactionary Church. They looked for a compromise, peaceful, but clear about the demand for justice. It was found, in Wales as in England, in the Methodist Movement. It is often said that John Wesley saved England from a French-style revolution. Wesley remained a faithful member of the Church of England all his life, but he and his followers established a Methodist Conference of Churches, sending their ministers out travelling to convert the sinner. They preached sobriety, morality, honesty, faithfulness in marriage and a lifelong compassionate union. The Rhondda needed this message, but it also needed to hear the minister speak of the poverty of the people and of the injustice of the mine owners. Methodist preachers were not slow to do this. They trained their young people to think and to put their case with cogency. They trained them in the ways of democracy and to take the side of the poor.

But it was not only the Methodists who took up the Rhondda's cause. There were chapels of many denominations, some having the name of Methodist (to this day the Welsh Presbyterian Church is called the Calvinistic Methodist) with many varieties, such as Primitive Methodists and Wesleyans. In addition there were Welsh-speaking churches and English-speaking churches which divided all denominations. They all flooded into Wales like the charismatic movement of today. They brought enthusiasm, so often lacking and suspect in the Established Church, and they would not confine themselves to religious matters. For them, religion involved the whole of life. Their ardent followers spent all their spare time at chapel and learnt how to live more fully. The strength of the chapels lay in their determination to influence every aspect of life.

Religion was for them inextricably bound up with life itself, here and now, educating the children, cultivating the native instinct and expression in poetry and song, adding joy and happiness to every activity of life. It was only when the bitterness against injustice became too great, or when prosperity offered wider diversion, or the political parties seemed more effective in bringing about change, that the chapels began to decline. But there is always a feeling in the Rhondda that it could all come back again on a tide of religious revival.

The beginnings of Nonconformity in the Rhondda itself, however, were not so exciting, but rather slow to take off. In 1738 the Revd Henry Davies of Blaen Gwrath gathered a fellowship of the Independents at Cymner and five years later a meeting house was opened. It was not until 1784 that the next Independent fellowship was gathered, Baptist this time, by the Revd David Williams. In the following year, he baptized six people in the river and in 1786 the first Baptist chapel in the Rhondda was opened. It was named *Ynysfach* and cost sixty pounds to build! This was a very slow beginning. The tempo rose early in the nineteenth century when the Methodist preachers began to travel through the farmsteads. The first Methodist chapel was then built in 1830 at Dinas and was called *Ebenezer*. George Thomas was to preach there regularly in the 1930s and 1940s.

The naming of chapels with sonorous Old Testament names seems to have been the favoured approach of these nonconformist pietists: Bethel, Pisgah, Moriah, Mount Zion, Ararat can frequently be seen etched in the blackened stone of these sturdy little chapels, many of which have outlived their original purpose and nowadays welcome only congregations of Bingo players and discount furniture shoppers. As soon as the Methodists grew, the Baptists did too, and *Ynysfach* became a thriving cause.

Education was an early priority. Private schools existed, but they were exclusive and only for those who could afford them. The majority of the population had limited access to state schooling, which taught only the basic reading and writing skills. The Welsh Sunday schools soon took over the education of the children. They taught the tenets of the Christian faith, but did not stop there. Music, dramatics, singing and even mock parliaments featured regularly in the syllabus. They helped to form the culture of the valleys and brought out the genius of the Welsh people. But they also achieved something which many a country with an immigration problem might envy. They blended the cosmopolitan population of the Rhondda Valley into a unity. Even the English-speaking people from England became as Welsh as the Welsh. Many of them learnt Welsh, but not all. The devotion to the Welsh language does not alter the fact that bilingual Wales has no second-class citizens. At least that was true when George Thomas's grandfather, John Tilbury, came to the Rhondda in 1872 and was completely accepted. For him, as for so many who had come as "foreigners", the chapel was the centre of life—Welsh life. John Tilbury joined with six other English immigrants to form the Tonypandy Wesleyan Church. They met in an upstairs room of the White Rock Hotel, Penygraig, until their chapel was built. In the chapel life there were choirs, outings, discussion meetings that did not rule out politics, class meetings with much further education for adults, preaching by ministers and laity alike. Many a Welsh MP learnt to put his case in chapel before he persuaded Parliament.

The Eisteddfod was an event where excellence counted in word and in song. The male-voice choirs were famous throughout the valleys and soon became famous throughout the world. One is not surprised to find an opera singer, as good as any Italian, from Wales, and as likely as not he or she first learnt to sing in chapel. This is true of Sir Geraint Evans, Stuart Burrows, Gynweth Jones and many others. Chapel life had colour and those whose daily lives amounted to little more than drudgery found in that colour new possibilities in life. The quality of such art was high. The women in particular, whose lives were relentlessly hard, found a fullness in chapel. They were refreshed rather than tired by their voluntary service and they learnt to work in communities. A woman's social life was catered for through chapel guilds, choirs and prayer meetings. The chapel was so much more than a Sunday centre. It offered weekday activities for all members of the family, and these activities were not narrowly religious.

Most townships had also their parish church. Some retained the loyalty of a section of the population, but before the growth of the chapels church attendance had been declining for some time. A few social churches maintained by local squires or tenant farmers kept a good congregation. But the establishment of the Church, with its legal powers, tended to separate it from the mass of the population. This, in fact, continued until David Lloyd George brought about the disestablishment of the Church in Wales on the grounds that the great majority of the people of Wales were chapel people. From the moment of disestablishment, the Anglican Church in Wales has grown in influence in the life of Wales, unfettered by links with the state. But in the great days of chapel the balance was very much against the parish church. There were twelve parish churches in the Valley, but a hundred chapels, and they were all full.

So the ground was fertile in 1904, when the great Welsh revival led by Evan Roberts swept through South Wales, leaving its mark on the valleys for many years after the short episode of the revival itself was over. Until the First World War, the chapels were booming. Decline did not begin until after the bitter experience of war. God seemed irrelevant in the trenches except for a few credulous people. If God was powerless to stop the stupidity of war, man must take his destiny into his own hands. Pacifism became a creed as enthusiastic as the preaching of the chapels. Men turned to politics. Then came the Depression and soon the Labour Party won the support which the reformers had once given to the Liberals. The hero figure of David Lloyd George was replaced by men like Aneurin Bevan. The prospect of a National Health Service seemed more to the point than an offer of salvation or the cultural activities of the chapel. Men and women took their chapel enthusiasm and their chapel training into the world of politics.

It was against this backdrop of passionate religious fervour, physical struggle, bitter disappointments and frustration, met with an unfaltering and proud dignity by people of all kinds, that George Thomas passed his childhood and adolescence.

The Labour Party in the Rhondda

The Labour Party then had two distinct roots. There were the majority who found the basis of their social concern and desire for reform in the teaching they had received in the chapels. Thus the Labour Party included a substantial number who believed that they were supporting Christianity in practice. Some continued with their chapel activity but supplemented it with Labour Party activity. This was the group to which George's family belonged. His grandfather remained a Liberal, but had the same attitude; the reforming party was Christianity in action. He had to admit later that the Labour Party was now the true reforming party, but by then he was too old to change.

There was also a minority in the Labour Party who had never been influenced by the chapels—the Communists, whose roots were in Marxist doctrine, and those who had left the chapels because they found the congregations were not prepared for radical action. The Labour Party has never ceased to have its two sections—Christian-based and Marxist-based. There was inevitable conflict, but also much agreement about the results to be desired.

At first the Communists formed a separate party, but as Labour became effectively the only party in the Rhondda, many of them joined it. There remained a Communist Party and also an Independent Labour Party, both hostile to the chapels and prepared to fight the Labour Party in an effort to win over its supporters. The chapel men were constantly doing battle with the Marxists, but they soon had too much to do for such a peripheral activity. The Rhondda Urban District Council, Labour controlled, from 1920 concentrated much of its effort upon education, using what resources it had for that, and as far as it could it tried to help with employment. Injury and sickness were also a constant threat to a miner's life and they were all aware of this. The Labour Party fought the mine owners for compensation and always had in their sights the objective of nationalizing the mines. They did not dispute the owners' right to the land, but asserted that the minerals under the earth belonged to the people. When eventually the Labour Party came to power in 1945, the nationalizing of the mines was as inspiring as the storming of the Bastille by the French in 1789. The difference, of course, was that this post-war Labour Party had retained the deep compassion and understanding which are the hallmarks of a genuinely Christ-like way of life. Those who suffered were of their own class. They knew the terrible catastrophe of underground explosions, which were not an unfortunate accident for them, but stark tragedy, measured in terms of men whom they had known and lost. The poverty of a family which lost its wage-earner, the fatherless children living on the edge of existence—such suffering could not be solved by compensation, alone, but conditions could be eased.

They knew not only the public tragedies, which filled newspapers for a season, but also the private tragedies in which a man's health was destroyed, that needed compensation and legislative reform. Dust disease, now called pneumoconiosis, was more sinister as a threat, because it was hidden, than the loss of a limb caused by the crashing down of rock or shale upon a man's arm or leg. The inhalation of dust over a long period, causing obstructions in the lungs, together with poor housing and inadequate food, led to tuberculosis—an all too frequent occurrence in the South Wales valleys. Compensation was minimal and difficult to obtain. The regulations for granting such compensations were heartless and unjust. Even former miners who had been in receipt of pneumoconiosis benefits were registered as dying from heart failure rather than pneumoconiosis. This meant that no pension was paid to the widow and her family. Poverty and injustice, the lack of proper health care and inadequate security in the mines, were the devils these crusaders of the Labour Party set out to exorcise.

George's Inheritance

Into this background John Tilbury brought his family, and into this world his grandson, George Thomas, was born. It was his birthright. Nowadays he marvels that out of this grinding poverty and severe handicap could come a Speaker of the House of Commons. But for all the handicaps and the improbabilities, it was good soil. His father had come from Welsh Carmarthen, a chapel man who later spoiled himself by drink. His grandfather had come with the wave of English people, and because he had capital, he started both a shop and a building contractor's business.

His mother had chosen her own man, and had chosen badly. As a child George had known little happy family life, but he had felt the power of a warm Valley community and had a grand person for a mother, who cared and did not let her poverty prevent her from helping others. From her he grew into Methodism and a Socialist commitment, causes which did not conflict, but fitted like a glove over a strong hand. He suffered privations, he knew poverty; but he learnt honesty and how to love. When he looked back, he appreciated the comments of Raymond Williams, the distinguished writer on English literature and politics in the 1960s, who was asked whether his resentment against Cambridge arose from class envy, to which English privilege habitually ascribes all insubordination. Raymond Williams, like George Thomas, had been brought up in a poor Welsh rural home. His reply was: "Nobody fortunate enough to grow up in a good home, in a genuinely well mannered and sensitive community, could for a moment envy those loud, competitive and deprived people."

CHAPTER TWO

"Mam"

A VISIT TO THE HOME of Viscount Tonypandy in Cardiff leaves one in no doubt about the dominant influence in his life. The home is a museum of George's life, decked with photographs of the great, noble and royal friends whom he has known. It is stacked with books that authors have given to him. It is a tribute to a great and successful life. But it is also a shrine—a happy shrine and a proud one—to the one person without whom George could have achieved very little.

His mother was known by everybody as "Mam". It was a term of respect and affection. She was English with a tincture of lively French blood in her, but she was born and brought up in the Valley and no one there thought of her as anything but Welsh. If we are to understand George, we must know the strength and goodness of this most powerful woman, who bred him and formed his values, moulded his character, made possible what he could not have done without her and inspired him with a faith and a passion for justice that he has never lost. There were other influences, of course, especially his grandfather, Mam's father, and his stepfather, Mam's second husband. There was the Valley itself, with its strength and sorrow and the "genuinely well mannered and sensitive community" of which he was part. But all these influences were personalized and wrought into his system by the gracious tenacity of Mam.

John Tilbury

The influence of grandparents on a young life can often be quite considerable. Of George's two grandmothers he knew only one—his father's mother, whom he called his Welsh grandmother. She spoke no English. George spoke to her in the Welsh he knew as a second language. She died when he was six. Of the two grandfathers, the overwhelming influence was Mam's father, John Tilbury. The house George now lives in, and which he bought for Mam when she could no longer manage the stairs in the old house, is called "Tilbury". George remembers him as a hero, taking the place of his father who early deserted the family, a grandfather who had all the attributes of a Father Christmas—a genial and patriarchal figure of great wisdom and firm convictions in politics and religion. He is remembered as of ruddy countenance, "a cherubic, reddish face with a big white beard". He lived to the age of eighty-five, a strong man, greatly honoured in the community as one who kept his word. He was a pillar of the Methodist church.

John Tilbury was a Hampshire man with family roots in Clanfield, near Petersfield, where his parents had been prominent in founding a Methodist church in 1840. This greatly displeased the vicar, who until then had been able to say, as many did, "Mercifully we have no dissenters here." To be a Methodist in a rural area in mid-nineteenth-century England was to be greatly disadvantaged. If you were a tradesman, the influential Anglican community, sometimes encouraged by the vicar, would dissuade people from trading with you. It would be difficult to find a job and every hindrance was put in the way of your continuing your religious allegiance. In those days, even non-Church burials were difficult and weddings were only just beginning to be authorized in Nonconformist chapels. John Tilbury had to find work over which the vicar had no influence. For a time he bought and sold fruit and vegetables in distant markets, and he saved every penny that he could. We know that he went as far as Bristol, because it was there that he met his future wife, who was a lady's maid. This was a very respectable occupation, where girls could learn how to behave in society.

Elizabeth Loyns

George's maternal grandmother was the granddaughter of a Frenchman who had fled from the Terror which followed upon the French Revolution. Her family name, originally Lyon, was pronounced Loyns by the Somerset people. There are several entries in the records of births, deaths and marriages for the nineteenth century in West Buckland parish church register. Her father had settled in Somerset and Elizabeth grew up on a farm in West Buckland, not far from

Wellington. She was "in service" at the time John Tilbury met her in Bristol. A lady's maid would have to work hard and she could ply her needle with skill. No doubt a touch of French elegance added to her attractiveness and John Tilbury was a handsome man. They met and soon fell in love and married. John Tilbury had found a good wife and she a reliable husband. They settled in Petersfield and rented a shop which seems to have combined many functions. John sold vegetables from it, in addition to trading in the markets, and it was also a drapery shop, which Elizabeth managed. Theirs was a very happy marriage, with both working; their two eldest children, John and Elizabeth, were born in Petersfield and occupied more of Elizabeth's time, in days when children were not planned or spaced to suit household budgets, but were seen as blessings from the Lord, the natural fruit of love. The family lived above the shop, where the first two children were born. Soon a larger income was needed and John looked out for different work.

The Move to the Rhondda

The industrialization of South Wales, the opening of new pits month by month, the rapid expansion of the population and the consequent need for ancillary services, made South Wales an attractive place for a trader to go. John Tilbury took his family to Tonypandy where he thought at first to set up as a greengrocer. It soon became evident to his quick mind that the greatest demand would be for housing. He became a building contractor and prospered. There was plenty of work as the demand for colliers' houses grew. His rows of terraced houses helped to form the new landscape of the Mid-Rhondda.

It was in 1872 that he and his family moved to Tonypandy. The family increased and there were already five healthy children in their quite comfortable house when on 12th January 1881 their sixth child was born during a raging blizzard. She was named Emma Jane.

John Tilbury would often tell the story of how he first learnt that he now had to conform to the ways of the Rhondda, and he had no hesitation in doing so. He was received into the warm community without difficulty and he wanted to be one of them. In Hampshire, he had always gone to church in frock coat and top hat, no doubt as a way of showing the Anglicans that the Methodists were gentlemen too, but also because, at that time, most Nonconformists thought it right to go before the Lord at church or chapel in the apparel they might wear to approach a monarch. On his first Sunday in Tonypandy, he went to worship with the local group of Methodists, dressed in his accustomed way, but found that he was alone and very conspicuous. The other men and women had put on their Sunday best and took pride in their appearance, but there was no frock coat or top hat among them. He said to his wife afterwards, "I'll not wear my frock coat and top hat to go to church again, Elizabeth. People were turning to stare at me as we passed." A first lesson, but there were others. He learnt to talk of "chapel" instead of "church". There were adjustments to be made. It was a happy and comfortable family, all staunch Methodists and supporters of the Liberal Party.

One adjustment he could not make. Most of the chapels were Welsh-speaking, and learning Welsh as well as building up a business was too much. He picked up a little, but he wanted to worship God in his own language. He soon discovered that there were many others in Mid-Rhondda, in fact the majority, who were more at home in English than in Welsh. There was a need for an English-speaking chapel.

John Tilbury had made friends with a fellow businessman, also in the building trade, called John Hearn. They were both Methodists and both from England. They were involved in building houses for the colliers and, as Bible men, could hardly forget the condemnation of Haggai against those who had built themselves "ceiled houses" when they returned from Babylon, but had left the Temple in ruins in their midst. They, who had built houses, must now build a chapel for their fellow English immigrants. The English-speaking Methodist chapel was soon finished and grew apace. It became later the Methodist Central Hall in Tonypandy. Towards the end of his life, John Tilbury had the pleasure of seeing it being rebuilt to hold a congregation of a thousand people, with facilities for a wide range of activities. He did not live to see the larger chapel completed and opened for worship, so that it was in the smaller chapel he had built that he and his family worshipped.

This happy and closely knit family centred its life on the chapel and became as Welsh as any immigrant family could be. Even though they spoke no Welsh, the warmth and friendliness of the Rhondda made it home for them. Almost all the people in Tonypandy could speak English. John Tilbury came to the Rhondda at a boom time and saw it grow. Within thirty years of his coming the population had climbed from 17,000 to 117,000. These mining families formed a remarkable community, blending the characteristics of many different regions. If America was a melting pot of nations, so was the Rhondda. They came not only from many parts of Wales, but also in large numbers from England and to a lesser extent from Scotland and Ireland. The records show that some came also from Australia and the West Indies. Some may have been people who had been disappointed with prospects in Australia after the gold mining boom collapsed. For whatever reason, they came and stayed. In the days of a flourishing British Empire, families moved freely from one part to another. All these very different people melted into a community with recognizable characteristics. They had all been received without suspicion and they knew how to receive other strangers who came. Within a short time they were one community with a strong local pride. Unlike the gold-diggers of California or Australia, they came to South Wales to settle, not to make quick money and leave. The Valley, marred and smudged as it now was, had about it the fascination of age and its steep sides still held communities together. It was still a difficult journey to the outside world. When the trains came they were a lifeline. It was only later that they appeared to be tragic points of departure into exile for the unemployed. At this period of growth the railway meant that those who could afford the time and money were beginning to make contact with the outside world. Already the closeness of the communities, fostered by their chapels and motivated by their politics and their faith, increased the sense of kinship and belonging.

Where there was need, people helped. They received help from one another as from family, but it was only with the greatest resistance that they accepted help from the state. What made the pension acceptable eventually was to call it "the Lloyd George".

Industrial Relations

There were good and bad employers, but the miners usually recognized that mine owners and miners had a common interest in the success of the mine. Capital was needed to sink a mine shaft, and unless coal was found the money was lost and work was lost for the miners. This mutual interest in success led to some excellent industrial relations which we may read about today with envy.

A good example is that of David Davies of Llandinam. He had been a successful railway engineer, laying tracks in Britain and in Russia. He decided to risk his capital on mining for coal in the Upper Rhondda, but his venture looked set to fail as he ran out of capital before striking a seam. There seemed to be no alternative to giving up, which meant sacking the men and cutting his losses. That would have been a double disaster, for men and employer. He called the men together and talked the matter over with them and they decided to work for two more weeks without pay. It was a costly decision. The miners had few resources. But it was also a wise decision. If they were unemployed there was little prospect of relief until they had been reduced to paupers. They worked on, and before the fortnight was up they struck one of the richest seams of coal in the area. David Davies made a fortune and the men kept their jobs, demonstrating to the world that industrial relations do not always need to be confrontational. It was for men like these that John Tilbury built houses, long rows of them in Tonypandy and throughout the Mid-Rhondda.

A Defiant Daughter

Emma was one of the brightest in the family, but suffered from the considerable age gap between herself and her five older brothers and sisters, who thought they knew what was best for her. Alfred Adler, in his *Individual Psychology*, portrays the youngest child of a large family as fiercely independent, seeking to compensate for the disability of being younger and smaller than the other children. Emma compensated, by her rapid intellectual development, her tendency to lead and her fierce independence. The most significant example of this latter tendency concerned her one and only boy friend. She was seventeen, had never been much attracted to boys and certainly had never had a boy friend. The first boy she really noticed was a miner, whose family had come from rural Carmarthen. Four thousand others had come from that county into the Rhondda. They had no experience of mining, as they were more skilled with sheep than in heavy pit work. He was the same age as Emma Tilbury. His name was Zachariah Thomas. He noticed Emma and they walked out together. Emma was a totally innocent girl, who even after her marriage had to ask an older woman where babies came from! She liked talking with the boy who seemed to come from a different world. He was strong and brave and lived dangerously. One day, as they were standing at the corner talking, Emma's oldest sister Elizabeth saw them. Very unwisely she went up to Emma and said, "Go home! Leave him!" She should have known Emma better. The family might well have judged Zachariah Thomas unsuitable for Emma; they wanted a better marriage. But her sister's interference in public had angered Emma. She determined to defy them all and marry Zachariah. She accomplished her goal when they were both only eighteen. Many years later, when the marriage proved disastrous, she did not complain. That was not her style. She did, however, confess to George: "I probably would not have gone with him, except that I wanted to show off to Lizzie."

Zachariah and Emma were married in 1899. Things went well for some years, as long as they were in the protective chapel community of Tonypandy. In the first seven years, three children were born, two girls, Ada May and Dolly, and then the first boy, Emrys. Zachariah was Welsh-speaking and Emma wanted him to teach the children his native tongue and she would gladly have learnt it with them. He refused. In his wife he had a built-in English teacher and he saw some advantage in being able to speak English well. Emma would have liked them all to go to the same chapel and was prepared to go with her husband to his Welsh-speaking Methodist chapel in Penygraig. For some reason he resisted this. His family was as strongly chapel as hers, but Welsh-speaking. Emma was clearly more intelligent than he was and he may have felt threatened by her. So he spoke only English at home and attended with her the English Methodists in Tonypandy. The marriage seemed stable enough, although George comments that the father probably felt his freedom limited by the growing number of children around him. However, Emma had the man of her choice in defiance of Lizzie, and she was not the person to give up. She worked at the marriage and with her defiant spirit never admitted to any strain.

The Breakdown

So long as they lived in Tonypandy, Zachariah was supported by his chapel and he conformed to the usual pattern of chapel life; but he appears to have been a man easily influenced. For some reason, probably for better wages, he decided to move from Tonypandy around 1908, and take work in Port Talbot. The next two years were disastrous for the marriage. Zachariah was away from the restraints of chapel, unknown and in need of friends. Emma was preoccupied with the children and life was hard. He could not withdraw to his familiar chapel community and talk with old friends. The new ones he met in Port Talbot were not held within the moral restraints of a chapel culture. He began drinking with his new-found friends during those two years in and around Port Talbot. It was there in 1909 that both George and Ivor were born within eleven months of each other, so that Emma nursed them almost like twins. It was a busy life for her, and her husband's drinking bouts made it worse. He was still a young man in his late twenties and was already finding family life restrictive. By 1910 they were back in Penygraig and living in Hughes Street, but the drinking continued. He had lost all his interest in the chapel and continued to spend far too much money on drink. He would return home on Saturday nights, violent, smashing furniture and hitting out indiscriminately at his wife and children. His rages were uncontrollable. "Saturday nights," George records, "were a nightmare." The older children were ashamed of him. Years later, when the Boys' Brigade was on parade for the opening of the Methodist Central Hall in Tonypandy, the boys in full uniform unexpectedly met their father after a long absence. It was 1923. He simply walked up to them and said, "I'm your father." Emrys and Ivor stayed with him, but George walked away. George also has an earlier, more pleasant, memory of him at the outbreak of war when George was five: 'I can remember my father carrying me on his shoulders right down the main street of Penygraig.'

Friends and neighbours of Emma Thomas understood the hardship of bringing up five young children with a drunken husband. They saw her striving to support the children, taking on extra work, and protecting the children from their father. It was not Emma's way to admit that the marriage had failed or that the children should write off a father because he was drunk from time to time. She provided moral as well as financial support, but the poverty was hard. The neighbours did what neighbours do in a sensitive community. They saw where they could help without taking away the dignity of the one they helped. George was admitted to school even before he was three.

The family lived across the road from Penygraig Infants School, where their Methodist Sunday school superintendent, Miss Gould, was a teacher. She could see the pressure on Emma Thomas and invited her to send George over despite his tender years, well before the statutory age for school.

A Wartime Drama

There was some relief when war came and Zachariah, like many miners, volunteered for war service. He joined up at once and looked forward to an unrestricted life, away from his moral wife and brood of kids. He would be disciplined in the army, and maybe he saw that he needed this, but he would also be free in his leisure time. There was enough reproach from the community for Zachariah to find the army attractive. He went off, breathing a sigh of relief. The children were glad to see him go. Emma had mixed feelings. She knew that she had made a mistake in marrying him, but believed she had the strength to influence him and thought that she could make something of him when the children had grown up. How far he would be described today as an alcoholic is doubtful, but he was an undisciplined man. Emma thought the army discipline might do him good. She would certainly have quieter Saturday nights. But he was her chosen husband and the father of her children. After the war, perhaps, they could make a new start. He wasn't all bad. All the women of the valleys had found some pride in reforming their men and holding on to them. There was shame in losing your man or in giving him up. Financially, she would not be much worse off. His drinking had eaten into his earnings and although a soldier's pay was not much and the allowance to his wife even less, she did at least have something which he could not spend. She was also much less under stress, and found time and energy to work more herself. George tells a very moving story of waking up in the night and finding her sewing at two in the morning. She worked hard. Of course, financial hardship continued. Then, even the meagre army allowance was threatened.

Zachariah had not gone overseas at once, but like many others was processed in a camp at a home base before leaving for Salonika. He was billeted for a time with a family in Kent. He felt himself an unfettered man and there was a girl in the house. Before leaving for Greece, he married the girl and assigned his allowance to her. Emma, of course, knew nothing of this, until she went to the post office to collect her weekly sum, and was stunned when told that there was no money. The effect on the family was instantaneous. It was a household that lived very near the margin and, despite Emma's careful spending and supplementary income from her work, there was never much reserve. The children were too young to earn. George watched his mother wrestle with this insuperable problem and he vowed to himself that as soon as he could he would work and bring riches to the family. But neither his vows nor his dreams could help the immediate crisis and at the age of six he could hardly understand what was happening. Somehow, a malevolent force, vaguely connected with the army and his father, had robbed his mother of the money she needed to support the family. Their belts were not very loose, but they had to pull them in further!

Emma, of course, fought. After enquiries the army notified her that the allowance was being paid to the woman he had designated as his wife. Emma had to go to a tribunal to prove that she was the legitimate wife. She was intelligent enough to know the procedures and she had her first lesson in real politics. Again, the community helped, but the battle was personal and in her determination she won it. The army allowance flowed once more into Penygraig. What happened to the girl in Kent we shall never know. Years later, when George was driving through Kent, he turned off to see the place where she had lived, but did not try to contact her. It was a painful memory and at the time it was a battle for survival.

Poverty

Even with the army allowance restored, the house in Hughes Street was too expensive and the family moved to what was virtually a cellar in 139 Miskin Road, Trealaw, across the stream from Tonypandy proper, but really an adjunct to it. It was called an "underhouse". It is no longer used for a dwelling, but in those days there were many such homes in the valleys. An underhouse is a basement. It consisted of a small living room with one window, with a door that opened on to the pavement. Off this small living room were two much smaller rooms—poky box rooms— with no window at all. An outside lavatory was shared with other families. There was no room to do the washing, but Mam, as she was already called, soon discovered that there was room on the pavement. The rent for this underhouse was suitably low, but collected regularly each week on behalf of the owner of the whole house. You can still see the door to the underhouse in 139 Miskin Road, but today it forms the cellar to the main house. Although this move aligned the Thomases with the poorest families in Tonypandy, Mam's genius transformed the underhouse, at least in the eyes of her children, who never felt deprived.

Mam gave them more than riches. She gave them the basis of a good human life. Some of the lessons were hard, but they were valuable, and never forgotten. When the young George picked up a book which had been on display outside a shop and brought it home, he was promptly sent back. Mam insisted, not only that he return the book, but that he confess to the shopkeeper that he had taken it. Open honesty was required, and an admission of wrong done. Even harder was the lesson of the silver threepence! In Tonypandy there lived a Jewish man who in orthodox fashion kept the Sabbath. One of his problems in the winter, was the lighting of his fire on the Sabbath. One morning, he asked George to light his fire for him and gave him a bright threepenny piece. It was wealth untold for the little boy. But his joy was cut short when he returned home with the news. Mam would not have her boy rewarded for doing a kindness. He had to give the threepenny piece back! But it turned out all right eventually when George was allowed to keep the threepence on condition that he lit the fire every future Saturday for nothing.

It seemed a strict home, but it was a happy one. Contacts with Grandfather continued. Why did he not help in their poverty? He probably did, but Mam was independent and it couldn't have been easy to do what John Tilbury must so often have wanted to do to help them. Mam did not want charity, even from her father. She would manage. One of her oft-quoted responses when faced with a financial problem was: "We'll manage somehow!" And she always did.

The two girls went into service—as their grandmother had done —and that left Emma with her three boys: Emrys, George and Ivor. They had a happy childhood. They learnt in a kind school the satisfaction of honesty, the grace of courtesy, concern for others, the value of learning, the virtue of hard work and a genuine respect for the Sabbath. It was a school that produced integrity, not subservience. Mam never allowed poverty to become squalid in her hands. Even that underhouse lingered in the memory of the boys as a warm and

attractive home, bright with love, care and decency. George described
it seventy years later in terms that may have been softened by memory,
but reveal the loving care of a good housewife and mother:

> Our sparsely furnished living-room had a stone floor which was
> scrubbed with a hard brush every day, and was dominated by a
> splendid overmantel above the fireplace. It had a large centre
> mirror and three smaller ones, each with a shelf in front, decor-
> ated with twelve large brass candlesticks, which my brother and
> I cleaned every Saturday morning. There was also a mounted
> picture of the Wellington Monument near my grandmother's old
> home in Somerset. In front of the fire we had a home-made rag
> mat, and whenever it wore out, Emrys and Ivor and I made a
> new one. Friday night was bath night. We put a large tin bath
> in front of the fire and filled it with water that had been heated
> in saucepans on the open coal fire. After taking our turn to bath,
> we would gather round Mam's rocking chair, where she sat
> wearing her black sheen apron, and kneel to say our prayers.
> She would finish our prayers by asking God to help us to grow
> into good men and to bless our home.

Many a person brought up in the wealth of a rich suburban house
will read that description with envy.

George and Ivor were near enough in age to be like inseparable
twins. They shared the same bedroom, in fact the same bed, until
they moved in 1925 when George was sixteen. It was quite a ceremony
going to bed after prayers. The living room was lit by an oil lamp and
that had to be lowered while each child went to bed with a candle.
There was much variety in their life. All three joined the Boys'
Brigade as soon as they could and enjoyed the simple uniform and
the parades. There were all kinds of events at the chapel, where they
had some status as John Tilbury's grandchildren. But at home, too,
there were events. Hallowe'en was a family festival. The tub had a
different function then. Emrys, George and Ivor filled it with cold
water, stripped to the waist and "bobbed" for apples—nearly drown-
ing themselves in an attempt to bite an apple! There were peals of
laughter in the dark underhouse. Poverty did not rob them of joy.
Many who had much more than they had less fun.

Although Mam managed and did not go to her father for help, the
family was not isolated. In chapel, where despite their poverty the
three boys always wore their Sunday suits (for Sunday only, and to
be taken off after service!) they sat in front of Grandpa in his second

row. He would often come back home with them and give a father's guidance to the boys. He was old-fashioned, but loved. When George innocently began to whistle a hymn tune on the way back from chapel, Grandpa asked gently, "George, do you know what day it is?"— "Sunday, Grandpa!"—then equally gently, not in the imperious tone of a command, but in a caring voice, "Well, it's the Lord's day. You don't whistle on the Lord's day." Trivial? Perhaps. George did not resent it. In fact, he kept that deep respect for the Sabbath all his life. There have been few more eloquent speeches in his later years to match his defence of the Sunday trading laws in the House of Lords. And as he made that speech, surely old John Tilbury stood behind him saying, "You don't whistle on the Lord's day!" To this day, there is still nothing sad or legalistic about George's Sundays. He enjoyed his chapel and his Sunday school as a boy, and he enjoys it still.

The Scholarship Boy

There is no evidence that Mam had any favourites among her boys. Like any Welsh mother she wanted them to avoid the fate of the pits. She had that fervour for education that seems to belong to the Celtic race and is accentuated in Wales, because it offers the best way to find alternative work to going down the mines. Emrys at thirteen had won no scholarship, and without hesitation or discussion he went to the pits as his father had done. The family needed the money and Emrys played his part in support without complaint or comment. When he received his pay envelope at the end of the week he never opened it, but handed it at once to Mam, who handed him back two shillings. His habit then was to put the two shillings on the overmantel and say, "It's there if you need more money before Saturday." Three years later, when Ivor was thirteen, he took another route by working in a shop. Some years later he was apprenticed to Masters and Co., outfitters, at a salary of seven shillings and sixpence a week. That was 1928. Meanwhile, George was the one to be educated. "Why?" I asked him. "How did your family choose?" There was no special favour. His reply was quite simply, "Because I won the scholarship."

Although most mothers wanted to save their boys from the pits this view was not shared by the boys. They wanted to do a manly job and listened with excitement to stories of life underground. They felt envious of those who had already started work in the pits. George at first shared this envy, but not Ivor, who was frightened by Emrys' account of "rats as big as cats". After that George too lost his enthusiasm for going down the mines. This reluctance was accentuated one day when he was about ten. On the way home from school he saw a procession of miners carrying home the body of one of their mates who had died in an accident. Doffing his cap, he looked at the burden they were carrying. The body was covered with dirty sacking and George said to himself, "It's like carrying a dead dog." He recalls this experience as prompting the first stirrings in him of resentment against injustice, even of the beginnings of his dreams of reform. It also increased his determination to win that scholarship and go on to higher education. Dreams were not enough, nothing could be achieved without education. Like any good Welsh mother, Mam had told him that, and she backed it up with her own reading and determination to do something about the conditions in the Rhondda. Her own political views were already taking definite shape. She had left the Liberal Party of her father and had become a fervent supporter of the Labour Party. She saw hopeful signs in George and was not surprised, although delighted, when he ran home to tell her that he had passed the scholarship exam. She was out on the pavement with the washtub balanced on two chairs. George was full of excitement but also of anxiety. Could they afford it? The Labour council had abolished school fees for those who passed for the grammar school, but there was the school uniform to pay for and George would not begin to earn at fourteen like the others. The family would have to sacrifice to pay for him. Mam would have to break into Emrys' two shillings more often now. The budget was as close as that. "Can we afford it?" The smile which greeted the news of his success did not go away as she replied, "We'll manage somehow!'

Dad Tom and a New Life for Mam

A little frightened at the beginning of his new life at Tonypandy Higher Grade School, but determined, despite the persistent bullying of the larger boys, to fulfil his mother's hopes, George worked hard. He enjoyed the school and eventually did well. He liked the teachers and later paid tribute to the English teacher in particular—a Miss Llewellyn—and also to Miss Firstbrook who came all the way from Cardiff on a noisy motorbike. While he was there the school changed

its name from Higher Grade, to Tonypandy Secondary Grammar
School. But much larger changes were afoot at home.

In 1925, Mam married again. For ten years the three boys had had
her to themselves. She was theirs! Her commanding presence in the
home as father, mother, teacher, friend and guide did not alter the
fact that they assumed that she existed for them. Their lives could
change, but not hers. Of course, as they grew older, she could give
more time to political matters. She became President of the local
Co-operative Women's Guild and Chairman of the Tonypandy Ward
of the Labour Party. She was eventually elected as the representative
for Wales on the National Council of the Co-operative Women's
Guild. She spoke at meetings and the boys, especially George, went
with her. That was fine, they were proud of her. But at home she
was not expected to change. Now came this bombshell—Mam was
to marry!

Tom Davies was an old childhood friend, once an underground
miner, now a winding engineer, lowering and raising the cage with
miners or trucks of coal. It was a good job, well paid and not usually
susceptible to strikes. Winding engineers usually stayed on during
strikes to lower the safety officials and prevent harm to the mine. The
miners had learnt that they gained nothing by damaging the pits. It
took the children quite a time to adjust to this new man in the house.
Eventually they grew very fond of him and gave him the affectionate
name of "Dad Tom".

The marriage to Tom Davies made an immense difference to the
financial state of the family. He at once moved them out of their
underhouse into a pleasant three-storey house, built by John Tilbury,
who had died two years before. It was at 201 Trealaw Road, a great
improvement, but the house was in a poor state. They all set to work
to clean it and make it ready for their new home. One of the problems
was black beetles. Tom knew how to get rid of them. He bought a
load of cucumbers and together they laid slices all round the skirting
of the house. It got rid of the beetles, but put George off cucumber
for life! When all was finished, they had a fine home.

Life now changed dramatically and George began to forge ahead
with his studies. For the first time, he had a room to himself where
he could work harder on his books. His mother was still his main
encourager. She had accepted that Emrys should go down the mine;
she was glad that Ivor had found a cleaner and safer job; but her

hopes were in George. She knew that a poor boy from South Wales could do nothing without a higher education; but with it there was no limit to what he might achieve. She talked to George of a friend whose son had "letters after his name". But she was not interested in education for its own sake. She saw that there was much wrong with the country, that there was injustice and exploitation. George could do something as an educated man and no doubt she already saw him one day in Parliament arguing the case for justice in the Rhondda. At least, with education and wide reading he would know what he was talking about. She might also have seen him as a Methodist minister, guiding men and women in the ways of righteousness and meaningful life. She did not look for wealth or fame, although she would have welcomed both for her son. She looked for usefulness and a good influence upon society. This meant a faithful adherence to the faith he had embraced for himself and for which she had prepared him. He did not disappoint her. He inherited her values and made them his own. He admired her industry and roused himself often from lethargy by the memory of her example. Her strength of political feeling never left him and her independence of thought and action were his constant admiration. She was the greatest influence in his life.

It was a happy and busy household at 201 Trealaw Road, a miner's family, with one boy down the mine, another serving his time in a shop, father in a senior position in the mine and the hope of the family studying successfully. But it was all held together by Mam. She kept in contact with her girls "in service", guiding them and being available when there were troubles or anxieties; she looked after her husband and made a good home for him to return to after hard work at the mine; she discussed domestic matters with Emrys and watched him become a man of the mines; she advised Ivor carefully in his work and watched over him as the most delicate one of the family; but in George she put all her hopes of accomplishing something for God and the people. He was just sixteen at the time of the marriage and she helped him to adjust to his new father. Her ambitions for him were far beyond those he could understand at his age.

CHAPTER THREE

◆◆◆

The Chapel and the Labour Party

"METHODIST FAITH and Co-op food" encapsulated the two sources of George's strength and conviction. He both inherited them and acquired them for himself. The Methodist faith came through his grandfather and his mother. He could hardly have avoided it, but it had to become his own by conviction and not inheritance alone. What he calls the "watershed" of his life came at the age of sixteen in Judge's Hall, not very far from the underhouse where the family once lived. It was a special youth service at which the minister, the Revd W. G. Hughes, appealed to the large congregation of young people to commit their lives to Christ. He called upon them to "get right up out of their seats" and give public proof of their commitment by walking up to the platform where he stood. George tells his own story: "I felt myself go hot and cold. The challenge seemed directed straight at me. I said a silent prayer, and stepped forward."

He never went back on that decision, and every day of his life since, he has started the day with silent prayer.

It is permissible to speculate what might have happened had George not experienced a personal conversion. So many successful politicians had been brought up in the chapels and churches of Britain and remained no more than nominal members. In South Wales it was an advantage to be a member of the chapel, a dwindling asset in England. If George had remained only nominally a Methodist, the connection would still have helped him keep his parliamentary majority. But the moral restraints of a personal faith might have been loosened and he might have become an ambitious man. His own career might have become more important for him than his concern for those in need. He would not have been the first politician to forget his humble origins and the suffering of his own people in the glamour of success. As a Christian, he knew he could still do wrong, but he had to answer every day to his Father in heaven. That can be a powerful rebuke. He would have been more successful at many points in his life if he had not been hindered by his personal faith, but he would not have lived to be so happy and at one with his people and his God.

The second element was equally inherited and acquired. His grandfather had been a staunch, reforming Liberal whose hero was Gladstone, "the Grand Old Man", and there was no doubt about his achievements. David Lloyd George had his support, with his establishment of social services and improved conditions in industry. But John Tilbury was of Gladstone's generation and that was his brand of Liberalism. There had been no Labour Party in his youth. No doubt he recognized Lloyd George's failure to reconstruct the coal mines, but unlike others, including his daughter, he did not desert his loyalties to the Liberal Party. George was as yet too young to make an informed decision about whether the Liberals or Labour were most likely to right the wrongs done to the miners. He might have become a Communist, but that was never likely. He accompanied his mother as she went about speaking, and admired the way she calmly faced large crowds and dealt with noisy Communist hecklers. About the same time as his commitment to Christ, he also decided to join the Labour Party. He says of that decision that it determined the course of the rest of his life.

These two elements were brought together at a crucial moment both in George's own development and the development of the political consciousness of the people of South Wales. It was a little before the General Strike of 1926. The Revd R. J. Barker was appointed minister of Tonypandy Methodist Central Hall. His preaching was persuasive and crowds queued for a seat to hear his three-quarter-hour sermons. This was not revival, but radical preaching. Barker came from that section of the English middle class which had an acute social conscience. He knew the wealth of Britain and was shocked at the poverty of the miners. Adrian Hastings in *A History of English Christianity, 1920–1985* has written:

> In the England of the nineteen twenties, as much as in many a previous age, there were two nations. The prosperous, possessing nation had grown a great deal larger and rather more homogenous than it had ever been before. It was too large . . . but there was another nation. Millions of people were far too

31

poor, far too remote socially or geographically from the mechanisms of advancement and novel opportunities of entertainment, far too miserable in their living conditions, far too trapped in the mouldering stages of the Industrial Revolution . . . The miners were the single largest, most obvious case, but the inhabitants of all the major slums of Britain and most farm workers too belonged to this other nation for whom "the golden age" of the mid-nineteen twenties was no other than the bitterest of bad jokes. There were always over a million unemployed.

Barker preached reform vigorously. The conditions of the poor, contrasted with the comfort of his own class, convicted him and he preached with burning passion for justice. George drank it in. The memory of the dead miner carried like a dog by his mates, which had appalled him at the age of ten, quickened his sense of injustice. With other young people from the chapel he went about talking of revolution. But Barker had seen the danger in stirring these young people into action that could be exploited by the Communists. He was not going to make them into fodder for Communist revolution. In his preaching he attacked the Communists too, and insisted upon the importance of the individual and of the individual conscience, which he argued was the basis of our form of democracy. This remained the basis of George's political understanding as he worked towards a just society, but not for a violent overthrow or a dictatorship of the proletariat.

Barker found his source in the Bible, not in Marx. This was, of course, also true for George, but it was going to take him the rest of his life to work it out. The conditions imposed upon the miners had left him angry with an unjust society. He found in the prophets of the Old Testament a sympathetic anger. He hated social injustice and one of the many examples of it which he found was the leasehold system which drove people out of their inherited homes. He found it in the lack of compensation for injuries sustained at work. He found it in the treatment of old people in workhouses. He found it in poverty while the country counted its riches. In all this he did not find the Bible difficult to understand. The prophets, such as Amos, denounced the rich, those who ground the faces of the poor. He could understand Jesus' saying that it was harder for a rich man to enter the kingdom of God than for a camel to go through the eye of a needle. He had no need to read Karl Marx to denounce unjust capitalism. And Barker's preaching was just what he needed at that stage.

The General Strike

Tonypandy had a tradition of radical political views and George, like any other boy in the Rhondda, must have heard many stories of injustice and radical protest. The miners had combined in 1910 to strike and riots had followed. George knew of these riots only through the stories that he heard, but they had become legendary by this time in the mid-twenties. Older men who had been involved fifteen years before told their stories with increasing colour: of troops sent to subdue the rioters; of rioters coming from other valleys though local men went to gaol; of police behaving savagely; of police reinforcements coming from outside who couldn't understand the Welsh accent let alone the Welsh language; of people being beaten up in their homes. As George tells it in his memoirs, "The people of Tonypandy retaliated as the Celts had against the Romans; they went up the mountains to find the huge stones left by the Ice Age and rolled them down the slopes to keep the police away." All these stories were revived in 1921 when the government gave up the wartime control of the mines, and again in the 1926 General Strike. Miners clashed over wages, control and nationalization.

A nationwide coal strike began. Safety men were withdrawn from the pits, many of which were flooded and ruined. The miners called upon their partners in the "triple alliance" (the railway and the transport workers) to join them in a General Strike. At the last minute, the other unions, fearful of rising unemployment, backed down. Tonypandy was in the thick of all this and George was growing up with it happening all around him. Emrys was just beginning his work in the mine.

From the distant chambers of Westminster, it looked like ugly revolution. The Communists saw themselves as following the example of Russia and the men who had returned from the war to face unemployment were bitter. The heroes, those who in 1910 had rolled the stones down to keep back the police, were in George's adolescence leaders on the Council, solid burghers and supporters of the Labour Party. They were also the men who made up the male voice choirs in the chapels. They were George's heroes. The mythology of those days was ever ready to blossom fourth and the event which occurred when George was seventeen encouraged soul-stirring memories of those heroic days.

On 1st May 1926, the miners were locked out for refusing to accept a reduction in wages. After attempts at negotiation with the government of the day, the TUC called a General Strike. This decisive move sent Tonypandy into action. George was seventeen, small but strong, looked upon as a clever lad with a good education. He had been a member of the Labour Party for less than a year, a new Christian with crusading zeal. Truly it was "bliss in that moment to be alive and to be young was very heaven". All Tonypandy seemed to be on the right side of a great battle for the rights of man. There was a solidarity among the workers, all divisions were forgotten. Miners packed the main street. There was an anxious atmosphere, as though a new war had begun. Nine days later, the shattering news came that the TUC had capitulated. The General Strike was over.

The Miners Fight On

Everybody had expected success—even to speculate about less was treason—but now the high morale was gone. Despair gripped every heart. The miners must stand alone, and most of them knew that of themselves they had little strength. George walked home on the day the TUC gave in, fearful of what would happen. The family had just begun to taste a little prosperity with the new marriage and the new house. He was succeeding at school and was considering whether he should continue his studies to be a teacher, or possibly become a minister of the Church. Now, he might have to give all that up. Emrys would earn nothing on strike, Dad Tom might stay on as safety man for a little while, but he too might have to come out eventually. As unemployment took effect in the Valley, Ivor could soon lose his job. If the mines were damaged there might be long-term unemployment after a defeat in the strike. The owners could certainly hold out longer than the men. There would be no strike pay, and no one knew how long it would last or what would be the consequences for the Valley. In fact, the strike went on for seven months, with increasing hardship and little relief at the end.

The outlook was grim, but mining communities are strongly bound together by common danger. The women who ran to the pithead when the hooter sounded to tell of another disaster in the mine, supporting one another in their anxious grief, knew how to rally in time of adversity. The battle was fought by the whole community. There were no non-combatants. Men, women and children knew that they were fighting for their very existence and for the future of their community. They shared a common way of life and common values, fashioned in the chapels and the political parties, now pre-dominantly the Labour Party.

Food was the first requirement and the women organized soup kitchens. What they were ashamed to receive from the state, they received from one another with dignity. The soup kitchens were mostly located in the chapel halls and Mam was at the centre of the organization. They were mainly for the children of the strikers and the objective was to provide one nourishing meal a day for every child whose father was unemployed or on strike. George eyed these meals with a little envy. At seventeen he had a healthy appetite and they were good meals. His step-father was not at first on strike—the miners took care that the mines were preserved intact and encouraged safety men to continue at their task so long as they were permitted to do so—and because he was working, George was not entitled to one of those meals. Mam put much of her new-found prosperity into helping others. George was recruited, when not at school, to act as a courier, carrying messages from one soup kitchen to another. It seems to have been run with all the precision of a military operation. The women saw his hungry eyes and, although Mam would make no exceptions, the other women did. This lad, they said, who worked so hard, should have the privilege of one meal. He enjoyed his free helping of fish and chips, but only once. Mam would have no privileges for her own.

The Hungry Valleys

It was not easy to finance the soup kitchens, although the poor gave what they could. The generosity of the rest of the country soon dried up when the miners hung on after the General Strike was over. The TUC advised the miners to settle. Appeal to the rest of the country was ineffective. The valleys were hungry and resources gradually dried up. The Lord Mayor of London set up an Appeal Fund to help miners' families.

The Co-operative Women's Guild, of which Mam was president,

sent one of her predecessors, Joanna James, to London to raise funds. The miners never forgot her. For years afterwards, at Labour Party meetings, a point could be made with emphasis when punctuated with "Remember Joanna James". She was the first martyr of the strike. George did not see her on her return, but he remembers with feeling the shattering effect on those who did when she came back from her unsuccessful mission. She had found sympathy in London, but little else. Her story as well as her appearance shocked the miners. She had been given lodging in a house where they could not afford to feed her. Day after day she had stood on street corners, speaking to working people and collecting their coppers. They had also given her cups of tea and buns, but they were mostly people who had not much more to give. She lived on scraps for more than three months. Eventually, in George's words, "she was completely worn out and came home to die."

The Breaking of the Strike

The General Strike had lasted only nine days. After a compromise had been worked out and all except the miners had gone back to work, Baldwin felt that the government had interfered enough and washed his hands of the miners' stubborn continuance. Despite appeals from Lloyd George, he treated the miners' continued strike as a matter which concerned the mine owners. They must come to terms with the miners without government help. This was bad news for the Rhondda. They knew their mine owners and rightly expected the terms to be harsh. The miners' slogan, "Not a penny off the pay: not a minute on the day" was simple enough. It cut no ice with the coal owners. They had only one objective—to crush the strike—and they had no need to compromise. Wages were reduced at a time when prices were rising. The number of miners per pit was also reduced and those sacked were carefully selected from the so-called "trouble-makers". The owners were determined to break the spirit of this "radical" movement. They had no desire to encourage a Labour Party and many miners were dismissed because of their political activities. The owners dictated the terms of the return to work; they did not negotiate. And they knew that the miners were so reduced that they had to accept. Many left the valleys and sought work else-where. By November, seven months after the lock-out for refusing to accept lower wages, the miners returned to work on the imposed conditions, a defeated and dispirited people.

George felt this keenly and determined that one day he would do something about it. Would he be a preacher and denounce the wrong in the name of God, or would he become a Member of Parliament? He dreamed, as many of the young men did, of a Labour victory and a majority Labour government. It seemed an impossible dream. Would he become a teacher and train a whole new generation of young people to stand up and demand justice in the way the Revd Barker had said? At seventeen, he did not know which way he should go, or which way was possible.

The strike left a legacy of great bitterness among the miners, which continues to this day among the working people in South Wales. Pits closed, the industry of South Wales was crippled and the area became depressed. A long period of unemployment began for increasing numbers of miners. From 1926 South Wales suffered until 1939, when war demanded coal from British mines. There is no doubt that the government bore the larger responsibility for the suffering even though they blamed it on the stubbornness of the miners. The Labour Party believed that the wrong would never be righted until a Labour government came to power and nationalized the mines. Lloyd George continued to protest against the biased and unfair way in which the government had played its part in the dispute, but the miners had transferred their loyalty to the Labour Party.

The Experience of a Lifetime

Those seven months of strikes and their painful consequences influenced George Thomas for the rest of his life. He remembered them vividly in his later years, and as the superb storyteller that he is, he filtered his memories through a lifetime's experience in chapel, school and Parliament. The way he recalls that turning point in his life may not be objective reporting, but it reflects his mature consideration of how it shaped his life.

At the beginning, there was the thrill of solidarity. Then it appeared to him that the Trades Unions had let the miners down. The Liberals seemed to be a spent force, lost in internal disputes, despite the brave but ineffective protests of Lloyd George. The Tories, however, were the enemy. They were in power and their legislation imposed humiliating conditions upon those applying for the dole. Little as it was —fifteen shillings a week—an unemployed man did not receive benefits unless he could prove that he was "genuinely seeking work". As the only source of possible work was the silent pits, the miners were thus reduced to deception. They compiled fictitious lists of pits they claimed to have visited to ask for work. George felt the sense of degradation that had come over the community. Yet he retained his sense of humour, as the miners did. He would remember years afterwards the story of the miner who called at the Naval Colliery, Penygraig, to look for work, and was sharply sent away with the familiar words: "You know there's no work here, Dai. Come back in the spring." Dai's reply was instant: "What do you think I am? A bloody cuckoo?" You cannot kill the humour of the valleys.

The worst plights were of those who failed to qualify for unemployment benefits. They were driven to seek help from the relief officers. These, in George's words, were "usually brutal men whose insensitivity made them loathed", who applied the means test with heartlessness. This included a rigorous investigation into what other members of the family were receiving, and often meant the undermining of family relations. A sister earning a few pence for her hard work cleaning and washing clothes, scrubbing floors and doing whatever a richer family required, would have her pence taken into account when assessing the relief money paid to her brother.

It was no wonder that young people left the valley to seek work elsewhere. Tonypandy gradually emptied. George watched his friends and fellow teenagers leaving for distant parts. There is an air of remembered sadness in his brief account:

> On my way to school every Monday morning during the great exodus I would see little family groups on the platform of Tonypandy railway station saying tearful farewells to somebody who had found work in Slough or Birmingham or Coventry or Nuneaton. In these days that was like going to China, because they did not know when they would be able to save enough to pay for a visit home.

One type of work aroused a deep anger among the proud people of the Rhondda: domestic service in English homes. "Our daughters," they said, "are cheap skivvies for well-off people." No doubt Mam and George were as angry as anyone else, but Mam was practical. If this particular evil had to be, then she would help where she could. In addition to her work in surpervising the soup kitchens, work which had to continue beyond the strike, she also helped to clothe three hundred valley girls who had found jobs as domestic servants in England. Essential clothing and their railway fares were subsidized from a distress fund set up by the Lord Mayor of London. In the Mid-Rhondda it was administered by Mark Harcombe, while Mam was put in charge of caring for women with special needs in Tonypandy and Trealaw. She would visit the families and give them credit notes from the fund. George often went with her on these visits. One incident stuck in his mind. He saw a pregnant woman and noticed that she was different from other women! But he also noticed that she was hungry and proud. As Mam gave her a credit note, she broke down and cried as she said, "I never thought that I would come to this!" Mam's eyes filled, and George gripped her hand as tears poured down her face.

Preparations for Life

George learnt much from those years of poverty in Tonypandy. His soul was angry with the injustice of it all. And he was more than a spectator. During the strike he helped Emrys dig coal out of the mountainside. You can still see the hillside scars that are left where they dug a level, or a trench, into the side of the mountain, to get the coal for themselves and also to sell. No miner would regard that as stealing. The mountains were free—only the pits belonged to the owners. When the mine owners put up fences to stop them, they were pulled down in the same spirit with which years later the young Germans pulled down the Berlin Wall. Emrys was strong enough to dig a level and he had one about twenty-five feet into the mountainside. George went with him and as Emrys crawled into the level he handed the coal out to his younger brother. One day, George felt Emrys give him a mighty push which sent him hurtling away from the level. As he fell away, a huge rock missed him by a narrow margin. It was enormous and would have killed him had Emrys not shoved. George could not understand how Emrys could know that the rock was about to fall. "By the sound," Emrys said. This explained why at that time miners were reluctant to wear helmets. They trusted their ears for danger signs rather than helmets to cushion the shock.

It was a hard school in which the future Viscount Tonypandy grew up. There were no entertainments, except at chapel or at meetings of the Labour Party or the local cinemas. He learnt to rely upon his own resources, to love good books and to take pleasure in singing and speaking. George was nourished on the freedom that comes from self-evident values of honesty and integrity which were not enforced but expected. It was not a life with a set of rules, but one governed by faith in the God and Father of our Lord Jesus Christ who had set him free. George's character was developed in this school, against the background of a harsh and suffering valley. It was not surprising that he felt the call to the Methodist Ministry while he was still a teenager.

Minister, Teacher, or Politician?

When he was eighteen, George's schooldays came to an end. He had done well. But what next? Three dominant interests vied for decision. What was to be his life commitment?

His first choice was the call he had undoubtedly received to full-time Christian service. Whatever decision he took, he would give his whole life to Christ. The ordained ministry seemed the right choice already before he left school. George had always played a significant role in the life of the chapel. He was the grandson of the founding member of the English Methodist Church in Tonypandy, and many of the people in the chapel must have seen him as a future preacher. After his conversion at the age of sixteen, this was always a possibility.

There was one other claimant for his loyalty, almost as powerful as the chapel. It was the Labour Party. Mam's example in the political life of Tonypandy encouraged this and he shared her passion for social justice. But it was not at all evident that there was any future in politics except on a voluntary basis. At eighteen, it offered no career for him, despite his deep concern that justice should be done in the valleys. It is unlikely that he was aware of Labour's growing strength, largely because of the strike. Kenneth Harris, in his biography of Attlee says categorically that "The outcome of the strike improved Labour's long-term prospects of coming to power. It toughened Labour supporters and it made friends for the Labour Party among many floating voters who felt the miners had been treated harshly and unjustly."

This was not evident in Tonypandy, and an eighteen-year-old with merely local backing and no political experience could hardly consider a future in Parliament. What he could do was work for the return of another and stronger Labour government, and this he did with Mam's support. The first Labour government had been short-lived and a great disappointment. It was doomed from the start because Labour was not even the majority party in the House. It was only the larger of the two parties which had defeated the Conservatives, who still held the largest number of seats: Labour, 191; Liberals, 159; Conservatives, 258. Despite this result, Ramsay MacDonald had formed the first Labour government in January 1924.

It was not all that easy to find work in 1927, but there was a tradition of school teaching among the brighter sons of the valleys. It was not surprising that, as George recalls, "gradually the idea formed that I should become a school teacher." Although he was still grappling with the overwhelming feeling that he was called to the life of an ordained Methodist minister, practical considerations prevailed: and at the age of eighteen he became a pupil teacher at a school in Trealaw.

CHAPTER FOUR

◆◆◆

A Teacher in the Making

A PUPIL TEACHER was the very first rung on the ladder. All of George's teaching was supervised and he was liable to have to do any job in the school. To use a term more appropriate in an office, he was the "dogsbody". In Alaw School at Trealaw, he was at everybody's beck and call. He did not mind, because he was having his first taste of teaching. But the wages were very low and he looked out for a more responsible, lucrative position in every available advertisement. He was not alone. There were others in exactly the same position. Eventually four of them found jobs as "uncertificated teachers" in Essex.

The one big positive achievement of the first Labour government had been the Wheatley Housing Act, which became law in August 1924. By increasing the state subsidies and by negotiating with the building trade, Wheatley produced "the basis of a vast expansion in municipal house-building". Among these council estates, there was an area to the east of London—Dagenham and Rainham, where Fords eventually put their factory. It was mostly the badly housed families of East London who were moved out to Dagenham, and new schools were needed and new teachers. It was here that George found his first real teaching post as an uncertificated teacher, teaching children eight years old in Fanshawe Crescent in Dagenham. An uncertificated teacher was a great deal further advanced than a pupil teacher, and with the rapid growth of the child population there was no difference in duties between a certificated and an uncertificated teacher, except in the salary! George's salary was one pound five shillings per week. One pound a week went on lodgings, which he found in Chadwell Heath, three miles from the school. The five shillings remaining was divided equally between pocket money and his contribution to Mam's budget back home. With only two shillings and sixpence disposable income per week he usually walked the three miles each way to school.

He enjoyed his teaching, despite the enormous size of the class—sixty-three pupils. The statutory size of a junior class was then sixty and therefore George kept two registers, one for the inspector, containing precisely sixty names, another with the three extra children "under cover". They were very different from the children he knew in Tonypandy and he felt a bit of a foreigner among them. But his love of children was growing and it would stay with him all his life. None the less, the strange accents and the different values of these children left him homesick.

The other three who had come with him to Essex, Griselda Lewis and Margaret Howell from the Tonypandy Secondary School and his classmate Trevor Bennett, were all teaching in the same area. They met every week to share news of home and remember it nostalgically. Since they came from homes which did not have telephones, the post and copies of local newspapers were their only source of news. But they were Welsh and no evening passed without some singing with Trevor playing Welsh folk tunes on his violin. George recalls how they indulged their homesick emotions.

> After a while, I would invariably say, "Give us 'The Picture of my Mother on the Wall'". Every time he played it we would have tears in our eyes and we would insist that he must never play it again. The following Tuesday he was always asked for it.

They were only nineteen and far from their beloved valleys. All of them were away from home for the first time.

It was good experience and they were growing up, but they knew that teaching without qualifications had no future. But training was costly. As the son of an ex-serviceman, George applied to the British Legion for help and they gave fifty pounds, but that was nowhere near enough, and he knew how difficult it was for the family to manage at home. They needed his small contribution, and although Mam would have managed without that, even with her diligent determination it would be hard. She was, however, well aware that he needed training and determined that he should get it. Back home, after a school year in Dagenham, he discussed the situation with Mam and Dad Tom. He applied to three colleges and was accepted by the University College of Southampton. Even that meant a heavy sacrifice for the family, but they reckoned they could manage for two years, which was the regulation period for teacher training.

Away from Home Again

After that one school year in Dagenham, George was glad to be home again. He was soon throwing himself into all the activities at chapel. But the autumn term in Southampton began in September and George had to leave. He entrusted his close friend Annie Thomas to Trevor and took his sad farewell. He was glad of the opportunities that Southampton would offer, but he was going to miss Annie and his family. Twice a week he wrote to Annie. He was in love. New experiences and new friends at college made their demands, but his thoughts were always of returning to find Annie waiting for him at the end. He soon discovered that Trevor had looked after Annie all too well. They were beginning to fall in love with each other, and eventually they married, to George's great concern and perhaps resentment. At least he had nothing more to do with Trevor for a time. Meanwhile, the course in Southampton demanded all his attention. Despite the exciting political events on the national scene, he kept his head down and studied hard.

In the 1929 General Election, Labour was elected as the largest party in the House, although without an overall majority. Ramsay MacDonald had declared that he did not want confrontational politics, but announced that "by putting our ideas into the common pool we can bring out legislation and administration that will be of substantial benefit to the country as a whole."

That attitude did not please all members of the Labour Party, who wanted to try to introduce a full socialist programme, even if the attempt was defeated. At the time, Clement Attlee shared this view. But MacDonald had recognized many more serious economic issues on the horizon. World trade faltered and unemployment in Britain rose ominously from 1.5 million in January 1930 to 2.5 million in December. By August 1931, when George had finished his two-year course, MacDonald was discussing with the Opposition his proposed cuts of ten per cent in all benefits and in wages. The economy of the country was shattered and before long the Labour Party would be divided on the issue of a National Government, which MacDonald would lead, but which the Conservatives would dominate.

Reduced Circumstances

Another reason why George did not engage in many outside activities while in Southampton was quite frankly his lack of money. He had virtually no pocket money. It cost nothing to lie on the grass and read books from the library, but it was on Saturday nights that he felt the pinch. That was when the other students went down town to relax and unwind after the week's work. He could not afford to join them. He found a substitute which stood him in good stead later. The college had a magnificent library and on Saturday nights he had it to himself. He could unwind by reading books on subjects that were not in his syllabus. It was then that he developed that wide range of interests which was later to characterize his rich conversation and enable him to take up with eagerness tasks of great variety in government. Much later, it made him a better Speaker of the House. He read omnivorously, developed a passion for history and discovered his photographic memory which could recall the very page on which he had read something he wanted to refer to subsequently. As Speaker of the House it was to enable him to remember the faces of every member, simply by studying their photographs beforehand. Meanwhile, it made his essay writing much easier, because he could more quickly find the passages he wanted to quote. He was a lonely student, bravely finding compensation for his poverty.

This difference between him and other students, many of whom were well-endowed by their families, did not embitter him, though it may have embarrassed him. His politics were not affected; he was already committed to the Labour Party and there were far worse injustices in the Rhondda than he ever saw in Southampton. There was no bitterness, but he recalls one incident which illustrates his awareness of being deprived. It concerned plus fours! In one of his regular letters home, he remarked that the male students mostly wore plus fours and then added a comment which he later regretted, "Of course I know we cannot afford them." He should have guessed the effect of that upon Mam and Dad Tom. They were finding it hard to manage, but they could not let their boy feel deprived. Money for the plus fours soon arrived and he knew how much that had cost the family back home. To this day he is ashamed of that careless "whinge". When he returned to Tonypandy on the next vacation, he sported his plus fours, to the sniggering comments of his old friends. He tells of his humiliation with an appreciation of Welsh humour:

> My big mistake was to wear them when I went home to Tony-pandy. As I walked down Trealaw Road I passed a group of miners squatting low on the ground, talking. As I passed them, one miner spat about three yards, looked up and said, "What's the matter, George? Are you working in water?" The group collapsed in laughter. They knew that miners who had to work in water invariably tied their trousers below the knee. I coloured and hurried home to change.

He never wore them there again.

Testing a Social Conscience

The Professor of Education at Southampton, Joe Cock, took a special interest in George. He too was a socialist and a Christian. A strong believer in practical Christianity, he always attempted to go where the need was. He also enlisted the help of the students in his good works. One day he appealed for volunteers to accompany him to a school for mentally handicapped children. George volunteered, but found the task too emotionally disturbing. When he saw, for the first time, "the twisted bodies and over-large heads", he was literally sick and had to go outside to vomit. He was afterwards afraid to go back into the classroom. Joe Cock knew what had happened to this healthy young man, but he also knew that he had something to learn. He did not let the incident pass as George hoped he might. Rather, he met him head-on and asked why he had deserted after volunteering. George was ashamed of himself. He met Joe Cock's frankness with equal frankness. He apologized, but told him that it made him sick, that he couldn't bear it. Joe Cock did not accept his excuse, but quietly replied, "And what if it was one of your own family?" That hit George hard and made him feel even more of a worm. He learnt his lesson as Joe explained how hard it would be for handicapped people if society shared his reactions to them. He went back to the school and continued to work there for the whole time he was at Southampton.

George had found in Professor Cock a good tutor and a good friend, who recognized his potential, but saw that he lacked experience and confidence. The Rhondda had been an excellent but limited training ground, where ideas were firmly held but not always thought through with careful consideration of alternatives. George was now beginning to think independently. What he needed, however, was a university education, and Joe Cock encouraged him. He was offered an exhibition to study for an honours degree in history, but to Joe Cock's disappointment, he refused it. The exhibition would have paid for fees and some maintenance while at university, but George saw that this was not enough. After two years of being supported by his family, at the age of twenty-two it was time he earned a living and contributed to the family budget.

But he did not forget Joe Cock, who had taken him to lectures at the Workers Educational Association in the New Forest and discussed with him his career and his abilities. He had certainly been tempted to accept the offer of higher education, particularly if it meant reading history. The professor had opened up a new world to him and talked not of "letters after his name" but of an academic post. If he wavered, it was because of his love for the Rhondda, accentuated one vacation period when he was at home, by a mining disaster. The hooter at the pit head sounded the alarm and George rushed, like the rest, to the scene. Dad Tom was the winder who lowered the rescuers down and brought the bodies up. This was familiar enough to George. The deep sense of sorrow when a body was recognized, the rending sobs, the solidarity of the whole community, all reminded him of his roots. Watching the cage, he recalled that Emrys was day by day facing that danger in the mine and that Ivor was working long hours for a small wage. Dad Tom was not in the danger of the pit itself, but he bore the anxiety of the winder. Mam was not in the depths of poverty which she had known, but theirs was a working family with a struggle to keep going. His great desire was to work for his family, and if possible in this valley. At least, he must put out of his mind any thought of further education. He was a certificated teacher now, and he decided to look for a teaching post in South Wales.

A Qualified Teacher

In Southampton, George had followed with great interest the progress of the various Education Bills which were fiercely debated in Parliament. The county councils were beginning to take over responsibility for education from the churches. Early in the century a great deal of

47

education had been in Anglican or Nonconformist hands, the former called "National Schools" and the latter "British Schools". The Liberal Party, particularly David Lloyd George, had rallied around proposals to secularize the schools and bring church control of schools to an end. Lloyd George had won the support of the chapels when he had pleaded—albeit unsuccessfully—for freedom of the schools from sectarian influence:

> Give the children the Bible if you want to teach them the Christian faith. Let it be expounded by its founder. Stop this brawling of the priests in and around the schools, so that the children can hear Him speak His own words. I appeal to the House of Commons now, at the eleventh hour, to use its influence and lift its commanding voice and say: "Pray silence for the Master!"

His appeal was unavailing, but he emerged as the champion of the chapels and Mam undoubtedly referred to that speech many times. Welsh Nonconformity especially delighted to honour David Lloyd George as the incarnation of its spirit and purpose, representing them in the highest political places. This was the generation of George Thomas's grandfather, John Tilbury, and it explains the neighbours' horror when Emma left her father's party for the Labour Party. John Tilbury understood Emma's decision, because he also saw the relationship of the new Labour Party both to reform and to the chapels. When George took up his post as a qualified teacher, the Act under which he was required to work was the Fisher Act, drafted during the war and on the statute book with the royal assent by August 1918. It raised the school leaving age to fifteen, developed central schools, and authorized the multiplication of secondary schools and continuation classes up to eighteen for all who left school before they were sixteen. Much of that was left as intentions, but one proposal was of great significance. This was the setting up of a Standing Joint Committee under the chairmanship of Lord Burnham to fix teachers' salaries. The "Burnham Scales" were devised and gave secure guidelines for regulating teachers' salaries, thus ensuring for teachers a reasonably well-paid profession. It was this that made it so important for George to be a certificated teacher.

His teaching career began, however, in the financial blizzard of the summer of 1931. It was the beginning of "the greatest crisis in the Labour Party's history". An Austrian bank had failed in May and this was followed by the collapse of the German banking system. There was a run on the pound in July. Philip Snowden, then Chancellor of the Exchequer in Ramsay MacDonald's Labour government, faced a deficit of £120 million—an unprecedented figure in 1931. Cuts in public spending were absolutely vital. Public works were suspended, unemployment benefits cut and a means test applied to "transitional" benefits. The Rhondda suffered again from the hated and humiliating means tests, and the unemployment benefits were not enough to live on. The dole was calculated on the number of calories needed to keep a person in reasonable health. The mining valleys knew how to manage on far less than most. They chose their food with instinctive care to make it most nourishing in times of dire poverty. They were no strangers to this, but many unemployed families could not manage. It was at this time that so many leases came to an end and deeds to houses had to be handed in. To lose one's home was the ultimate degradation to the proud, hard-working, independent people of the Valley.

There were inevitably cuts in public service salaries and this affected teachers also. The recently established Burnham Scales were severely modified.

George looked round for a teaching post with as good a salary as possible. He would have preferred South Wales, but could only find a satisfactory post in London. This was in Southwark, at Rockingham Street School. From the start he kept his eyes open for another post, in Wales. He did not like London, but found satisfaction in the teaching, and also in his discovery of Westminster Central Hall, the Methodist headquarters in London, and the nearby Houses of Parliament. Both were quite a long way from his south London school, and even further from his lodgings in Brixton. But his spare time was taken up mostly with walking and he walked all round London, usually ending in Westminster, either attending a meeting of Methodists at the Central Hall or sitting in the Strangers' Gallery in the House of Commons.

Apart from Sundays and Tuesdays at the lively Central Hall, his eye was on the Houses of Parliament, across the square. He was at first slightly ashamed by the behaviour of members during debates. They seemed to pay little attention to what others were saying and were often quite rude. He was most angry when the Tories laughed at the speech of Will John, the member for Rhondda West. He disapproved also of the Speaker, E. A. Fitzroy, who mumbled the names of those he called to speak, so that visitors in the Gallery did not hear the MP's name. This inexpensive form of entertainment taught him a great deal about parliamentary procedure. It was a stormy time inside and outside of Parliament. MacDonald could not hold his cabinet together in the face of fierce cuts in unemployment benefits, upon which the American bankers had insisted. A National Government was formed with the two Opposition leaders, the Liberal Lord Samuel and the Conservative Stanley Baldwin serving under Ramsay MacDonald as Prime Minister. There was bitter opposition from the Labour Party supporters. Demonstrations became a nightly occurrence and they were sometimes quite violent. George noted that some of this violence was in reaction to police provocation. In his memoirs he has a lively description of how he was caught one Tuesday evening in the autumn of 1931 when leaving a meeting at the Central Hall and encountered a demonstration of chanting protesters:

> I began to make my way through the crowd, but as they pressed forward mounted police pressed them back. Thoroughly fright-ened by the surging violence, I jumped clean over the railings which then surrounded Parliament Square. I was safe on the green, but had great difficulties in getting back on the pavement as the spiked railings were more than four feet high. I was lucky to get home without being arrested, for that night the police were in a mood to push anybody into the van.

It was an exciting if lonely time in London, but George enjoyed the teaching. His classes were smaller than they had been in Dagen-ham and he was more confident now, as a trained teacher. The Methodist Central Hall, the long walks around London and the Strangers' Gallery formed the framework of his life outside the class-room. He was stimulated by the life of London, but not yet ready to contemplate making it even his second home. He had only been there a matter of weeks and his mind was often in South Wales. In fact, his determination to get back there prevented him from taking up other opportunities which were open to him. Professor Cock had given his name to a colleague, a professor of history in London University, and had written to try to make an appointment for him. He could have studied at an evening school and taken a diploma in history while he was teaching. Many did this, and George had the ability and the aptitude. He might have become a distinguished historian and fulfilled all the hopes Joe Cock had for him. George knew this, but he concentrated his energies elsewhere: he was determined to find a school in Wales. He scoured the advertisements for teaching posts, hoping he might find one nearer home, and after only one term he was successful. Shortly after arriving in London he saw a post advertised at Marlborough Road School, Cardiff.

He applied and was given an interview in the very impressive Cardiff City Hall. He was not the only applicant. There were twenty in all. George knew that he was up against stiff competition, but he very much wanted this job. He planned the interview with the care of a military operation. Appearance was important, he considered, and, always very particular about his clothes, on this occasion he must look his best. Again the family came to his support. Ivor had just bought a splendid new belted overcoat and that was made available to George, who wore it on the day as though this was his style! He prepared himself for all the questions that might be asked. The experiences of Dagenham, Southampton and London were carefully thought through so as to present himself to the committee as an experienced teacher. He anticipated the question, "Why do you want to teach in Cardiff?" He realized that he had a lot to offer and was anxious, but confident, as he waited in the corridor, which later was to become familiar territory, with the other applicants. This job meant everything to him. It must have counted against him that he had taught for only one term in London. Was he reliable, and could they count on him as a teacher who would stay? It must have become evident to the committee that this young man was Welsh to the core and wanted to teach his own Welsh children; that home meant so much to him that he needed to be in close contact with it; and that he was conscientious and a good teacher. They chose well. He was appointed as the new teacher at Marlborough Road School under a Mr Francis, who was headmaster.

George was only partly aware of the crucial change which had taken place in his life and what it would mean for his future. Looking back as Viscount Tonypandy, full of honours and admired by all, he tried to recapture his feelings at the time and anticipate what he could not have known. In his memoirs, he writes of this appointment:

> When I learnt that the committee had decided to appoint me, I could not have begun to guess what a difference their decision was going to make to the rest of my life. It meant that I never

fulfilled Professor Cock's ambition for me, but many other doors opened within months of my return to Wales. At that moment I just felt satisfied to be coming home; that I would be able at last to contribute my full share to the family income. I returned to London to complete the school term, and came back to the Rhondda for Christmas.

That was Christmas 1931.

CHAPTER FIVE

❖❖❖

Cardiff and Tonypandy

AFTER A TONYPANDY CHRISTMAS at home, George travelled to Cardiff to take up his new job at Marlborough Road Elementary School for Boys. He knew that it took boys straight from the infant school at about seven years old, and that some of them would take a scholarship and go at eleven to a grammar school. The rest stayed on at Marlborough Road until they were fourteen. What he did not know was which class he was to teach. The fact that it was a good school, and in Cardiff, and gave him the opportunity to live at home, weighed more upon his mind than the kind of teaching he would have to do. He soon discovered that he had to be prepared for anything.

He had a shock on his very first morning. The headmaster assigned him to the youngest class, fresh from the infants school, and told him, "You will teach them to read." George had taught young children in Dagenham, but had no specialized training in teaching reading. After Dagenham he had thought in terms of older children and at Southampton had specialized in the teaching of senior forms. He was lucky to have a sympathetic headmaster, who did not let him off the hook, but helped him. He took the first few lessons with George until he grasped the method. Then George enjoyed the satisfaction of seeing little boys discovering the delights of reading. He eventually taught hundreds of boys to read and was always grateful to that kindly headmaster who insisted, but also helped.

There was another shock in store. Looking down the timetable, he noticed that he was also required to teach singing. He had never been taught to do this. Again he turned to the headmaster in panic and suggested that the children would run out of the class if he started singing. This time he got no help. The head merely smiled and said, "In that case, you'd better lock the door." George was in at the deep end, but before long he was enjoying the music lessons more than

53

anything else. He taught the boys to sing Welsh airs and hymns.

After that start, he was prepared for anything. Soon the boys grew very fond of him and he of the boys. The school was small enough for him to know and notice all of them. Because the journey from home was a little awkward by public transport, he bought a second-hand motor cycle, which became the pride of the school. Its noise could hardly be missed. The boys gathered round him as he left, and pushed the bike until it started. In class and outside he was their friend, and they learnt from him not only to read and to sing, but also how to behave. He knew that his example was more important than what he said. He tells an amusing story of how his pupils imitated him. He always kept a handkerchief tucked in his sleeve, to wipe the chalk off his hands and so protect his clothes from chalk dust. This was typical of his carefulness with his appearance. It was not long, he noticed, before every boy in the class had a handkerchief showing from inside his cuff! He realized he was becoming their model even in little things. That taught him to be careful how he behaved in more important matters. The boys could duplicate his vices as easily as his virtues.

Poverty in Cardiff

The Depression hit Cardiff just as hard as it had hit the Rhondda. George saw the effects of unemployment among the parents of his children. The dole was scarcely enough to live on and there were no reserves. What you bought had to be paid for and families lived a day at a time. The family of an unemployed man could pay only for the immediate necessities. Some kindly shopkeepers would put it "on the slate" until the next payment came. But as the Depression deepened, even this practice became rare and the more familiar sign was "No credit". George learnt the effect of this one day in class. A boy named George Edgebrook suddenly fainted and collapsed on the floor. When he came round, George asked if he had eaten anything which might have upset him. "What did you eat at breakfast?" he asked. The reply shook him: "Nothing, sir. I never have breakfast, we can't afford it." In those days it was possible for children to buy a small bottle of milk at school. They paid only a halfpenny for it, but they had to pay for the week in advance. The Edgebrook family could never spare twopence halfpenny on Monday. From then on, George

Thomas paid for that milk and then he enquired about other boys. He was anxious to know exactly the conditions of the homes from which the boys came.

George would learn much more about Cardiff in subsequent years, particularly when he won a Cardiff seat in Parliament. But already the iniquities of the property leasehold system were evident. Through the schoolchildren, he learnt of the poverty in Cardiff and did what he could, but determined to do more. He was already politically involved, a member of the Labour Party, and as a student he had joined the National Union of Teachers. The formation of the National Government had shaken the Labour Party. MacDonald was a traitor. Philip Snowden had cut the unemployment benefits and been expelled from the Labour Party "for his disregard of the poor". George had no sympathy with the National Government, and supported the brave band of forty-nine members of the Labour Party whose major concern was the poor. Many of these were trades union members from the mining valleys. Only a few of this small party in Parliament could stand the pace of committees and debates. They were the heroes in Cardiff and although he could no longer listen in the Strangers' Gallery, George read their speeches. Aneurin Bevan made speech after speech on the plight of the depressed areas; Tom Williams spoke on agriculture, Jimmy Maxton on domestic affairs. Besides these three, the weight of the work fell on a small number of MPs: George Lansbury, who was already growing old, a veteran pacifist and irrepressible defender of the poor; Stafford Cripps, very left-wing and later opposed by George Thomas when he came to Tonypandy; Margaret Bondfield, the first woman cabinet member; Arthur Greenwood and Herbert Morrison. Clement Attlee became their leader, elected because he was the only one, except Lansbury, with previous government experience. George followed this political scene with mixed feelings. He was opposed to Communism, but a good trades union socialist. The poverty of Cardiff and the continuing unemployment in the mining valleys led him more and more in the direction of the veteran George Lansbury.

Life in Tonypandy

While he was teaching in Cardiff, George lived in Tonypandy—quite a distance to travel, but the old motor bike carried him to and fro.

Shortly after he started teaching at Marlborough Road School, the family moved from Trealaw Road to 62 Ely Street, which is still remembered as his home in Tonypandy. In fact he lived there for twenty years. It was not luxurious, with no hot water, no bathroom, and only an outside toilet, but to his great joy, it had electric light! It also had a double-bay window, which was something special.

His political activities started at once. Already a member of the NUT, he became Press and Parliamentary Secretary of the Cardiff Association of Teachers. This brought him into contact with the media, both the local press and the Welsh BBC, whose head office was in Park Place, Cardiff. With his wonderful speaking voice and his ability to turn a dull political issue into an absorbing story, he was a gift to the media and he never forgot how important it was to use them rightly. Had he been Welsh-speaking, he would certainly have been offered a career in radio. But he was content to teach by day and follow the issues of the teachers' union in his free time. He worked with Mam in Tonypandy and was able to supply newspapers and radio with copy about the Rhondda Valley. He also had to keep an eye on Parliament and report on what the Welsh MPs were doing. It was a stormy time in the National Government. The father of those forty-six Labour MPs was George Lansbury. Kenneth Harris' description of him at that time shows why George Thomas was attracted to him of all Labour leaders:

> He was the only one of the veteran Labour leaders who had survived the carnage of 1931. He had been the wartime pacifist idol of the ILP [Independent Labour Party] ... He had built up the *Daily Herald* ... In the 1931 crisis, nobody had more strenuously resisted the cuts in unemployment pay than he had. More than any living Labour leader, Lansbury represented Socialist idealism—under no other leader could the little band of forty-six have marched into the voting lobby singing "The Red Flag". His followers loved him, and trusted him.

Apart from George's preference for "Cwm Rhondda" over "The Red Flag", Lansbury represented his socialism at this stage. It moved him towards pacifism. But his major influence was still Mam, who continued with her political activities in Tonypandy and recruited George to her local party.

Mock Parliament

Among the activities at chapel was a novel idea, initiated by the new minister, the Revd Cyril Gwyther. He started a mock Parliament in place of the regular meeting. The men formed themselves into parties and chose a Prime Minister as well as a Leader of the Opposition. They debated the issues of the day and called for divisions. The Speaker was always Mr Gwyther dressed in his gown to suit the part. The hall rang with indignant debates, but the members were better behaved than in the real House of Commons! George enjoyed this charade and in his turn played many parts, but he was never allowed to be the Speaker. Among motions debated were "The abolition of the death penalty", "The reform of prisons", "The institution of a National Health Service", and "The right of every person to work". On all these issues there were party lines and party whips, much discussion, regulated by Mr Speaker, and divisions. It was all very real and entertaining, and gave George the feel of Parliament.

Police Hostility

George became well known not only to the media, but also to the police, who kept a wary eye for troublemakers, usually indiscriminately called "Communists"—they were not too clear about the distinction between Labour and Communist. It was all too easy to confuse a politically active young man, speaking out about the injustice of poverty in a potentially rich country, with a violent agitator. Though conditions were improving in the Rhondda, unemployment was a major issue still. It was a national problem and people were hungry. Hunger Marchers from all over the country converged on Westminster and were joined by crowds of sympathizers. The police expected trouble and were sometimes the cause of it. George was given charge of organizing the Tonypandy contingent by the local Labour Party. The police marked him as a potential troublemaker and informed him that no collecting of money *en route* would be permitted. It would be regarded as begging and therefore illegal. It was only on the night before the march that the Chief Inspector of Mid-Rhondda Police informed George of this restriction and added, "Tell the others". George spent the rest of the night contacting his helpers—"No collecting *en route*," he told them, "or we have trouble with the police." This was disastrous news, because the marchers could only survive on their long march to London if they could depend upon help from sympathizers on the way. George was surprised that they all took it so calmly. "Leave it to us, George," they said. His helpers were mostly miners and older men with experience of outwitting the police. What a respectable schoolmaster could not do, they could! Once the march was well away from Tonypandy, George saw one of his helpers moving surreptitiously among the crowds lining the road to cheer them on, carrying his cap in his hand. When George spotted him, he got a broad grin and a wink.

At that time, the Rhondda was a centre of political activity and leading politicians were prepared to travel from Westminster to talk to the miners. They wanted to be able to say that they had been to the Rhondda when the debates came up in Parliament. George and Mam were both actively engaged in looking after these important speakers. The Communists also brought their big guns, because the Rhondda was one of the places where they might win seats. There was one evening when they brought two of their top men: Tom Mann, the veteran Communist leader, now almost eighty; and Harry Pollitt, a founder member of the British Communist Party. There were others there, as well as the plain-clothes detectives. George was also present to listen to what was effectively his main opposition. After the meeting both Tom Mann and Harry Pollitt were charged with sedition. Both were acquitted, but not before George had witnessed an attempt by the police to charge the speakers with things they hadn't said. He was both disturbed and amused by the way in which the defence counsel revealed the police hostility. Under cross-questioning, the policeman who at first claimed he had written everything down in shorthand, later confessed that he didn't know shorthand, and then admitted that he had only written down what was seditious. The defence counsel then caught him with the question: "Do you hold as seditious anything you disapprove of?" to which the policeman answered simply and firmly, "Yes." It was difficult to convict the two men after that, but for George it was one more example of police hostility. He did not agree with the Communists, but he wrote a large question mark against the police.

Fascists in Tonypandy

The "unemployment march", for that is what it really was, had aroused sympathy among some but hostility in others. Chief among its opponents were the British Fascists and Blackshirts, led by Oswald Mosley. Though George shared their opposition to the Communists, he had no sympathy at all for Fascism, and the more he heard about their methods, the more he disapproved of them. He did not welcome the meeting in Tonypandy to which Mosley had been invited by local sympathizers. He had read of brawls in the East End of London when Mosley marched through Labour territory, and he saw that there would be trouble in Tonypandy, which was a Labour stronghold with a substantial Communist Party. The fact that Mosley had left the Labour Party in February 1931 made him even more disliked. He was, to many in Tonypandy, a Judas, a renegade and now the very opposite of what a good socialist should be. If the Communists opposed him, Labour really hated him. He usually encouraged violence to show the strength of his followers. The local Labour Party therefore decided to boycott the meeting in order to avoid the expected trouble. George went to the local cinema to avoid temptation. Before buying his ticket, he chatted with the manager who always stood outside his theatre, dressed with black tie, to receive his guests. George knew him well. Some hours later, when he emerged from the cinema, George was approached by a policeman who also knew him, and knew him to be chairman of the local Labour Party. The policeman wanted to arrest him, saying categorically, "You tore my coat." It was fortunate for George that the cinema manager could vouch that George had been in the cinema all evening. The police sergeant eventually knew that he was beaten and moved away.

Pacifism

These were violent days and the visit of Mosley made things worse. The local Communists brawled with his followers in the streets before and after the meeting. At the meeting itself, the Blackshirts kept order by their superior numbers. The police protected the Fascists and the only people who were arrested were Communists and Labour supporters.

George was not a violent man and he had learnt—and taught—

that Fascism could not be overcome by violence. Much as he hated what the dictators were doing in Europe, he did not see war as a way to handle the situation. The uselessness of the Spanish Civil War was daily becoming obvious and it was clear that Franco could count on much greater military support from Germany and Italy than all the democratic countries in Europe could muster on the other side. Within the democratic countries, there was some sympathy for Fascism. In Britain, it helped the Fascist cause that Sir Oswald Mosley was of the aristocracy. Men like George Lansbury and others in the leadership of the Labour Party were convinced that if the workers in the belligerent countries refused to fight there would be no war. The trench warfare of the First World War had deeply affected the ordinary soldier and there was a great deal of pacifism in Britain in the thirties.

As an idealist, it was not surprising that George tended to involve himself with the good causes associated with the Labour Party. In this mood, he joined the Labour Temperance League, and no doubt the memory of his father helped in that. An efficient, conscientious young man like George was not likely to remain a member only. The Temperance League saw in him a good local secretary and they were very wise. He was in a position to influence young people in the school, he was in touch with the media and he was well thought of in chapel and in the Labour Party.

In the midst of all this activity, with the discovery of new opportunities almost every day—"never a dull moment"—he decided that he must take his stand as a pacifist. It was not easy and he was never quite convinced. What he heard about the behaviour of Mussolini and later of Hitler led him also to listen to those who said the dictators must at all costs be stopped. Yet the spectre of the Great War haunted him and eventually he declared his hand by joining the International War Resistance Movement. The founders of the movement determined to resist war and believed that if the different peoples of Europe knew each other better they would not want to fight. For this reason they organized international trips. George was invited to attend one of these projects, in Denmark. Denmark had been neutral in the war and like all the Scandinavian countries had a strong peace movement. The Danes welcomed visitors from England as well as from Germany and tried to help them make friends in peaceful Denmark.

This was George's first overseas visit. He was excited as he boarded the ship at Harwich. He had much to learn. The first was his limitations as a sailor! He was miserably seasick all the way to Eskjerg. But that did not prevent him from enjoying Denmark and learning much from the new experience in a strange land speaking a strange language. There was a group of several from the War Resistance Movement and each stayed with a Danish family. It was not surprising that George was well received. He was still in his twenties, excited about everything he saw, with that childlike pleasure which he never lost. He knew no Danish, of course, but Danes are used to that and like to practise their English. George soon discovered this when he apologized for speaking no Danish. He made fast friends and no doubt left them with a slight Welsh accent to refine their command of English. His hosts took him round to see the sights and talked of their way of life, asking questions about his. They must have found it difficult to understand the peculiar life of the Welsh valleys, and to picture the landscape. George, for his part, drank in the beauty of the flat land with its immense sky. He left Denmark full of all he had seen and heard. It was a new world for him. So confident was he that he had gone through a great change that he boarded the ship back to Harwich without a fear. His own words describe the disillusionment: "As soon as I put my feet on the boat, the smell of the oil upset me. And before we had even sailed out of harbour, I knew I was a confirmed poor sailor."

But he had learnt that in order to understand people of another country you have to face the twofold truth, that there is a common humanity, but also a diversity of cultures. In some things, people are all the same, but their differences are also of great importance.

Number 62 Ely Street

The home where George lived for twenty years, 1932 to 1952, saw many a drama. It was a simple home, lit by the magical electric light —three rooms downstairs and three up. There the family gathered, and even though his two sisters were married by then, they always came back to Mam. One of the sisters had made a very bad marriage and she suffered much from her husband; but she could escape to Ely Street. George found it a strong base with Mam in control. It was a sober household, with George a strong temperance worker, but he never took objection to Dad Tom, who enjoyed his drink on the way home from work on Friday, pay night. He would arrive home, merry and bright, with none of the unpleasant violence of George's own father. Dad Tom was a social drinker and wise in his cups. George remembers that he never lost his values in drink. "Be sincere," he advised George, "and always pay your turn." He was fond of George and proud of him.

The house was also the centre of political activity. Because of her position in the Co-operative Guild it often fell to Mam's lot to entertain leading politicians from Westminster. During the disturbing years of the thirties, the Welsh valleys were important to Labour members of Parliament. George recalls one member in particular, who stayed with them when he was speaking at a meeting in the Rhondda. He tells the story of this rather pompous man without malice, but with the kind of humour that must have characterized the household in Ely Street. It was Dr Salter, the member for Bermondsey; a safe Labour seat. Dr Salter, in Tonypandy, was an important man. He arrived, announcing he was a "vegetarian". Mam took that in her stride, but when she was out of range she took George to one side and asked him, "What is that? A vegetarian?" George explained that it meant he didn't eat meat. This was beyond Mam's comprehension: "He doesn't eat meat! Then what does he eat?" They settled for vegetables, not without much stifled laughter. He was not the sort of man one chats with. He was ill at ease in the Valley. Mam gave him the middle room downstairs to work in and retired with George to the kitchen. They talked as quietly as they could, but when those two were together there was always some laughter. Dr Salter was working at his speech and had his window open. Suddenly, in the kitchen, they heard a roar: "Will you stop talking, please. I am working!" Dad Tom was with them and he was not amused. Mam quietly calmed him down or he might have exploded. The two conspirators put their fingers to their lips and Dad Tom walked out with an angry look.

There were many unsettling incidents in the disturbing thirties before the war broke upon them. But nothing disturbed the solidity of this household, whose foundation was in Mam who made it and which gave George that balance in his life that he never lost. He was equally at home with paupers and with princes. Such a balance served him well in his political life.

The Shaking of the Foundation

Mam was always so strong that it was a shock to that happy group when she was taken very seriously ill with uraemia, a kidney complaint from which few people recovered in those days. The doctors gave up hope as her condition worsened, until one day they talked to George privately and admitted to him, "Your mother's life is now in the hands of her Maker. We've done everything we can." The two doctors, one old and experienced, the other young, left the house and George was devastated. He would have to tell the others and he knew that for all of them it was the shaking of the foundation. About half an hour later, the young doctor returned, saying that he remembered a formula he had been taught as a student, which might help. He had looked up his college notes and gave George the prescription. George flew like the wind to the nearest chemist. The medicine looked like water, but it worked. Mam recovered and, as George says, she lived another forty years, adding mischievously, "long enough for me to attend the funeral of both doctors."

It was like a miracle. That was the kind of miracle George believed in all his life. He prayed and he expected God to work through the knowledge and skill of those to whom he had given it, the doctors and surgeons. But that miracle was not enough. No sooner had Mam recovered from the kidney complaint than an open sore broke out on her leg. She was taken to Cardiff Royal Infirmary and given bad news —she was told she would never walk again. This time, Ivor and George took over the miracle-working. They could not bear the thought of Mam stuck at home all day. After so much activity, she had to get out. The two brothers had a financial discussion and decided that between them they could afford the deposit on a Morris 8 car, which they would buy by hire-purchase. This "old banger" proved a good investment. The boys used it to take Mam away from home, and chose the little seaside village of Llantwit Major in the Vale of Glamorgan. The verdict of the specialist had shaken her badly and she was in a despondent mood. The boys knew how to handle her and gradually they coaxed her out of the car—much as she had coaxed them as children to walk—and within a year she was walking again, almost as well as ever, "having proved the doctors wrong", said George, "for the second time."

The Sisters

It is remarkable how easy it is to tell the story of George's life without any mention of his sisters. That would be unfair, although it is true that they did not exercise the influence that his brothers did, and certainly not as much as his mother. The figure of Dad Tom is also a slightly hazy figure, but he is always there and his influence, although late, was considerable. After the initial shock of Mam belonging to someone else, the family discovered that he brought a steady background to the whole family. He was a great support to Mam, although she was the stronger character of the two.

But the sisters? Ada May and Dolly were already married at this period. Ada May was thirty-seven and Dolly thirty-five. Older sisters tend to have a remoteness from younger brothers, and George had been only a child when they married.

In his eighties, George could still recall vividly the effect of Ada May's marriage to a young farm bailiff. It introduced him to a new kind of country life. He wrote of his memory of this time when his childhood in Tonypandy took a turn for the better. This was in a one-page article in the November 1991 issue of *Country Living*. The owner of the farm where William Webb, Ada May's husband, worked was a Mr Radcliffe. Ada May's house was about a hundred yards from the Radcliffe residence, but, George recalls, "the gap in social status was enormous. I always took off my school cap when I went there to buy a jug of milk." One of the jobs he remembered doing for the Radcliffes was being a scarecrow for sixpence: he stood in a cornfield and shouted to keep the birds away from the corn.

> I would stay in the field all morning and again for hours after lunch. Somehow, the trees surrounding the field held as much attraction for me as the birds and I would wander from my duties and accept a tree's unspoken challenge to climb it. Yet, even while doing this, I would keep looking back to the field and would shout until my lungs were nearly bursting if the crows took advantage of my absence. There is no doubt that I earned my sixpence from Mr Radcliffe.

Everything about the farm fascinated him. The barn, where chickens and geese strutted in and out at their pleasure, mesmerized him. There were also dangerous moments which he recalled vividly.

When I was eight years old, I nearly lost my life there. As a town boy I was ignorant of the ways of animals. One day seeing a sow and her piglets in a corner of the barn, foolishly I picked up one of the tiny animals which naturally squealed on top note. The old sow snorted angrily and began to run towards me. I screamed in terror and was fortunate. Will Webb, my brother-in-law, came rushing in. Beating off the sow with a rake, he shouted at me to drop the piglet. I was trembling with fright.

Despite such a moment of danger, and partly because of it, George remembers his days on the farm with much pleasure.

He remembers also that during the miners' strike in 1926, the pit ponies had been put into two fields rented from the farm. After adjusting to the light the ponies enjoyed their freedom for a few months, before they returned to "the pits and eternal darkness". But they left behind a harvest of mushrooms in the fields, which Ivor and George gathered until their baskets were full. The breakfasts of mushrooms and fresh farm bacon were among the most delicious meals he can remember! Palla Farm was another world from Tonypandy and it has remained in George's memory all his life. His conclusion to the article in *Country Living* is, "I love the green fields and the green trees but, above all, I love the village people.'

CHAPTER SIX

$\diamond\!\diamond\!\diamond$

The Pacifist Faces the Reality of War

EVERYTHING in his background led to George Thomas being a pacifist, but the events of the thirties imposed a great strain upon his principles. The Great War of 1914–1918, with its massacre of the youth of Europe and beyond, bred patriotism and pride in Empire, but also a growing conviction that the war had accomplished nothing —and at great sacrifice. In the valleys of South Wales and in the Trades Union movement, war was seen as a game played by old men, capitalists, who sent young men into battles to defend their interests. Like many others, George must have vowed that he would never fight in a capitalist war. The twenties were years of unchallenged pacifism among the majority of socialists. George's Christian beliefs also supported his pacifist inclination. Donald Soper had a following among Methodists for his pacifist views; Fenner Brockway among socialists. George Thomas belonged in both camps.

In 1928, the Kellogg–Briand Pact, signed by forty-five nations, denounced recourse to war as a means of settling international disputes. The churches strongly supported this and went so far as to say that Christians should not support their government if it declared war without first accepting an offer of negotiation. The young ecumenical movement and the Lambeth Conference both passed resolutions to this effect. There is no doubt that this was George Thomas's position in 1930. The change came with news of Hitler's aggressions and atrocities, following hard upon the behaviour of Italian troops in Abyssinia. The shift in the attitude of the Labour Party can be detected first at the Brighton Conference of October 1935.

At this point, George went along with the imposition of sanctions against Italy which was also Labour Party policy, but he was among those who held still to a pacifist position. Sanctions, yes; but war, no. But sanctions were either not applied or were ineffective. Meanwhile things were growing worse in Germany. The situation in Europe posed fearful problems for George, because it was obvious that sooner or later war would come and he would be called up. He was beginning to question whether he was prepared to register as a conscientious objector. It could not be said that the imminence of war had brought on his pacifism, as it had in so many other cases—the Peace Pledge Union, for example, had a rush of new members as soon as it was clear that there was a possibility of war and conscription. George's problem was the opposite. He was a convinced pacifist on religious grounds, but he questioned the right to stand aside and do nothing while Hitler pillaged Europe and massacred Jews.

The Special Police in Tonypandy

The year preceding the outbreak of war brought news of atrocities which George could not ignore. The treatment of the Jews in Germany troubled him. How could he hold a pacifist view now? Should he do nothing? In face of all this, he could not retain his pacifist position, however good it might have seemed in theory. This led to an agonizing period of self-examination. But eventually he decided to report for action in one or other of the armed forces. He appeared before a medical board and to his surprise was graded "C" which meant he was unfit for active service. No one explained what was wrong with him. There was no arguing with the army. But what now? He was still a schoolteacher, but he had to do something more for the war effort. He took a decision which must have angered his friends and even surprised him. He decided to join the police as a part-time reserve officer.

The very idea of the chairman of the local Labour Party in a police uniform was too much to contemplate. George was thirty now, and quite able to take a lead. He did not forget the behaviour of the police in former days, nor their continuing prejudice against the Labour Party as a bunch of dangerous "bolshies". The other officers of the Special Wartime Police must have been as surprised as his Labour Party colleagues when they received his application. Why did they accept him? There was a shortage and there was no good reason for refusing. His army exemption had not mentioned any debilitating disease. The police could not refuse him and they knew that they had a well-equipped, intelligent officer who was perfectly capable of carrying out his duties. The head of the Glamorgan police force, however, did have some hesitations. Chief Constable Lindsay was a man of very strong opinions and prejudices. He was politically a Conservative and personally opposed to any representative of the Labour Party. He had a record of prejudicial action which had destroyed public confidence in him and his police force. To the miners of the Rhondda, the police were the enemy, and George was about to join their ranks. Lindsay must have been puzzled and annoyed. But there was little he could do, except try to make life uncomfortable for his new recruit. His major problem must have been to fit George into his prejudiced view of the Rhondda miner and the typical Labour Party supporter. George was an educated man, an experienced teacher in a Cardiff school and of impeccable behaviour, well dressed and polite. If he had met him socially he would have assumed that he was a Conservative!

Police Unfairness

George was often unhappy about the activities of the police and, although he did his job well and was soon promoted to sergeant, this was not a congenial environment for him. At school he was caring for boys and helping them to grow up as law-abiding citizens; at night he was with the police who were after the boys to "book" them if possible and show them who was master. He tells a story of a night in Tonypandy when Ron, a young war reserve officer like himself, but younger, was on duty with a regular sergeant. There was a party of some kind going on in a marquee and the sergeant was looking for trouble. Nothing of the sort happened. Ron, himself only nineteen, never expected trouble, because he had been at many of these parties himself. The sergeant was getting impatient. Then a young man came out of the marquee, probably just to relieve himself behind the bushes. "Ah!" said the sergeant to Ron, "book him." The young man who had stepped out of the tent was frightened and began to cry, protesting he had done no wrong. When Ron took his side, the sergeant was infuriated and insisted that he charge him. Ron was also scared and did as he was told. Of the four regular officers with whom George worked in Tonypandy, this was the only one who showed such bullying tactics. It was enough to illustrate that the old ways of the police were not completely gone. Ron was troubled at what he had done, and came to George to ask his advice. George was the obvious one to go to, because of his age and experience and because he was a sergeant by now; but most of all because he was George. Throughout his life, young men came to him when they were in trouble. He should in this instance have reported the matter to a senior officer, but instead advised Ron to go to the sergeant and tell him that Sergeant Thomas knew what had happened and was very angry. It was good advice and required courage in the young man. He did as George had said and had a very hard time with the sergeant who blustered and threatened, but decided to drop the charge.

Apart from such unpleasant incidents, George rather enjoyed the work of a part-time policeman and thought it no bad thing for the people of Mid-Rhondda to see the chairman of the local Labour Party in a police uniform. The incident with Ron worried him for a long time, because he felt he should have done more, but he was much involved in other things at that time. It was 1942 and the bombs were already falling on Cardiff where he taught and where his boys lived.

Political Ambitions

George was always a trades union man and, from the beginning, active in the NUT, the largest schoolteachers' trades union. It was a slightly élitist union, not wishing to take on the political colour of the larger industrial and transport unions, and was not, like them, a member of the Trades Union Congress. George clearly thought it should be, and he made his views known. As chairman of the Labour Party in Tonypandy he had political ideas about where his union should stand. He wanted Labour votes from members of the NUT. As a single member there was little that he could do, but he had learnt the power structures from his mother. He knew that you had to take office when asked and from that office use your position to advance your political ideas. He was no passive member of the NUT. Locally, his active work among teachers and his efforts to understand the ways the machinery for wage advancement worked, led soon to his appointment as President of the Cardiff Teachers' Association. By 1942, his activity had been noted, and when Wales came to elect their contingent for the National Executive of the NUT, George was one of those chosen. That election gave him a broader vision and a wider recognition. "It was like a second university to me," he recalls.

In London, where the meetings were usually held, he met teachers with very different backgrounds from his own. He was expected to represent the interests of Welsh teachers, and did so, but he could not fail to recognize wider and different interests among teachers from England. Not all of them were Labour supporters. Many were Liberals and some were Conservatives. He found himself working in a multi-party committee for the welfare of teachers, where he held his own as a Welshman and a left-wing Labour supporter. He talks about these years as "developing years" and they certainly changed the focus of his thinking. In Tonypandy, he supported the cause of the miners, who were the main constituents of his Labour Party; in Cardiff, involved with teaching and as President of the Teachers' Association, he saw the problems of South Wales as a whole and of the "capital" city in particular. He understood the needs of the schools in Cardiff. There he met and discussed with teachers who had similar problems to his own. But he was lifted out of that world, even though he had to represent it, when he became involved in the wider national work of the NUT. The future of education in Britain as well as the status of teachers was often on the agenda. He began to see the need to understand the wider problems, and even to compromise. The Executive Committee was not a place for speeches or sermons. Wales was not their only concern. He was cutting his teeth on political issues, developing new skills in debate. He was also learning something of the pressures and temptations of power—"a second university" in fact.

A good example of the lessons he learnt and did not forget concerns his proposal that the NUT should join the TUC. The strongest opposition came from the General Secretary, Sir Frederick Mander, who was trying to keep the militant left wing from taking over the NUT. He advised George not to press his proposal. Most new members of the Executive Committee would have listened to the wise words of this senior official, who obviously knew the strategy and nature of political life in the trades union movement. Most members as new as George might have submitted for the sake of the influence which Sir Frederick could bring to their career. He was a powerful man. Or such a new member might have been modest enough to recognize that Sir Frederick knew better than he did what was good for the union. But George suffered neither from fear nor from undue modesty. He stuck to his point. Sir Frederick Mander was furious and threatened to get him off the Executive. No doubt he tried, but George had more support in Wales than he realized. George represented Wales, and they knew what to expect of him, but they also knew that his pressure for solidarity with the other trades unions was right. At the next election he received the highest vote in Wales. It was an early sign that George belonged to the future. He saw that the TUC was becoming a power in the land and that the NUT needed to be part of it.

A second example of his lack of fear in the face of threat came when the Communist group in the NUT tried to use him. They saw his proposal as an indication that he was a man of the left, and obviously spotted leadership potential in him. For the Communists, membership of the TUC meant a movement of the NUT to the left, and a new member of the Executive who sponsored and carried through a proposal to take their union into the TUC was one they could use—at least so they thought. George did not at once succeed in his proposal, but it brought him recognition. G. C. T. Giles, the first Communist president of the NUT, an annual appointment, approached George and suggested that he stand for the presidency. Giles promised him Communist support. George had had trouble with the Communists in Tonypandy, but times had changed and the Soviet Union was now fighting with the Allies against Hitler. George hesitated and finally refused, for two reasons. The first he expressed openly—he was not yet ready for such an office; the second was an uneasy feeling that he was being used. Giles came to him with great friendliness, expressing his appreciation of George's courage in making the proposal. Of course George felt flattered. He was also aware that with his own large Welsh support and that of the Communists he would probably have won. But he refused. He had been on the Executive for only one year and he was not prepared to attempt a task which he felt was beyond him at that point. He suggested that he might reconsider in the following year. His would-be supporters began to feel that this was not the pliant man that they could use. They threatened that if he did not stand then, they would support Ralph Morley, a Labour man from Southampton for whom George had high regard. But they added that if he refused now and stood next year, they would brand him as a careerist and do everything to ruin his reputation as well as defeat him. Much to George's approval, Morley was elected. George voted for him.

For a year he served under Morley as an active member of the Executive, still a full-time teacher and a part-time policeman. If he were elected the following year as President, he decided, he would resign from the police. There were several who wanted him to be President but the Communists kept their word and blackened him. George was defeated. He learnt several good lessons from this experience. It was his first contact with the king-makers, who appeared at first to be frank in their admiration but turned nasty when their chosen man was not a puppet doing their bidding. He realized that he had had a narrow escape. Had he been elected with their support, he might have been beholden to them. His loyalty was to the Labour Party and he had given it freely. He continued as a very active member of the National Executive and a free man. He learnt that it was worth sacrificing position to be your own man.

It was a full life and meant a great deal of travel. Mam was also on the move. She was on committees for the welfare of domestic servants and often in London. "She travelled more than I did," says George. His travel was between three points: Tony-pandy—Cardiff—London. He made other visits, but these three were his constant destinations. In the course of his journeys, he loved to meet and talk with people, quite casual acquaintances. It was a habit he kept up all his life. He was never suspicious of a stranger and his first reaction was always to want to help. Although he has always loved talking, he could also listen. He recalls one of these surprising contacts:

> Once when I was returning home [from a meeting of the National Executive] I went into the grill room at Cardiff station while waiting for my train to Tonypandy. Before the war nobody would sit at a restaurant table with a total stranger, but in the war years all this changed, and a young airman came and asked if he could share the table. We started to talk and he told me that he was going to make his very first broadcast that night in a BBC production of *How Green was my Valley*, playing David, the leading part. I told him I would listen with great care and then write to tell him what I thought, adding only half seriously, "Do you want me to be honest, or just kind?" The poor fellow had no choice, but fortunately his performance was brilliant. He told me that although his real name was Jenkins, he had taken his school-master's surname, and acted under the name of Richard Burton.

This kind of chance encounter seemed to happen to George more often than to most, perhaps because he was more open to them.

A Change of School

On the nights of the bombing of Cardiff, George and his family listened with growing concern to the thumps of the bombs and the anti-aircraft guns. Cardiff seemed near and George's friends were in danger—the teachers belonging to the Cardiff Teachers' Association, many of whom lived in Cardiff, but even more the boys of his own class. They would be sleepless and tired, anxious, with stories to tell. Some might be killed, others rendered homeless. Each morning he travelled into the city by car or motor bike, or perhaps by train during the petrol shortage. Each morning he was relieved to see the whole class there and listened easily to their stories of the bombs. He was a fairly strict teacher but he knew when to relax with them, and when they needed to talk. For all his nightly anxieties, he was not prepared for the night when it really happened.

He arrived at Marlborough Road School to find it flattened. Fortunately no one had been using the building that night and it was empty, but many people had been killed in the surrounding houses. This meant, first of all, a hunt to find if all his boys were safe. They were. Then, to their disappointment, for like schoolboys the world over they looked forward to a long holiday now their school was bombed, another school was found for them and Mr T. G. Thomas was assigned to Roath Park School. Several of his boys were also sent to that school, and he had one extra pleasure. He was asked to teach Scripture throughout the school. This experience confirmed two principles from which he never departed. He enjoyed the teaching of Scripture and realized how much it meant that the Bible was more than literature to him. He was teaching the Word of God and he believed it. This meant that the boys listened and he saw the effect upon them. The two principles he confirmed were: a) that Christian knowledge should always be taught in our schools; and b) that it should never be taught by anyone who does not believe it. The two men from the wartime coalition government who were at that time working on a new Education Bill for England and Wales, Butler and Chuter Ede, both desired and secured the first of those principles—

Christian knowledge was a required item on the curriculum. What they did not secure was the second.

A Candidate for Parliament

George had no desire to leave teaching. It seemed to him to be an ideal job and he could happily have taught all his life. He was a good teacher, with a real concern for his boys and the world in which they were growing up. He had accepted the necessity for the war to destroy the evil thing in Nazi Germany. It was, however, not enough to destroy evil. You had to build good, and he saw no way of changing society for these boys he was teaching, except through politics. He read of work on the Education Bill and of the Beveridge Report. He could see the possibilities of a Labour government after the war putting these things into action and building a Christian Britain. Gradually politics took over more and more of his interest.

Early in 1944, Elizabeth Andrews, the women's organizer for the Welsh Labour Party, who knew Mam and had watched with interest the growth of her son George, asked him if she could submit his name to Transport House as a candidate for Parliament. George had not openly expressed an interest in going into Parliament, but it is most likely that his growing involvement in political affairs would have led him to consider it. Elizabeth Andrews was a persuasive and influential woman, the very first woman to become a Justice of the Peace in Wales. If she believed in him, then he could hardly say no. After all, she was not offering him a seat in Parliament, only to let his name go forward to be considered as a possible candidate. He agreed and his name was sent to Transport House. He was interviewed and considered suitable. His name was put on the list. To his surprise he soon received invitations. One came from Blackburn which had two seats in Parliament, and had to nominate two candidates for the same constituency. The local party therefore was looking for two likely candidates. He went to Blackburn, faced his first selection committee and met as his partner a *Daily Mirror* journalist, the red-headed Barbara Betts, who later became better known as Barbara Castle. They were both adopted with enthusiasm by the Blackburn Labour Party.

George travelled home in great excitement. He could already see himself entering Parliament at the next election as one of the two members for Blackburn. It was a pity that Blackburn was in Lancashire. If it had been in Wales he would have been delighted. Problems began to arise in his mind. He had no intention of moving to Blackburn, but how could he manage to nurse his constituency so far from home? Could he afford it? Over the next week his enthusiasm for Blackburn diminished and then the letter came for which he had hoped and prayed. It was an invitation to be considered as a candidate for Cardiff South. He wrote at once to Blackburn, explaining his doubts about getting to know the constituency before the general election, and to Cardiff to say that he was willing. He was not being asked to be adopted, but to be considered for possible selection. There were others also invited to Cardiff South. One of them was Leonard James Callaghan, dressed in his naval lieutenant's gold-braided uniform. George couldn't compete with that, but he lost by only one vote! Later, he would get to know James Callaghan much better, but now he rather envied him. His humour did not desert him as he said, "That uniform was worth more than one vote." Callaghan responded warmly if somewhat patronizingly, "I am sure that this young man will get adopted by another constituency." The "young man" was, in fact, older than James Callaghan! Cardiff had seemed ideal, he had lost it, but George was never one to despair. He never mentioned that Blackburn had been a fairly safe seat.

He went back to his teaching at Roath Park School. One day an old miners' leader, Methuselah ("Meth") Jones came to the school and asked him if he would let his name go forward for the Cardiff Central constituency. He did not accept at once, but asked for time to think and consult with his family. That night he talked it over with Mam and Dad Tom and they both said he should seek selection. Why he hesitated was no doubt partly the fear of missing selection again, but this time he was successful. He attended the Labour Party Conference held in Blackpool, in May 1945, just ten days after the war in Europe came to an end, as the prospective parliamentary candidate for Cardiff Central.

The Blackpool Conference

The main issue at the conference was obviously to be the coming general election. Attlee had already spoken with Churchill. The

Conservatives wanted a snap election which they thought they could win on the enormous reputation of Churchill as "the man who won the war"; Labour wanted an end to wartime coalition, but it was Attlee's view that they should keep the government together until the end of the war with Japan, which both expected to last several months. The favoured date was October. Both Attlee and Churchill seemed to agree to this. Attlee made a condition, that the coalition government would do its utmost to implement the proposals for security and full employment already laid before Parliament. He thought that this would enable him to persuade the conference to stay in coalition until the end of the war with Japan. George was not of course aware of these discussions, nor of the divisions in the National Executive of the Labour Party between Attlee, Bevin and Dalton, who wanted to stay in the coalition, and Morrison, who thought the party would not brook continued participation in the coalition with their enemies, the Tories! At the conference, Morrison carried the day and Attlee wrote to Churchill while the conference was still in session. Churchill thought that Attlee had let him down and went at once to the King to tender his resignation.

At Blackpool, the news that the coalition was over was greeted with loud applause. Ellen Wilkinson, the Party Chairman, said: "Never before was Labour so united or in such fighting fettle." The *Daily Express*, reporting the conference, hailed Morrison as "the present idol and leader of the Party". Several, including Ellen Wilkinson, began some lobbying to get Attlee to step aside and let Morrison lead the party to election victory. They failed and Attlee remained leader. The reason was not his rhetoric, for Morrison was a much more exciting speaker, but his ability to hold the party together. *Picture Post* summed it up: "Though overshadowed by his colleagues he co-ordinates the Party."

George was more concerned with the policy and programme speeches than he was with disputes over leadership. He listened to Morrison on domestic affairs and then to Attlee on "the war, the San Francisco Conference, India, the treatment of Germany, the peace settlement, the need for world economic planning and the need for Britain, the United States and the Soviet Union to continue to work in peace as they had in the war". It was a good survey, an effective speech, and George applauded with the rest. He probably followed with more interest the policy discussions on education, social security, full employment, and the Beveridge Report, because they all came nearer to the concerns he felt at home. But he knew that he would have to inform himself about party policy in foreign affairs too. In particular he was moved by Ernest Bevin's "tremendous speech on international co-operation", which, he comments, "was later to earn him the Foreign Secretaryship". Like everyone there he tried to catch the chairman's eye so that he could speak and make his presence known as "the prospective candidate for Cardiff Central". The mood of the conference was exhilarating—"We all voiced our determination to build a better Britain and prevent the unemployment of the pre-war years." It was a chance to meet the other candidates and to be known by the leaders of the party. They all expected to win the election, which they had agreed should be as soon as possible, rather than remain in a coalition which masked their identity as a party. They discussed the issue and, as George summed it up later, "Clem Attlee and his team in the National Government were given their marching orders and told they must be prepared to leave the government and insist on a general election."

The coalition ended on 28th May with a farewell party in the cabinet rooms for ministers and ex-ministers. Lord Chandos recorded that "Attlee adopted a very correct but rather chilly attitude" (quoted in *Attlee* by Richard Harris). He described Ernest Bevin as "shaken and anxious; Morrison expectant". The attempts to replace Attlee did not succeed at the Blackpool conference. As soon as the coalition ended, Harold Laski wrote to Attlee, suggesting that he should resign. He was offered the Companion of Honour and accepted, while Ernest Bevin, offered the same distinction, refused. But Attlee did not resign. Laski's letter had been colourful with analogies from wartime changes, but Attlee's reply was in one line, "Thank you for your letter, contents of which have been noted." Churchill called the general election for 5th July 1945 and Attlee led the Labour Party into battle.

The Campaign

George had never fought a campaign before, but neither had his opponents. Charles Hallinan, a well-liked local solicitor, a member of the Cardiff City Council, and Deputy Lord Mayor, was the Conservative candidate; Peter Morgan, a very friendly young man in his twenties, who had been on active service during the war and worked much with refugees in Europe, was fighting the seat for the Liberals. All three fought a good clean campaign and became firm friends. The sitting member, Sir Ernest Bennett, who was National Labour (as George says, "who had abandoned Labour to support Ramsay MacDonald in 1931") was not seeking re-election. In the 1931 election, he had had a majority for National Labour of more than 13,000; in the 1935 election when Labour, but again no Conservative, contested the seat, he was less than 5,000 votes ahead of the Labour candidate. So this constituency, while nominally Labour, had voted for National Labour in the last two elections. It was by now no longer a safe Labour seat when opposed by a good Conservative candidate with local support.

George had to ask for leave of absence from the school while he fought the campaign. With his supporters he walked the streets of his prospective constituency and knocked on doors. He had a great advantage in that he was known as Mr Thomas, the teacher, and some of the families knew him already through their children. He had taught in Marlborough Road and then Roath Park School for thirteen years and some of his boys were voters now. He met one of them at a campaign meeting. It was the first he addressed in Cardiff. When it came to question time, a young man stood up and said, "I want to say something." That always sounds ominous. The interrupter usually wants to let off steam and parade his own ideas rather than draw out the meaning of what the speaker has said. The chairman wisely reminded him that he must either ask a question or be quiet. "But I want to say something," he repeated. George did not recognize him, but he looked familiar and rather than create a scene, he suggested that the young man be allowed to speak. As soon as he started speaking, George recognized the boy who had fainted in class twelve years before. It was George Edgebrook! He simply told the story of his poverty and George's kindness. That was all. It gave George a powerful emotional support.

George's main platform had been a determination that the poverty of the thirties should never return. He could not have had a more sincere tribute to his continuing concern. He had not whipped up this concern for the poor as an election ploy. For more than twelve years he had lived with that deep desire to eradicate poverty and he was now seeking the means to accomplish it. His own appeal was personal: "I will fight to ensure that no mother suffers as mine has done." He knew what he was talking about and his insistence was that private enterprise should not be allowed to put profit before people. He also fought as a Christian, believing that politics should be used to translate Christian values into practice, and determined so to use any political influence he might achieve. Then as now, George believed utterly in the British parliamentary system and thought that Parliament was one of the means for Christian people to make the world more closely resemble God's world.

He was a Christian socialist, as many Labour candidates were in 1945. He wanted the chapel vote, but he did not approve of church or chapel telling a person how to vote. Each one must vote for what he thought right. The local Roman Catholic Church in Cardiff Central had a notice pinned to the door reading, "To vote for George Thomas is a mortal sin." The official Roman Catholic condemnation of Communists sometimes took the form of opposition to Labour, and George was both left-wing and chapel.

The visit of Churchill to Cardiff was a blow to Labour morale, but George's supporters lined the route with Labour posters in every window! There was a concern about the forces' vote. Many thought that as Churchill was leading the Conservatives, the forces' vote would be for him across the board. However, one incident during the campaign gave George hope. At an open-air meeting, a sailor asked for his megaphone. George handed it to him with trepidation and was encouraged to hear him say with confidence: "All the forces want you to vote Labour." Eventually it was the forces' vote which gave Labour its landslide victory. That vote was so massive that the final results were not published until three weeks after polling. The results staggered the world. Britain had rejected her hero. Personally, Winston Churchill won his seat, but the country turned to Labour for its rebuilding; to Clement Attlee instead of Winston Churchill.

The Result

In Tonypandy the people were not thinking of Attlee or Churchill, their whole heart was with George. When the day came for the official count, the boxes from overseas joined the others from Cardiff, and George went to the City Hall to watch and wait. He stayed for several hours watching the counting and grew more and more depressed—

every ballot paper he saw was a vote for Hallinan! When it became clear that the result would not be known until morning he went home to Tonypandy and told Mam he thought he had lost. Next morning he was not allowed to return to Cardiff alone—Mam went with him as though to conjure the votes in his favour. The morning was wet and grey, not unusual in the valleys, and it matched George's feelings. He entered the City Hall amicably with his principal opponent, Charles Hallinan. The count was still going on and George brightened when it became apparent that the votes were going his way. Then at the crucial moment of the announcements the candidates assembled in their raincoats outside City Hall to hear the Lord Mayor read out the results:

Hallinan, Charles—Conservative	11,982
Hopkin Morgan, Peter—Liberal	5,121
Thomas, George—Labour	16,506

Outside, it was pouring with rain, but the crowds remained waiting for the result. It had been a long time since an election and this one had a very great significance for the future of the country. As no one knew the exact size of the total vote, the cheering of Conservative supporters at the announcement of nearly 12,000 votes for Hallinan died down quickly to hear the expected small Liberal vote and then to know whether or not Labour had passed the Conservative 12,000. As the voice of the Mayor came to "Thomas, George, 16,000 . . ." the rest was drowned in cheers which went on for some time. The rain was forgotten and the only interest now was how the other Labour candidates had done. Hilary Marquard had won Cardiff East and Jim Callaghan Cardiff South. It was a wonderful night for Labour and soon the news filtered through that there had been a Labour landslide throughout the country.

George, numbed at first, soon recovered his buoyant spirit and exulted in the fact that he was elected a Member of Parliament in a Labour-led House. He thanked his supporters who were jubilant in their praise of him. They drank his health and wished him well, but his strict teetotal habits did not desert him. Even on such a night he drank to the victory in lemonade. Mam was there too, as proud as she could be. He could not go back to Tonypandy that night. It was a night of celebrations, and only in the morning did he take the train to his Valley. As he trudged up the familiar slope to his home in Ely

Street, every house had a flag hanging from the window, and outside number 62 was a chalked message, much like the message for soldiers coming home from the war. It read, "Congratulations George on your good work in Parliament."

A little later, but before they took their seats, George invited Jim Callaghan to spend a week with him in Tonypandy so that they could get to know each other. It was a wonderful week. They walked and joked and dreamed together. They went one day into Cardiff to meet the officials of the City Council with whom they would be expected to work over the years of their membership of Parliament. As they walked around St John's Square, Jim suddenly asked, "What are you going to do in this Parliament?" George was taken by surprise. It was a new world and he simply thought of learning to become an MP and making sure that he represented Cardiff faithfully. He was already making some plans, but mostly concerned with looking after his constituency. Jim had no such inhibitions. He declared quite firmly, "Before the end of this Parliament I shall be in the Government." This was far from George's thoughts. He was simply happy and excited. Parliament and his new life as an MP seemed enough to fill his vision of the future.

CHAPTER SEVEN

◆◆◆

The Member for Cardiff Central

M ANY YEARS LATER, after a distinguished period of office as
Speaker of the House of Commons, loaded with honours and
praised on every side, George Thomas could still remember the pride
and the thrill of walking through the Carriage Gates of the Palace
of Westminster for the first time, as the member for Cardiff
Central:

> I felt eight feet tall when I walked through the great Carriage
> Gates into Palace Yard, Westminster, for the first time as a newly
> elected Member of Parliament. I thought of Palmerston and
> Pitt, Gladstone and Disraeli, and all the other giants of our
> parliamentary history.

He never lost that deep sense of privilege of being an MP. He had
always worked hard, as schoolteacher, policeman, chapel man,
Labour Party official, but now it was a new sense of privilege and of
standing in a great historical succession that made the mature man
approaching thirty-seven aware that privilege carried responsibility.
He vowed to give his all to this new honour bestowed upon him and
to work harder than he had ever done before.

The House of Commons had been bombed during the war
and the assembly on 1st August was in the House of Lords, adap-
ted for the use of the Commons. George sat between Jim
Callaghan and Michael Foot. A whole new world was opening up
to him.

He had already worked out his pattern of life in London, carefully,
because the salaries of Members of Parliament were low and there
was no expense account. He could no longer earn money teaching.
Together with other members from Wales, he booked a room in a
friendly Welsh hotel near Russell Square. It had the advantage, not
only of being Welsh, but also strictly a temperance hotel. He went

home at weekends to nurse his constituency, but while in London, this hotel was his base. Each day he left early to collect the morning mail and take it to the library of the House of Commons before other members arrived. The library was soon crowded, because MPs had no office accommodation, but had to answer their letters there or in the corridors. There were, of course, no secretaries provided, and this meant personal replies written in longhand. The habit of working in the corridors was helpful to MPs getting to know each other. George very soon made friends with Anthony Eden, who gave him some good advice. George, still fascinated by the corridors of the great, expressed to Eden his admiration of the wonderful people in Parliament. Eden warned him that there were also some of the other sort and added, "The good thing is that we can choose our friends. You be careful in your choice." George chose many who were not of his own party. From the beginning he was not above all a party man. He represented Cardiff and he had a Nonconformist conscience. He would not be fodder for the lobbies.

George was a new boy, but he was not alone. The country had not had a general election for ten years and the majority of members were new. J. E. D. Hall in *Labour's First Year*, puts it quite dramatically: "When the new Parliament assembled on 1st August to re-elect the Conservative Colonel Clifton Brown as Speaker, the familiar faces were islands in a sea of strangers." When Churchill entered the chamber to take his seat among the Opposition, the Conservatives rose as one man and roared out "For he's a jolly good fellow". The Labour members were silent—with one exception; Ellen Wilkinson's sense of history overcame her party loyalties. But she joined in the counter-demonstration also when George Griffiths rose to his feet and, conducting vigorously with his arms, began to sing "The Red Flag". Raggedly at first, but with growing volume, his colleagues joined in. Most stood, but the front bench was indecisive. Some ministers, momentarily transported to a Labour Party Conference, rose promptly and then, recollecting themselves, sat down again. George joined in as heartily as any.

The State Opening of the new Parliament

Parliament opened on 15th August, the day Japan surrendered. On that day, George saw the full panoply of the institution whose ceremony he later learnt in detail and loved with a deep and enduring respect. A description of J. E. D. Hall may help us to capture the atmosphere of that day. He wrote it while the occasion was still fresh in his memory as a member of the parliamentary press gallery:

> The House met in the morning in St Stephen's Hall—it was 111 years to the day since the Commons last sat there—and were summoned to the House of Lords by the Gentleman Usher of the Black Rod to hear the Speech from the Throne. In the afternoon they reassembled in their own Chamber where the Prime Minister made the statement of the surrender. Afterwards they attended a service of thanksgiving at St Margaret's Church, returned again to the House and voted an address of congratulation to the King on the achievement of final victory and restoration of peace.

And so on the day when the Second World War finally ended, Britain began the difficult experiment: a new era with the first Labour government in power with a large enough majority to carry out its policies. George was among the victors and he listened with his characteristic care to the King's Speech, outlining the proposed programme of the Labour government during its first year in office.

George listened for his own special interests which were his reasons for going into politics in the first place. What did his party intend to do for poverty, for unemployment, for justice; and particularly, how could he fit in a plea for leasehold reform? Many details flashed through his mind, but it was general issues that filled his thoughts now. Cardiff was his immediate concern, but as an MP, he had responsibility for the country as a whole. After the sacrifices of war, he would be able to play his part in building a happier Britain, where there would be no poverty, no enervating insecurity, families with assured homes, schools well equipped and staffed, a prosperous Wales in a prosperous Britain, with overseas responsibilities and trade. Above all he thought of peace and a world nearer than ever before to God's world. How could he fail to pray at such a moment, "Thy kingdom come, thy will be done, on earth as it is in heaven"? He listened.

The Speech from the Throne

After stating the most obvious task of converting industry from the purposes of war to those of peace and expanding the export trade, came the first Labour objective: "securing by suitable control or by public ownership that our industries and services shall make their maximum contribution to the national well-being".

The first significant proposal was to bring the Bank of England under public ownership. Then, as George expected: "A Bill will also be laid before you to nationalize the coal mining industry," adding "as part of a concerted plan for the co-ordination of the fuel and power industries". The government also declared its intention to take what powers were necessary to secure the right use of resources and distribution and to set fair prices for essential supplies and services. This clearly meant the continuation of rationing. It also declared its determination to increase the number of homes. This meant organizing the resources of building and manufacturing industries to meet the housing and essential building needs of the nation. There were other measures concerning compulsory purchase, compensation, then, "You will be asked to approve measures to provide a comprehensive scheme of insurance against industrial injuries, to extend and improve the existing scheme of social insurance and to establish a national health service."

For George, next to the nationalizing of the coal mining industry, the National Health Service was one of the most exciting plans. But the legislation to repeal the Trades Dispute and Trade Union Act was also of immediate relevance to him. This Parliament obviously had a full programme before it and not all could be done in the first year.

The end of the Speech explained something dear to Attlee's heart and, although at the time he did not know it, which would involve George in world travel. For years Clement Attlee had believed that Britain must fulfil its promises to India and set her free. The Speech therefore included: "In accordance with the promises already made to my Indian peoples, my Government will do their utmost to promote in conjunction with the leaders of Indian opinion the early realization of full self-government in India." That full self-government came in 1947, amidst much bloodshed, which caused Churchill to issue his rebuke that "The great ship of India is going down." But India was ultimately grateful and it became common parlance that "Gandhi was the father of modern India, but Attlee the father-in-law." George was to remember this years later when he visited Pakistan and India and was mildly rebuked by Mrs Gandhi for the partition of India.

The government had a lot to do. It was therefore a relief to all its members when the ceremonies were over and it could get down to business on 16th August. Just one more ceremony—the Reading of the Outlawries Bill "for the effectual preventing of Clandestine Outlawries". Sir Alan Herbert explained the extraordinary character of this Bill which is "not recommended or introduced by any member. It is not printed and it is quite impossible to find a copy in the Library" (quoted by J. E. D. Hall in *Labour's First Years*). No more than any other member did George know what it was all about. But he learnt that it was a historic reminder of the right of the Commons to discuss whatever they pleased before the King's Speech. This reinforced the independence of the House of Commons from the domination of the monarchy.

The gesture of independence duly made, the Commons discussed the King's Speech. The debate was unusual in that the wartime coalition had accustomed the old members to co-operation and the new ones were all making maiden speeches. Matters of policy also had to give place initially to the victory, which required tributes to Churchill, while the atomic bomb foreshadowed unimagined horrors. Churchill defended it, Attlee was noncommittal. The debate on the King's Speech was not acrimonious.

The Maiden Speech

The member for Cardiff Central was called, but by the wrong name, which gave George Thomas an opportunity to make clear to the Speaker, as well as to the House, that George Thomas was there! His maiden speech was on the second day of the debate on the King's Speech, which lasted four days in all. It was a composite speech containing many of the issues which he would raise in the course of his parliamentary career.

He called for equality of status for Wales, comparable with that of Scotland, leading to the appointment of a Secretary of State for Wales; he asked that other employment might be found for those miners who suffered from silicosis and pneumoconiosis and were no longer fit to work in the mines; he spoke up for his constituency, which is common in maiden speeches, saying that the port of Cardiff should be the exporting centre of the west country, rather than merely an importing centre; he drew attention to the housing problems in Cardiff and asked for a larger degree of public ownership of housing, in the form of council houses and estates; he supported the attention the new government was giving to raising the old age pensions. He was not yet ready to make his major attack on the property leasehold system, but it was already hinted at.

It is customary for members to be congratulated on their maiden speech and George Thomas was, with unusual warmth, because he had at once caught the sympathy of the House. These were matters that concerned many of them and they were made with "good common sense".

Within the next few days, the House became well acquainted with the member for Cardiff Central. He was forever asking questions and usually requiring the details of a written answer. On 21st August, he asked how many ex-service men in Cardiff had applied for help in setting up in business during the period 1944–1945 and how many were refused. The reply came precisely; "In the period, 1st January 1944–31st July 1945—62 requests granted, 19 refused, 22 outstanding." He found these times for questions, particularly the written answers, valuable for his constituency and to inform himself. His quick mind soon grasped the important questions to ask. On 23rd August he was twice on his feet and the questions were detailed. "How many pensioners in Cardiff receive supplementary benefits, and how many applications have been refused?" Regarding the emergency training scheme for teachers, "How many recruits have been accepted?" and addressing the Minister of Education, Ellen Wilkinson, he asked "whether it is her intention to give equal opportunities for recruitment in the near future to the 'uncertificated teachers' who have already rendered good service?"

National Insurance

The Coalition government had been concerned with the prosecution of the war, but it had also had responsibility on the home front and much of what Labour was about to do now had already been talked about in the Coalition government during the progress of the war.

Nothing fired that government more than the Beveridge Report on Social Insurance. Conservative, Liberal and Labour were at one in commending it. There was much debate and several White Papers and the legislation had got under way during the war. The Ministry of National Insurance had been established and the Family Allowance Act was on the Statute Book. The foundations were already laid. The Labour government lost no time in completing the structure and by October the House was busy with the National Insurance (Industrial Injuries) Bill which was of much concern to all those members representing industrial and coal mining areas. But all were concerned. The Bill was comprehensive, embracing all persons under any contract of service or apprenticeship. There was no income limit, the managing director also paying his fourpence a week and receiving the basic benefit of forty-five shillings with appropriate allowances, just the same as the farm worker and the dustman.

James Griffiths was the Minister of National Insurance and his warm Welsh temperament must have encouraged the eager George Thomas as he listened to a man who had himself spent seventeen years in the pits. As he spoke of the National Insurance Bill, and came to the more positive proposals which linked into the Disabled Persons (Employment) Act to train injured men for employment, the minister could not resist an emotional appeal from his own experience: "I still have boyhood memories of buying a threepenny raffle ticket to provide a peg-leg for a miner." He paused for a moment, recalling days that George could also recall. In his Memoirs, George lists Jim Griffiths with Arthur Pearson, Harold Finch, Eirene White, Cliff Williams, James Idwal Jones and Tudor Watkins as members of the Welsh Parliamentary Labour Party who were deeply steeped in the traditions of the party. At their retirement some years later, he wrote that they "heralded the end of an era. The new intake was very different." That was in 1970. At the beginning of this Parliament in 1945, these people were his models. And not least James Griffiths. He carried the Opposition with him as he presented the National Insurance (Industrial Injuries) Bill for its Second Reading and as it became law. Some of the Opposition speakers were as enthusiastic as Labour members. George was in an unusual House of Commons. The issues were too serious for petty party strife. The Bill was what the Conservative minister, Osbert Peake, had described as "a scheme born in a new atmosphere of free and equal partnership between

88

employer and workman". And George could hardly fail to be moved by Jim Griffiths' final speech:

> All the time I have been working out these details, I have tried to remember that behind the contributions, the benefits, the rates, behind them all are human beings, men and women with their hopes and dreams, their fears and their disappointments. For a generation I have lived with the consequences of insecurity, but to those who profess to fear that security will weaken moral fibre and destroy self-respect, let us say this. It is not security which destroys but insecurity. It is the fear of tomorrow that paralyses the will; it is the frustration of human hopes that corrodes the soul. Security in adversity will, I believe, release our people from the haunting fears of yesterday and make tomorrow not a day of dread but a day of welcome. It will release their gifts and energies for the service of the nation.

Then he concluded:

> This Bill represents an act of faith, of trust in the British people. I ask the House to accept it, in the sure confidence that our people are worthy of our trust.

There were other bills to follow. For Labour it was a holy war, but their enemy was not the Opposition, who often agreed with them, but the poverty which so many had understood and experienced in their youth, as George had. In connection with some of these bills, he says: "The Government pushed ahead vigorously with other social and economic reforms. There was a feeling of crusade as we took into public ownership the essential industries of coal, gas and electricity." In these nationalization crusades, of course, they had a growing opposition from the Conservatives and the lobbies became like jousting fields. The voting was secure because of Labour's large majority. The enthusiasm was electric and often almost religious in its fervour. To quote George Thomas's Memoirs again, "Each night as we trooped through the division lobbies someone would call out, 'Come on, George. Strike Up!' and I would start to sing 'Guide me, O thou great Jehovah'. Instantly there would be a mighty choir singing its way through the lobby."

In its first year, the Labour government presented a staggering eighty-three bills to Parliament. The fifty-seventh was the bill to establish a National Health Service. Beveridge had said that the success of the plan for social insurance would depend upon three assumptions: that unemployment should never rise above 8.5 per cent of the insured population, that family allowances should be paid and that there should be a national health service. The Labour government was well aware of the need to tackle unemployment, and family allowances were being paid. The third remained—the creation of a national health service. The bill was presented by another Welshman, the dominating figure of Aneurin Bevan.

The National Health Service

Civil aviation was nationalized on 24th January 1946; the coal nationalization had its Second Reading on 30th January, its Third on 20th May; Cable and Wireless communications, road and rail transport, electricity and gas were all nationalized during the 1945/46 sessions of Parliament. Attlee, in his autobiography, comments that apart from iron and steel, there was "not much opposition to our nationalization policy".

The National Health Service Bill, published on 22nd March 1946, was much more controversial. The reason probably lay in the difference between the two Welshmen in whose hands were the two major components of the new social structure: James Griffiths and Aneurin Bevan. Although they were both most certainly loyal Labour men, they were heirs of the great Welsh pioneer in social legislation, David Lloyd George. George Thomas must often have remembered the story of his mother's move to Labour and John Tilbury's wise comment that Labour was the radical party now. James Griffiths had characteristically taken the existing Coalition national insurance scheme and carried it through in substantially the same form. Aneurin Bevan's style was to sweep the board clean of previous ideas and to start afresh. The universal health service involved a general practitioner and specialist service, general and special hospital treatment, maternity and child welfare clinics, eye and dental treatment, spectacles and deaf aids and so on, to be provided free to all persons insured under the National Insurance Act. No one expected the tenpence a week to pay for this vast structure and therefore money would be required from the Exchequer (or the general taxpayers) and the local authorities (or the ratepayers).

"When this scheme is carried out," Aneurin Bevan announced, "it will place this country in the forefront of all countries in the world in medical services." One ancient institution which was abolished by this bill was the "workhouse". George felt this most keenly, because he loathed the place where old people were treated with indignity, almost as though they were criminals. He had often had to approach almoners in the other hospitals to get an old person's charges reduced, and sometimes succeeded. But the workhouse remained the largest building in his constituency and was his Bastille which would be destroyed by the revolution of the National Health Service Bill. The superintendent of the workhouse in Cardiff acted like a beadle from a Dickens novel. He insisted upon being called "Master" by inmates and visitors alike. That was merely laughable, but the treatment and the attitude to the inmates offended George greatly. At tea time he saw the inadequacy of the food and complained to the Master who snapped back at him, "They are paupers. They should have taken greater care not to come here." A sharp response from George that they had never had enough income to save for their old age was shrugged off. His anger against the system was clear. It had to be changed, and the new MP gave his enthusiastic support to a service that would put an end to all that. One other incident during a visit to that same workhouse moved him to tears. His own words are best to describe that rainy day.

> An old couple I knew were sitting on a bench outside. I told them they should go inside. They would catch pneumonia in the drizzle. The old lady replied, "George, they separate us when we are in there." The image of that couple remained in my mind throughout the health service debates.

Aneurin Bevan piloted the bill through the House against considerable opposition and threats that the doctors would withdraw or emigrate to America. But Bevan was formidable and his bill was passed through both Houses and received the Royal Assent on 6th November 1946. There was much more to be done before the National Health Service was established. Throughout 1947 several doctors attempted to fight a rearguard action against many of its provisions. Then Bevan secured cabinet approval for a debate in the House on 9th February 1948 on a motion reaffirming the government's determination to introduce the Act on the appropriate day, 5th July 1948. This date was kept. It was Aneurin Bevan's crowning achievement, and until he died he fought against every effort to dilute it.

A Visit to Warsaw

The work of a member of Parliament is accumulative—the longer you are in Parliament, the more approaches are made to you. George had an increasing correspondence, particularly from his constituency, and he dealt with this conscientiously. But there were also many opportunities for broadening his education and experience. He faced the usual dangers too. Pressure groups tried to involve him in their particular causes. Several of the new MPs, particularly those with pacifist leanings, fell for the attraction of invitations to the Peace Conference in Warsaw. The Soviet Union adopted peace as a political weapon. The USA had the atomic bomb and Russia did not. The Soviet Union posed as the champion of peace and invited influential people in the West to peace conferences. Picasso, known to be sympathetic to Communism, designed the posters and stationery they used to impress. The logo he used was his own type of dove of peace. When Karl Barth, the famous Swiss theologian, was invited to the Peace Conference, he declined the invitation, but added with his typical humour, "What is that bird that looks like a vulture on your notepaper?" George was not so discerning. He was in fact a little naive when he received an invitation. The only country he had visited outside Britain was Denmark and he rather liked the idea of a visit to Poland. Communism was not quite what it had been before the war, the Russians had been our gallant allies. Why not? The invitation came to him in the autumn of 1945 when he was quite new to Westminster and he accepted it. As it turned out it did him no political harm but it gave him what he called "the most harrowing experience of my life".

He visited the site of the Warsaw ghetto and Auschwitz and he spoke with young Poles at the conference. This was a broadening experience he would not have missed. At the ghetto he wept and in Auschwitz he was shocked into numb silence. He was seeing evidence at first hand of the horrors he had condemned in Nazi behaviour, but he was also learning something about the real fate of the Jews in Eastern Europe. His visit to Warsaw made him sympathetic all his life to the Jews, who insisted that the world should never forget the atrocities of Auschwitz and that those guilty should be hunted down as long as they lived.

Meeting young Polish people at the Peace Conference enabled him to begin to assess the terrible price that Poland had paid for the war. Two of these encounters stood out in his memory. One was in a circle of young people which included a girl with a six-figure number tattooed on her arm. He innocently asked her about it but she gave no reply, although he was aware that he had asked a fearful question. The silence of the whole group was explained to him afterwards. It was her number in Auschwitz, tattooed for the rest of her life. He was told that she still woke screaming after nightmares, and was fighting to get back to normality. His comment on that indiscreet moment was, "I still cringe when I remember my ignorance."

The other encounter was with a young Pole who spoke frankly about his future hopes. Bereft of any qualifications he nevertheless said, "I want to go to the United States." This didn't make sense to George. Why should a young man who appeared to be a convinced Communist want to go to the leading capitalist country in the world? His answer to George's puzzled enquiry was, "I am a Jew. If you look at Polish history you will see that we have a pogrom every fifty years or so. I want to get out."

Although George may have been naive to accept this invitation which seemed to support the Soviet Union's propaganda for peace, it can be said in retrospect that he got more out of the trip than they got out of him. His visit to Auschwitz was also a very good preparation for a later visit as an observer to the Nuremberg trials. A former inmate of Auschwitz had shown them round and pointed out the human incinerators with charred bones still there, the room full of human hair for stuffing cushions, the mountain of sandals and shoes, many of them in children's sizes, which shocked everyone who saw them. Auschwitz dried up any springs of compassion for the monster who had perpetrated such things.

The Nuremberg Trials

Long before 8th May 1945 when the war in Europe came to an end, the Allied leaders had issued public proclamations to the effect that after the war was won, those responsible for its outbreak, ensuing deprivation, suffering and atrocities, would be dealt with as war criminals. On 8th August, the four major powers, Britain, America, France and the Soviet Union, signed the London Agreement, which resulted in the International Military Tribunal. Much earlier, in 1943,

Churchill, Roosevelt and Stalin had agreed that those responsible by act and consent for committing crimes against peace and who were guilty of atrocities in occupied countries, would be handed over to the Allied governments as soon as Hitler was defeated. However, at the end of the war, the four major powers, in order to highlight the awful crimes of the Nazis, saw an opportunity to present a public demonstration of the leading Nazis against whom all twenty-three Allied nations wished to bring charges. They planned to do this before a single court. The list of those to be tried was published and the city of Nuremberg chosen for the stage. The so-called legal basis of the Nazi treatment of the Jews and those of Jewish origin had been fashioned in Nuremberg. The city was heavy with German history and its name was given to the Nuremberg Laws (1935) which defined the degree of Jewishness that deprived a citizen of human rights. Nuremberg was a good choice for the trials.

The London Agreement named twenty-four Nazis and six institutions. The indictment was on four charges:

1. The crime of being a party to a common plan to wage aggressive war.
2. Crimes against peace—planning, preparing, initiating or waging a war of aggression—or a war in violation of international treaties.
3. War Crimes—violation of the laws or customs of war, which included wanton destruction and the mistreatment of prisoners of war.
4. Crimes against humanity—inhuman treatment of civilians, extermination and persecutions on racial and religious grounds.

A common indictment was presented at Nuremberg by the twenty-three nations, with the trial scheduled for 20th November 1945. The ancient medieval town was in ruins, with the rubble concealing 30,000 dead. Hardly a building was undamaged. The Allied air forces had done their work well! The Palace of Justice, however, which is away from the centre of the town, was still useable. There the trials were opened at 10 a.m. on the appointed day and continued—meeting five days a week—until 31st August 1946. Judgement was delivered on 30th September and 1st October. All but three of the twenty-four indicted sat in two rows against the wall to hear their sentence. Robert Ley had hanged himself in his cell, Gustav Krupp was declared senile, and no one could find Martin Bormann.

The trial was already in progress when a group of British MPs went as observers to this historic and chilling event. Under normal circumstances, one might have expected George Thomas, who was one of the delegation, to feel compassion for a defeated people facing trial by their victors. There was no one on trial from the winning side. But the experience of Auschwitz had hardened him. In a room outside the court he talked with the French prosecuting counsel, who showed him some of the evidence he was going to submit. There was the shrunken head of a Polish boy whose crime had been that he had fallen in love with a German girl. The head, mounted on a plaque like some trophy of the hunt, had been found in a German official's house, used as an ornament. Another exhibit was a jar of soap made from human fat. There was also a lampshade made from human skin "torn from the chest of a Polish prisoner while he was still alive". These horrors revived George's worst memories of his Warsaw visit. In the court, he looked down at Goering with horror. He seemed no longer a human being, but "a python in my path". These were new emotions for George. He had never looked at human beings in that way before. "When I saw an American military policeman push a truncheon in his side to make him stand to attention when addressed by the judge," he commented, "I felt no sympathy for him." That was a unique moment in the life of George Thomas. He left Nuremberg after a few days convinced that he had been right to put aside his pacifist principles and report for military service in 1939. It was right to use force against this demonic power of evil. Yet, with the war over now, he was returning to his earlier pacifism, not fanatically, nor without qualifications.

The MPs who visited Germany returned profoundly disturbed by what they had learnt. This led to many questions in the House, and George Thomas was not slow in asking his. He was concerned about German schoolteachers, and on the 23rd October 1945, he asked, "What proportion of schoolteachers now employed in German schools by the Military Government in the British Zone were previously employed by the Nazis in a similar capacity?" It was an oral question and the minister was not able to answer it. Figures were not available. George did not stop there. He made his own enquiries and came back a month later to say that "Denazification is being hindered by the presence of 80 per cent of the German teachers who were Nazis, now employed under our authority." The Minister assured him that the figure was nothing like that, but George persisted. He was, perhaps, not fully aware that the British Military Government had extreme difficulty in finding any teachers who had not been in some way involved with a Nazi organization. But he was proving himself a probing MP, who would not let the government get away with confused or unsatisfactory answers.

Leasehold Reform

For twenty-one years, George Thomas campaigned for leasehold reform and eventually he succeeded. Tony Greenwood presented the Leasehold Reform Bill to the Commons, along the lines he had been advocating, in February 1967 and it was on the statute book by the autumn. The campaign was a persistent one, and although George developed many interests along the way, from Nyasaland to Cyprus, Greece and Germany, he never forgot that he represented the people of Cardiff, and their suffering was his first concern. He had already hinted at the housing problem in his maiden speech and he kept the issue of Cardiff housing alive in that first Parliament of 1945–1950. At this stage in the story, it might be well to quote from the first speech in which he overtly argued the need for leasehold reform. It was during the debate on the King's Speech in November 1946. The Speech had drawn attention to compensation and the betterment of conditions for the poor. George Thomas rose to speak on the afternoon of 14th November:

> I believe that we shall not be a full democracy until we have, hand in hand with our political democracy, economic freedom for our people. The people of South Wales have long since learnt that political democracy means little unless there is security, unless there is work and unless there are the general amenities that make life worthwhile.
>
> I could have hoped that the government would promise to introduce legislation to deal with the leasehold system of this country. Under the protection of the law, people in all parts of the country are being blackmailed and robbed at the present time. Electors in my own constituency whose parents bought their houses, are having their homes filched from them by great corporations who enjoy the protection of legislation laid down by this House in earlier days. The legislation is a relic of the days when the House of Commons was filled with people who

represented only the great landowning section of our community
. . . I would like to give the House some examples. In May 1938,
the Marquis of Bute, who is "the rich man in his castle" in the
city of Cardiff, sold half of our great city to some London concern which calls itself Western Ground Rents Ltd. That trans-
action included the ground rents of no fewer than 20,000 houses
in Cardiff, 1,000 shops, 250 public houses, some theatres,
cinemas and even a large part of Cardiff Docks.

There was something of a disturbance when George quoted the *Daily
Express* and turning to a fellow MP (probably Callaghan) said, "He
knows all about this racket." There was a protest about the use of
the word "racket" which the Speaker professed not to hear. Then
George continued:

> This is a question about which I feel deeply. The wretched
> ground landlord system is robbing the people . . . Within the
> next ten years the majority of leases in Cardiff will be falling due.
> It will only be possible for householders to keep their homes, and
> business people their shops, if these people are prepared to pay
> the prices which will be demanded of them by WGR or Mountjoy
> Estates which is the estate of the family of the Earl of Bute.

George spoke passionately and brought forward another example.
Cardiff City Council wanted to build a public hall which entailed the
purchase of a car park, but they could not start on it until they had
paid £10,000 to the ground landlord. In the midst of his eloquence
he was challenged by a Conservative member with the intended rhe-
torical question: "Who built the Cardiff Docks?" George was quick
to reply:

> The people of Cardiff built the docks and they have made Cardiff
> what it is today. But now we are trying to build new schools,
> and factories, new housing development; all handicapped by this
> leasehold system.

The debate went on and George ended with an appeal:

> I hope that the government will at last give the people of Wales
> the right to sing "Land of our fathers", and know that it is their
> land and not the land of some corporation in London.

Although George had not yet learnt the art of tactical manoeuvres,
his preaching skills came in useful. He could denounce injustice as
a preacher denounces sin and could appeal for a just decision and

compassion as a preacher appeals for conversion. The Welsh accent did not diminish but rather enhanced the power of his political preaching.

This was his first considerable salvo but there would be others. George Thomas had made his mark and Cardiff knew that it had a champion.

Hastings Banda and Nyasaland

Apart from Warsaw and the Peace Conference, there were other opportunities to be involved in overseas matters. The major involvement was to be in Greece, but quite early an exchange of views and a meeting occurred with an unknown doctor in London who represented Nyasaland. His name, Hastings Banda, later became much better known and George would meet him many years later in his own country where he ruled almost absolutely as Life President.

The first contact came after George had raised questions about teachers in Nyasaland (now Malawi). Dr Hastings Banda wrote to him on 7th April 1946, requesting a meeting. He described himself as "an African of Nyasaland, now resident in this country". He had seen Dr Rita Hinden of the Fabian Colonial Bureau and learnt from her of George's "interest in colonial affairs". He also saw there a copy of the Questions on Nyasaland that George had raised in the House of Commons. His letter continued:

> No doubt, Dr Hinden mentioned to you the existence of a political organization, formed by the Africans, under the title of "Nyasaland African Congress". Last year, the Nyasaland African Congress appointed me as their representative in this country.

He then described his duties as, to bring to the attention of the Colonial Office and the people of this country, questions affecting the Africans in Nyasaland. Among the questions were those concerned with education, and Hastings Banda pointed out that he was approaching George because he had raised questions in the Commons on this very matter. There were other issues also in which he believed George had an interest—political representation, land laws, protection of African women, colour bar, etc. George could hardly fail to respond to such a letter.

He replied almost at once, confirming his interest in the colonies and suggesting a meeting in the House of Commons. They met on 9th May. Hastings Banda was obviously delighted at the quick response and sent a letter giving the details of what he wished to discuss, promising further material when he came.

The heart of the letter (20th April 1946) was:

> The Africans of Nyasaland feel that they must be directly rep-resented in the Legislative Council of the country. There are in round figures 2,000,000 Africans, as against 2,000 Europeans. The Legislative Council is composed of twelve Europeans, six official and six non-official, but not a single African. We feel that we form the greatest majority of the total population. The very existence of anything in the nature of a country or a state in Nyasaland depends entirely on us, since 2,000 Europeans could never form a country or a state.
>
> What is even more, twice within thirty years, we have given our blood and labour in defence of the Empire, both in Africa and outside Africa. We feel that by every and any standard adopted, we are entitled to the rights of full citizens, which include political and civil rights in all their aspects.
>
> As you probably know, land in Africa is very often given away to various speculators or prospectors by Colonial Governments. In all cases, the people are not consulted. The Government, where scrupulous enough, simply tells or orders a chief to sign papers, giving land to any buyer or would-be buyer. We in Nyasa-land have been deprived of our land in this way many times since the British occupation. We feel it is now about time this should stop. We ask that no more land be given to Europeans or Asiatics without our free consent. And by our free consent, we do not mean the consent of a single chief or group of chiefs. The land does not belong to chiefs in Nyasaland, if it does to any other chiefs in Africa at all. It belongs to the people. Chiefs are, accord-ing to our tribal laws and customs, only trustees or custodians. They have no right to give land away to anyone.

Dr Banda added that colonial governments had the habit of looking upon chiefs as representatives of the people, which they are not. He then pointed to the changed situation, now that so many Africans had received advanced education. He was himself a trained doctor, practising in London:

> Almost all over Africa now, there is a large body of educated Africans, politically articulate, who should be taken into con-sideration in deciding any questions affecting Africans. In Nyasa-

land, these educated and articulate Africans have organized themselves into a political body, called the Nyasaland African Congress. We feel therefore that in Nyasaland, the Government must no longer deal with chiefs alone, without consulting the Congress, on any subject affecting Africans. Just as the earls, barons and dukes are not the people of Britain, so too are not chiefs and headmen the people of Nyasaland. The Government does not content itself with consulting dukes, earls and barons in Britain. We see no reason why it should be different in Nyasaland.

These were the lines of discussion on 9th May, when Dr Banda also brought a sheaf of documents including minutes of meetings of the Nyasaland African Congress and letters from Church leaders in Nyasaland. This letter, however, showed clearly what the African Congress was seeking through Hastings Banda. An MP without office, who had been only a few months in the House, was obviously not competent to deal with such issues without consultation. George readily referred the matter to the Secretary of State for the Colonies, George Hall, a mine-worker for eleven years, the member for Aberdare since 1922. He had been Under Secretary of State for Foreign Affairs in the Coalition government during the Second World War. Such a man would surely understand the appeal of that letter. It was returned to George with the comment—typed—"No Action Taken".

Hastings Banda in Power

Later, in 1967, George met Hastings Banda when he was paying an official visit to Kenya, and flew to Malawi with him in his private plane. But these countries were independent by then, and Dr Banda in power was a very different man, although he still had nostalgic memories of Willesden where he had practised as a doctor. He was out of patience with many of his fellow African leaders, and thought Britain very foolish not to look after her own interests in Rhodesia. She should forget all this clamour about racial discrimination and cultivate friendship with South Africa. George had liked him better in London more than twenty years before. His kindly comment in 1967 was: "A maverick among the African leaders, I liked him and respected his spectacular achievements in Malawi." That was probably influenced by his warm reception and protected visit.

A further twenty-five years later, when George Thomas was Viscount Tonypandy, he met the eighty-five-year-old Life President and was upset. A representative of Amnesty International drew George's attention to the lack of human rights in Malawi. There was a man in prison because he had addressed Dr Banda as "President" when he should have said, "Life President".

Age had taken its toll of him. He was frail, but as shrewd as ever. He had ensured that his visitor talked with his senior ministers before coming to him, and he was therefore well aware that George Thomas would be raising the question of people held in detention in Malawi without charge or trial. Amnesty International, having been alerted to the interview that had been arranged between the Life President and the former minister in Wilson's cabinet, had sent George a list of distressing cases where torture and imprisonment without trial were involved. At least one senior Malawian minister told their visitor that he had read the Amnesty International report. This meant that the Malawian government was aware of world anxiety about human rights in their country. Pleasantries were exchanged between the two veteran politicians and conversation was directed towards the efforts of the Life President to improve the education of the brightest of his young people by establishing an academy based upon lines similar to an English public school. But when eventually George tried to raise the issue of the detainees by referring to the long record of fighting for African freedom by the Life President, Dr Banda suddenly decided that he was tired and the interview was at an end. Dismay and frustration filled George's thoughts as he contrasted the young Nyasaland African of long ago with the power-clinging President who did not want to talk of his detainees.

CHAPTER EIGHT

◆◆◆

Defending Democracy in Greece

T HE DIVISION between the Western Allies and the Soviet Union became apparent as soon as the war was won. Stalin was not consulted about the atomic bomb and any plan he had to invade Japan was thwarted. The possession of the atomic bomb by the West was a source of great concern to the Soviet Union. As its forces moved west, especially in the south of Europe, the Western Allies became uneasy. At Potsdam they were able to agree to Stalin's terms which gave him a slice of Poland and of Finland, together with the inclusion of the Baltic states in the Soviet Union. But southern Europe was less clear. One country of dispute was Greece. Its natural trading partners were Yugoslavia, Bulgaria and possibly Albania. All these went under Communist governments eventually, although Yugoslavia was less subservient to the Soviet Union than the others.

George Thomas first made contact with Greece early in 1947. There had been a clash between the Greek government and the students of Athens, and he was asked by the National Union of Students to investigate. He was a new MP, still vulnerable to pressure groups, and inexperienced in foreign affairs. By the time he reached Athens the government had closed down the university. George Thomas was a radical idealist but no Communist. He was aware that America had determined to keep Greece within the sphere of influence of the Western world, and he could hardly disapprove of that, but he was shocked at what he saw in Greece. The Royalist government, supported by the British and the Americans, was behaving in a most undemocratic way. It seemed to be using those who had also been used by the Germans to enforce a new totalitarian rule. The guerrillas were the same men and women who had fought against the Nazis. George saw British forces being used to prop up an undemocratic government and was horrified by what he saw of the treatment of prisoners and guerrillas. In later years, he would look on this visit to

Greece in a different light and admit that he had been used by the Communists.

The contrast between the way in which George describes his Greek adventure in 1947 and his memory of it after reflecting for almost forty years, is instructive as showing his development from the raw idealist who went to Parliament to change the world and the retired Speaker of the House of Commons who had learnt to see things in balance and to understand the necessary compromises of politics. The published account of this adventure is that of Viscount Tony-pandy, the greatly honoured and respected elder statesman, looking back. He calls it "A Lesson in Greek" and it fills an exciting chapter in his memoirs. But there are earlier accounts which portray the events as they happened.

The League for Democracy in Greece

A pressure group in Britain presided over by Compton Mackenzie was supportive of the Greek trade unions and left-wing political movements. It was not Communist, but it was strongly supported by left-wing Labour MPs, some of whom were on its Executive Committee: Bessie Braddock, Donald Bruce, Fred Peart, D. N. Pritt, KC, Captain Swingler, S. Tiffany—and George Thomas. Hannen Swaffer was also a member of the Executive. The aims of the League were spelt out quite clearly:

1. To rebuild and strengthen the traditional friendship between the peoples of Greece and of Great Britain on the basis of the establishment and development of democracy in Greece.
2. To enlighten the British public about the situation in Greece and to promote cultural relations between the two countries.
3. To organize relief to those Greeks who have suffered for their democratic beliefs and activities and to their dependants, and to the dependants of those Greeks who died fighting for democracy.
4. To work for (a) A general amnesty for all Greek democrats imprisoned for political reasons;
   (b) The restoration of trade union and civil liberties generally in Greece;
   (c) The suppression of armed terrorism and the trial and punishment of collaborators.

The assumption behind those aims was that the existing Greek government, restored to power by the British and further supported by the American forces, was a right-wing government, made up largely of those who had been collaborators with the Germans until they were defeated. The brave Greek resistance, as the British Army knew, were the left-wing Greek Liberation Army (ELAS). Many of these were now imprisoned by a government which had not resisted the Germans until the last phase of the war. These men and women of the Greek Liberation Army were now "rebels", hunted down, tortured, and murdered. As George learned these facts, his sympathies went naturally with the oppressed.

The Labour MPs who supported the League saw the "rebels" as their kind and the rebels saw hope in the Labour government of Great Britain.

Colonel Sheppard

One of the most informed members of the Executive of the League was an Australian, Colonel A. W. Sheppard, who first went to Greece with the Australian Imperial Forces in 1941. He was in command of part of the evacuation when German forces overran the mainland, and went to Crete. Early in 1945, when the Germans were on the run, he was in charge of two Australian relief teams and later transferred to UNRWA in charge of relief camps. In July 1946, he was appointed Director of the Northern Greece Office of the British Economic Mission. It was not until he returned to England on 6th March 1947 that he spoke about conditions in Greece. By then he had retired from office. One of the first things he did for the League was to write a pamphlet called *A Study in International Interference*. George Thomas wrote a foreword for this pamphlet, which is his first account in print of the Greek adventure.

First Impressions

The pamphlet by Colonel Sheppard seemed to explain a great deal which had puzzled George Thomas on his visit to Greece. He realized the depth of the tragedy of modern Greece and was aware that many progressive people throughout the world were dismayed and bewildered by it. His visit and this pamphlet convinced him that the atmosphere in Greece provided "a special challenge to the Labour and trade union movement of Great Britain". The British press had not helped. He expressed his judgement of the British press quite strongly: "With a few honourable exceptions there has been a reluctance to give the story of the barbarism unleashed by the quisling Governments who have been maintained in power by the presence of British troops." There is a nice *double entendre* in his assessment of the value of the British troops to the Greek Government:

> When I visited Greece in the early part of this year [1947] it was to be assured by all political parties—from the extreme Left to the extreme Right—that the presence of the British Military forces and the various Missions were of incalculable advantage to the Government in power.

This being so, and considering the cost in money and manpower tied up in Greece, Britain should surely have been concerned about the kind of government it was supporting in Athens.

George Thomas attempted, by giving examples of things he had seen and people he had spoken to in Athens, to show what kind of government it was:

> In Athens I visited an overcrowded political prison. There was pathos in the eager trust which these helpless people placed in the activities of the Labour rank and file in Great Britain. Many of the prisoners were charged with activities against Hitler's Security Battalions during the Occupation! Since some of the leading quisling collaborators are now in the Greek Parliament, this is understandable.

With his superb storytelling style, George tells of a young man in Piraeus, the port of Athens, who was just out of hospital after the amputation of a leg as a result of being shot by a gendarme. He comments, "This same gendarme had been in his house to arrest him during the occupation—for activities against the Nazis! The gendarme was still in the service of the Government."

George was not content with Athens, but asked to go to Larissa and then to the mountains. He then discovered that the only way that he could contact socialists and liberals, apart from prisoners, was "by using the underground movement that had been active during the war". He was aware that the British authorities were worried about his safety as well as about what he might find out. They shadowed him and he comments, "So much for the freedom of movement of a British MP seeking to talk to the workers!" But he did contact the guerrillas. The British lost track of him and there was a scare at home. The newspapers reported him as missing. One typical headline was: "MP Vanishes on Visit to Greek Guerrilla HQ". He had been missing for four days. The newspaper reported:

> Mr T. G. Thomas, 37, Labour MP for Central Cardiff, has vanished since he went on a visit four days ago to a guerrilla HQ in Thessaly, Greece.
>
> He flew to Greece three weeks ago to attend the trials of members of EPON, the Greek left-wing youth organization charged by political opponents with "deviating from its original aims" and indulging in forbidden political activities.
>
> He was representing the Student Labour Federation and other British youth organizations.
>
> Four days ago he was reported in Trikkala, in Thessaly, and was believed to have set out from there on a visit to a guerrilla HQ in a neighbouring mountain range.
>
> The British Military Mission at Edessa, north of Salonika, had previously told him they could not guarantee his safety if he tried to contact the guerrillas. (*Daily Mirror*, 1947)

George had a dangerous and difficult journey, but he was safe. His first-hand account of life among the guerrillas gave him unrivalled authority when he returned to England:

> It was in the shades of Mount Olympus that I contacted the guerrillas. For five days and nights in the peasants' homes of the mountains, sharing not only their hardships but their fellowship as well. The only time that I had any real sense of freedom was in these mountain villages. The young people gathered together to sing the songs of the Resistance Movement against Hitler; this was the first time for me to hear these songs, for it is forbidden to sing them in those parts under the control of the Athens Government. The stories of the persecution with which I was regaled convinced me that the policy of the Government was creating guerrillas. Tyranny always produces its own antidote! Undoubtedly large numbers of guerrilla forces would have been quietly pursuing their daily work had it not been for the ever-present fear and dread of sudden arrest, exile without trial, or even worse.

He concluded that the Greek government must be made up of frightened men, using first British professional help and now American dollars and arms to suppress their own people. His emotions were on the boil when he accused America: "The land where lynching of coloured men goes unpunished rushes to the defence of Greek democracy by helping to keep the tyranny in power." He could not influence America, but he could speak out as a member of the British Parliament. After recounting the number of political executions, including women, and the exile of intellectuals, he states firmly:

> I am convinced that this is the way to breed Communists and not to destroy them. It is a short-sighted and dangerous policy that drives even moderates to resort to extreme policies to defend themselves.

George welcomed the pamphlet by Colonel Sheppard, which confirmed his views and was written from more prolonged acquaintance with the situation. Colonel Sheppard had made quite clear that he was not a Communist. George also accepted his "Ten-point Programme for Improvement" and campaigned for it. Because of his adventures in Greece he was asked to speak at various meetings and he joined the British all-party parliamentary delegation which presented its recommendations to the British Government.

The Recommendations of the All-Party Delegation

> We, Members of Parliament who have visited Greece since the Liberation, have repeatedly warned the British public that the continuation of the repressive and anti-democratic policy of successive right-wing governments, supported by Britain and America, could only lead to a further deterioration of the situation.
>
> The British All-Party Parliamentary Delegation recommended the formation of a new all-party government, a general policy of clemency towards political prisoners, the release of the political exiles, new elections on an up-to-date register, the restoration of trade union freedom and the early withdrawal of British troops.
>
> Those recommendations were ignored by the British Government. The consequence has been an intensification of the terror which has drawn thousands of Greeks to the mountains to form guerrilla units and led to the formation of General Markos' Democratic Army and now the Provisional Democratic Government.
>
> The large-scale civil war which now rages in Greece need

never have taken place had the recommendations of the British Parliamentary Delegation been adopted.

Our Police and Military Missions have so far been unable to purge the Greek forces of collaborators or prevent beatings, decapitations and other atrocities and have presumably acquiesced in the incarceration of at least 10,000 young conscripts, suspected of democratic views, in the military concentration camps of Makronisos and Psytaleia. These Missions should therefore be withdrawn. There is grave danger today that the 5,000 British troops still in Greece may once more be involved in a Greek civil war. They should be withdrawn at once.

(Signed) . . . George Thomas

Trouble at Home

On 10th March, George Thomas spoke in the House about the mass arrests and secret trials of leading members of EPON and EAM in Athens on 4th March. These were the trials for which he had gone to Greece in the first place. He was eloquent and convincing: "People of this country regard with horror the subsidizing of a system which enables people to be exiled after secret trials, without any opportunity of defending themselves." A few days later he was putting forward the same views in the lengthy debate on assistance to Greece. It was in that debate that he first referred to his visit: "During my recent visit to Greece . . ." (14th March 1947).

Ernest Bevin was furious. He had a difficult foreign policy to carry through and it was very definitely anti-Soviet Union and anti-Communist. It was no help to the Labour Party to be branded as sympathetic to Communists. The Conservatives were always ready to talk of the Labour Party as "Socialist", implying in their propaganda that they were in league with the Union of Soviet Socialist Republics. Bevin sent for George and in his usual direct—George says rough —language, told him that he was being used by the Communist Party. George reacted sharply to Bevin's lecture. No one likes to be told that he is being used, that he is an innocent abroad. George was not a schoolboy. He was thirty-eight, an experienced teacher and had been involved all his life in political activity for the Labour Party. Moreover, he had first-hand experience of Greece. Bevin had not been to the guerrilla HQ! However, looking back, he admits that he began to eye the people who surrounded him at the rallies. They were very much on the left of the party. He remembers his gradual acceptance of the fact that Bevin was probably partly right. In any case, he turned his attention away from foreign affairs for a time and learnt to use more discrimination when approached by pressure groups. It was all part of his education into national politics. He was greatly helped by the kindness of Clement Attlee, who recognized that many of his new MPs were getting themselves into strange entanglements. Attlee was a wise and gentle person with great compassion. The rough language of Ernest Bevin was foreign to him although in political controversy he could be devastating when necessary.

Recollected in Tranquillity

When writing up the Greek adventure for his Memoirs, the Viscount could afford to laugh at himself. He told the story eloquently and never left out the adventurous parts, but he could rebuke himself and see how he had been used. He confesses that he should have learnt from his Polish experience just how vulnerable newly elected MPs were to outside political exploitation. Commenting on the man who had met him at Athens airport, Professor Georgiou, he says, "I did not know it but I was already in the hands of a group determined to indoctrinate me with Anti-Greek-Government propaganda." The following day his interpreter Christos took him to a prison in Piraeus and showed him the dreadful conditions of the "political" prisoners. He comments, "I left the prison burning with anger but my anti-Government indoctrination was not complete. It was next put to me that I might like to visit Macedonia before returning to England. When I think back at what had happened, I am ashamed at my gullibility." He had no need to be ashamed. The important thing was that he eventually saw through it. But not while he was in Greece. And he enjoyed the excitement of it all.

Nearly forty years later the thrill he felt as he went into the dangerous territory of the guerrillas was still apparent. If anything, the story told later is more exciting than when he was writing for the League. His description of Christos, his interpreter, is vivid and he stops to comment, "By this time I should have realized that Christos was a Communist." He had warmed to Christos with all the deep sense of friendship of which he was always capable. This comes out most clearly in a letter he wrote to him on his way home. He had stopped at Rome and wrote on the last sheet of hotel notepaper:

> My dear Christos,
> I arrived at Rome at 1 p.m. today (2 p.m. by Athens time). When my plane took off from Athens, I saw you standing in the doorway and waved to you—but you did not see me. I felt quite sad, Christos. You have been a wonderful friend to me and I shall always be grateful for your friendship. I always feel that parting from friends is so distressing! Tonight I am alone in Rome and I feel really homesick—*for Athens*. It was a great delight to me to see a copy of Monday's *Daily Herald* here. My interview is splashed in big headlines and the report is quite extensive. There are parts of the article with which I am not too pleased, but on the whole it is good. Christos, my friend, I am going to work as hard as possible to help you boys in the magnificent struggle you are putting up for liberty. Greece is fortunate— even in her misfortunes—to possess young men like you who are ready to risk so much for democracy. From time to time you will be reading my speeches. Always remember, old chap, that it is you who inspired me to greater effort. When I return to London, I shall write to you for EPON. I return a humbled individual, having learnt that we in Britain accept our liberty too lightly. From the depths of my heart, I thank you, Christos, both for your friendship and for your countless acts of kindness. Believe me *filos mou* [my son, one of George's familiar forms of address still], I shall do my utmost to justify your confidence . . .
> Always your sincere friend
> George

That letter from Hotel Flora, Rome, on 18th February 1947, should have been sent from London on his return, but he was persuaded not to send it. A little later he learnt that Christos had been shot dead by government forces while trying to escape from a house they raided. They had no scruples about a "shoot to kill" policy.

The warmth of the welcome by the villagers was remembered vividly. George had always liked meeting people. His meeting with General Marcos and the mountain villagers is described in detail, with the dangerous return journey through guerrilla country into no man's land and then Larissa.

He had on him a letter from General Marcos to the United Nations and a roll of film of the guerrillas. "They seemed to burn in my pocket," he wrote. The army were angry, believing that he had deliberately planned to meet Marcos. When he reached Larissa, he discovered that his absence in the mountains had made world news and Jim Callaghan had persuaded the Foreign Office to make a statement. The sense of terror comes through the remembered night in the house of the Mayor of Larissa. He felt safer with Marcos and the mountain villagers. But at last he left. He took Marcos' letter to the United Nations. He had given his word. Then he returned to London with great relief. At once the League for Democracy sprang into action, organizing enormous rallies. He was well received in the universities, "but the ensuing publicity became an embarrassment to the Labour Government".

His final comment on the episode, "recollected in tranquillity", is: "The whole Greek episode was a major political blunder on my part, and I was fortunate that Clem Attlee understood that my behaviour was due to naivety rather than malice."

Affection and Admiration

It may have been naivety but his actions inspired admiration and his personal danger brought out the depth of affection in which he was held by many different kinds of people. When he returned to London, there was a mountain of correspondence awaiting him and hardly one failed to mention concern and affection, distress at the news he was missing and delighted relief at his safe return.

Mrs K. Bookham of the World Federation of Democratic Youth in Prague wrote:

> You really have become famous. We have just received the English newspapers out here in Prague of last Friday and photographs with your report of the story of your mission and that you are "missing". I cannot, of course, believe that you are missing, although there was no news of you for several days. In such circumstances as you were, I imagine that it is very difficult to maintain contact. What I am really writing to say therefore, is how very appreciative indeed we all are of your efforts in Greece, and how tremendously impressed we are with the letter you sent back from Paris.
>
> PS Did I say that the Czechoslovak youth came rushing in to me with the English papers—*Herald* and *Telegraph*—as soon as they saw the reports—in terrible consternation.

But it was not only in Prague that deep concern had been felt. The Rhondda and Cardiff hummed with the news—first of the loss of contact, then of the relief that he was safe:

> I shall be very glad when I hear that you have arrived safely home from Greece, and I am sure your mother will. The News in the *Herald* quite startled me, and I can assure you that I was fit for nothing until the good news came through that you were found. Somehow I believe that the great Faith you have in God will always bring you through. (Lilean James)

> Cut out these capers, my lad, or some of us will pass out with nervous anxiety! (Albany Road Boys School, Cardiff)

> My mother cried when she heard the news, but when she heard the glad news of your safety she was delighted. Yes! George I can say that you have so many friends here that I can never count them. (NUT, Caernarvon)

> We congratulate you on your safe return. There were gloomy faces at Cardiff last week when the scare concerning your disappearance was raised. We thought we had lost our St George. (A Cardiff teacher)

Another teacher, presumably from Roath Park School, wrote:

> What a terrible fright you gave us all (I know it was not your fault). I was so terribly miserable. I wandered into St Peter's School. Miss Lane said the whole staff had met her with the awful news. Then I went across to the Prince of Wales Hospital School, where none of them had opened their papers. You would have been flattered if you had seen the reaction, and I was getting ready to go and visit your mother to beg her to keep on hoping when a yell of joy from the kitchen brought me downstairs and Lizzie, my housekeeper, told me the joyful news given out by the BBC that all was well (I suppose you didn't get a snapshot of that donkey you rode—or occasionally didn't ride). What marvellous experiences you are getting—doesn't travel widen one's horizon? Teaching in Roath Park School was all very well, but . . .

There were hundreds of letters like that, which illustrate the immense affection with which George was regarded and the growing recognition of his importance in the political life of the country.

Of course there were some who said that he should be in Parlia-

The Tilburys in Hampshire, about 1855

Happy trio – Mam, Dad Tom and George

Annie Powell, 1928

Mam, 1959

Homegrown entertainment by the Tonypandy Women's Labour Section, 1926.
Mam is wearing the mortar-board

Brother Ivor *(back row, extreme left)* at the Bargoed Central Hall in the early 1930s

A diminutive George *(centre of the back row)* in Form V of
the Tonypandy Grammar School, 1922

George Thomas, schoolmaster, with his class at Marlborough Road School in 1934

Mock election at the Labour Youth Conference in Filey, 1947

Under guerrilla guard, Macedonia, 1947

Opposite: George worked his passage to Canada and back
aboard the *SS Hawkinge*, 1948

An annual good deed at the Court Road Infants' School, Grangetown, Cardiff

Cardiff West pensioners at the House of Commons

Election winner shaking hands with cheerful loser, Sir Charles Hallinan, 1951

Ex-Prime Minister Clement Attlee comes to Cardiff, 1951

Electioneering in Cardiff West, 1955

ment or looking after his constituency instead of gadding round the world!

Illness and Worry

The whole episode had been a great strain. George Thomas was looking ill and his closest friend in the Commons, Tony Greenwood, son of a very senior colleague who had sat in the House almost continuously since 1932, took him in hand. Tony Greenwood entered Parliament in February 1946 when he won the by-election at Heywood and Radcliffe. He was a few years younger than George, but came with experience of the Ministry of Information in Russia and the Middle East. His background was very different from George's; Oxford and a former president of the Union. He had served in the RAF as an officer and after the war was with the Chief of Staff organization and the Reparations Commission. He liked George and sent him off to his own family doctor in Harley Street. All that was wrong with him was that he had been overdoing it. Physically and emotionally he needed a rest. This diagnosis made him feel better, but he was anxious again when the Prime Minister wanted to see him. It was like being called into the headmaster's study! He had never had a private interview with Attlee. It sounded like trouble. He was probably expecting a rebuke for the Greek escapade. The scene was remembered vividly years later:

> Attlee could not have been kinder. He sat behind his desk with his pipe in his hand. A plain white saucer served as his ashtray. He had apparently received a letter from one of my constituents expressing anxiety about my health. I explained that I had just had a check-up but he told me crisply to be in Palace Yard the next morning at ten, when I would be taken in his car to be examined by his doctor.
>
> He sent for me again a week later to say that the doctor had recommended that I should go to Switzerland for six weeks' rest. When I said that I could not possibly afford the trip, Attlee replied, "You have friends in this House, George. The bills will be paid." I was deeply touched but went on to say that I could not leave my constituency for so long a period. Attlee explained that a neighbouring MP would look after it for me. This time I was emphatic that I would not go to Switzerland. We agreed that I would rest at home for six weeks.

The way in which Attlee brushed aside George's Greek escapade when he knew that he was ill made him one of George's folk heroes. He was a man of compassion and, although he could not possibly have agreed with what George had done in Greece, he was more concerned with his well-being than with his political peccadilloes.

Mam

Enough has already been said to indicate the stature of George Thomas's mother, who was an accomplished and influential political figure in her own right. Throughout the war she was much involved in committees dealing with welfare, some of them meeting regularly in London. Locally, she was President of the Women's Co-operative Movement. Her writing shows profound political insight. It was she more than anyone else who encouraged George in his political career. She was intensely proud of him and backed him all the way. He was closer to her in his interests than any other of the children and a deep affection developed between them. She saw him achieving all the things she could not do. At first she was a more impressive figure than he was and supported him on platforms, by writing commendations of him as a hard-working MP, and by suggestions that made him more effective. Tom Davies was never the political figure that his wife was, nor did he always understand what George was doing, but he too never failed to support him. In the spring of 1948, George was persuaded to take a short break in Canada. When he returned, anxious for Dad Tom because he had been ill for some time, he found the house in Tonypandy full of sadness. Dad Tom was dying. He seems to have hung on so as to say farewell to George and he was able to do this. George, who had developed a great affection for him, was overwhelmed with a sense of loss on his own account as well as a deep concern for his mother. When the sorrowing was over, George realized how much closer he had come to his mother and that she had now only him for the immense amount of affection and loyalty she was capable of giving. She remained a great source of strength to him in his work so long as she lived.

Anthony Eden wrote to him with full understanding of the grief at the loss of his father, a long two-page letter, telling of the bereavement he had felt at the loss of his own father. George shared this letter with Mam and never forgot Eden's kindness and care. Attlee and Eden, men in the full glare of public life, knew how to care for people. George vowed that he would never forget that lesson. And, of course, he did not. However high he climbed, he could always pause to help someone in need of encouragement. Not all political climbers learn that lesson.

The Making of a Mature Politician

In 1945, George had had a lot to learn about parliamentary life. The eager new member who at first jumped up to ask questions on every possible occasion learnt that the life of an MP consisted of more than this. His first lesson was of the paramount importance of caring for his constituency. He was in Parliament to represent Cardiff and he did this conscientiously and well.

The next lesson he learnt was that he was in a national Parliament and the welfare of the country as well as its honour was in his hands. He had to listen to the concerns of other MPs whose constituencies had needs that weighed against the needs of Cardiff. He was helping to fashion a policy for the nation.

After the Greek escapade, he had to look soberly at his enthusiasm and even his idealism. The inexperienced MP in the Greek guerrilla camps needed to look at the national and international policy of the government of which he was a part. He was in Parliament, not only to carry through his own ideals, but to support the Labour Party, even when he thought it could have modified its policy nearer to his own ideas. He was learning the art of compromise.

Like any MP he wanted to equip himself for office. He was not over-ambitious, but he wanted to increase his influence. Those who chose men for office watched the new MPs and some qualities were already emerging in George Thomas. He was known to be on the left wing of the party. He was known to have an interest, even a passion for social justice. He had often pleaded for fair treatment of underprivileged people. He was conscientious in following up requests for help. That seemed to point towards some place in the Home Office. But he was showing interest in foreign affairs, even if he had been a little indiscreet so far. He got on well with people, and as the Colonial Office had some tricky deals to do with African and

Asian politicians, he might be useful. He had not quite emerged during the 1945–1950 parliament and, unlike Jim Callaghan, he was not in office at its end.

CHAPTER NINE

———◆◆◆———

Cardiff's Champion: 1947–1950

AFTER THE EXULTATION of victory in 1945 and the steady progress of Labour's first year, there was bound to be a reaction. By the beginning of 1947, the Labour government could claim that its two main objectives were well on the way to achievement: the programme of social legislation to which they had committed themselves in the 1945 election, and a long-term export drive which had balanced the Budget. Rationing was still in force, but Labour was optimistic.

The change came in early 1947. There was a long, hard, freezing winter. Industry was put on part-time because of fuel shortage. Morale was at rock bottom among the people. Motorists had slogans on their cars, reading, "Don't blame me. I didn't vote for them."

The crisis was both national and, for George Thomas, personal. He could be described at this stage as a loyal supporter of the Labour Party, deeply concerned with the plight of the poor, passionate for social justice at home and abroad, a convinced Christian and practising Methodist, inclined to pacifism and certainly opposed to war except as the very last resort, and with a growing interest in foreign affairs. He liked travel—except by sea! He was a backbencher and therefore not privy to the detailed problems of the cabinet, although he was as receptive as any member to leaks that told of conflict.

Trouble over the National Service Bill

In the earlier part of the year, George Thomas was preoccupied with his Greek adventure, but he was soon in the midst of the disputes about expenditure on defence or social services. The issue came to a head for him personally with the National Service Bill. It was clear that though cuts were being made in overseas commitments, the level of military manpower needed could not be met by voluntary means only. Already in February 1947, a White Paper had hinted at a new National Service Bill, which would mean conscription in peace time. In the Labour Party, pacifists, anti-imperialists and those who objected to the financial strain of Britain's military commitments, continued to form a formidable opposition to any peace-time conscription. The Liberals called it an interference with the liberty of the individual. The bill was passed on 1st April, but only because of Conservative support. There were eighty-five who voted against the bill, and these were mostly Labour. The spearhead of the opposition had been the Keep Left Group, who were very much the left wing of the Labour Party. George Thomas voted against the bill. He was not a member of the Keep Left Group, but his conscience prevented him from supporting the government on this matter. It was a personal decision; there had been a three-line whip and he had defied it. As he says in his Memoirs, "I had already said that even if there were a forty-three-line whip, I would not vote for it." George Thomas's involvement with the League for Democracy in Greece, his statement in the Foreword to Colonel Sheppard's pamphlet ("I believe that British troops should be withdrawn") and above all his speech in the House on 14th March 1947, when he roundly attacked the government's policy in Greece, marked him as left-wing. This vote confirmed the opinion of some that if he were not a Communist, he was apparently a "fellow-traveller"; but they were wrong—he was a Methodist, a chapel man from the Rhondda.

Like many others he was on the carpet next day for having ignored, in fact, defied, a three-line whip. He was summoned to appear before the Chief Whip, William Whiteley, and the Leader of the House, Herbert Morrison. George knew that he could expect little sympathy from Herbert Morrison, who dealt roughly with any backbencher who failed to support Labour in a division. He accused George of disloyalty. But Willie Whiteley was a Durham man, formerly a miners' agent and most important of all, a Methodist. George did not attempt to argue with Morrison, but he did with Whiteley and insisted that there were times when a man had to follow his conscience. All Whiteley said was, "You can go, George. But remember you were sent here to support the Labour government." Morrison was angry that Whiteley had not insisted upon a promise that he would not do it again, but George's argument had affected him. Whiteley knew the difference between a dangerous rebel and a convinced Christian. He ignored Morrison's angry remarks.

Constituency Care

In hundreds of incidents, trivial to all, perhaps, except the people involved, George had learnt that as an MP he had influence. If anyone in his constituency was being treated unjustly or suffering because of neglect or inability to obtain justice, George was there arguing his or her case in the highest office. No case was too trivial for him if a person was being wrongly treated. His warm heart, his personal experience of hardship and his passion for justice earned him many successes and the nickname "our Saint George". There was one particular case in which he failed and its memory never left him. It compelled him to give a very black mark to the Home Secretary, Mr Chuter Ede.

This incident concerned two young men from Aberavon separately accused of murder, the one guilty of a particularly brutal murder, but the other, innocent of any intention to kill. Both were condemned to be hanged. George was approached by the parents of the latter and he interceded with the Home Secretary for a reprieve. Chuter Ede at once made it clear that he would not recommend the exercise of the royal prerogative of mercy. George was dumbfounded. It seemed a clear-cut case. Chuter Ede said, "You know that there were two murders in the Aberavon constituency that night, and in each case a young man has been sentenced to hang. The young man you have come about is a Protestant, and the other is a Roman Catholic." George was even more confused and asked what that had to do with his decision. The reply was shattering: "I am not going to offend my Catholics in South Shields by reprieving a Protestant and allowing a Catholic to hang." Chuter Ede had a 7,000 majority in South Shields, but whatever the proportions in question, no such argument would ever have justified such a decision. George made no secret of his disgust. He tells the whole story with some vigour in his Memoirs as though it were yesterday, and his involvement illustrates something of the commitment he showed to his constituents although this family was from a neighbouring constituency. George's comment thirty years later shows how deeply that sense of injustice had cut:

When Chuter Ede left the Home Office he told the Commons that he had changed his mind about capital punishment. As I listened to him say that the case of Timothy Evans, whose innocence was proved after he had been hanged, had made him opposed to the death penalty, I recalled my own unhappy dealing with him and wondered if the boy from Aberavon was also on his conscience.

George's reaction to Chuter Ede's announcement to the Commons that day, not recorded in Hansard, was, "It's a bit late now!"

From the moment he entered the House of Commons, George Thomas was careful of the needs of his constituency. Cardiff was constantly the theme of his questions and his interventions. During the recess, he based himself in Cardiff and his "surgery" was constantly visited by people who had problems, which they hoped George might solve for them. In addition, there were letters which poured in, asking for his help. At first these dealt with problems of pensions, compassionate release of sons from the armed forces, training opportunities, allocations of food to relatives, even the need for shelters at bus stops! No problem was too small for George to deal with and, if necessary, raise in Parliament.

Although the Greek adventure caught the headlines, his constant work was for Cardiff and he was hardly ever silent about its needs in Parliament. Turning over the pages of Hansard is enough to show his insistence. In 1947 half his interventions were on behalf of Cardiff specifically: the distribution of biscuits, the condition of a secondary school, the availability of elastic anklets, the shortage of electrical components, the opening of a training college, the use of premises for a local football pool firm, the need for nursery schools, the unsuitable accommodation in a remand home, salvage collecting, allowances for schools, their development and reorganization, bus shelters in Scott Street and Cathays Park, and the persistent problem of unemployment. It was no wonder that he had the nickname of Saint George. There were dragons in Cardiff and he tackled them. He was not always successful, but it is amazing how often he was. This success was due to a persistent advocacy and a recognition by others of his sincere concern. Every letter in those days received a sympathetic answer. And he was tireless in his efforts, never giving up at the first rebuff.

Second to Cardiff was his concern with education, but he was also developing wider interests: Greece, Palestine, Nyasaland and a growing interest in the colonies, perhaps due to his friendship with Jim Griffiths, who became Secretary of State for the Colonies.

An Anxious Backbencher

The National Service Bill (1947) which had involved George personally also made clear to him the divisions in his own party. The first Labour government was running into trouble. There were divisions among the "lions" in the cabinet and rumours of calling an early election. Attlee presided over a very powerful cabinet, all of whom he had chosen himself, but it was a cabinet of individualists who threatened resignation when financial crisis made it impossible to carry through cherished plans. Kenneth Harris sums up the situation in 1947 when Hugh Dalton was pressing for defence cuts and Attlee feared the effect of this upon the Americans:

> Political circumstances did not encourage Attlee to do more than temporize. Only a few weeks earlier he had had to do with Crossman and the Keep Left Amendment. Dalton was known to have sympathies with Crossman and his group. With Bevin so much absent and Morrison ill Attlee could not afford to have a showdown with Dalton on this issue at this time [i.e., the issue of the Defence Cuts]. As well as precipitating a domestic crisis, it would give an impression of national disunity which would disturb the Americans. On the other hand, if Attlee had given Dalton all he wanted—withdrawal from overseas commitments on a major scale—the Americans would have been even more alarmed. So Attlee ... made the maximum concessions to Dalton which were consistent with minimum damage to the main objectives—to avoid political upset, and to keep on the closest possible terms with the Americans.

The year of crisis, 1947, was only a few weeks old when a wave of strikes hit the country. An unofficial strike of road haulage workers at Stratford in the East End, caused meat rations to be reduced in the London area. Porters in Billingsgate and Smithfield came out in sympathy when the government used troops to move food supplies. Almost immediately, 50,000 Glasgow shipyard and engineering workers struck and a general dock strike was threatened. A coal shortage loomed.

In addition to all this, Attlee had to deal with dissension in the cabinet. Dalton's memoirs (*High Tide*) contain the most lively accounts of the dissensions which were becoming common knowledge among the backbenchers. The Ministerial Committee on Economic Planning consisted of Morrison, Cripps, Isaacs (who was Minister of Labour) and Dalton. They made proposals about dealing with the manpower shortage by reductions in the armed forces. Dalton wrote: "A very bad and rowdy Cabinet in which a substantial group ganged up against Cripps and myself." He complained that Morrison and Bevin were always ill. Of the others, he said, they displayed "easy-going, muddle-headed irresponsibility". He was also impatient with Attlee who seemed to think that the shortage of manpower could be handled by greater productivity. He is not fair to Attlee, but that is how he saw it and he was exonerated from blame when the financial crisis came. Dalton was serious enough to write a 700-word "Note on a Difference of Opinion", complaining that the cabinet was failing because it would not "face unpleasant facts". Attlee gave in enough to ask the Defence Minister, A. V. Alexander, to make a small concession. Dalton recognized that the matter was only shelved: "And so for the moment, it ended," he wrote, "leaving a faint trail of antagonism, I fear, between me and the Prime Minister." In his covering letter to the Prime Minister with the "Note on a Difference", he added as Chancellor, much to Attlee's annoyance: "At least I have gone on record against future possibilities." This division of opinion in early 1947 was not resolved.

The severe winter, with the railways frozen and little road transport, added to the problems of the Labour government. A coal shortage and devaluation of the currency again showed rifts in the leadership. There were differences also over the nationalization of steel. The National Service Bill divided the rank and file as well as the leadership. Then the convertibility crisis broke and compelled Attlee to take on new powers with the Transitional Powers Bill on 6th August 1947. Once sterling became convertible into dollars, devaluation and uncertainty caused a run on the pound. When investors and the banks rushed to sell their pounds, the country was near to bankruptcy. The only hope was aid from America and many felt that this curtailed Britain's freedom. Attlee was curtailing it in another way. The Transitional Powers Bill meant that the government had emergency powers to control supplies and demands. Churchill described the bill as a "blank cheque for totalitarian government", but it was finally passed after an all-night sitting. George was less concerned with the possibility of the Labour government becoming totalitarian—he trusted his colleagues—but he was concerned to maintain independence from America. In reply to a correspondent earlier in the year who had said that a speech by Truman had been a call to a Third World War and that the United Nations Organization was condemned to death, he wrote, "I think you may rely upon me fighting bitterly against American imperialism reducing your country to slavery." He was referring to Greece, but he would have fought as bitterly to defend the independence of his own country from America.

All these disturbances affected George, who was by now becoming experienced in political life. He avoided joining pressure groups after his experience in Greece, but there was little doubt where his sympathies lay. He was concerned lest the Welfare State be diluted by financial pressures, sympathized greatly with Aneurin Bevan in his defence of the National Health Service and feared that American pressure might force a Labour government to go slow in its reforms. There was one man to whom he was attracted quite early—Harold Wilson, a younger colleague who was appointed to the Board of Trade in 1947 at the early age of thirty-one, and the youngest person in the cabinet. The attraction was to last. It was Harold Wilson more than anyone else who later brought George into the centre of political life. At this stage, however, George Thomas was active and made influential friends, but held no office in the government. He spoke often, but was not marked out as a future leader. He was an anxious backbencher, wondering if the quarrelling cabinet might call an early election, if there would be a change of leader and if there was danger of the country going bankrupt. This last prospect carried the haunting fear that a Tory government would take over and undo all the good that Labour had done. In this tense atmosphere, despite all its setbacks, the Labour government did not lose a single seat in a by-election throughout the whole of its five-year term.

The End of Empire

George Thomas described the Labour landslide victory of 1945 as almost universally approved throughout the Commonwealth. He had in mind those countries seeking independence and expecting a Labour government to support their efforts. They were right. In

India, fervour for the Labour government ran particularly high and Attlee did not disappoint them. Despite the financial crisis at home, which eased a little as 1947 came to an end, Attlee kept his promise to give India independence. India and Pakistan became independent countries, breaking with Britain on the most friendly terms possible, which considering the long conflict and widespread disaffection with the way Britain had behaved as masters of the Raj was a considerable achievement. It was illustrative of Attlee's authority and skill that India, although a republic, remained within the Commonwealth. Many resented the partition, which involved much bloodshed, but Attlee allowed India to take the transfer of power into her own hands. The bitter clash between Muslim and Hindu made partition unavoidable. Jinnah and Nehru were intractable foes.

In 1947, George nowhere expressed his view about partition, but he was wholehearted in supporting independence. He found no occasion to speak in the House about India, although in the 1947–48 session he did make one small intervention concerning Burma Independence Day. Apart from Greece, he had not ventured further into foreign affairs. That was yet to come.

The government's diplomatic skills seemed much less in evidence over Palestine and, after some clumsy and unfortunate negotiations, the sequel to Britain's abdication of power, after much violence, was war. Arabs and Jews alike blamed the British. But that sad story does not belong to the career of George Thomas. Attlee had to take the consequences of Ernest Bevin's strong dislike of minority views. In addition, Bevin's anti-Semitism reflected the Foreign office policy even then.

The Left Wing and Eastern Europe

Ernest Bevin took a pragmatic approach to world affairs and cared little for arguments about the importance of "international socialism", but there were those in the Parliamentary Labour Party who differed from him. They objected to Bevin's alliance with the Tories, particularly Churchill and Eden who had a high regard for him and supported his foreign policy. Attlee complained to his old friend Fenner Brockway that some members of the Labour Party over-simplified foreign affairs. Many Labour members wanted to concentrate all their efforts on a Third Socialist Force in Europe and were suspicious of

America. Attlee as well as Bevin saw that there were neither material nor spiritual bases for this. Russia was a world power and would sweep across Europe if it was not resisted by a world power. America was essential for the security of Europe. The absorption of Czechoslovakia, Yugoslavia, Poland, Hungary and Bulgaria into the Soviet Empire gave increasing weight to their fears.

Konni Zilliacus represented the extreme left view and was active in bringing the issues of Eastern Europe constantly before the House. He arranged a broadly-based delegation of MPs to visit Eastern Europe during the long summer recess of 1948. George was one of that delegation, which visited Czechoslovakia, Yugoslavia, Poland and the Soviet Union. He was cautious this time and did not involve himself in any left-wing causes. The visit to Yugoslavia was exhilarating. At that time an international team of youth workers had volunteered to build a railway and a road to help restore that war-ravaged land. George appreciated the idealism of the youth workers and saw the value of such work for good international relations. He does not appear to have liked Tito very much, whom he found too bombastic:

> Tito received us in his magnificent home, resplendent in his field-marshal's uniform weighed down with the highest decorations he could bestow upon himself. His Alsatian dog was the one that had saved his life during the war by alerting him that enemy troops were approaching.

The picture contrasted very much with his impression of Stalin, whom they also met: "Stalin's plain drill suit bore no decorations, and he clearly felt no need to buttress himself with medals." George was impressed by Stalin, a friendly man, but had one little murmur at that time: "It struck me as odd that he sent greetings to neither Churchill nor Attlee." It was only much later—many years later in fact—that George could look back and contrast his pleasant impressions with "the ruthless murderer of his own people".

In Poland and Czechoslovakia he felt much more troubled. Poland had no choice but to be absorbed within the Soviet sphere of influence; she was dependent upon Russia, her old enemy, but the people seemed to fear her. Only a short time before George's visit, Gomulka had been deposed by the Soviets and the Socialist Party was absorbed into the Communist Party. This Catholic country was obviously uneasy under atheist control. Czechoslovakia was even more disturbing. Earlier that year there had been a Communist *coup d'état* and Jan Masaryk had been found dead beneath his office window.

The British delegation met with Masaryk's successor, Clementis, and talked with him at length. They were aware of a very fragile situation in Prague and an even more fragile democracy. The delegation had come from a government which was hostile to the Communist regime while Britain, France and the USA had protested that the change of government was in fact "the disguised dictatorship of a single party under the cloak of a Government of National Union". They were troubled by evidence of anti-Semitism and dictatorship. It was not long after the visit that pogroms broke out against the Jews in Poland, Czechoslovakia, and along the Danube. Britain was in a difficult position, trying to hold a balance in Palestine and suffering appalling atrocities from Zionists, including the blowing up of the King David Hotel. Jewish refugees from Germany, for whom there had been world sympathy, were refused entrance to Palestine and sent to camps in Cyprus or even turned back to Germany. Relations with America were strained over this issue. The talk with Clementis must have been very difficult. He was clearly in favour of the kind of independence from the Soviet Union which Tito had won for Yugoslavia and he was sympathetic to the Jews. His position was very unstable and in fact in 1950, he was forced to resign and was executed. This visit marked the end of George's flirtation with the Communist powers. His speeches in Parliament made little mention of the visit. His Memoirs comment simply, "I was relieved to get out of both countries."

The eager new MP who had looked upon Europe as a place where his ideas of justice and righteousness should be applied, now saw the wheels within wheels which made issues much more complicated than he had believed. He was becoming wiser and sadder!

The Remaining Sessions of the 1945–1950 Parliament

After returning to Britain at the end of the summer of 1948, George Thomas found himself fully involved in domestic matters. Cardiff was high on the agenda and leasehold reform was his crusade. He showed some interest in colonial and Middle East services, protested about the atomic bomb, never failed to rise on matters concerning education. But he was aware that the government was facing a national financial crisis and that there were rumours of an early general election. The government had until July 1950 to run, but it was thought the election would come earlier. Some argued for autumn 1949.

The final troubles began with Cripps' Budget speech on 6th April 1949. His problems have since become familiar to this country—the dollar gap, inflation, lack of investment, the need to create new wealth. He saw and said that social services must be cut, or at least their progress slowed down, wages and prices must be stabilized and the restrictive policy continued for at least another year. He greatly displeased the trades unions and disappointed his own party. Oliver Stanley, a Conservative MP, summed up the effect of the Budget speech upon him by describing it as "the end of an era of socialist policy and socialist propaganda". The Labour Party lost heavily in the ensuing County Council elections. In the London County Council, Labour's membership was reduced from 90 to 64, while the Conservatives had risen from 28 to 64. The Liberals, reduced from two members to one, held the balance! The main debates in the House now seemed to be about nationalization and the economy. The Labour Party conference met in Blackpool on 6th June 1949. There was little recrimination and Attlee enjoyed a triumph. Zilliacus, who had been expelled from the party, with Solley, was refused permission to address the conference. It was in no mood to hear expostulations from the far left. The main dispute of the conference was between Morrison, who wanted to consolidate the considerable reforms that the government had initiated, and Bevan, who wanted to press on further. It is difficult to determine which side George Thomas was on. His past record would have suggested that he was with Bevan, but he was changing and it was probably about this time that his disillusion with the left wing and the growing influence of Attlee were having their effect. But he was not yet in the limelight and for a time was content to listen to the arguments of both sides.

The General Election of 1950

Late in November 1949 things seemed to be improving for the Labour government. The country had responded sensibly to the necessary cuts, the TUC announced eight recommendations for a wages policy to meet the crisis, the long wrangle over the Steel Bill was in sight of settlement and the government had come to terms

with the House of Lords about the date of transferring ownership of
the steel industry. The new date was to be after the election, and
Churchill gave notice that if the Conservatives won, the Steel Bill
would be removed from the statute book.

The date of the election was normally a matter of discussion at the
cabinet meeting with all present, but Attlee called senior members
only to advise him on the final choice of date. The choice was between
February and June 1950.

Morrison thought that the weather in February might affect the
Labour turnout, but all the others supported this date. That was
decided, but they all knew that their own Representation of the
People's Act would militate against them. The old 1918 Act had
enabled them to win a massive majority by the inclusion of several
safe Labour seats with small constituencies. Attlee believed firmly in
every vote bearing an equal value and reformed constituencies according to fairness. He knew the price they would have to pay. Yet they
were optimistic. The reform would certainly cost Labour about thirty
seats, but they had a majority of 146. Since 1945 they had not lost a
seat in a by-election and there had been thirty-five of them. The
government was also aware that it had not called the election because
it was forced by the Opposition, nor to catch a popular vote. Attlee
had called it because Cripps thought it politically irresponsible to
present a budget before the election, that is without a further
mandate.

The year 1950 was the Jubilee year of the Labour Party, although
the birthday did not fall until 28th February, after the election. There
were many indiscreet speeches made in the days before the election,
but Labour expected to win. George Thomas was confident enough.
He had benefited from the constituency reform. Three-fifths of his
constituency of Cardiff Central was merged into Cardiff West and
there he fought a safer seat. Cardiff West now included the largest
council housing estate in the city, in Ely. It was solidly Labour!

George Thomas and James Callaghan

After the reorganization there were three seats in Cardiff—two held
by Labour—L. J. Callaghan, Cardiff South-East, and George
Thomas, Cardiff West. Cardiff North was held by a Conservative,
D. T. Llewellyn. George Thomas and James Callaghan were friends,

but had very different views of their careers. George had come in by way of the chapel and supported by the trade union movement. He retained a sense of surprise and delight to be in Parliament at all. He enjoyed everything he could and marvelled at the stature of the men he met, of all parties. He wanted to be friends with everyone, but he had a passionate love of liberty and justice. He made no secret of his future dreams.

James Callaghan, who was three years younger, made no secret of his ambition. When they were first elected, Callaghan had said: "Before the end of this Parliament, I shall be in the government." In 1947, he was appointed Parliamentary Secretary to the Ministry of Transport, where he served until the dissolution in 1950. He had his eye on office. In the 1950 general election, both won comfortably, James Callaghan by nearly 6,000 votes and George Thomas by more than 4,000. Their colleagues throughout the country did not fare so well. The large Labour majority of 1945 was swept away. An important factor was that the government was already tired of the burden of office. It had fulfilled its main programme and it gave every impression of being rudderless. At least that was George's view.

Attlee was left with a margin of only seventeen members over the Conservative opposition, and of only six over the rest of the House combined. With 315 supporters the government faced 297 members of the Conservative and associated parties, and there were nine Liberals, whose intentions in the lobby were uncertain from the start.

Labour's Defeat

The general election result was a crushing disappointment for Labour and although George came safely through, he entered a very different Parliament in February 1950 from that he had embraced so enthusiastically in the summer of 1945. The Labour Party Manifesto, *Let us win through together*, was brave enough, but its very title seemed a mockery before long. It rested upon its record:

> ... Britain has accomplished a recovery unsurpassed by any other country. No doubt there have been mistakes. But judge on what basis you will—by the standard of life of the general body of citizens, by employment, by the infrequency of serious industrial disputes, by the stability of the nation, by social security—by any fair comparison, the British people have done an infinitely better

job than was done after the first world war. By explaining to the
people what needed to be done, by giving the facts, by appealing
to the patriotism of the people, by vigorous, sensible leadership,
the Labour Government has led Britain to the first victories of
peace. Now let us win through together.

George had no difficulty in fighting an election on such a proven
record and the manifesto continued by maintaining the supreme aim
to be full employment. The details of the policy also raised his vision
of what was yet to be done. There were to be special measures for
Areas of Special Need (The North-East, Scotland, Wales and other
areas of high unemployment), a workable policy to maintain the cost
of living at a manageable level and a better supply of essential foods,
and an insistence upon world peace and plenty. There was support
for the United Nations and a determination to move towards a new
economic and political unity in Europe.

George could almost have written the last paragraph himself:

> The fundamental question for the men and women of the United
> Kingdom to determine when they vote is this: Shall we continue
> along the road of ordered progress which the people deliberately
> chose in 1945, or shall reaction, the protectors of privilege and
> the apostles of scarcity economics be once more placed in the
> seats of power, to take us back to the bleak years of poverty
> and unemployment? Those years must never return. We are
> successfully going forward with the great and inspiring adventure
> of our time. Let us win through together.

But all that required a workable majority in Parliament. George soon
learnt the truth of what Bevan was saying, that Labour had achieved
from 1945 to 1950 "a greater degree of unity" than he had ever
known, "and the reason why we achieved that unity was that we
achieved it in activity. We are always better when we are getting on
with the job." Bevan had been restless enough in the 1945–1950
government, but then he believed that at its own pace it was introducing socialism, and moving in the right historical direction. In 1950–
1951, he had no such confidence and his fundamental loyalty came
under increasing strain. It led eventually to his resignation from the
cabinet and this was a traumatic action, as George saw clearly when
he urged Bevan's wife, Jennie Lee, to keep Bevan from resigning and
was rudely repulsed. Bevan was right in his judgement. It soon
became clear that this government was going to do nothing that could

look like progress. In fact at its very first cabinet meeting on 25th February 1950, with Bevan absent through illness, it was decided that "there could be no question of attempting to carry through any of the controversial legislation which had been promised." When Bevan returned he argued against such a possibility and at least persuaded them to put through the nationalization of steel. Otherwise there was nothing of significance in the King's Speech, for in John Campbell's words, Bevan "rumbled like a volcano", but did not resign until 23rd April 1951. (Campbell was Editor of *The Daily Worker* and stood as a Communist candidate in Greenock in 1945 and 1950, and against Winston Churchill in Woodford in 1951.)

Leasehold Reform

Meanwhile George Thomas was anxious to do some unfinished business. Just before the summer recess of 1950, he tabled a motion calling for an immediate standstill order to give temporary protection to those tenants whose leases were falling due in the near future. He saw this as a matter of urgency in any case, because parliamentary procedure can be very slow. This was no political manoeuvre, but a deeply human concern for those in danger of eviction in Cardiff and the valleys. He collected 125 signatures from Labour MPs for his motion and felt fairly confident that he would be successful. Nothing could be done before the summer recess, but if he was to get his motion through in this Parliament before it went into the next election, it would have to be mentioned in the King's Speech, because it was reasonable to suppose that the election would interrupt business, probably as early as February 1951. George waited anxiously and it seemed ages before the point came, but there it was towards the end of the Speech. The government acted quickly and by Christmas 1950 the Leasehold Property (Temporary Provisions) Bill was passed, assuring a two-year protection period for tenants whose leases were due to expire. George faced the electors with confidence. Here was something that made a more immediate appeal to Cardiff than democracy in Greece.

A Glimpse of the Speaker's Chair

Early in 1951, when Parliament had only months to go before the inevitable general election, George Thomas was invited by Sir Charles MacAndrew, Chairman of Ways and Means and a Deputy Speaker, to join the Panel of Chairmen who assisted the Speaker, then Colonel Clifton-Brown, by presiding over standing committees in the House, and even over the whole House, when the detailed examination of a bill was taken on the floor of the House at the committee stage. George enjoyed this work and it gave him an appreciation of the work of the Committees of the House as well as a taste for presiding over them. He had not until then thought very seriously about where he might serve in Parliament. Perhaps it was along these lines that his services would be most valuable. It is doubtful that he thought at this point of becoming Mr Speaker, but he was interested in the duties surrounding his task and the ceremonies that accompanied it. He began to study closely the qualities that were required.

Sir Charles MacAndrew was a good Deputy Speaker, greatly respected by the House. George decided that he had two secrets: first, his complete impartiality—he never favoured his own party; the second was that he never tried to make a member feel small in front of his colleagues. The Speaker needed much more than those two qualities, but both of them were essential. Only thus could the Speaker be respected and trusted and, by treating members with such courtesy, they found it hard to resist his plea for co-operation. Sir Charles was at that time working very closely with the Speaker, Colonel Clifton-Brown. George says of W. S. Morrison, who succeeded Clifton-Brown after the 1951 Election: "His commanding presence and resounding voice made him a great Speaker."

There is a marked change in George Thomas during this period as a member of the Speaker's Panel of Chairmen. He was learning about the manners of the House, its traditions and ceremonies, which helped to maintain its authority. Of course, every member represented a party, but a Member of Parliament was more than a representative. He was also there to govern the realm and to maintain the honour of Great Britain. There was dignity in his office and a member must live accordingly. George was still left-wing, Nye Bevan was still his man, and he felt close to such men as Harold Wilson and Tony Benn, but he never let himself go in debate in the way that they did. His rhetoric, of which he was eminently capable, was now always restrained by the dignity of the House.

CHAPTER TEN

◆◆◆

Tory Pressure and Power

I T SADDENED GEORGE to see the newspapers filled with stories of bitter divisions in cabinet, of undignified attacks on one another by Members and an apparent disregard for the importance and honour of their office. Very soon the Opposition saw the value of these divisions. The Labour majority was so small that even one vote against the government could be fatal. Tiredness and absence through illness could be used to weaken the Labour hold. The internal quarrels in the Parliamentary Labour Party inevitably led to loss of support in the country. The Conservatives saw their chance and put on the pressure in a way that, as George said, made parliamentary life a misery.

> Night after night we were kept in the Commons until the small hours. The Opposition knew that the Government could survive only by bringing in sick members from their hospital beds. With a majority now reduced to five, we were limping along. Robert Boothby revealed Conservative tactics when he publicly declared, "We will harry them to death!"

Finally, Attlee called a general election for 25th October 1951.

Another Election

Churchill had noted that in the 1950 election more than one third of the Labour Party candidates who were successful had been sponsored by trades unions; of 140 known to have been nominated, 111 were returned. He therefore decided to seek the goodwill of the trades unions, both during the election and after. He was not above flattering TUC leaders and calling them "the Fourth Estate of the realm". George noted this, as a trades union representative himself, and commented, "The old man's cunning political instinct enabled him to lay firm foundations for a long Tory rule."

The Labour manifesto was not as confident as it had been in the 1950 election, but its main emphases were clear. It set four main tasks for the nation: to secure peace; to maintain full employment and increase production; to bring down the cost of living; and to build a just society. George Thomas had no problems with that, but the details of how it should all be done were not so clear. However, he had his own local interpretation and his own battles to fight and he concentrated on leasehold reform. He had evidence that in Parliament he had fought for this and given notice that he would do so until successful. His Conservative opponent this time was the son of the one he had fought in 1945 and 1950—A. L. Hallinan, much younger than George, a barrister and a member of Cardiff City Council. He had failed to win a by-election at Aberdare in 1946. He had not stood much chance in Aberdare, but Cardiff West could have gone to the Conservatives if the swing had continued. His father had polled almost 23,000 votes against George Thomas's 27,000 in 1950. As president of several old age pensioners' committees, and with his British Legion association, he was a formidable opponent in the atmosphere of 1951, which was critical of the government.

The gentlemanly politeness of 1945 was gone and it was a tough fight. A Conservative pamphlet aimed against George and his mother, issued in Cardiff during the 1951 election, gives some idea of the nature of the opposition he faced and would face in the future. George had campaigned with his mother and she had been articulate in expressing her own preference for him and the superiority of socialism.

The Conservative handbill, headed, "The Truth ... Please", denied George's claim that he had acted for the leaseholders of Cardiff and that the Conservatives had voted against the bill. "No!" says his opponent, "the Conservatives were trying to amend the Bill and make it better." It quoted Mrs Davies campaigning on behalf of her son, the Labour candidate, as saying, "Australia and New Zealand warn us of the heavy increase in the cost of living whenever the Conservative Party are in power." This, the Conservatives denied, with figures to support their argument. Mrs Davies had said, "The cost of living has increased everywhere in the world, but less here than in any other country except Norway and Sweden." This was refuted, and Switzerland, America, Belgium, Italy and Eire quoted as examples of smaller increase than Britain—"and they have not

Socialist governments." The Conservative pamphlet also attacked Labour for not building houses, and tore George's election address to pieces, accusing him and his party of being Communists in disguise. His trip to Greece was also remembered, as well as his earlier support from Communists. The pamphlet added: "Mr Thomas has not denied that he accepted Communist support in 1945. He cannot ... It's in print for the country to see! ... in *Picture Post* and the *Daily Worker*! Which side is he on?"

The strength of George's appeal, however, was his personal care for his constituency and it comes clearly through in his letter to the voters:

> Dear Friends,
>
> Six years ago when I first had the honour to be elected to Parliament, I vowed to myself that I would give my whole time serving the people whom I had the privilege to represent. "No other mother should suffer as mine had suffered," was the promise that I made.
>
> I have never forgotten that vow and promise. It has been my full-time task to seek to serve you. Thus I have now dealt with roughly 10,000 individual cases in each of which I have done my best to act as a friend. If my work as MP had been a part-time occupation it would have been impossible for me to have undertaken so much.
>
> Although there are very few streets in the Division which my mother and I have not visited some time or another, we shall probably again be calling at your street during this campaign. It will be a joy to be with you all.
>
> I hope that you will take the opportunity to come to some of my meetings where I shall explain our programme and, of course, gladly answer your questions. We shall be glad to welcome you.
>
> Thank you all regardless of Party, for the unfailing friendliness and kindness with which you have upheld me during these past years. I hope that the Election Campaign will be of a high tone, enabling the electorate to reach its decision after a clean contest in the best interests not of ourselves alone, but of the world brotherhood of which we are a part.
>
> Every blessing to you all,
> Very sincerely,
> George Thomas

He won with an increased majority—5,400 from 4,300. This was against the run of the country. Jim Callaghan was re-elected, but with a reduced majority. Winston Churchill was back as Prime Minister with an overall majority of seventeen. The *Times* reported: "Thus ended a Parliament which had survived precariously since February 23 1950, largely in a condition of frustration and stalemate."

Nye Bevan and Health Charges

The loss of the election did not depress Labour anything like as much as their slender victory in 1950 had. The Conservatives were in much the same position as they had been prior to the election and another general election was probable in the near future. Labour was encouraged that it had polled 200,000 more votes in total than the Conservatives had achieved and their highest vote on record. The division caused by Bevan's resignation had not done significant harm. Although a group of Bevanites gathered around him, he was loyal to the party's interests. Bevan withdrew from full parliamentary activity, refused to join the shadow cabinet and spoke very little in the House. Instead, he worked quietly on his pamphlet, *In Place of Fear*, by which he hoped to fire the imagination of a new generation with pure socialism. He tried to show the unalterable objectives of the Labour Party in setting people free from fear of poverty, disease, unemployment and exploitation. Those who had gathered around Hugh Gaitskell put forward the alternative view of a changed socialism in the future, which was not shackled to old dogmas. Tony Crossland represented this revisionist group with his pamphlet *The Future of Socialism*. It was that pamphlet, not Nye Bevan's, that charted the course ahead.

Nye Bevan returned to full parliamentary activity on 31st January 1952 with a brilliant speech during an economic debate. George followed this with an attack on the health charges, which Churchill had immediately increased. George Thomas organized a motion, much as he had for leasehold reform. His power to persuade was increasing and he was at his best talking to members one by one. He wanted to commit the next Labour government to the complete abolition of health charges. He noted and reported that many had lost their seats because they had supported Hugh Gaitskell in his imposition of health charges. He recalls that he had no difficulty in getting more than half the Parliamentary Labour Party ready to sign the motion. This roused Herbert Morrison's anger once again. He told a crowded parliamentary meeting that it was undemocratic to collect signatures before there had been any chance of discussion. He strongly urged the meeting not to tie the hands of the future Labour government. There was a stormy debate, but George was unrepentant, and his motion was carried easily. Gaitskell and Morrison, at least, regarded George as a strong Bevanite! He had certainly grown in confidence since Morrison had rebuked him for voting against the National Service Bill. There was no real Bevanite party. Nye Bevan himself would not have approved of that. He was an individualist and liked to have people with comparable standards around him, but he was not a leader. The leadership of the ill-defined group was in the hands of three men who greatly influenced George Thomas, as he was becoming aware of his own strength. Not all three exercised a comparable influence. George was antipathetic to Richard Crossman, admired the independence of Ian Mikardo, but found his strongest affinity with Harold Wilson. All three, however, influenced him. It was with the group sympathetic to Bevan that George stood, regarding the "revisionists" as untrue to the basic tenets of socialism.

A Visit to Israel

Shortly after this meeting, in which George triumphed over Morrison, Elwyn Jones (MP for West Ham and one of Labour's strongest lawyers, who ultimately became Lord Chancellor) invited him to accompany him to Israel. It was a visit arranged by Ian Mikardo, whose brother-in-law was the Clerk of the Israeli Parliament. George found the Labour leaders in Israel well informed about the machinations of the British Labour Party and perceptive of the division between the Bevanites and Gaitskellites. What he did not expect was to meet Bevan himself on that visit. Bevan at fifty-six was beginning to get impatient of the daily grind of parliamentary business. His rhetoric called for a world stage and he was developing a taste for world travel. He had often said that the real problems of modern politics are global problems and he had a special interest in the colonies, where subject peoples were struggling for their independence. It was during one of these prolonged trips in 1953 that George had his triumphal meeting over health charges. Bevan was visiting India, Burma and Pakistan in February and March. On the way back he stopped in Israel, at the same time as George Thomas and Elwyn Jones were there. They all met at the British Embassy residence in

Tel Aviv. Bevan had heard about the Parliamentary Party meeting from Jennie Lee. They, Nye Bevan and George Thomas, both laughed at Morrison's discomfiture. Elwyn smiled discreetly, but the three Welshmen enjoyed the thought of the rather pompous Morrison being defeated by George Thomas. They relaxed and shared a common interest in news of progress in those countries which had been so recently under colonial rule. How were they fashioning their independence? Bevan expanded on his theme of global problems and was able to give first-hand examples from the Indian sub-continent. The three countries he had just visited had quite different destinies. India was making miraculous progress, Pakistan as an Islamic state was deficient in freedom, Burma after its civil war was looking to the Soviet Union for its political philosophy. George learnt a great deal from the more experienced and highly respected Labour volcano. George liked Nye.

The stay in Israel was short and George began to study the situation in that country. Years later, he could recall the shock of what he saw:

> It was only four years since the modern state of Israel had been proclaimed, and the scars of her recent conflicts were raw. Tanks lay abandoned in the desert, and people used to gather in the King David Hotel to look towards Old Jerusalem in Jordan, and across the valley outside Jerusalem where the tombstones of Jewish people had been smashed by the Arabs.

He was moved, much as he had been in Greece, to see the signs of brutality. He might have pondered that the very hotel he spoke of had been blown up and British servicemen killed by Israeli guerrillas not so many years before his visit. He was in a violent land where the distrust of Arab for Jew and both for the British was endemic. But George responded with a deep concern for the suffering Jews and it all added to his dislike of war.

The Hydrogen Bomb

On 1st March 1952—"St David's Day!" said George later, with injured pride—the Americans detonated their first hydrogen bomb. This was a degree of terror beyond the atomic bomb which had shattered Hiroshima and Nagasaki. Its unbelievable capacity to destroy and leave lingering elements of disease for future generations was known. The Bevanites rallied to oppose this monstrosity. Fenner

Brockway called a meeting in one of the committee rooms of the House of Commons and it was natural for George to be invited. Others there were also predictable, both members and visitors— Tony Greenwood, Donald Soper, John Collins, Sidney Silverman, Lord Beveridge, Victor Yates, George Craddock and a few others. There was no doubting the sincerity and deep concern of all those present. They were bent on forming a protest movement, which would have as its objective the banning of all nuclear weapons in the world. The movement would be launched in the Albert Hall with prestigious persons present. The whole country must be impressed by a vast and significant gathering saying, "No!" It was important to have the right chairman for such a rally and George found himself playing an amusing role, which he remembered years later and still marvelled at the vanity of famous men. His own words catch the flavour of his disgust:

> We had to select a chairman to preside at the rally and to my great surprise, Lord Beveridge, the father of the welfare state, announced, "My wife has said that in view of my status and position, I should be chairman of this meeting." I intervened to point out that we were not interested in Lady Beveridge's views on this particular matter. He went on to say that his wife had told him to withdraw if he was not going to be chairman. The meeting agreed with me, and Beveridge left to telephone her. When he returned, he said his wife had told him to withdraw and he left the meeting.
>
> More was to follow. John Collins, then Canon of St Paul's, announced, "Well, now Lord Beveridge has gone, I think that I should be chairman." I could hardly believe my own ears; the sheer vanity of people who were professing to hold such high ideals. The rest of the meeting shared my view that we should not allow the Canon to nominate himself. Collins also left. When he had gone, my proposal that Donald Soper should be in the chair was agreed. Even in the peace movement there are people who think of themselves first.

The incident shows how persistent George could be and the standards he expected from others. Words applied to Bishop George Bell at his funeral might be apt for George Thomas: "He was the most humbly obstinate man I have ever known!"

The Meeting in the Albert Hall

The Albert Hall holds a lot of people and it would be disastrous to have a meeting that made it look empty. So publicity was called for. Fenner Brockway, Tony Greenwood, Tony Benn, Richard Ackland, Victor Yates, George Craddock and George Thomas decided to advertise the Albert Hall rally. They thought that the best way to express their horror at the hydrogen bomb and draw attention to the rally would be for them to walk from Victoria Station to Piccadilly Circus by way of Westminster with sandwich boards. An old photograph of 1954 shows six of our heroes assembled at Victoria Station with boards reading "Hydrogen Bomb" in large letters with something like a cross or an explosion in the background. In small letters the heading is "Hydrogen Bomb National Campaign" and the rest of the poster reads, "Challenge to Mankind" with details of the meeting in the Albert Hall, 7 p.m. on Friday 30th April. It is interesting to study their embarrassed faces! George Craddock stands like a soldier on parade, Fenner Brockway and Richard Ackland are talking to each other in an uneasy atmosphere, Tony Greenwood is grinning a nervous smile. Tony Benn looks very young and sincere, gritting his teeth for the ordeal. But George Thomas looks completely composed and happy, as though he had gathered this reluctant group together for its unusual parade. But his composure was a mask as his own memory recalls:

> We gathered at Victoria, only to be told by the police, who were not very polite about it, that we should not be allowed to walk together. There had to be four hundred yards separating each of us. I soon discovered that walking on your own with a sandwich board can be a very embarrassing business. I will never forget the big fat clergyman crammed into a small car, needling me all the time, saying things like, "Go back to Russia, you Communist!"
>
> I felt terribly awkward as I passed the Commons, and hoped no members would see me walking along with the board. Eventually I reached Horse Guards Parade, and the clergyman was still following, niggling and sneering all the time. At last I could bear it no longer, turned to him and said, "If you don't go away, I'll lift this board and bring it down on your head." That, of course was what he wanted: "There! I knew you were all men of violence inside."

George never joined the Campaign for Nuclear Disarmament which grew out of the Albert Hall meeting, but he was glad to have been involved at its inception. Canon Collins took an active part and support mushroomed. It continues to be a very effective movement, having learnt to influence policy and move far beyond its simple message of "Ban the Bomb". George did not lose interest, but was becoming aware that he must concentrate on his role in the Labour Party.

He was in the House as usual on 5th April, when Attlee made one of his finest speeches against the detonation of the H-bomb in the Pacific. He called for immediate three-power talks and a ban on further tests. The whole Labour Party was for once united and two Scottish by-elections showed how the country responded favourably to the protest against the H-bomb tests. Mallalieu, writing in *Tribune* said, "Labour, in fact, had just begun to bask in the unaccustomed and unexpected luxury of unity, to profit from the mistakes of its opponents, to assume once again the leadership of Britain." At that point they could probably have won an election, but there was another year to go.

Leasehold Reform Again

In 1954, Sir David Maxwell-Fyfe, Home Secretary and Minister for Welsh Affairs, proposed the Landlord and Tenant Bill, which was a setback for George Thomas's campaign for leasehold reform. Maxwell-Fyfe claimed that to grant tenants the right to purchase the freehold of their own houses would pose too many practical problems. An improved security of tenure was as far as he would go. But this left the main problem unsolved. Eviction might be more difficult, but the landlord still had the right to raise ground rents and charge for repairs when the lease ran out. When the bill had its final reading, George Thomas opposed it strongly and ended by saying that this was not his final word.

Later, he was successful in the ballot for a Private Member's Bill and was able to introduce his bill to give leaseholders the right either to renew their leases or to buy the freehold of their homes at a reasonable price. The bill was presented for its second reading on Friday 18th March 1955. He suffered what many have suffered since who have with passionate belief introduced their own Private

Member's Bill: there is no automatic government or party support. You are on your own and have to drum up support privately. George Thomas was good at this and had high hopes of success. But Friday is a bad day and it is the usual day for Private Member's Bills.

There is no better way to illustrate the liveliness of George Thomas in debate than to transcribe a few paragraphs from Hansard. The debate on the second reading of the Leasehold Enfranchisement Bill on that Friday, 18th March 1955, is as good an example as any. He was confident of success as he rose to speak at 11.30 that morning to support the bill. He reminded the House that there had been previous bills, one as early as 1884. Early supporters had urged this bill as calculated to "remove a powerful stimulus to Socialism (and) conditions likely to bring about revolutions". He pointed out that this was not his motivation. He also reminded the House that in 1906, David Lloyd George had driven the Tories out of Wales by his support for this very measure. The bill had long been his crusade and as early as 1947 he had intended broadcasting in favour of such a bill, but the BBC, which at first agreed, was persuaded by Western Ground Rents not to let him go on the air. He gave various examples and concentrated his attack principally against Western Ground Rents. They were the owners of half of Cardiff which they had purchased in the 1930s from the Marquis of Bute for a reputed £20 million. The member for Buckinghamshire rose and made a slight point in favour. George was quick to respond and from that response we shall take up an edited version of the transcript in Hansard:

> *Mr Thomas*: The hon. Member for Buckinghamshire South (Mr R. Bell) talks as a lawyer.
>
> *Mr Hale*: No, he does not.
>
> *Mr Thomas*: Well, the hon. Member talks—and we will leave it there. All that I am sure of is that the people who buy their homes believe that they belong to them. Perhaps I can give the illustration of a little piece of land which I lease from Cardiff Corporation, for which the Corporation will receive, over 90 years, a sum of £1,000; but at the end of that period the Corporation will expect the property on top of it as well. People in Pembrokeshire have had this happen not in 99 years but in 50 years ... Swansea, Llanelly, and the whole of South Wales is in a revolt against this system. The result is that we cannot find a Tory down there who will defend it—not in public, at any rate.

Mr Griffiths: What about the hon. Member for Cardiff North (Mr Llewellyn)?

Mr Thomas: The hon. Member for Cardiff North is on record as being in favour of enfranchisement, and no doubt he will say so today, Mr Speaker, if he has the good fortune to catch your eye.

Mr David Llewellyn (Cardiff North): I am in favour of it on fair terms.

Mr Thomas: In that case, I welcome the hon. gentleman's support.

My hon. friend and Member for Rhondda East (Mr Mainwaring) who will second the Motion, will no doubt give his own illustrations from my native valley of the Rhondda, but it is impossible to find any part of South Wales where this injustice does not rankle in our breasts.

In London there is a powerful non-political organization, the London Leaseholders' Association, with an energetic secretary to whom I personally am greatly indebted. This movement has been established because throughout London there is the same burning injustice as that which exists in South Wales. The hon. Member for Hampstead (Mr H. Brooke), who now serves in the Treasury, told us in an earlier debate that a thousand houses in the borough of Hampstead alone are owned by leasehold estates. In Lewisham and Windsor, in Dulwich and Paddington, in St Pancras and Holborn, there are great slices where these finance corporations own the land and are exploiting it.

I have inevitably received a lot of correspondence about this Bill, but I will quote from only two letters. One is from Newport, Monmouthshire, and the other from Grantham. The letter from Grantham reads:

"A case was brought to my notice a few weeks ago of a man who after war service bought a leasehold house, the only one he could get, with 25 years unexpired. He is now compelled to change his town of employment and finds he cannot sell his house, even at a great loss. He has appealed to the ground landlord to whom he pays £2.15 a year ground rent, for reasonable enfranchisement. He has not had any satisfactory reply."

The letter gives a lot more details about the property. I read it only to illustrate that the present leasehold system imposes an unfair handicap upon people who wish to move from one part of the country to another.

The second letter is from an elderly lady in Newport, Monmouthshire, and it reads:

"The lease of my house expires in 18 months and I am being asked £750 and all legal charges for the freehold. I pay £3.15 per year ground rent. They therefore want 200 years' purchase price for me to have the freehold. I am a widow and have lived in this house 58 years."

There is something immoral and cruel about a system which allows an elderly person like that to be robbed of her home. The Landlord and Tenant Act, introduced by the present Government last year, is quite inadequate to protect the householder from the grasping hands of the finance corporations. When the lease runs out, he is now guaranteed security of tenure at an economic rent. (But) from paying a ground rent of £6 a year, he may well find that he has to pay a rent of £16 a month. This is not at all an exaggerated illustration. If he cannot afford the rent —the new inflated rent—there is no security for him, because he will have to leave.

The 1954 Measure is a Landlords' Charter. The morality of capitalism apparently discounts human considerations. The human aspect does not seem to count. The fact that family associations with a home mean much has not entered into the Government's considerations.

In the very first Clause this Bill establishes the right to enfranchisement for tenants except those in one category—those who acquire

"the tenancy in consideration of money or moneys' worth within ten years of the end of the term for which the money was granted".

There are speculators, and I am not interested in speculators, big or small; I am interested in the man who is living in his own home and who wants to stay there.

Clause 5 deals with the terms of payment, and they are not ungenerous to the landlord. The provision of 20 times the average ground rent is compensation which in the opinion of all of us who prepared the Measure, gives justice to the ground landlord and justice to the tenant.

Mr Hale: Very fair terms.

Mr Thomas: In Clause 6 the authority of the courts is established to determine questions of disagreement where the lease concerned a property which is part of other premises. It also establishes the right of the court to permit the tenant to pay the enfranchisement fee by instalments. If the tenant changes his mind after giving notice that he intended to purchase the freehold, he is entitled to do so, provided that he satisfies the court that it is not reasonably practicable for him to continue with his purchase. But, if he exercises this right within three years of the end of the tenancy, the right of enfranchisement will thereafter lapse.

Clause 9 gives to tenants of Crown or Government property the right to enfranchisement. This clause will be received with special welcome in Windsor and Greenwich, Camborne and Falmouth, and Cornwall and Devon. During my recent visit to Cornwall I found that everyone I spoke to about Crown Property paid a tribute to the Crown Estate as being a very good landlord. They all recognized that it was a good ground or estate landlord. There may have been others who thought differently, but I did not meet them. But even those to whom I spoke asked me to do my best to obtain for them the right to buy the freehold of their own homes. Local authorities will be exempt only where they require leases for the exercise of distinctive public functions which have been laid upon them by statute.

The usual argument put forward against a proposal of this sort is that the principle of the sanctity of contract must be honoured and recognized in this country —

Mr Hale: And at Yalta.

Mr Thomas: That does not come within the terms of this Bill. A contract which is entered into almost under duress is recognized by everyone as not having the moral sanction of the rest of the community. Where there is a monopoly in the ownership of land there is no equality among the parties negotiating the contract. I could not buy the freehold of land in the city of Cardiff upon which to have my home built. Like everyone else I was obliged to buy a piece of land through the leasehold system.

Mr R. Bell: *indicating dissent.*

Mr Thomas: The hon. Member shakes his head. If he can tell the hon. Member for Cardiff North, (Mr Llewellyn) or myself where in Cardiff we can buy the freehold of land we shall be very pleased.

Mr Callaghan: I will buy it.

Mr Thomas: My hon. and wealthy friend will buy it. An unfortunate effect of the present system is that it sets neighbour against neighbour. In the little mining village of Treharris in South Wales the leases of some mining cottages were due to fall in and the ground landlord sold the leases of five of them to one of the tenants who, in turn, by the charges he imposed upon his neighbours, exploited them. It is not only the big people who can behave badly. This system has a bad effect upon individuals.

George Thomas went on to say that at the last election, the Conservative Party had talked in favour of a "property-owning democracy", but they forgot to say who is to own the property. Most of the speakers that followed him spoke against the iniquities of the leasehold laws, but the Attorney General defended them: "Why should the reversioner get the house which he himself did not build?" The debate went on for about four hours and the arguments by the Attorney General carried little weight, especially after the member for Gower spoke with such clear examples of injustice: "We are asking for a square deal," he said at the end of his speech, "and I hope the House will give it to us." The House divided and there was a clear majority in favour of the Bill—87 to 38. There were not enough members present, however, and George's victory was turned to disappointment as the Speaker ruled, that "it was not supported by the majority prescribed by Standing Orders". The debate stood adjourned.

He had come so near to winning, but the rules of the House, which later he would be proud to defend, defeated him. But still he had not had his final word on the subject of leasehold reform.

Another General Election

It had been obvious for some time that Mam was frail and George, who was now her main support, moved his house from 40 Plasterton Gardens in Cardiff to a bungalow in King George V Drive, overlooking Heath Park, where he continues to live. This was necessary if Mam was to continue the active life, which was the only kind she knew. The stairs of the old house defeated her. George called the new house "Tilbury"—her maiden name. They had been settled in the bungalow for more than a year when the Prime Minister, Winston Churchill, called a general election. He had held his government for four years with a small majority. When asked earlier why he persisted with so small a majority, he characteristically replied, "One is enough!" But he was growing old, and two strokes took their toll of his energy. In April 1955, he resigned in favour of Anthony Eden. It was Eden who led the Conservatives into the general election of 25th May 1955. Many thought that Clement Attlee should also have resigned before the election, but he had his reasons for staying. He was ill but he stuck it out until he was quite sure that Hugh Gaitskell and not Herbert Morrison would succeed him.

That election was not an easy one for Labour. George fought it well and successfully. Mam was still there fighting for him. She appealed to the housewives of Cardiff and dealt with grass root problems: "My son George lives to serve . . . He brings his Christian faith to his public work. His entire life is given in service to other people. He is a man of principle and will never let you down."

Mam had not changed in her support and appeal to the reliability of a Christian believer. George had to express his views in hard facts, although the heart of his appeal was still the careful pastoral work which he did at his surgery in 208 Cowbridge Road East. In setting out what he believed, George was consistent. He denounced the use or testing of the H-Bomb. "Fear," he declared, "is an inadequate base for maintaining peace." He insisted that the government should hold down the cost of living. Of course, he pledged his support for leasehold reform, pointing out that Cardiff was one of the worst victims. He argued for full employment and good social services, and again appealed for Liberal support.

George Thomas had no difficulty in retaining his seat, and neither did Jim Callaghan. Throughout the country, the Conservatives did much better and were returned with an increased majority. Six months later, Attlee resigned. There were three candidates for his successor: Hugh Gaitskell, whom Attlee favoured and had built up by making him Chancellor of the Exchequer; Herbert Morrison, the veteran; Nye Bevan, the controversial figure. Gaitskell won with 157 votes against 70 for Bevan and only 40 for Morrison. George Thomas voted for Nye Bevan. So both parties had new leaders—Eden and Gaitskell.

The Suez Crisis

George was not in England when the Suez crisis broke. He had been invited to America earlier in 1956 and combined the function of a visiting British Member of Parliament with that of a Methodist preacher. It enabled him to attend the Ninth World Methodist Conference which was held in North Carolina, 1st–12th September. He was listed among the visiting preachers open to invitations to preach throughout the USA. Among that list of visiting preachers were William Sangster and Gordon Rupp, Eric Baker, Harold Roberts, Maldwyn Edwards and Benson Perkins, a veritable galaxy of British Methodists. George Thomas was much in demand and, according to his own account, "I ended up preaching in every one of the states except Florida." He was in Mount Vernon, New York, on 22nd July; Selby, North Carolina, on 7th September and San Francisco, California, on 28th October. It was during that last engagement that he heard news of the invasion of Egypt by British and French troops. The action taken by Eden astounded all who knew him. Attlee was in India when he heard the news and wrote of his surprise that Eden had done such a thing: "Couldn't reconcile it with his whole career —inexplicable." Denis Healey declared that he had never been so angry in all his life. "Reggie Maudling claimed that steam was actually coming out of my ears." The country was divided. America was furious and stopped the escapade. "Eisenhower," wrote George, "made what I thought a very cruel speech attacking the British," adding by way of explanation, "Because he was electioneering, principles did not appeal to him very much just then." In San Francisco, George was with a Tory MP, Joe Godber, and they decided upon the customary policy of British MPs abroad, "always to defend our own country", with the result that when either of them addressed a Rotary or Lions' Club meeting, he took a strong line of defence of the UK action. To the hostile Americans, George would say, "If it were the Panama Canal that was to be closed, you would take a very different attitude." His view was clear and simple:

> President Nasser of Egypt had nationalized the Suez Canal Company, whose headquarters were in Paris and most of whose directors were French or British. The canal was of enormous international importance, and Britain and France took the controversial decision to land troops in Egypt to secure its free navigation.

He returned from his lengthy stay in America, to find petrol rationing and anger in the country and in the House of Commons. The country was bitterly divided. Old friends would not speak to each other. Passions were roused and accusations flew wildly about. The Conservatives felt that the Labour Party had behaved treacherously by supporting the exercise at first and then pulling back later. They accused Labour of letting down the troops and Britain. But even Harold Macmillan, originally in favour of the invasion, later distanced himself from the Prime Minister. The affair destroyed Anthony Eden and after a short while he resigned, broken in health as well as prestige. Writing in 1985, when the documents were all public and a considered opinion could be formed without emotion, George Thomas did not greatly change his view as he had expressed it in San Francisco in 1956:

> Looking back at Suez now, it is clear that if the exercise had been successful, the whole history of the Middle East would have been transformed. The Arabs learned that, although they were weak militarily, they had the strength to defeat big powers through the force of world opinion and the United Nations. Both America and the Soviet Union were determined to block us over Suez, and under those circumstances it was impossible to succeed. It was a watershed for us ... The country was deeply wounded by the whole affair but even now, looking back from the distance, it is not easy to assess the merits or demerits of the exercise.

Writing about the same time, Denis Healey, looking back, saw more than George did and was much more hostile. He lived up to George's comment on the first day they met: "Denis, you have the most wonderful gift of vituperation!" Denis Healey wrote in his autobiography in 1985, not so much with his vituperation, which he must have exhausted in 1956, but with deep sorrow:

> The final obscenity was that Eden's invasion of Suez coincided with Russia's invasion of Hungary. Port Said fell to the British and French troops on the same day as Budapest fell to the Red Army. I asked Eden if he had exchanged congratulations with Bulganin. While I was driving to a protest meeting in York against Suez, I heard on the car radio that last broken appeal from Hungary for help from the West. I had to pull in to the side of the road until I had stopped weeping.

George Thomas and Denis Healey, both loyal and intelligent members of the Labour Party, illustrate the division in the party itself over Suez. And that division went through the House and the country.

A Rounded Life

At this period, George Thomas was branching out in all directions. He was much in demand as a public speaker and many organizations wanted to have so lively, articulate and influential a man on their platform. He retained his key position in the National Union of Teachers. His Methodism was never more important to him as he continued as a preacher and took part in Methodist activities—the extended visit to America showed that. He was unusually conscientious in the care of his constituency, following up cases in detail. Already in 1956, there was some evidence that he was overdoing things.

In April 1956, he attended the Scarborough Conference of the National Union of Teachers. He was in relaxed mood as his diary notes show: "We came on Good Friday. Wonderful run up. Arrived 3.30—tea, wash, Welsh meeting. Stayed in bed for breakfast. After dinner, shops with Cath [Minton, wife of the Secretary of the Cardiff NUT]. Pictures at night."

Then he added, "I made up my mind to rest each morning." That may simply have been in order to be fresh for the evening meeting. But it could also have meant that he realized that he was getting tired —and who could be surprised, with his programme. In May he was at the Annual Conference of the National Brotherhood Movement in Leamington Spa. The Brotherhood Movement was an organization of Christian men, drawn almost entirely from the Free Churches. Its first National President was John Clifford, a politically-minded Baptist preacher. It embodied the "Nonconformist conscience". George Thomas was welcomed in Leamington Spa as the incoming President. That was 11th–15th May. He was in full flood: "On the home front the moral challenge is full employment"; but there was a warning for his fellow socialists: "Selfishness and irresponsibility can pull down the pillars of the Welfare State." "In the foreign field," he added, "the moral challenge of world hunger has priority. If we face the problem as brothers we shall the more surely face the challenge of the hydrogen bomb."

Earlier in the year he was attending the reopening of the Tonypandy Methodist Central Hall by his mother, and his diary is full of engagements great and small. The trip to America which took up so large a part of 1956 was no holiday, as we have seen. Anthony Barker of the *South Wales Evening Post* summed him up about this time in his column, headed, "Cardiff Socialist of the Week".

> One of the most popular men in the House—jovial, always trying to make life a little more pleasant for someone—astute Parliamentarian, quick to size up any situation, never lost for sound or reasoned comment. He seldom minces his words, speaks with the authority one would expect from a member who is one of the Chairmen's panel, and what he says comes straight from the heart. Ardent Socialist, never too proud to proclaim it. "Rocking the boat" is not his speciality. A man of deep and sincere principles, a pacifist. On Monday 1st April [1957], Gaitskell and Macmillan agreed to continue with the H-bomb tests—divides the Labour Party—George leads the opposition to make a compromise—the Parliamentary Labour Party has a secret meeting with George on Wednesday 3rd—George puts forward a resolution—George meets with the Shadow Cabinet. They agree to "postponement of the British H-bomb tests for a limited period". This left open the possibility of talks with the USA and with the USSR, to reduce tests and ultimately end them.

Nye Bevan and the Nuclear Deterrent

The disastrous outcome of the Suez adventure in 1956 led to the change of Prime Minister from Anthony Eden to Harold Macmillan, and changes in leadership of the Labour Party. There began a period of adjustment between Hugh Gaitskell and Nye Bevan which was undoubtedly influenced by Bevan's desire to be Foreign Secretary in the next Labour government. He considered that he could talk with the Russians and did not regard the Americans as the successors to Britain in greatness. In all this, George Thomas agreed with him. In particular, both seemed to support the abolition of nuclear weapons. There were three issues involved—abolition of nuclear tests, refusal to make nuclear weapons and proliferation of nuclear powers. There is no doubt where George stood. He would have banned tests and manufacture and unilaterally given up nuclear weapons. Britain could then say, "Nuclear power stops here!" On the whole the Bevanities should have supported that view. But at the Labour Party Conference in Brighton in 1957, the most extraordinary thing happened. Nye Bevan did one of his emotional somersaults and supported the retention of nuclear weapons. It was his worst speech and his heart was not in it. His reasons were obscure, but George certainly thought that he changed his views because he wanted to be the next Labour Foreign Secretary. Bevan himself argued that you could not separate the nuclear issue from the general foreign policy of the Labour Party. Bevan's followers were furious at this change, George Thomas among them. Months later during a debate on defence, 27th February 1958, George argued the unilateral line. The step should be taken boldly he said, even if the other countries retained their nuclear weapons. The majority view in the Labour Party was that if this line was taken they would lose the next election. For the sake of victory now—the Tories were still suffering from the Suez disaster—they closed ranks. George was in good form that day. "Fear is not enough for a defence policy," he argued, and he referred to the speech at Brighton in which Bevan had "disappointed his friends and pleased other people." Then as he looked at the front benches—Tory and Labour—he said in cutting words, but not without humour even then: "Consistency is, I know, no virtue in this House—it is a great handicap; I have only to glance at either front bench, to realize this." He went on with a little anger to defend Earl Russell, who had been summarily dismissed as a "superannuated philosopher". It was at that time that he said, "I never had the distinction of being a Bevanite; I never belonged to that group, although for much of the time my views coincided with theirs."

Laughing at Oneself

One of the characteristics of George Thomas, all his life, has been the ability to make people laugh, even in the most serious situations. And many times he has shown his readiness to take the butt of the joke himself. It was about this time, when the wounds of Suez were just beginning to heal a little and jokes were at a minimum in the House, that George appeared to attract undue attention when he came into the House. He often sat next to Jo Grimond and when he noticed that the Tories were staring at him in an amused way, he asked Jo Grimond why they were pointing at them. Jo said, "I think it's you!" Then he added, "I think it's the way you're dressed." George was puzzled and looked down to see if all his buttons were done up. Then Colonel Robin Chichester-Clark, an Ulster member who sat on the government bench as a Whip, motioned him to go to the Bar of the House. He dutifully went, still puzzled. The House erupted in laughter and Colonel Chichester-Clark said, "Do you know that you are wearing an Old Etonian tie?" George answered quite truthfully, "I bought it in the Co-operative store in Tonypandy. I liked the look of it." The Colonel grinned and said, "You're probably safe to wear it in Tonypandy, but not here—too many members are entitled to wear it." With a final touch of humour, George gave the tie to an old age pensioner. That was in 1957 and his innocent transgression endeared him to the House. "One of the most popular men in the House"—that journalist was right.

CHAPTER ELEVEN

◆◆◆

The Road to Wales

IN HIS MAIDEN SPEECH in the Commons in 1945, George Thomas had given notice that he believed that Wales was as much entitled to a Secretary of State as was Scotland. Equally he never wavered in his belief that Cardiff was the natural capital city for Wales.

His path in fighting for official recognition of capital status for Cardiff was anything but smooth. The people of North Wales looked on Caernarvon as the Welsh cultural capital. The Welsh language was overwhelmingly the mother-tongue in that part of Wales, whereas in Cardiff only a very small minority of people claimed Welsh as their first language. Poor communication between North and South Wales did nothing to break down the mistrust that existed between Caernarvon and Cardiff.

Even in South Wales sharp rivalry existed between Swansea and Cardiff, so it was no surprise that when George submitted to the Welsh Parliamentary Party (which included every party in Wales) a motion that Cardiff should be declared the capital city of Wales, he met with a storm of abusive opposition. Megan Lloyd George, although she now represented Carmarthen in the Labour interest, was fiercely for her native Caernarvon, which had been represented for fifty years in the Commons by her late father. She rallied her friend Aneurin Bevan to make one of his extremely rare visits to a meeting of the Welsh Parliamentary Party, where he poured vitriolic scorn on the idea that Wales needed a capital at all.

Percy Morris, the right-wing Labour MP for Swansea West, shared Bevan's hostility to Cardiff even being considered as capital city. Historically there had been no love lost between Cardiff and the valleys, so no support was forthcoming from there. The proposal was rejected by an overwhelming vote.

Seven years of campaigning were to elapse before Megan Lloyd

George's brother, Gwilym, member for Pembrokeshire and Home Secretary of the day, received an official petition from the Lord Mayor of Cardiff, the Town Clerk and George Thomas, MP, asking for the city to be granted capital status. His reply was affirmative.

The Welsh Grand Committee

Another sop to the growing awareness of national feeling in Wales was the establishment of the Welsh Grand Committee. The Committee was the brain-child of two MPs—Ness Edwards for Caerphilly and Goronwy Roberts for Caernarvon. They had pursued the matter in the Welsh Parliamentary Party and eventually obtained unanimous support for their idea.

The government agreed that a Welsh Grand Committee, consisting of all Welsh MPs, should meet from time to time to discuss matters appertaining to Wales. Hitherto there had been only one day a year allocated in the Commons timetable for consideration of Welsh affairs. "Welsh Day", as it became known in the Commons, was soon seen to be a farce. Each Welsh MP who was called to speak in the debate tended to concentrate on issues affecting his own constituency. There was no single theme on which members would concentrate. Even when an attempt was made to choose a subject, such as "Unemployment in Wales", the debate became so broad that ministers had an easy time in winding up speeches. Thus it was hoped that Welsh MPs would be content with a Grand Committee that took no decisions, but would be only a talking shop.

It was not easy for either of the major political parties to acknowledge the growing clamour in Wales for a recognition that it was not just an appendage to England. At this time George was undoubtedly inspired by more than one motive. He wanted to establish himself as a true son of Wales, but equally he was well aware that his campaigning was making him a well-known Welsh MP. Personal ambition blended comfortably with his Welsh ideals.

The First Chairman

Because George Thomas was the only Welsh MP on the Speaker's Panel of Chairmen, he was almost automatically appointed as the first Chairman of the Welsh Grand Committee. His political instincts warned him of the danger to his position in Wales when it would be realized that he was the only Welsh MP unable to make a speech in the Committee. He thereupon set about building up the significance of the honour of being its chairman. In his public speeches he constantly referred to the success of Welsh MPs in getting the Committee established, and how great an honour it was to be its chairman.

Because of the preponderance of Labour MPs in Wales, it was impossible to have a balanced Committee without Conservative MPs from English constituencies. These co-opted members never asked to speak and therefore the handful of Welsh Conservative MPs had more than their share of being called. They were soon speaking at every sitting of the Committee.

Despite his campaigning for Wales and his agitation for parliamentary time to be made available for Welsh affairs, George Thomas never ceased to be actively opposed to the devolution of parliamentary power from Westminster to Wales. Remembering how the Commons itself had grown by demanding more and more powers, he feared that any Welsh National Assembly that was set up, would similarly demand greater and greater autonomy, leading eventually to the break-up of the United Kingdom.

The Labour Party Divided

In 1959, Hugh Gaitskell led the Labour Party to defeat in the general election, with the Conservatives increasing their majority. George challenges the view that Hugh Gaitskell was a "moderate" leader, a healer of divisions. He claims that Gaitskell was well to the right of the party and "could not be bothered with anyone who did not share his views". The Parliamentary Labour Party looked increasingly like two parties and the Welsh MPs were mainly on the opposite side to Gaitskell. One of the issues dividing the party was that of unilateral nuclear disarmament, and most of the Welsh MPs were unilateralists. This was evident both in the Party Conference at Scarborough in 1960, after the death of Nye Bevan, and in the subsequent leadership election.

At the Conference, Gaitskell's official statement of his defence policy was narrowly defeated, while a resolution calling for unilateral disarmament was narrowly passed. Hugh Gaitskell was emerging as the leader of "half a party".

Feeling in the Parliamentary Labour Party ran so high that it was inevitable that Gaitskell's continued leadership would be challenged at the annual selection of Shadow Cabinet members and Party Leader. Normally there was a contest for the leadership only when there was a vacancy. This time, Tony Greenwood, well known to be only slightly left of centre in the Labour Party, announced that he was going to stand against Gaitskell for the leadership. This was interpreted as a direct challenge to Harold Wilson, who had been generally regarded as Aneurin Bevan's successor as leader of Labour's left, to come out and fight. Wilson immediately picked up the gauntlet and announced his candidature. Tony Greenwood then declared that he would withdraw in favour of Wilson. George Thomas immediately announced his support for Wilson.

When the result of the voting was declared Hugh Gaitskell had 166 votes while Harold Wilson had 81. In the new Shadow Cabinet, Gaitskell showed his awareness that steps had to be taken to try to get the party united. He appointed Harold Wilson as Shadow Chancellor of the Exchequer, but within a year had switched him to Shadow Foreign Secretary. Wilson was rattled by this switch, as he made clear to George Thomas and others of his friends in the Commons. None the less, it was George's view that the switch was to prove tremendously beneficial to Wilson in his subsequent bid for the leadership.

An Offended George Thomas

It was fairly obvious that George Thomas neither liked nor approved of Hugh Gaitskell. The dislike, it seems, was mutual. Their policies differed on defence and most other issues. If Gaitskell was "way to the right of the Party" at that time, George Thomas was certainly to the left. George had also mobilized as many Welsh MPs as he could against Gaitskell in the leadership election. But there was a personality clash too, which comes out in one of George's frank comments: "In the members' tea-room he would sit only with his cronies, making it clear to anyone that he was content to lead a divided party as long as his supporters were in the majority."

George had always made friends in the House with members of all Parties—Eden and Jo Grimond, as well as Nye Bevan. He loved the solidarity of the House and hated personal divisions, even on policy grounds. He was, of course, not without his prejudices and he had those he liked and those he disliked, but Gaitskell's narrow sectarianism offended him.

An incident in Cardiff, which he describes with hurt feelings years later, illustrates this very clearly:

> He [Gaitskell] came down to Cardiff on one occasion to speak for Jim Callaghan. He had not given me any indication that he was coming, but I had read about it in the Cardiff newspapers. On Friday night I was at home watching the television news and saw Gaitskell being received at Cardiff station by Callaghan. I was just about to go out to a meeting when the telephone rang.
>
> It was Cliff Prothero, the Labour Party's regional organizer in Wales, who asked me to go to a Transport House press conference in the morning to meet Hugh Gaitskell. I refused, not just because Gaitskell had been discourteous to me in not telling me he was coming to Cardiff, but because I felt strongly that he only wanted to lead half the Labour Party. And I had no intention of doing anything other than let it be seen that he was leading half a party. Prothero, an old friend, begged me to put in an appearance. I finally agreed that I would, after I had finished my constituency surgery.

The surgery was allowed to go on longer than usual and George arrived after the press conference was over. George had made his point. Hugh Gaitskell, with apparent affection, put his arm round him and asked him to walk down Queen Street with him. George Thomas was angry and replied: "I've seen you and Jim several times this week, and neither of you told me you were coming. If you want to lead half the party, you lead it; but I'm not going to make it any easier for you."

That occasion also marked a growing division between George Thomas and James Callaghan, which did not get easier with the passage of the years. Both Gaitskell and Callaghan underestimated the influence of George Thomas with the majority of the Welsh MPs and with others on the left wing of the party.

Another Effort for Leasehold Reform

Out of sympathy with the leadership of his party, George Thomas might well have been expected to turn for support to the Welsh MPs. He was Chairman of the Welsh Parliamentary Party, and at times he did this. For example, in 1959 he appealed to them to support a petition which would force the government to act on the scandal of leasehold exploitation. To his disappointment, they bluntly refused to co-operate. Although he did not know it at the time, that refusal was the best thing that could have happened. He went over the heads of the Welsh MPs and appealed to the people by organizing a national petition for leasehold reform. His friend David Rosser of the *Western Mail*, wrote many articles on his one-man campaign for an All Wales Leasehold Reform Petition. He was deluged with letters of support. This encouraged him to form an all-party committee, not in the House, but in Cardiff, which sent out letters to groups and individuals throughout Wales. The whole "leasehold scandal" was now seen as primarily a Welsh, rather than a party, affair. The committee set five weeks as the target period and proceeded to collect signatures. For five successive Saturdays, George stood outside the entrance to the Cardiff city market with a table loaded with petition forms. The people queued to sign, and George, always sensitive to good publicity, showed that the Archbishop of Wales had signed and that the lease-holders could tell their own sad stories. Within five weeks, more than 60,000 signatures were obtained. The support crossed all party boundaries, as George had forecast to the unco-operative Welsh Parliamentary Party. His triumphant moment in the House must be savoured in his own language:

> The next step was to present the petition to Parliament. Cheers from my Welsh colleagues were music to my ears when I rose to my feet in the Commons. My hand was shaking as I read out the top copy. Then I bowed to the Speaker and made my way to deposit the petition in the big green bag behind his Chair. The whole House gave a generous cheer.

Within a few days of his presenting the petition to Parliament, George received an urgent request to go to the Ministry of Local Government and Welsh Affairs, whose Minister, Dr Charles Hill, wished to discuss the matter with him. Dr Hill was a National Liberal MP, who supported the Conservative government and who had become popular as the "Radio Doctor", specializing in broadcast health talks on the BBC.

When George was admitted to his impressive office in Whitehall, Dr Hill greeted him with warmth, declaring, "Well done, George!

You have had a great triumph." Then he closed the door so that the secretaries could not hear and asked George what terms he would settle for. George stubbornly refused to compromise. He insisted on the right of people to buy the freehold of their home, even if the ground landlord did not wish to sell. Charles Hill, a National Liberal in a Tory government, made much of his sympathy for the cause, but added, "You know this Tory government will never agree to that. Be reasonable, George, and settle for half a loaf now." The two parliamentarians parried with each other for a while, but it became clear that they had no common ground. George's speeches, both in Parliament and in Wales, had totally committed him to demand total reform of the leasehold system. He could not afford to compromise on the issue even if he had been so inclined. It so happened that it was an issue on which he felt more strongly than on anything else. He commented: "I left knowing that the Government was worried by the success of the campaign, but I also knew that reform of the leasehold system would have to await the coming of a Labour Government."

Taking on the Cardiff City Council

George Thomas was showing a remarkable resilience in returning to local issues and ensuring the solidity of his seat in Cardiff. In these battles he was "no respecter of persons". The Cardiff City Council had condemned some houses in the Riverside area of Cardiff and were not generous in their offer of compensation to the owners, who had been granted mortgages only two years before. George spoke and campaigned in Cardiff. On 4th April 1962, his statement was reported in full in the *South Wales Echo*:

> I am astonished at the speed with which the local authority have moved to condemn houses for which they granted mortgages so recently. I can show them plenty of houses in Cardiff unfit for human habitation which they are very reluctant to condemn. There are people in Cardiff living in intolerable conditions in other privately owned properties, and I would have thought that these were entitled to a demolition order and the occupants rehoused before the Riverside houses, which were considered fit one, two years ago. There is something wrong in Cardiff if this can happen to thrifty people who are struggling to buy their own homes.

He promised that he would raise the issue in the House of Commons before the Easter recess and he did so. He called for legislation to protect Cardiff house owners threatened with the loss of their homes with little or no compensation. No new legislation was forthcoming; indeed, the government's response was that sufficient existed, but the issue had been raised and the Cardiff City Council had been exposed.

We find him a year later photographed with a confident Mrs Anne Rees, one of his more militant supporters, escorting her to the City Hall with a petition for compensation.

George Thomas, for all his admiration for Parliament and its dignity, which he never lost, belonged first and foremost to Wales and to Cardiff in particular. He was never content to be a remote Westminster legislator, neither was his career ever more important than his constituency.

A New Leader

The two great rivals for power in 1959 had been Hugh Gaitskell and Nye Bevan. They represented the two distinct halves of the Labour Party. But in that year, Bevan seemed to mellow, as though he had some premonition of the cancer which would cause his death in 1960. Denis Healey tells of the visit all three of them made to the Soviet Union in 1959, and maintained that it was the "first time Hugh had an easy relationship with Nye". Macmillan announced the general election while they were in Moscow and it was Bevan who faced the press. Later, at the Party Conference in Blackpool after the electoral defeat, it was Bevan again who rescued Gaitskell. Hugh Gaitskell also died young, three years after Bevan, at the age of fifty-six. Healey's comment is, "Politics is one of the most demanding professions. It tends to kill many of its most active leaders before they are sixty." In his typical style he adds, "Those who survive often live beyond ninety!" There was much praise for Hugh Gaitskell in his death— far more than he received when he was alive. He died in January 1963. George tells with displeasure of the in-fighting that accompanied the struggle for the succession, particularly the rumours circulating about Harold Wilson. There could be no doubt that Wilson was George's choice. It was embarrassing for him, however, because Callaghan was the other candidate. In fact, Callaghan seemed to assume that he would have George's support—so much so that he leaked to the press a conversation he had had with George Thomas. The fight was between right and left of the party and George was definitely on the left, as Wilson was. But *The Times* printed a report that "over the weekend George Thomas, one of Wilson's keenest supporters, had indicated that he was switching support to Callaghan". When Wilson showed him the piece, George was angry and protested that Jim was jumping the gun. He referred Wilson to that evening's *South Wales Echo*. George had telephoned the editor to make it clear that he was supporting Wilson. That evening the paper carried the two pictures of Thomas and Callaghan, with the heading, "Cardiff MPs divided".

The first ballot was for three candidates—George Brown, James Callaghan and Harold Wilson. For the second ballot, Callaghan dropped out and Wilson won. Denis Healey recalls, "Harold won the succession without great difficulty, against George Brown and Jim Callaghan." George Thomas did not see it like that, but thought it was only the Callaghan–Brown split which ensured ultimate victory for Harold Wilson. Whatever the reason, the result greatly pleased him. He had always liked Wilson and he trusted him as a man who kept his promises. He wrote of him, "It is rarely easy to get him to commit himself, but when he does so, his promise is binding."

A Welsh Baptism for Wilson

At least a year before his election as leader of the Labour Party, Wilson had promised George that he would visit the Cardiff West constituency in his support. A date had been fixed and a school hall booked for the public meeting.

A week before the arranged meeting, Harold Wilson was elected leader of the party. George offered to release Wilson from his engagement in Cardiff, but the new leader resolved to make his first public speech in his new capacity in George's constituency.

Excited by Wilson's decision, George immediately cancelled the school hall venue, and booked the Sophia Garden Pavilion which would accommodate 3,000 people. He thought that this would please Wilson, but he soon learnt otherwise. Underestimating his own pulling power, Wilson feared that the television cameras would focus on a lot of empty seats. He need not have worried, for Wilson's appointment had inspired a new enthusiasm in Labour ranks. Not only was the Pavilion packed to capacity, but 3,000 people stood outside listening to a broadcast of the proceedings. Twenty Welsh Labour MPs were assembled on the platform when George led Harold Wilson to his place. A storm of applause greeted the new leader and the audience burst into song, "We'll keep a welcome in the hillsides". Wilson was visibly moved and said, in an aside to George, "I'm not an orator, George. I'm a House of Commons man." One wonders what he must have felt at George's reply, intended to encourage: "Nonsense. There's a lot of Nye Bevan in you."

Harold Wilson's speech proved to be a super launching for the long two-year campaign to the general election in 1964. Taking full advantage of the wide age gap between himself and Prime Minister Macmillan he jested freely at the latter's expense.

George Thomas was convinced that that meeting, so soon after the leadership election, at which Wilson was a great success, was his baptism of fire—Welsh fire! His considered comment on reflection was: "It was a firm conviction of mine that that tremendous public meeting gave Harold Wilson a new confidence in himself. No man could have asked for a more auspicious beginning to the Party leadership."

Harold Wilson and Labour's Victory

There are many different views about Harold Wilson, both as a politician and as Prime Minister. The two extremes might well be those of Denis Healey and George Thomas. Healey talks of Wilson packing his cabinet with yes-men, and George Thomas shows how he held the party together by deliberately choosing his Shadow Cabinet from the left and right. He did not want to lead a half party, but "he was intent on having both wings of the Party sharing responsibility."

By 1964, the Conservative government was in disarray. Macmillan had retired soon after the "night of the long knives" when he had sacked six senior Cabinet ministers, and after the Profumo affair had shaken the administration. Alec Douglas-Home had given up his earldom to follow as Prime Minister and had limped along for a year until the Parliament Act required him to go to the country. Wilson won the general election in 1964 and ended thirteen years of Tory rule. There were those who said with some reason that it was not so much Labour who won the election as the Conservatives who lost it. George was told by the Chief Whip that if Labour won the election, he would be Chairman of Ways and Means and Deputy Speaker. He was delighted, but there must have been a worry in his mind. As Deputy Speaker, he would have all the limitations customarily imposed on Mr Speaker, without enjoying the prestige and status which protects the Speaker in his constituency. As Deputy Speaker he would be outside the party political battle. His long cherished fight for leasehold reform could not be pursued. No longer would he be able to raise constituency issues in the House. George was well aware that by long tradition the Commons disliked promoting Deputy Speakers to be Speaker, for it gave Prime Ministers an indirect power to choose the Speaker if a vacancy arose. The Deputy Speaker is always the choice of the government, whereas, in theory at least, the Speaker is the choice of all parties in the House.

But the thought of being Deputy Speaker appealed so strongly to him that his pleasure showed itself to the Chief Whip, who said, "Of course, George, if we have a majority of only half a dozen, we will have to give the job to a Tory, for we will need the vote."

The election came. Douglas-Home made the nuclear deterrent an issue and nearly carried the country with him. It was a near thing. Labour won, but by a majority of only five.

On the Sunday morning after the election, when George arrived home from chapel, he found his mother quite excited. There had been a telephone call from Number 10 Downing Street and the Prime Minister's secretary would ring again in the afternoon.

When the call came, it was an invitation for him to make himself available in the Commons on the Monday for the Prime Minister to summon him to Number 10 when he would be ready to see George. In the event it was seven o'clock in the evening before the summons came that he was wanted. When he learned that, because the Deputy Speakership had gone to the Conservative who had held it previously he was offered the post of Parliamentary Under Secretary of State in the Home Office, George was thrilled.

Within a week of joining the Home Office, George learned that the former Deputy Speaker no longer wanted the job. When he contacted the Prime Minister he was told that if he wanted to switch to being Deputy Speaker, he was free to do so. But by now, with the intoxicating delight of having his own impressive room and savouring the unspoken flattery of having his own private secretary, he swiftly opted to stay as a junior minister. The Deputy Speakership was given to Horace King, who became Labour's first Speaker in the following year when Mr Speaker, Hylton Foster died suddenly.

The Press commented on what might have been when Hylton Foster died. The *Sunday Express* on 12th September 1965 made this the subject of "Cross Bench", a political gossip column:

> Another politician who can sigh over what might have been is Mr George Thomas, MP for Cardiff West. This charming and popular fellow looked like landing the job of Deputy Speaker last October. The move was stopped by Mr Harold Wilson who told him, "I've got something bigger in mind for you." And the post went to Dr Horace King. Today, had he not been deflected Mr Thomas would be enjoying Dr King's likeliest chance of becoming Speaker, with all the perquisites of the great position: a salary of £8,500, a magnificent house under Big Ben, and in due course, a £4,000-a-year pension and a certain viscountcy. What did the "something bigger" promised by Mr Wilson turn out to be? A paltry Under-Secretaryship at the Home Office.

Learning the Ropes

When George Thomas started his first assignment as Parliamentary Under Secretary of State in 1964 he was excited but also confused. There were so many civil servants in the Home Office that he found it difficult even to learn their names. That was an unusual embarrassment for one who all his life had tried to relate personally to everyone with whom he was in contact. The civil servants seemed to operate more like functional objects than real people. The hierarchical structures seemed to him not unlike the army or the police. He soon realized that a new minister has to learn many lessons before he is on top of his job, and in that initial period the civil servants are at their strongest and most able to manipulate the minister. Sir Charles Cunningham, the Permanent Secretary, was a formidable person with whom George had to come to terms. George describes the breaking of the ice with this dour Scot:

> One day, after he had greeted me with an aloof, "Good morning, Parliamentary Secretary," I said, "Sir Charles, I think I am a little afraid of you, and I don't like it. I'm the son of a miner, and I've never been afraid of people." His face wrinkled into the bare hint of a smile, and he replied, "You're not afraid of me, Parliamentary Secretary." To my quick rejoinder: "Everyone is

afraid of you," he said, "No, they are afraid of my expression. I cannot help it. I was born like it." From then on, I felt much closer to him.

That little transcript of conversation encapsulates George Thomas. He found it necessary to know people before he could work with them. Then he engendered true affection and loyalty, and gave it in return.

What was true of the civil servants was also true of his boss, the Home Secretary, Frank Soskice, who had been Attorney General in the last few months of Attlee's government. George learnt quite a lot from him, particularly how to delegate. Soskice presided over the Home Office with a lightness of touch, always trusting each junior minister to do his own job, interfering only to help or co-ordinate. This trust was rewarded with loyalty and affection.

Michael Head

George was fortunate in having a first-class private secretary, Michael Head, whose advice proved to be invaluable. One of the very first tasks in the Home Office was to share out the respective responsibilities to be allotted to each junior minister. Once Michael Head discovered that George was interested in the maximum work possible in the House of Commons, he advised him to try to get the General Department included in his portfolio. In the event, Immigration, the Police, and the General Department were allotted to him. The latter involved night after night answering Adjournment Debates in the Commons. It also involved considerable work when Private Members' Bills were discussed on Fridays in the House. George knew that more marks were gained by a high profile in Parliament than by desk work in the Home Office. He was in his element.

Racial Issues

One of the issues which George Thomas had in his responsibility was the application of the immigration laws. The Parliamentary Labour Party put pressure on him to introduce a bill making it an offence to discriminate against anyone on grounds of race. There were also many in the party who wanted to ease immigration control. George asked for a conference of junior ministers with the Home

Secretary to discuss this. It soon became evident that Soskice was in favour of stringent immigration controls. He is reported to have said, "If we do not have strict immigration rules, our people will soon all be coffee coloured!" George's protests were not heeded. Frank Soskice was equally adamant in opposition to a bill dealing with racial discrimination. He feared the loss of freedom of speech and believed that the state should not interfere too much in human relationships. George agreed with him on that, but wanted better education for life in a multi-cultural—and multi-racial—society.

Sir Frank Soskice delegated "prisons" to Alice Bacon. Among his many stories of this period, George tells how Harold Wilson came up to him in the tea room about the time when the train robbers had escaped. "What's this about prisoners escaping?" Wilson said. "You need to pull your socks up in the Home Office." George was quick to respond: "Prime Minister, I'm responsible for immigration; Alice Bacon is responsible for prisons. She can't keep them in and I can't keep them out!"

Despite his light-hearted reply, George's compassion and humanity caused him many a pain when he had to send immigrants back to unknown situations in their country of origin. He was quick to respond to questions, as when Eric Lubbock, Liberal MP for Orpington, protested that immigration officials at Heathrow were sending back to South Africa a teacher who had arrived that day. At the last minute George managed to recall him from a plane due to take off in a quarter of an hour. He examined the case but he was not convinced that the young man was in danger and sent him back to South Africa, where he had left behind a family of six children. In all such decisions, he agonized. It was so easy to get it wrong. Control of immigration caused him more heartache than anything else at the Home Office. Years later, he could write: "I used to feel ill with worry when I had to order some poor man to be sent back to his own country." The story of the teacher from South Africa, whom he took off the plane, but eventually had to send back, has a tailpiece, which he tells in his memoirs:

> Later that evening, I was in Frank Soskice's room when Michael Head unexpectedly and unusually came in. His face had a sickly pallor as he said, "Parliamentary Under Secretary, a man sent back to Africa from Heathrow today has committed suicide in flight over Rome. He cut his throat." I felt sick as I asked whether

it was the man I had sent back. Head told me that it was not. That decision had been taken by an immigration officer. Relief that it had not been my decision blended with sympathy for the officer concerned. It was a wretched job trying to bring justice to immigration control.

George the Brewer

Harold Wilson once asked, "George, is it true that you are responsible for drink, gambling and Sunday observance?" To which George had to reply in the affirmative and Wilson's reaction was, "Heaven help us! We face enough trouble without that."

Gambling and Sunday observance were matters of control and gave George no problems of conscience, but the drinking was another matter. The Home Office had responsibility for 206 public houses, off-licenses, hotels and bingo clubs, in Carlisle and the Border country. When George met the managers of these in the course of his duties, he referred to them as brewers. They reacted at once, saying, "No. You are the brewer." The sternly teetotal Methodist found that title difficult to wear and his first reaction was, "I'm afraid to tell Mam about it!"

The Welsh Office

The Labour Government was greatly hampered by its small majority and Harold Wilson watched carefully for the opportunity to call another election and gain a workable majority. This he did for 31st March 1966, after only eighteen months in power. The Conservative Party was weak after a series of resignations and poor leadership. Alec Douglas-Home had resigned and had handed a demoralized party over to Edward Heath. Wilson took every advantage of Conservative weakness, fought a sparkling campaign and ended his tour of the country in Cardiff. Jim Callaghan and George Thomas, as usual at general elections, combined to fight a successful campaign. As had become their custom, they lunched together on the eve of polling day and speculated about the result. They expected to win, not only in Cardiff, but with an increased majority throughout the country. The result was beyond their hopes or calculations. Labour won by 110 seats over the Tories. Wilson could now lead a government with a mandate from the people. At the pre-polling lunch, Jim Callaghan had told George that he was in for promotion if Labour won. Jim always seemed to know. He was right. George Thomas was appointed Minister of State at the Welsh Office. This meant that much of his work would now be based in Cardiff.

The Welsh Office had been set up shortly after Labour came to power in 1964 with James Griffiths as the first Secretary of State for Wales. He stayed only until 1965 and was succeeded by Cledwyn Hughes. There was a difference between George and Cledwyn Hughes from the beginning. George Thomas had already shown his disapproval of aspirations to Welsh Nationalism, which Cledwyn Hughes favoured—in fact, he was one of the six Welsh Labour MPs who had campaigned for a Parliament for Wales in the 1950s. George describes the differences between the two men in unmistakable terms:

> By setting up the office, the Labour Government had opened the floodgates for nationalism. Cledwyn Hughes was Secretary of State, and his nationalistic fervour led to periodical tensions between us. Despite a genuine pride in my Welsh heritage, and my eagerness to advance Welsh culture, I have never believed in Welsh nationalism.

After all, George Thomas was the grandson of a Hampshire man and the son of an English mother, albeit born in Tonypandy. On his father's side he was thoroughly Welsh. Although his strong Welsh accent and his love of Welsh culture might have suggested a passionate Welshman, he resented the anti-English emphasis among so many who pleaded for Wales. The Valley and his upbringing, as well as his family, engendered a love of Wales and its culture. His mother had wanted him to learn Welsh and had urged his father to teach the children as well as herself, but none the less she also nurtured a deep affection for her parents' counties of Somerset and Hampshire.

The Welsh Language Act

The creation of the Welsh Office in 1964 led to Parliament passing the Welsh Language Act in 1965. This Act gave equal validity in Wales to the Welsh and English languages. The Welsh Nationalist Party were quick to seize the initiative. As soon as the Measure was given royal approval the Nationalists encouraged their supporters to demand Welsh language forms for registering births, deaths and marriages. Unfortunately the Welsh Office had totally underestimated the extent to which such forms would be in demand. The Labour government tried to moderate these demands and was pushed on to a defensive position. Whatever action they took was denounced as inadequate by a now confident Welsh Nationalist Party.

Every government department in Wales was under pressure to produce bilingual forms. The same was true of all local government. Pressure was also put on the police forces and demand was understandably made for Welsh-speaking people appearing in courts of law to be able to give evidence in their own first language. This was an overdue reform, but in some courts the absence of Welsh-speaking lawyers created problems. Language difficulties caused frustration and in the media, radio and television, advantage was given to the Welsh-speaking minority over the English-speaking majority.

George Thomas's Welsh grandmother could not speak English, so as long as she lived, which was until George was ten, he had to speak to her in Welsh. Later, when he wanted to become a pupil-teacher in the Rhondda Valley, he had first to pass a viva voce examination by Rhondda's Director of Education. Thus he had a good grounding in Welsh speaking on which to build during his service in the Welsh Office. In rural Wales and in the Welsh-speaking areas in North, West and Mid-Wales he would conduct his conversations in Welsh where necessary. In the heavily populated industrial areas of South Wales his conversations were almost always in English. His attitude to Welsh issues was summed up in a statement he made in 1970.

> Wales is a proud nation with its own traditions and its own cultural values, but its central problems in the present day depend for a solution on the recognition that for economic purposes it must not be a separate entity from those across the border.

Welsh Culture in Glyncorrwg

When it came to defending the culture of a community, however, George Thomas was as nationalist as anyone. This was well illustrated in his dealings with a lonely village at the top of the valley leading down to Port Talbot. Glyncorrwg was entirely dependent upon coal. Its culture was built around the pit and there was no other industry there. Whether they spoke English or Welsh was irrelevant. The

National Coal Board had decided to close the pit. The Ministry of Fuel and Power decided about pit closures, but in Wales the Welsh Office had first of all to be consulted before the closures were effected. The community, fearing for the social consequences for the village if the pit was closed, asked the Secretary of State for Wales, Cledwyn Hughes, if he would meet representatives in Glyncorrwg to discuss the proposed closure.

George Thomas fully understood the helplessness of Cledwyn Hughes' position, but as a Valley-nurtured man himself he felt obliged to go to Glyncorrwg to meet the community leaders. He was well versed in the agony caused in mining villages by pit closures, and he could not stay away. Accompanied by John Morris he met the community in a local schoolroom. Church leaders, councillors, teachers, trade union leaders and especially the NUM, pleaded for further efforts to keep the mine working in Glyncorrwg. George relived the anxieties of the pit closures of his youth in Tonypandy. The meeting turned out to be not a confrontation but a sharing of sorrow. The National Coal Board, led by Lord Robens, was utterly resolved that the high rate of absenteeism amongst the miners made it uneconomic to continue working the mine. In an attempt to ease the troubled community, George spoke of the government's Industrial Grants Scheme to attract new industries into the Development Areas, but he was under no illusion about the difficulty of attracting industry to such an isolated mountain village. The assembled people in the school hall felt the sympathy of the son of Rhondda, and they knew that he was as genuinely grieved as they were. He left them with a promise to do all he could to attract alternative industry to their area.

Lord Robens had been a friendly colleague of George when he had served in the House of Commons, but George did not find any sympathy when he raised the subject of the Glyncorrwg pit closure. This surprised him, because as Chairman of the National Coal Board Robens had generated a great deal of goodwill from the National Union of Mineworkers. Alternative employment had already attracted many mineworkers to the Port Talbot area, where more congenial factory work was available. To George's dismay Alf Robens seemed unable to appreciate the scale of the disaster to a single-industry mountain village when its pit was closed. Lack of understanding was also to divide George from Alf Robens later at the tragic Aberfan disaster.

Down the Mine at Nantymoel

Shortly afterwards, in June 1966, he visited another mining village and spent two hours down the mine of the Wyndham-Western Colliery at Nanytmoel. George had never worked in the pit. His father had been a miner at the age of ten and his older brother, Emrys, at the age of thirteen; while Dad Tom was first a miner and then a winding engineer. Mining was in George's blood and he had living contact with it in his family until Emrys died in November 1962. Going to Glyncorrwg when he had nothing to offer was part of that pull to the life of the pits and of the men who worked there. At Nantymoel he told the press that it was the first time he had been underground since he was a boy, when he had accompanied a visiting preacher's public school son down Llwynypia colliery. After his two hours underground the reporters wanted to know what he had found there. His reply was typical of his human interest in the miners: "I had a good chat with some of the boys and I must say they still have a wonderful sense of humour in the pits. I wanted to meet the miners at their place of work and wanted to see a colliery which is going to play an important part in the mining industry in the next quarter of a century." The Wyndham-Western Colliery at Nantymoel was, in fact, one of the show places of Welsh coalmining.

The Twenty-first Anniversary Celebrations

In 1966, George celebrated twenty-one years as a Member of Parliament. There were many friends who wanted to make an occasion of this and George always enjoyed a party. The celebrations were held in the Cardiff Connaught Rooms and everybody who had been involved with George in his multifarious career was invited either to attend or to send a message. It was a wonderfully happy occasion and George had much to be thankful for.

Mam, who was now eighty-five years old, was very seriously ill, but she insisted upon leaving her sickbed to be at the celebration of her son's twenty-one years as an MP for Cardiff.

Michael Foot praised his socialism, but insisted that he had much more to do, as socialism had much greater tasks ahead. Jim Griffiths said, "Politics is part of his religion and his life." Roy Jenkins, "George has become a legend in the Home Office. He has managed to convince me of the evils of gambling clubs, but I must confess that I have not managed to convert him from his teetotalism. A dogged fighter—he has the strength to take difficult decisions and, having taken them, to stand and defend them". Cledwyn Hughes acknowledged that "Mr Thomas was the man responsible for making Cardiff the capital of the Principality".

There were messages from the Prime Minister and the Chancellor of the Exchequer. He was presented with a silver chandelier from the Cardiff West division of the Labour Party. What Harold Wilson said of him was most perceptive:

> George is one of the most popular men in the House of Commons. His cheerfulness and kindly consideration win him friends wherever he goes; *but*, of course, he has a special place in the Party, for George's Socialism is of a special kind in which Wales is so rich. If George is our welcome, cheerful companion, he is also our conscience.

Those who had worked most closely with him were most aware that, apart from his infectious friendliness, he had a very hard core when it came to matters of principle and when outworn principles led to human misery. Jim Callaghan had good means of knowing George's work in the constituency and he paid a warm and generous tribute to him:

> One thing that is particularly notable is the deep personal links George has forged between himself and the people of Cardiff West. Everyone knows him and what he stands for. They admire and like him. They do so because he likes people. The fact that he so personally cares about people is one of George's strongest characteristics.

Of course, they were all being kind on this festive occasion, but their tributes ring true and each has picked out facets of George's character, his contribution to socialism, to the House of Commons, to the people of Cardiff and to the future of Wales as part of the United Kingdom.

The Severn Bridge was opened shortly after this celebration, on 7th September 1966. George appeared on television the night before with his persistent message to Wales: "The Welsh people have nothing to fear and a lot to gain from this bridge—the same is true for our cousins across the water."

The Days before the Tragedy

After the celebration and the coming of the Severn Bridge, there was a flurry of activity. George was improving his Welsh with the help of his senior, Cledwyn Hughes. There was much to do and George busied himself with matters that raised no controversy. He visited the Cistercian community on Caldy Island, Tenby, and ceremoniously raising a Welsh flag and offering a Welsh prayer, sealed the friendship: "I am claiming on behalf of the Welsh people", he said, "the friendship of Caldy Island. There is an ocean of good will flowing towards it." Then, with a typical nostalgia for the former beauty and peace in the Rhondda Valley, he added, "Caldy Island is an island that has retained the quietness and calm that we have long since lost in the industrial areas."

A few weeks later, he visited the Welsh Second Industrial Exhibition in Sophia Gardens, Cardiff, with Ted Heath. These parties and bridge openings and social visits were only pleasant diversions. The chill winds of an imminent economic freeze were blowing. These would soon plunge the Labour Party into crisis. They were felt most cruelly in the distressing effects of the mine closures throughout the country and particularly in South Wales. For much of the month following the exhibition in Sophia Gardens he was concerned with these closures. He assured the National Union of Miners that the government and the Welsh Office sympathized with their point of view, but the economic freeze was biting into industry. One of the most hurtful measures was the credit squeeze. A Labour government was being forced to take actions which they would have roundly condemned in a Tory government. In the midst of explanations, George addressed the government as well as the people, when he said, "It would be dangerous to panic in the credit squeeze." Throughout that month of September 1966, he travelled all over Wales.

None of this activity and travel, nor even the forebodings of a difficult winter, prepared him for a Friday in October, when the world's attention was focused in anguish on a small mining village in the Merthyr Valley: Aberfan.

CHAPTER TWELVE

◆◆◆

Aberfan and Africa

THE WELSH OFFICE was situated in Cathays Park, Cardiff, with a small staff also in Whitehall.

George Thomas found his work in the Cardiff Office pleasant. Although he travelled to London for the parliamentary sessions, most of his work was in Wales and he could go from home to the office within minutes. As Mam was getting older and was often quite unwell, it was good to be near home. It was an ideal situation. His heart was in Wales and much as he loved the House of Commons, he represented a constituency in the capital of his country. It was a happy period despite all the problems of conflict with Welsh Nationalists.

George had been enjoying his new job for only a few months when into this happy situation burst the most appalling human tragedy. He remembers every agonizing detail and in his Memoirs devotes a chapter to his involvement in it, which he calls "A Lost Generation". The detailed memory is evident from the first paragraph:

> One Friday morning in October 1966, I set off for the Welsh Office in Cardiff as usual, commenting to Mam that autumn was really here. There was a bite in the air, mist clung to the ground and there was no warmth from the sun.

These few words conjure up a picture of a man, happy and fulfilled in his home and work. They have an extraordinary poignancy considering what was happening in the mining village of Aberfan, not far from Merthyr Tydfil, which could be reached within an hour from Cardiff. The first news of the tragedy came by telephone from the Town Clerk of Merthyr Tydfil, about 10 o'clock on 28th October: "We have suffered a major disaster at Aberfan where a coal tip has slid down the mountain and covered the school below. We may have lost over a hundred children and their teachers."

George was on the scene within the hour. The tragedy was too terrible to take in. Miners were digging to get the bodies from under the slurry and rubble; strong men weeping like babies, mothers almost deranged with grief and shock, clawed with their bare hands. Chains of human hands carried away bucket load after bucket load of the black slurry. Every child brought out after the first hour was dead. George and the Chief Constable went to Merthyr Town Hall to organize the first relief work, and later in the day, at tea time, Cledwyn Hughes arrived by helicopter and Harold Wilson also came.

Everything they could do was done at once, but nothing could relieve the immense pain and suffering of the entire community. George was unable to leave the scene that night. He telephoned to Mam, who had been following the news on television, that he would not be home. His task now was pastoral and, working closely with the Chief Constable lest he should hinder the operations, he went from house to house. No one went to bed that night in Aberfan. George was soon beset by journalists from all over the world. What could he say? "Aberfan has lost one generation of children beneath the rubble," was his comment, and there was no more to be said. It was stark, unrelieved tragedy. It seemed quite natural that he should visit homes, even through the night. He had no comfort to bring, but just wanted to be with them, sharing their sorrows.

At two in the morning, a message came through to say that Lord Snowdon was on his way and George was to look after him. Typically, after the Chief Constable had briefed Lord Snowdon on the situation, George took him on his house-to-house visiting. But first into Bethany Chapel which was being used as a mortuary, where the dead children were laid out and labelled. Some teachers' bodies were there too, and George found himself confronted with the body of a teacher he had known well. It recalled the days of pit disasters at home in Tonypandy. But, amid the horror, there was a great deal more care and dignity than had been shown the dead miner who had so shocked him as a boy.

Then he took Lord Snowdon to the site of the disaster where more bodies were being brought out and identified. "We were numb with horror," he recalls. George's own account of their visit to one of the homes of bereaved parents is impossible to summarize. Here it is transcribed from his Memoirs:

At the first house, there was a young miner and his wife who was clearly expecting another child. The mother caught hold of me and sobbed. Her little girl was still under the rubble. She wanted me to say that there was still hope for her child, when clearly there was none. I could only talk about the wonderful way in which the miners had set about trying to rescue the children.

The father looked at me with agony in his eyes, and feeling the necessity to say something, he blurted out, "Will you have a cup of tea?"—the traditional Welsh way of expressing welcome. His wife still clung to me, so I shook my head. Lord Snowdon interrupted: "Yes, I would like a cup of tea, and the Minister can do with one also." When the young miner moved towards the kitchen in their two-down two-up cottage, Snowdon pushed forward. "Let me do it. I'm used to making tea."

In his absence I spoke gently to the weeping mother, telling her she must be brave for the sake of the baby waiting to be born. The father hovered around us, not knowing what to do. Snowdon re-emerged carrying a tin tray with roses printed on it, and I commented, "Here is the Queen's brother-in-law waiting on us." For a fraction of a second the darkness lifted from the father's face.

Suddenly the mother pulled herself away, and looking Snowdon straight in the face asked, "How would you feel if your child was under the tip?" Poor Snowdon, I felt for him as he replied, "That thought has been in my mind ever since I heard of the disaster. That is why I am here. I could not stay away."

George tells of other visits that night. That one description is enough to show how right it was for him to take Lord Snowdon into the homes and it shows much of the man, indeed both men, in critical and tragic moments. Snowdon returned to London eventually, but he left a trail of stories and a great affection for him in Aberfan.

George was overwhelmed with emotion, exhausted from lack of sleep and in deep distress. On the Sunday, Alf Robens visited the area. George met him in a building at the pit head. He was holding a large Havana cigar as he looked up to what remained of the mountain tip which had slid silently down until it submerged the school beneath. George looked up with him, but the two men saw quite different sights. Pointing at a bubbling stream which looked white from the valley below, Robens said, "There is the cause of the trouble. We are not to blame for the building up of the water force under the tip." George had no adequate comment at that moment, but the subsequent enquiry into the cause of the disaster by Lord Justice Davies did not confirm Lord Robens' view.

George Thomas visited every house in Aberfan where a child had died. It took him three weeks, travelling every day from Cardiff and leaving others to care for the office. He had a real sense of priorities. His presence was needed in Aberfan. For years, that scene in Bethany Chapel haunted him. But he was not finished with Aberfan yet.

Immediate Relief, the Appeal and an Inquiry

When Harold Wilson first arrived on the scene he was profoundly shocked. He put Cledwyn Hughes in charge of the rescue work, adding that he could call on all government agencies and the armed forces if he felt their assistance was required. Cledwyn Hughes at once took all the possible organizational steps that he could to help the community through the crisis. The full extent of the need was not at once evident. As George remained there for three weeks, he was able to see the immediate need and briefed the Secretary of State on what he believed was the situation and the need for help.

There was an enormous wave of sympathy throughout the country, which gradually turned to a sense of anger and questioning. The government was urged by public opinion to give what aid it could. There were demands for a nationwide appeal, and for a public inquiry.

The miners had not only lost their families, but their jobs were also threatened by the deepening depression and a freeze on wages and credit. Yet worse than anything else in Aberfan was the threatening shadow of the remains of the tips that loomed above the village on the mountainside. Every time a shower of rain fell, the remaining children would be called indoors, or taken from their beds to huddle against the fire downstairs. In other mining villages where slag tips hung threateningly over the small, steep streets there was also fear. George played his part in battling for the removal of those tips. Experts from the Coal Board said the tips were safe and it was not right to spend millions of taxpayers' money on an unnecessary and expensive operation. The battle raged. George was obliged to leave it for a while, but two years later came back to it, as Secretary of State for Wales.

Meanwhile the Aberfan Appeal called forth a most generous response and the only problem with that was how best to use the money. The Trustees of the Fund were determined to use it only for relief in Aberfan. They were not prepared to let this vast sum of money be used to relieve the government or the National Coal Board of their responsibilities! One of the fiercest defenders of this policy was the MP for Aberfan, which was in the constituency of Merthyr Tydfil. This was the formidable S. O. Davies, by then eighty years old and first elected in 1934. He had been a miner and a miners' leader, for sixteen years, a member of Merthyr Tydfil County Borough Council and Mayor in 1945–6. He had been at one time vice-president of the South Wales Miners' Federation. So far, George had had no quarrels with him.

An inquiry was set up under Lord Justice Edmund-Davies, who on the BBC news on 8th November 1966, announced in convincing terms that the Aberfan inquiry would undertake the "stern and relentless task of finding out the truth, and the truth will be found".

The Minister for Commonwealth Relations

In June 1967, for reasons he never fully disclosed, Harold Wilson transferred George Thomas from the Welsh Office to the Commonwealth Office. He probably thought that George had been under too much emotional pressure in Aberfan and needed to be away from Cardiff which was too near to the tragedy. It was what George needed and he certainly enjoyed his new job. It meant extensive travel to the newly independent Commonwealth countries, whose volatile state George soon discovered, "as though Pandora's box had been opened". Certainly, once he found himself in contact with the diplomatic staff he was more comfortable than in the Welsh Office: "I quickly found a greater sense of comradeship in the diplomatic departments than I had experienced elsewhere in the Civil Service," he confessed. This was greatly helped by his immediate rapport with Donald MacLeod, his Principal Private Secretary. George liked his sense of humour and appreciated his loyalty. Above all he admired his considerable ability.

George was quickly at home in the Commonwealth Office and looking forward to his travel. The main purpose of this was to make friends with leaders of the Commonwealth, and George always liked making friends. He did rather well. He had, of course, greatly matured since his adventurous visit to Greece, twenty years before.

His chief, Herbert Bowden, was a few years older than he was but had entered Parliament at the same time. He was MP for South-West Leicester where he had been member of the City Council and also President of the Labour Party in 1938. He had served in the RAF during the war, and already in Attlee's first government had been appointed Assistant Whip in 1949. He was a Lord Commissioner of the Treasury in 1950 and by now an experienced man in the Commonwealth Office. George compares him to Frank Soskice, whom he also enjoyed working with in the Home Office. There was no doubt that George was in more congenial company now than in the Welsh Office, where he had often felt frustrated. Bert Bowden was not afraid to delegate, and at their first meeting he told George that he was free to take decisions as long as he kept him informed. Among the diplomats in the department, whom George calls his "mentors" were Sir Saville Garner, Permanent Under Secretary, and Sir Morrice James, the Deputy Secretary. Both had been High Commissioners. He mentions as another close friend during these months in the Commonwealth Office, Sir Eric Norris, who later became High Commissioner in Kenya and Malaysia respectively. So he had plenty of good advisers.

A Touchy Business in Ghana

His first overseas assignment was in Ghana, formerly the Gold Coast, which had attained independence in 1957 under Kwame Nkrumah. It was the first of the African colonies to do so. Thus Nkrumah was setting a pattern for Africa, but he had no model to follow. Ghana had great assets in trade as well as in education. The high standards of Achimoto College set it above the rest of Africa and the University of Accra was soon functioning, with opportunities for higher education. All was set well for success. Many looked at Nkrumah and at first were pleased to see how well he did. But things began to go wrong in 1960. Ghana became a Republic within the Commonwealth. Nkrumah tended towards more centralized rule and there was corruption among his ministers. The wealth of the country was squandered.

In 1966, Nkrumah was ousted by a military coup, led by General Ankrah. There were trials for corruption and a former Ghanaian

High Commissioner in London was charged with the misuse of public funds, dismissed from his office and recalled. He refused to return to Ghana, fearing for his safety. General Ankrah applied for an extradition order and Roy Jenkins, then Home Secretary, refused. Anger was generated on both sides. The General had been in power only one year. It was a military government and although he had carried the people in opposition to Nkrumah, he was by no means certain that he could retain their loyalty. Others would attempt to overthrow him, and London was a safe place from which the General's enemies could plot a coup. General Ankrah had set up a committee to work on a new constitution and had promised elections, which were eventually held in 1969. It was far from being a politically stable situation, as Roy Jenkins knew. But the refusal of the extradition order was tantamount to saying that justice could not be expected in Ghana under General Ankrah. The situation was delicate to say the least. Britain appeared to be treating Ghana as though it were still a colony.

George went to Accra with Eric Norris to pacify the General and to suggest that he could prosecute his former High Commissioner in the British courts. George was to promise that there would be a fair trial and justice would be done. They were coldly received by the angry General, who for half an hour let them know what he thought of the British Government and Roy Jenkins in particular. George was impressed by the General's remarkable vocabulary. He had clearly been well educated. For a moment they crossed swords—George defended Roy Jenkins, Ankrah attacked him. An unfortunate comment was not heard and then George pulled himself together. He was not there to irritate the General any further, but to get his agreement to a London trial. Unexpectedly he found the right words. In order to impress the General with his sincerity, he said, "I am a Methodist, and I give you my word that the case will get a proper hearing in Britain." That broke the ice. General Ankrah was also a Methodist and his fine education had come from Methodist missionaries. In less than two minutes he agreed to the proposal and George had scored his first triumph as a Commonwealth negotiator. But at a price! General Ankrah, despite his Methodism, insisted that they celebrate their agreement by drinking a glass of champagne. George broke his pledge for Britain's sake and the story got back home, where he was teased unmercifully, not least by Harold Wilson.

Civil War in Nigeria

Nigeria became independent in 1960 and in the following year incorporated the territory of North British Cameroon. In 1963, it chose to become a Republic within the Commonwealth. A military coup in 1966 brought civilian government to an end. In 1967, Biafra seceded and civil war broke out, lasting until 1970. George Thomas was in Nigeria when the war began. The occasion of his visit was the secession, and fear of the prospect of civil war.

Colonel Ojukwu declared Biafra an independent state in May 1967. After his return from Ghana, George Thomas was sent back to Africa at once to see if he could obtain some agreement between Colonel Ojukwu and General Gowon, who was head of the military government of Nigeria. It was a last-minute impossible mission, but George went briefed for reconciliation. He was taken at once to the residency where the British High Commissioner, Sir David Hunt, a leading classical scholar and a cultured host, received him warmly and all but overwhelmed his guest with classical music! At tea, when they were about to discuss their conference with General Gowon next morning, the telephone rang and David Hunt answered it himself. He listened a moment and then called out to George, "The balloon's gone up!" Colonel Ojukwu had struck the first blow of the war.

They decided to go ahead with the conference anyway. Next morning they went to General Gowon's headquarters where his cabinet was already assembled. Gowon surprised them by saying, "Before we begin, let us have a reading from the Bible." It was becoming clear to George that in dealing with African leaders he had to do with men who had been schooled by missionaries. He responded warmly to Jack Gowon, "a slim, good-looking young man, whose single purpose was to end the civil war with maximum speed". Gowon asked for planes and bombs and a considerable increase in small arms and ammunition, together with a continuation of what Britain normally supplied, with some increase because of present dangers.

George was in difficulty. He had not been briefed on this situation. When he had left London, civil war had been feared but had not yet begun. He was there to reconcile, not to arm. He had to act upon his own initiative, which Herbert Bowden had always encouraged him to do. He therefore replied that although Britain would continue the supply of weapons normally directed to Nigeria, it could not agree to provide planes and bombs "to be used against Commonwealth citizens in a Commonwealth country". Gowon became angry, but his anger was controlled, as he responded: "We will get all the planes and bombs we need, but you are driving us into the hands of the Communists. We do not want to buy from them, but if you refuse to supply me, then we shall have no option but to turn to them."

When George Thomas returned to London, the cabinet confirmed his declaration to Gowon. Looking back, he realized that he could have done no other, because he did not have plenipotentiary powers on arms supply, but he considered that the government's stand was wrong. He thought personally that Gowon should have been supplied by Britain with what was needed so that the civil war might have ended sooner. As it was, the French ammunition industry supplied arms to both sides and kept the war going to their profit.

It is not difficult to understand George's dilemma as a pacifist in all these negotiations. He thought of resigning, but the propaganda for Ojukwu's cause was growing in Britain and he did not want to be seen to support that. He also saw that if he resigned he would be saying that when it came to the real issues, pacifists could only opt out. He had to show that as a pacifist he could bear responsibility. He remained to mitigate the consequences if possible. But, as he says, "the main consideration was my staunch support for Harold Wilson." Years later he could still question his motives: "Whether it was love of ministerial office or high principles that kept me in the government, I will never be sure."

Confrontation in Uganda

Herbert Bowden was away on holiday during August 1967 and had left George in charge of the Commonwealth Office. A crisis blew up in Uganda which led to direct confrontation between George Thomas and the President of Uganda, Dr Milton Obote. Uganda had been a British Protectorate since the First World War and achieved Independence in 1962. In 1963, the country became a Republic under the Kabaka of Buganda, with Milton Obote heading the government. Obote staged a coup in 1966 and introduced a new constitution in 1967. He was later deposed by Idi Amin, but returned ten years later, after Amin's notorious "terror". He was again elected President in 1977.

Even in 1967 he was a formidable opponent and a skilful politician. When George first met him, Dr Apollo Milton Obote had been President for just a year. The British High Commissioner, Roland Hunt, had repeatedly protested to him about Ugandan soldiers' ill-treatment of white civilians. Obote did nothing but express his annoyance at these diplomatic interferences. When a white woman was beaten by soldiers, Roland Hunt made his anger public and Obote was furious. A row developed between the High Commissioner and the Ugandan government.

George Thomas, taking the advice of Morrice James in the Commonwealth Office, recalled Roland Hunt for consultation. He understood that this would demonstrate the extent of Britain's anger towards Obote. It was a wrong decision. Obote interpreted the action as weakness and refused to allow Hunt to return to take up his duties. A petty dispute therefore blew up into a major inter-governmental row. George had to go to Kampala to meet Obote. Some face-saving was needed. Neither Britain nor Uganda would climb down. Harold Wilson instructed George to try to get Hunt returned for one month, on the promise that he would then be transferred to another post. He thought this assurance would appeal to Obote.

With these clear instructions, George called on President Obote, only to find himself face to face with the whole cabinet. George was as diplomatic as possible. He gave personal greetings and good wishes from Harold Wilson, expressed regret at the dispute, defended the High Commissioner's conduct and stated Wilson's proposal, inflating the one month to two so that there was room for negotiation. For two hours they argued, and Obote eventually said that he would have to discuss it with his cabinet.

The second meeting was in the garden of the President's residence, with fewer cabinet ministers present. Obote did not budge. Then George played his last card:

> Very well, Mr President, I will no longer try to reach agreement with you. I had hoped we could compromise on the formula I advanced to you, by which, although our High Commissioner has done no wrong, he would shortly be transferred. But you have refused to compromise. I will send the High Commissioner back to Kampala on Wednesday next. You have previously accepted his credentials so he is fully entitled to enter. If you block the admission of an accredited diplomat, you will cause a

storm of protest in the House of Commons, and the dispute will be reported all across the world.

George had noticed that until then, Obote had been making patterns in the dust with his stick. Now he stopped and spoke sharply, saying that he could do no such thing and most certainly would not do it.

"Wait four days," George said emphatically, "and Roland Hunt will knock on your door." Obote looked to see if George was serious and concluded that he was. They adjourned again so that Obote could consult his full cabinet.

That night, a fantastic state banquet was put on in George's honour in the floodlit grounds of Obote's residence, with African dancing and drums. During the evening, a huge and highly decorated soldier approached and Obote whispered, "I want you to meet my chief of the army. He is after my job, but I keep one step ahead of him. He is thick." And so George was introduced to Idi Amin! His handshake nearly crushed his bones and he noted, "It seemed unlikely that this smiling giant would have political ambitions."

Next morning, George met Milton Obote privately and they agreed to a compromise. Hunt was to return for six weeks and then he would be transferred. The confrontation was over and the whole atmosphere was quite different. Obote spoke of being "anxious to help"; George of "the interest of good will between our two governments". It was a triumph for George Thomas. Obote had realized that if this issue was blown up into a major issue, a severe rupture in diplomatic relations with Britain would follow, and he was aware that economic help from the UK was still important for Uganda.

Jomo Kenyatta

Sir Eric Norris went with George to Kenya at a time when President Kenyatta was annoyed with Britain over some financial matters which could easily have been settled, but the President was getting old and irritable. It was thought best to humour him and send a pleasant diplomat to negotiate with him. George was an obvious choice. It was not a very difficult assignment. George had been to Kenya before, in 1959, but now he noted a great difference. In 1963 it had achieved Independence under Jomo Kenyatta, who was revered as the father of his people. The High Commissioner warned George that he would probably be quite rough in his dealings. What the Foreign Office did not know was that George had a typical Tonypandy card to play. When he had been living in Britain, Kenyatta had stayed in Cardiff, in the area then known as Tiger Bay, near the docks. Only the Labour Party would have anything to do with this black rebel. Kenyatta was known to have led a sustained and vicious revolt against Britain as the colonial power.

In his Memoirs, George recalls with pleasure the card he had to play:

> When I was introduced to the old President, I said, "I bring you greetings from Cardiff, Wales, where you are remembered with much affection." Kenyatta's face creased into a huge smile. "Cardiff, Wales," he repeated softly, as though he were talking to himself. "Those choirs . . . and the cups of tea . . . and the Welsh cakes!" Turning with extreme cordiality, he asked me for news of the city and after a happy exchange of stories we soon settled the official business that had brought us together. Kenyatta insisted on coming out of the palace to have a photograph of us taken together.

South Africa

From Kenya George flew to Malawi where he stayed for a while with Hastings Banda, the Life President, whom he had known for a long time. Then, on his way to South Africa, he went to Botswana and there had a lesson which he never forgot from a brilliant young black woman minister. This sophisticated, highly educated and cultured young woman told her story lightly, laughing at the silliness of whites in South Africa, but it made George angry as is clear from the way he described her story:

> She talked about some of the ways that apartheid was practised and, laughing at her own experience, said that black people in South Africa were never allowed to try on shoes before they had bought them, so they often walked with a limp.
>
> She told me of one occasion when she had seen a bright red hat in a shop window, and had said to herself, "That's for me!" She went in knowing that she would not be permitted to try it on, but once she had paid for it, took it to a mirror to see how it looked. The shop assistant became agitated and said, "You know you're not allowed to try it on in here." "But it's mine," she answered, "I've paid for it." The girl was not satisfied:

"You'll get me the sack." She gave way and tried on the hat standing on the pavement.

It was in a slightly hostile mood that George Thomas and Donald MacLeod went on to South Africa, and their mood was not improved by their cool reception which amounted to impertinence. Sir John Nicholson, the British Ambassador, sent a Third Secretary to the airport. When the minister arrived at his residence the ambassador was sitting in the garden having pre-lunch drinks with his Number Two. He remained seated when the minister approached him, and George's Welsh temperament responded accordingly. "I thought", he wrote later, "of the people of Tonypandy who could have given the Ambassador a lesson in good manners." He was further irritated by Sir John repeating several times, "You know, Minister, apartheid is not as bad in practice as it is in theory." The visit to South Africa was not a success. When he returned to London, George told the Foreign Secretary, George Brown, that he did not think Nicholson was a proper person to reflect the views of the British Government. Nicholson continued his tour of duty and entered into honourable retirement two years later.

The Most Exciting Ministerial Office

After Africa there were visits to Asia—Pakistan, India and Ceylon. George enjoyed the Commonwealth Office, describing his role as "the most exciting ministerial office that I held". It gave him a taste for world travel which he would enjoy later to the full when he became Speaker of the House of Commons. He also met statesmen from all over the world and learnt to admire varying gifts. One whom he greatly admired was Lee Kuan Yew of Singapore, whom he called "one of the ablest Commonwealth Prime Ministers". However, he did not enjoy the endless rounds of cocktail parties and had to learn how dangerous it was to speak your mind on such occasions. What you thought you had said in confidence to a pleasant guest could be headline news tomorrow. But he enjoyed most of the work, contacts and travel. He enjoyed it as one enjoys a holiday! He knew where his real job lay and he had a longing to get back to the Welsh Office, which would mean a seat in the cabinet.

One Friday afternoon in September 1967 he had a message from the Prime Minister. He wanted to see George on Sunday at 5.45 p.m.

at Number Ten. He was to use the back entrance so that the press watchers would not know. George was very close to Donald MacLeod, who had been through many difficult moments with him, including the conversations in the garden of Sir John Nicholson in South Africa, so he discussed the possibilities with him. MacLeod told him that it might mean a move back to the Welsh Office. Harold Wilson had intended a reshuffle and was going to move Cledwyn Hughes and put George into the Welsh Office as his successor as Secretary of State for Wales. But for some reason, he changed his mind. George had to wait nine months until the next reshuffle, and then in April 1968 he was appointed Secretary of State for Wales. He and Mam were both delighted.

CHAPTER THIRTEEN

—◇◆◇—

The Secretary of State for Wales

T HE OFFICE of Secretary of State for Wales, created in October 1964, had given Wales for the first time direct cabinet representation and had also established a separate Department of State concerned with Welsh Affairs. Prior to this establishment a certain amount of devolution had already occurred. Home Office ministers, and later the Minister of Housing and Local Government, had represented the Welsh point of view at cabinet level. At the same time, a number of government departments had located offices in Wales. This limited devolution was frustrating to George Thomas as is most clearly shown in the debate on his motion on Leasehold Reform in the House of Commons in July 1961.

Leasehold Reform and Wales

The Opposition had requested and received time for two debates on 12th July. The first was on a motion by George Thomas:

> That this House, noting with grave concern the hardship caused in Wales by the operation of the current leasehold system, calls upon Her Majesty's Government to introduce forthwith legislation enabling leaseholders who are owner-occupiers to purchase the freehold of their homes at a fair and reasonable cost.

This was an attack on the unsatisfactory Landlords and Tenants Act of 1954. George Thomas argued eloquently for his motion, insisting that the landlords had exploited this Act. It was his old argument put persuasively, well documented and with severe attacks—and barbed humour at times. He spoke for just half an hour and ended with a Welsh appeal:

> The Welsh National Anthem begins with the words: "*Mae hen wlad fy nhadau ym annwyl i mi.*" "The land of my fathers is dear to me." We ask the Government to accept the Motion so that

the land of Wales can belong to the Welsh people and not to finance corporations as at present.

He was answered immediately by the Attorney General, Sir Reginald Manningham-Buller, with a tribute to his eloquence, but little respect for his arguments:

> The Hon. Member for Cardiff West has moved the Motion . . . with the eloquence and charm that we have come to expect from him. His eloquence and charm will not, I hope, lead the House to accept without question all the allegations and charges he has thought right to proffer.

The Attorney General reminded the House that George Thomas was a long-time opponent of the leasehold system and had repeatedly spoken in the House against it. The speakers who followed him were mainly Welsh MPs and they supported the motion. But in the end, the weight of the government's majority told. Henry Brooke, the Minister of Housing and Local Government in the Home Office, and Minister for Welsh Affairs, summed up and asked the House to reject the motion:

> So far as we can ascertain there is no specific evidence of hardship that would justify a fresh committee. The Government are very willing, as my right honourable and learned friend said, to examine any information on these matters which is put into our hands, but in our view, the Motion is not sufficiently supported by hard facts. I have explained that were it to become Government policy the proposal in the Motion would cause injustice between man and man and would give compulsory powers to private individuals, which is something which the House should be very reluctant to do. On all these grounds, I invite the House to reject the Motion.

The House did as it was told and rejected the motion by 245 to 179. This was a Welsh affair and the Welsh members had been outvoted. A careful examination of the way members voted shows that Welsh members were overwhelmingly in favour of the motion.

The debate that followed was less controversial, because it was not a motion, but a resolution to take note of the Report on Developments and Government Action in Wales and Monmouthshire for 1960. James Griffiths, who introduced the discussion on this report, for which largely Welsh MPs only stayed, was able to give George a new glimpse of hope when he said in his opening speech:

I suggest that in the Annual Report on Developments and
Government Action in Wales and Monmouthshire for 1961
there should be included one short paragraph referring to leasehold reform. That would bring the matter within the purview of
the Welsh Grand Committee and we should ask for two extra
days to discuss it in the Welsh Grand Committee.

Greater Attention to Welsh Affairs

The last opportunity to discuss Welsh Affairs at length in the House
before the 1964 election was on 25th June 1964. Sir Keith Joseph
was then Minister of Housing and Local Government and Minister for Welsh Affairs. When he had introduced the debate on the
Report on Developments and Government Action in Wales
and Monmouthshire for 1963, James Griffiths had replied by
pointing out the change that had taken place in attention to Welsh
Affairs:

> There was a time when we were able to discuss Welsh affairs
> only one day each year. But now we have more opportunities—
> and we hope to have even more in the future—of discussing in
> detail in the Welsh Grand Committee Government action and
> developments in Wales.

He pleaded for more recognition for Wales:

> For generations the ordinary people of Wales have struggled
> bravely to retain their identity and to preserve their language,
> the culture which is dependent upon it and the institutions
> associated with it. They have struggled for many generations
> against the full force of the Establishment. They fought against
> it, and in modern times they have fought against all the influences
> of the modern media of mass communications. For that reason,
> as the Minister knows, there is a demand in Wales for fuller
> recognition and an enhanced status within the Government of
> the United Kingdom.

He drew attention to Labour's proposals in the manifesto *Signposts
for the Sixties*, and reminded Sir Keith that for thirty years the Labour
Party had enjoyed the confidence of the majority of the Welsh people.
They had returned a majority of Labour members at every general
election in that period. The Opposition was in confident mood and

George Thomas in his long speech that day had the scent of victory in his nostrils:

> I was disappointed this afternoon by the Minister's speech. I did not think that he was quite himself . . . We know that he is a very able young man, but he is usually so ebullient and confident. He never gives me the impression of a man who is not sure of himself. Today, however, the very subjects that he left out of his speech told me how uneasy he was. I want to bring his mind back to things which are in our policy and in his. We heard nothing this afternoon of the property-owning democracy—or is that for England only?

And so he continued regretting the absence of ministers on the front bench and pointing with confidence to what Labour would do as though the result of the election was already a foregone conclusion. Then came his deep concern for the underprivileged in Wales:

> There are people who have to pay more than half their wages in rent. Surely that is far too high a proportion. Is this the Wales about which the Minister wishes to stand at the box and boast? We need a new Wales, but we will not have it until we have new men and new ideas.

By now it was clear that his next door constituency neighbour, Jim Callaghan, had set wider horizons for himself. Apart from the odd constituency question or two, Callaghan was content to leave Welsh issues to his neighbour.

In North Wales, both Goronwy Roberts (Caernarvon) and Cledwyn Hughes (Anglesey) had been strong supporters of a Parliament for Wales, and clearly took a keen interest in all things Welsh. If a Welsh Office became a reality, both the North Walians and George Thomas would expect to be considered for the office.

A Tribute to the Chairman of the Welsh Grand Committee

As Chairman of the Welsh Grand Committee, George Thomas had developed a good personal relationship with Sir Keith Joseph, despite their differences politically. On 15th July 1964, for example, George did not fail to note the birth of Sir Keith's daughter. He opened the proceedings of the Welsh Grand Committee with an introduction: "Before we begin our deliberations, may I say that right hon. and hon. Members know that this is a friendly committee. I know that everyone would like to offer felicitations to the Minister on the birth of his daughter. We wish them well." Although on the floor of the House of Commons George Thomas could argue as insistently as any against the minister, with humour, cutting at times, there grew up between them a sense of being one in their responsibility to the House. They were both "House of Commons men", a phrase used to indicate MPs who responded to the tone and atmosphere of the Commons. In an unusual act of warmth and generosity, Sir Keith Joseph paid a tribute to George at the end of the last meeting of the Welsh Grand Committee. In his tribute he indicated the qualities already emerging that would make George Thomas eventually one of the great Speakers of the House of Commons:

> Mr Thomas, I am sure that the whole Committee would, on the occasion of the last meeting during this Parliament, wish to pay a tribute to you personally. For four and a half years, ever since the Welsh Grand Committee was set up, you have presided as its Chairman. You have been, I understand, at every meeting except one sitting when you were ill. You have managed to bridle your ebullient desire to join in every controversy and have given us all an example of restraint and decorum which we have sought to copy. You have, above all, secured that despite the sharp words—and there have been sharp words—in this Committee there has been an underlying sense of good humour. I am sure that all hon. Members will join with me in paying a tribute to your chairmanship.

The 1964 Election

Sir Alec Douglas-Home had gone to the very last week allowed by the Parliament Act before he was compelled to call a general election. The *Message* sent by George Thomas to the voters of Cardiff West, asking for their vote for Labour, made very clear the two ambitions he had for Wales, which he supported with all the passion he possessed:

> Leasehold Reform will free the owner-occupiers from cruel exploitation by ground landlords.
> A Secretary of State for Wales will be established.

His support for these two principles had been consistent throughout his career in politics. The *Message* was balanced, making the assumption that Labour would be voted in this time after a long period of Tory rule; but these issues stood out crystal clear.

The fact that Labour won the election with only a small majority robbed George of both his ambitions. He could not be Chairman of Ways and Means, which could lead to the Speaker's Chair. The Government would offer the post to the Opposition, thus saving two urgently required votes. He also saw little chance for his Leasehold Reform Bill. Because of the small majority, Harold Wilson could not take the bill through the House until February 1967, after another general election in which he won a larger majority. It was not then proposed by George Thomas, but by his friend and colleague, Tony Greenwood. It was successful and on the Statute Book by autumn 1967.

Harold Wilson was able, however, to carry through legislation for a Secretary of State for Wales in 1964. George had no immediate part in it. The obvious choice for Secretary of State was James Griffiths. George Thomas might have hoped to be the Minister of State in the Welsh Office, when Goronwy Roberts became Minister of State for Wales and Cledwyn Hughes became Minister of State for Commonwealth Affairs. But for that too, he had to wait. The waiting was good for him. He needed experience and got it as Joint Parliamentary Under Secretary in the Home Office.

James Griffiths

Jim Griffiths was a miner, born in 1890, who studied at the National Labour College in London. At thirty-five, he became a miners' agent under the South Wales Miners' Federation, of which he later became the President. He entered Parliament in 1931 as member for Llanelly and continued to hold that seat at every subsequent election. In 1945, he became Minister of National Insurance and steered through the legislation necessary to implement the recommendations of the Beveridge Report and thus to establish the Welfare State. He and Nye Bevan were its two champions. Jim Griffiths was Chairman of the National Executive of the Labour Party in 1948–49. In 1950, he was appointed Secretary of State for the Colonies and as such engaged in discussions for the proposed federation of the Rhodesias and Nyasaland, which became the Central African Federation. These discussions had hardly started when Labour lost the 1951 election and he was out of office until 1964, when Labour regained power. He was an obvious choice for the first Secretary of State for Wales, but he was seventy-four and the office was given to him as a salute to his service to Labour and Wales. The first Secretary of State therefore stayed in office only for one year. When he took control the Welsh Office was not even furnished.

James Griffiths dined out on his accounts of his first day in the Welsh Office. There were no tools to get on with the job. He had to order pens and pencils, and then decide on the design and style of the Welsh Office notepaper! Official responsibilities allocated to the Welsh Office included environment, housing, local government, new towns, town and country planning, water, forestry, roads and national parks. What was to prove an embarrassment was that it was also given "oversight responsibilities" for all other government activities in Wales. This meant that in theory the Departments of Education, of Agriculture, of Fuel and Power and of Health, could not reach decisions affecting Wales without knowing the views of the Welsh Office or its Ministers. This knowledge, however, in no way obliged the Whitehall departments to defer to Welsh wishes. Thus the Welsh Office was given responsibility without power. Because of the collective responsibility of all ministers in every government, Welsh Office ministers found themselves having to defend decisions concerning government policy in Wales, even though they had often fought against those decisions having been reached.

The advantage for Wales, however, lay in the fact that the Secretary of State was a full member of the cabinet. At last, for the first time since Edward I had conquered Wales, her nationhood was recognized in the top councils of the United Kingdom. Within months of taking office, James Griffiths announced the production of the Welsh Language Bill, which would give equal status to the Welsh and English languages in Wales. This legislation would never have been forthcoming if the Welsh Office had not been set up by Harold Wilson. It is ironic that Wales is therefore in greater debt to the Yorkshireman, Prime Minister Wilson, for the protection of its language, than it ever was to the Welsh-speaking Prime Minister David Lloyd George.

David Lloyd George had ensured the disestablishment of the Church of England in Wales, but he never foresaw the advantage to Wales of having her own Secretary of State fighting for her interests at the cabinet table in 10 Downing Street.

Cledwyn Hughes

George Thomas was more than seven years older than Cledwyn Hughes, and their backgrounds were very different. Cledwyn Hughes was a solicitor, formerly town clerk of Holyhead, a member of the Anglesey County Council and Governor of the University of Wales. He had served in the RAF and contested Anglesey in 1945, but was defeated by the sitting Liberal Member since 1929, Lady Megan Lloyd George. Again in 1950 he failed, but in 1951 he defeated Lady Megan by a very narrow majority. He thus knew Parliament only in opposition until the 1964 election.

Conflicts and Changes

Despite his later observations, George Thomas was as keen as every other Welsh MP to see the Welsh Language Bill enacted. In their Welsh fervour, none of Wales's representatives in the House of Commons realized what a floodgate of nationalism they were opening.

George Thomas and Cledwyn Hughes had always held differing views about devolution. Cledwyn Hughes wanted the maximum possible and George wanted the minimum. During the period 1970–74 when George was Shadow Secretary of State for Wales, he felt obliged to compromise on a formula which would prevent the pro-devolutionists and the anti-devolutionists in the Labour Party from splitting apart.

Long before then, Cledwyn Hughes was moved from the Welsh Office and George Thomas was appointed Secretary of State for Wales in the cabinet reshuffle of April 1968. Harold Wilson then told George what he wanted to hear: "You are to be Secretary of State for Wales. You will be made a Privy Counsellor on Monday, and you will be a member of the Inner Cabinet." George recalls that he left the room walking on air. "I thanked God for the opportunity and for sparing my mother to share my happiness."

Ambition Achieved

George Thomas MP had really made it. When, more than twenty-two years earlier, the raw MP had made his maiden speech and called for a Secretary of State for Wales to put Wales on a par with Scotland, he had not dreamed that he might one day fill such an office himself.

Yet much of his parliamentary career had prepared him for it. His passion for Wales as part of the United Kingdom was important at this stage of its history. Wales was not viable as a separate entity, and yet with a Labour Government it had influence beyond its size. If Welsh matters were to be addressed, it was important to have a Labour government in which Welsh MPs would always hold a large number of seats. A Conservative government always put Wales—and Scotland also—in the Opposition. The solution, as George Thomas saw it, was not to form separate governments for Wales and Scotland, thus leaving England permanently in the hands of the Conservatives. The Welsh Nationalists saw the issue quite differently. It was therefore of immense importance both to England and Wales to have someone like George Thomas in charge of the Welsh Office. He was obviously popular with the staff, as he makes clear by his description of his first day back as Secretary of State: "When I arrived at the Welsh Office in Whitehall . . . the entire staff were assembled in the hall and greeted me with loud hand-clapping. A man would be a stone not to be moved by such a welcome home."

The Investiture

One of his first important tasks was to prepare for the Investiture of the Prince of Wales. This was already fixed for 1st July 1969. It was no simple matter of tradition and protocol. The Welsh Nationalists had already made it a controversial issue. A minority of them had resorted to violence and George, never very friendly towards them, warned that they were partly responsible for acts which the more serious-minded among them would regret. Evidence of this was there before George Thomas took over. Cledwyn Hughes had already formed the Investiture Committee, and while he was still Secretary of State he had held several meetings to plan the details. One meeting was due to be held at the Temple of Peace in Cathays Park, Cardiff, with Lord Snowdon, who was Constable of Caernarvon Castle where the ceremony was due to take place. Early that morning the Temple of Peace and Health was blown up by extremists. Later, when George was Secretary of State for Wales, the Welsh Office was blown up. George was quick to react. He used the occasion to attack the Welsh Nationalists, admitting that the violent action was only the work of a fanatical small group, but warning the more sober Nationalists that many of the things they said led less responsible people to action they would themselves disapprove of: "You have created a monster you cannot control."

Cledwyn Hughes' committee had had its tensions and on one occasion a Welsh minister of religion had insisted upon speaking Welsh. Cledwyn Hughes, a fine Welsh speaker, had no difficulty in translating so as not to isolate the members of the committee who did not speak Welsh. When George Thomas inherited that committee he had another solution to the problem, which illustrates the use he made of humour in the most difficult circumstances. He was a master of reducing tension. He ruled that "if anyone wished to speak Welsh, he would be quite free to do so, but there would be no translations!" Critics suggested that this was because George could not do what Cledwyn Hughes had so ably done, because his Welsh was not good enough. That may have been true, but the matter of principle held. All the committee could understand English, and only some could understand Welsh. It was simple courtesy, a virtue which Welsh people have always admired and most of them practised, to use an inclusive language. No one now chose to speak Welsh, because he would never get his point across.

The Duke of Norfolk and his "Daughter"

Cledwyn Hughes had chaired the Investiture Committee himself but George did not do this when he succeeded him. He recognized that the Duke of Norfolk as Earl Marshal was the natural Chairman of the Committee as he was responsible for all state ceremonial involving the monarchy; George himself, as Secretary of State for Wales, was Vice-chairman. There had not been an Investiture of a Prince of Wales since 1911 and the Duke of Norfolk had his father's complete record of the proceedings. George Thomas liked Bernard, Duke of Norfolk, and enjoyed working with him although it was not always easy.

In his Memoirs, George tells of the one serious clash, which was over the cost of the ceremony. The government had set a limit of £200,000 and the Duke insisted upon a further £50,000 being given. George records that, "to his angry declaration that the dignity of the occasion required more than could possibly be provided within the estimate of £200,000, I could only reply that I had every confidence in his ability to ensure success." The Duke was furious and demanded to see the Prime Minister. He did and was surprised to find George there too. "I asked to see you alone, Prime Minister," was the Duke's opening remark. Harold Wilson, who was always loyal to his ministers, explained that he had invited the Secretary of State for Wales, because he was the minister responsible for the Investiture. Diplomatic, but firm, Harold Wilson backed his minister and would not yield on the extra £50,000. There was a period of coldness and restrained anger, but it was resolved when eventually George welcomed the Duke of Norfolk to the Welsh Office with his usual, "Hello, Earl Marshal, how are you?", and the Duke replied, "I am going to call you George, and you will call me Bernard."

A more amusing misunderstanding was during rehearsals, and this time the joke was on George. This was one of three Investiture rehearsals, in the grounds of Buckingham Palace. The place of the Queen was taken by a young lady, whom George described as "a most regal-looking person". When he asked who she was he was told, "the Duke's daughter." When the rehearsal was over, George in his usual friendly manner told her how much he enjoyed working with her father. She was much amused and replied, "Yes, I know, Secretary of State; but he is not my father, he is my husband!" The joke went the rounds, improved by imitations of George's Welsh accent. At the next rehearsal, the Duke came up to him and asked, "Have you seen my daughter?" and roared with laughter. George was not allowed to live that one down—and he enjoyed it as much as anyone. His ability to see the place of humour as releasing tensions would later make him a very popular Speaker.

Threats and Disturbances

The bomb in the Temple of Peace in Cardiff, when Cledwyn Hughes was Secretary of State, was not the only angry threat from the Nationalists. George Thomas had many threats to his life throughout his period as Secretary of State for Wales, some general and some defining specific occasions when he would be allowed to walk to the place of ceremony but would be carried out! He had to take special precautions. The Welsh press was also hostile. But what worried him most were the threats to Mam. These struck him as the lowest of all and made him very angry. Mam, who had her eighty-eighth birthday in January 1969, was frequently awakened in the small hours of the morning by anonymous callers threatening his life. It was not only the secular press that attacked him, but also the Welsh religious press. He was even attacked from the pulpit. Students plastered his house, walls and windows with Welsh language literature. His response to the religious attacks was, "I came to the conclusion that there were some people in Nonconformist Wales who had replaced the worship of God Almighty with the worship of the language."

The Prince at Aberystwyth

Apart from its effect on Mam, George could weather the storm of hostility from those who he was convinced were a small minority of true Welshmen. But he was very worried when he learned that Prince Charles was to spend a term at the University College of Aberystwyth before the Investiture. The Principal of the college wrote a personal letter to George expressing grave fears about the atmosphere in Aberystwyth, and adding that he could not accept responsibility for the safety of the Prince. This was alarming. If the Prince could not come safely to Wales without an armed guard, the Investiture itself was jeopardized. George's deep concern is shown in his hindsight comment: "I felt it would be a terrible thing if there was any part of the United Kingdom which had to be declared closed to a member of the Royal Family." Harold Wilson, when consulted, said that the Queen must be informed. George was convinced that the Prince should go to Aberystwyth. He consulted with the Chief Constable of Dafydd and with the Principal of University College Aberystwyth. The Chief Constable was confident that he could deal with the security and that the Prince would be safe. But the advice to the Queen was the responsibility of the Secretary of State and George did not fail in his duty.

The Prince went, and turned the threatening situation into a triumph by his own personality and the speech he made at the Urdd Eisteddfod in very acceptable Welsh. "He had undermined his fiercest opposition by tackling them with their own weapons," George comments.

The Welsh Office

Though the Investiture was the most public of George's activities as Secretary of State, it did not consume the greater part of his time. The Welsh Office was still only a little over three years old when he was appointed. Neither of his predecessors had been there long and it fell to George to give the office its shape and discover its real potential. In his time the Secretary of State acquired direct responsibility for health and agricultural matters in Wales, which must have pleased him. But he was dissatisfied with the piecemeal nature of the office and worked with his staff to define the precise limits of his authority. The Welsh Office was organized into a number of divisions, each with a budget. The final document prepared by the Training Division spells out clearly the responsibilities of the Secretary of State through his staff.

> HOUSING
> This Division is concerned with the volume and quality of new house buildings; with the improvement (both structurally and environmentally) of older houses—about half the houses in Wales were built before the First World War; and with the eradication of unfit housing—there are nearly 100,000 houses being lived in today [May 1969] which are unfit for human habitation.

When we remember George's battle for Riverside, it is not difficult to imagine the enthusiasm with which he took up this part of his responsibilities. The range of work, undertaken in co-operation with the local authorities, was wide—the encouragement of better design, maintaining standards, improving layout, landscaping, costing and general improvement of the environment. He threw himself into this work, discussing loan sanctions, subsidies, rents and the acquisition of land. This division was responsible for much of the immediate background to an acceptable quality of life.

Housing was of prime importance and so was the related Town and Country Planning. In the context of "land use" he was soon busy on transport and improved the congested roads of Cardiff. As he drives today across the centre of Cardiff in a clear run, he talks with pride of the elevated road he was responsible for. Good houses and good roads, as far as the budget would allow, were supplemented by special attention to the preservation of the coastline and other beauty spots.

ROADS DIVISION
The Secretary of State is the Highway Authority for motorways and trunk roads and within his budget must pay for the entire cost of their construction and maintenance.

The Labour government had a major policy on road improvement in Wales and Monmouthshire and George carried it out with enthusiasm. The report of May 1969 says of the major trunk road programme, that it was divided into two parts:

a firm programme containing schemes which have been granted a starting date (schemes are usually in the *firm programme* two years before they are due to start); and a "preparation pool" which is virtually a reservoir of schemes designed to guarantee the firm programme a ready supply of prepared schemes.

The rate of supply is of course governed by resources available. It was estimated at that time that the value of the schemes in the Welsh trunk road programme was £100 million.

George Thomas was now daily involved in this kind of detailed work, which extended to divisions dealing with the hospital service, local government, economic and social planning and virtually everything to do with life in Wales except taxation and defence. Those matters that were not his immediate responsibility at least required his oversight. But there was one paragraph in that "Note on the Welsh Office" which had already caused him great concern and was to occupy his attention much of the time. It is modestly titled, "Other Responsibilities":

In addition to these responsibilities, the office is deeply involved in matters relating to the language and cultural and artistic vigour.
    Increasing funds are made available for the publication of Welsh language books. A Committee has been set up to advise the Secretary of State on the translation of official forms into Welsh and progress has been made in producing Welsh language and bi-lingual forms.

There were critics who felt that this part of his duties was not given the same enthusiastic attention by the Secretary of State as other matters. It must be admitted that he felt that good roads, good houses, a train service across central Wales, and adequate hospital and health facilities, were more important than bi-lingual forms. But he was a democrat and did what he was required to do under the Welsh Language Act.

Economic and Social Planning

The decline of the coal industry had brought great hardship into Wales, part of which was classified in the sixties as a "depressed area". Before George Thomas became Secretary of State this had been increasingly recognized, and he gave his attention to it at once. While Cledwyn Hughes was still Secretary of State for Wales in August 1965, the Welsh Development Area was greatly extended to cover virtually the whole of Wales. Incentives were given to attract industry to these Development Areas, including substantial grants and special assistance in retraining. Wales was to be transformed from a largely coal-mining area to a land of small industries and steel.

In 1967, still in Cledwyn Hughes' time, the President of the Board of Trade announced the designation of certain areas, which were expected to be hit very severely by colliery closures, as Special Development Areas. A large part of the South Wales coalfield was so designated. Special and additional financial inducements were offered to industry to go into these areas.

George Thomas inherited all this and gave his mind and energy to it. Much as he looked forward to the Investiture and much as he enjoyed the times of rehearsal and working with the Duke of Norfolk, that was not his main task. He had a massive job of restructuring the economy of Wales. And his heart was in it—defending the railway lines, improving living conditions, providing new employment, developing the health service and securing adequate pensions—such were the bread and butter of his life as Secretary of State for Wales.

The Shadow of the Tips of Aberfan

The fight of the people of Aberfan to have the menacing tips removed had been going on bitterly since the day of the disaster. George was deeply concerned when he was a minister and now almost three years later he was faced with demands as Secretary of State. It was on *his* desk now. He was advised that the tip on the hillside above Aberfan was not dangerous. Engineers from the local authority, the Coal Board and the government agreed that it was safe, but over the people of Aberfan it cast a shadow which reminded them of the day a whole generation was lost. George felt sympathy for them, but the cost of moving the tip was estimated at a million pounds. He argued their case to the Treasury, but failed. He had then to face the people of Aberfan, who did not trust the experts. He vividly remembered that dreadful experience as he tried to explain to the parents of the lost children that he was assured that the tips were safe:

> I knew them all as they sat in front of me in the Welsh Office. An old man, Alderman Tom Lewis, their leader, stood up and said, "Secretary of State, I never thought to hear such words from George Thomas' lips. I thought you understood the problems of Aberfan. That tip is a nightmare for our people. You can say that it is safe, but we were told that before. Nothing could do as much for the peace of mind of Aberfan as moving that tip." Others there who were less polite in their language than Tom, but not as effective, were shouting and very angry. I promised to take the matter back to the Government in London, which I did at once.

He took the first train to London, telephoned the Prime Minister at once and found that Harold Wilson knew all about his problems. "George, you've been having a rough time," he said. "I have just seen it on television." This was a surprise because George had not known that the television cameras had been inside the Welsh Office all the time. His dispute was now national news. He was deeply disturbed and told the Prime Minister that he could not carry out the government's decision—"I just can't tell those people that the tip has to stay. They are afraid. Their protest has not been manufactured, it's a genuine fear from people who have been through a terrible experience." He was invited to Number Ten and a solution was thrashed out; a compromise, but it would remove the threatening tip. The bank interest on the Aberfan Fund would contribute a quarter of a million pounds, the Coal Board the same, and the Treasury agreed to half a million.

One difficulty remained—the Aberfan Fund trustees. Public response to the tragedy three years before had been generous and there was quite a lot of money in the Fund. The trustees, however, were determined that it should be used only for relief of the people of Aberfan. George had a rough ride. He argued that he need not take a penny from the Fund, but use only the interest from the investments. He withdrew while they considered his argument and his proposals. He waited anxiously: "As I stood in my office, my private secretary looked out of the window and told me that S. O. Davies, Aberfan's local MP, had walked out of the meeting. It was the best sign so far, as it meant that the committee was moving my way."

George's assessment was right. S. O. Davies was determined that no contribution should be made from the Fund. When he walked out it was obvious that the committee was not going his way. It took some time after that, but eventually an agreement was reached. The dark satanic tip was moved. The Aberfan people held a dinner in celebration; George and Mam were invited as guests of honour. He never forgot Aberfan and its people, "scarred by tragedy".

The Investiture of the Prince of Wales

On Sunday, 30th June 1969, George Thomas MP, Secretary of State for Wales, went a little uneasily to Caernarvon Castle to see that all was in order for the following day. The square was packed and as his car crawled through the crowd, two tough bully-boys leaned through the open window of his car, spat on him and yelled, "*Bradwyr*" (traitor). While the royal train was travelling from London two men had blown themselves up trying to put a bomb on the railway line on which the royal party was to travel.

George was in a tense mood on Investiture Day as he waited for the royal party to arrive. Their train was delayed for two hours at Crewe because someone had cut the signalling wires. The Queen enquired if there had been other disturbances, and he had to tell her, but assured her that she and the Prince would have a real Welsh welcome. And so it proved; but this highlight in George's career must be told in George's own words as he remembered the event:

> The procession was headed by Prince Charles's coach, and David Checketts, his equerry, and I travelled with him. It was an uncomfortable coach with narrow seats, and I was quite unprepared when the Prince said, "This was Queen Victoria's coach, Mr Thomas, she rode in it herself." My answer came from the heart: "I hope she was more comfortable than I am."

About five minutes after we left the station, a shattering roar came from an adjoining field. An extremist had exploded a bomb. People watching television saw the police run after and capture a suspect, but neither Prince Charles nor I knew what was happening. He turned to me: "What is that, Mr Thomas?" I improvised. "It's a royal salute, Prince Charles." When he said it was a peculiar royal salute, I could only reply, "There are peculiar people up here, Prince Charles."

As we drove through the narrow streets of Caernarvon, the crowds roared their welcome and pressed hard to reach the coach. I looked up at the people reaching out of the overhanging buildings. A determined killer could easily have thrown a bomb that would have wiped us out. It was a comforting moment for us all when we reached the security of Caernarvon Castle.

I led the Prince into the Chamberlain Tower, where he disappeared from the public view. Inside the Tower, I was pleasantly surprised to see two little children sitting in front of a television set. These were the children of Princess Margaret and Lord Snowdon, who rushed towards Prince Charles as soon as they saw him.

My greatest ordeal was to come. I had to read the Letters of Proclamation in Welsh – very old, stiff Welsh. I thought particularly then how I wished my father had taught me Welsh. From what I can gather, the Proclamation is something like Shakespearian English. I had worked very hard on this. My friend, the late Idwal Jones, the then MP for Wrexham, had recorded the whole text for me, and I had gone over it with him many times. A friend of my mother's from Holyhead had also helped and corrected me, and my great anxiety was that I might have too strong a North Wales accent at the end of the day. I was thrilled with the reception my recital received, and with the splendour of the ceremony as a whole. The Duke of Norfolk had done his work splendidly, and every detail of the complicated procedure went like clockwork.

It was a relieved and contented Secretary of State who accompanied the Queen to her train and saw how happy she was that all had gone so smoothly. "I have never seen her so happy," he said. There was ample evidence that the Prince was going to be very popular in Wales.

It was clear that the Welsh Nationalists had misjudged the mood of the country. As the Prince toured Wales he was received with enthusiasm wherever he went. Even Gwynfor Evans, the Welsh Nationalist leader, who had been strongly opposed to the Investiture and refused to attend the ceremony, went down to his Carmar-thenshire constituency and stood in line to be presented to the Prince. This was on the advice of his agent, which George judged to be a mistake. The people of Wales do not like humbug. Gwynfor Evans lost his seat at the next election.

Unemployment in Wales

George Thomas, as Secretary of State for Wales, had carried through the Investiture and moved the Aberfan tip. He had also assessed the full potential of the Welsh Office and succeeded in widening its brief, responding to the natural sense of justice in the people of Wales, and had tackled unemployment caused by pit closures. He had created in the people of Wales a confidence in their Secretary of State and the Welsh Office.

But the pit closures were a major problem. In 1969, the Coal Board presented the Welsh Office with a programme of pit closures which the government had decided should go ahead on the basic assumption that uneconomic pits should be closed. George had fought this all the way, bringing forward arguments for saving pits that were border-line or had some prospect of becoming more profitable. He strongly argued the moral case for saving communities which would be ruined by closure of their only means of livelihood. Despite all his efforts there still remained a final list of pits that were due for closure with disastrous consequences for the local communities. Efforts were made to attract new industries, but every pit that closed meant 500 to 1,000 men out of work, while any new industry would employ only a few hundred of them. The problem seemed insurmountable, but remarkably by 1970, unemployment in Wales had fallen to 33,000. That was not achieved without effort and co-operation, patience and determination all round. In particular, George worked as a colleague side by side with the trades union officials. They knew that he was on their side and felt able to trust him, even when unpopular policies needed to be implemented. He names two in particular who helped him to resist closures, but also to ensure that law and order prevailed once a firm decision had been taken. They were Glyn Williams and Dai Francis, President and Secretary respectively of the South Wales NUM. George's visit to Glyncorrwg was remembered.

The 1970 Election

The government elected on 31st March 1966 was coming to the end of its course. Labour had not had good results in the opinion polls because it had had to do some very unpopular things, evidenced in Wales by the closure of the pits and subsequent unemployment. For three years this told against the government, much as rationing had told against Attlee's government in 1950. But the tide was turning. George saw things improve in Wales and unemployment fall. A similar picture was emerging in England. The opinion polls also were changing gear and rising in favour of Labour. Roy Jenkins, as Chancellor of the Exchequer, was in a position to relieve tax burdens somewhat. He resisted a "give-away" budget, having respect for the electorate whose votes he knew could not be bought with unrealistic concessions. But things looked good in April 1970. Early in May, Harold Wilson consulted his cabinet about going to the Queen to ask for a dissolution of Parliament. Every member was confident and in favour of an early appeal to the country. Throughout the campaign, the polls gave Labour a lead and the cabinet was sure that they would meet again after the election. Jim Callaghan's seemed to be the only doubtful voice. When he and George met on the eve of the general election in June, he remarked that he did not like the attitude of the young women voters. He thought the Conservative appeal to them by offering to cut the cost of living "at a stroke" would have its effect. He was by no means sure that Labour would win. In any case, he thought it would be a close thing, with only a handful of votes either way—no more than a majority of thirty, and it could as well be Tory as Labour. Callaghan's prediction was right; it was the Conservatives who won with a majority of thirty over Labour. The Welsh seats were fairly safe, although the Welsh Nationalists lost out. An analysis of why Labour had lost revealed that the young married women's vote had tipped the balance in favour of Ted Heath's "prices cut at a stroke". There was also a feeling in the country that the social services were being exploited by scroungers. Labour, it was perceived, was too soft on them and too easily conned. But when all is said, it was a shock to a party who expected to win.

The defeated cabinet met once more in grave and troubled mood to analyse the party's defeat. Harold Wilson asked each member to write down the state of things in his department when they left office.

George wrote his with great care and his thirty foolscap pages are a crystal clear picture of the Welsh Office in 1970. Much has already been said about the "Note on the Welsh Office" of May 1969 and most of these details are included in the thirty pages of 1970, but there is additional material on the investiture, Aberfan and the pit closures, as well as the impressive improvement of transport. George could not have been expected to write this up without expressing his opinion of the Welsh Nationalists, who throughout had been his main opponents. In fact, he was beginning to feel that his attitude to the Nationalists had been an embarrassment to the government. It was necessary therefore for him to summarize his conviction:

> Wales is a proud nation with its own traditions and its own cultural values, but its central problems in the present day depend for a solution on the recognition that for economic purposes it must not be a separate entity from those across the border.

That was his last word as Secretary of State for Wales. In the new parliament he would be Shadow Secretary of State for Wales and, predictably, he would not be silent in that role!

The Conservatives made an immediate mistake as far as the Welsh people were concerned. Ted Heath appointed Peter Thomas, MP for Hendon, as Chairman of the Conservative Party and Secretary for State for Wales. This was interpreted in Wales as a downgrading of the Welsh Office. It was not long before people were repeating the words of Anthony Barber that "Chairman of the Conservative Party is a full time job". Would Peter Thomas give only his spare time to Wales? He was soon labelled, "the part-time Secretary for Wales".

Moreover, the election changed the character of the Welsh Parliamentary Labour Party—the old champions were gone, their places filled by newcomers who could have been their children, and who inevitably brought changes in outlook. Devolution was again the issue to dominate the agenda and the new-look Welsh Parliamentary Labour Party was split over it. George did his best to unite the party. As Shadow Secretary of State for Wales, he also tried to unite the country in face of an increasingly vocal Welsh Nationalist Party. It was not difficult to get men like Cledwyn Hughes, Goronwy Roberts, John Morris and Elystan Morgan to make moderate speeches on devolution, even though they felt very strongly on the issue. It was quite a different matter with speakers like Will Edwards and Tom Ellis, who fanned the flames of Nationalism, but "their influence in Wales and Westminster was slight," although they were the new Nationalist heroes.

George's Political Creed

George set down his own personal attitude to the job which was consistently reflected in his actions:

> I am in politics because I believe that that is a field where a man's gifts can be fully used to serve his generation. My profound belief in the worth of every individual is matched by my deep conviction that politics are a means of creating a fairer society where every individual has a chance to discover and to develop his gifts. Because I believe that an MP is above all a trustee of the highest interests of the country, I commit myself to continue to work for a society where the dignity of man is recognized by practical measures as well as by words. To this I have dedicated myself.

This was not just electioneering talk, although it was contained in his message to the electorate in 1970, asking for their votes. It describes very well the conclusions of a convinced Christian who has been long enough in politics to know what is possible, but who has not lost his vision.

CHAPTER FOURTEEN

◆◆◆

The End of Party Politics

D ENIS HEALEY, who had enjoyed working in the Labour government as Secretary of State for Defence, expressed the feelings of many Labour MPs after the surprise result of the 1970 election: "After six years of hard work on something worth doing, it came as a bewildering shock to be thrown again into the Limbo of Opposition." George was now Shadow Secretary of State for Wales, but that was like moving from the team to the spectators.

The Welsh Parliamentary Group underwent very considerable change at the 1970 general election. The old guard who had been involved in manual work and fierce Trades Union battles, had almost entirely left the parliamentary scene. Coalminers James Griffiths, Harold Finch, Cliff Williams and Tudor Watkins all opted for retirement; Dai Mort, former Swansea steel worker and Arthur Pearson, former Pontypridd chain worker, also decided to retire.

In a watershed change the new Welsh Labour MPs were the firstfruits of the Welfare State set up by Labour's post-War government. Now there was only one former miner, Elfed Davies (Rhondda East) amongst all the Welsh Parliamentary Labour Group. Labour's 1970 parliamentary intake in Wales could well be described as representing "all the talents". Neil Kinnock, the fiery radical from Bedwellty, modelled himself on left-wing Michael Foot. Prior to entering Parliament, Kinnock, after graduating from Cardiff's University College, had been a lecturer for the Workers' Educational Association. This work took him into the South Wales valleys and established his reputation as a reliable left-wing Labour advocate. Bryn John, who replaced Pontypridd's chain worker Pearson, was a well-respected solicitor in Pontypridd. Denzil Davis (Llanelli) was a product of Pembroke College, Oxford and enjoyed a sparkling reputation as a barrister from Gray's Inn. Jeffrey Thomas (Abertillery) similarly entered Westminster with a shining reputation at the bar and also was a product of Gray's Inn. Barry Jones and Caerwyn Roderick were qualified teachers, already established as leaders in the NUT. Tom Ellis, who replaced James Idwal Jones at Wrexham, was a colliery manager. For the first time in its history, the Welsh Parliamentary Party had a majority of members belonging to the professional classes. Although they were all the sons of working class people, there was a change of style for Labour in Wales.

George Thomas, himself a former teacher, says clearly that it was a privilege to lead a team with such ability. This ability was, however, matched by high personal ambitions. Rivalries within political parties are almost invariably far sharper than inter-party rivalries. With a team of which any, or all, might prove to be of cabinet calibre, it was clear that to lead them in the 1970 Parliament would not prove an easy ride for the Welsh Shadow Secretary of State. When the inevitable differences of ideology concerning Welsh affairs surfaced, George was not slow to realize the advantages this could bring him, both as Group Co-ordinator and as spokesman in the House of Commons.

A Question of Retirement

Cledwyn Hughes and George Thomas shared adjoining rooms in the Commons throughout the four years in opposition that followed the 1970 election. Inevitably they became closer in their friendship and spent much time together planning possible policies for Wales. They also discussed their own futures. Cledwyn Hughes' persistent advice to George was not to leave it until too late to go to the House of Lords. At that time the custom still prevailed that former cabinet members were sent to the House of Lords on retirement from the Commons.

Despite the urging of Cledwyn Hughes, George felt a reluctance to leave the Commons. He had a profound attachment to his constituency, where he used to say with pride, "Even the children call me George." Yet at one stage he seemed ready to accept his colleague's advice. He also consulted Jim Callaghan, who similarly advised him not to wait too long. But Harold Wilson was incredulous, saying, "What on earth makes you think like that? If we win the next election you'll be back in the team." That was good enough for George, and all thought of resigning was cast aside.

The Death of Mam

It was only two years after leaving the Welsh Office that George suffered the severest blow of his life. His mother, Emma Jane, rebellious daughter of John and Elizabeth Tilbury, died after a very short illness. She was in her ninety-second year and she had helped to shape political life both in the Rhondda Valley and in Cardiff over a very long period. Above all she had laid the foundation of George's moral character, and had been the main inspiration in his Christian Socialist beliefs. Throughout his parliamentary career he had relied on her judgement when he was torn in conflict over party issues. She had always proved to be a shrewd judge of character and was invariably percipient in her assessments of George's political colleagues. Because he and his mother shared the same Christian and political beliefs, George regularly confided in her not only his anxieties and his ambitions, but his uneasiness about some of the people with whom he negotiated party matters. Thus her death was both emotionally and politically devastating for him. Like everyone who suffers a particularly close bereavement, George was for a while in a state of shock.

Mam's contribution to socialism in Wales, particularly during times of strife and war, deserves a book in its own right. She had that rare gift in mothers, that she did not try to own her son or to live her life through him. From the earliest age, she allowed him to make his own decisions, only providing the framework within which he could safely make those decisions on firm ground. He was his own man, but her influence was the strongest in his life. It did not make him dependent, but rather strengthened his independence. He was not likely to meet a stronger character than her in all his life, and this prevented him from modelling himself on any other person whom he admired. He had his heroes—Grandfather Tilbury, Nye Bevan, Keir Hardie, Clement Attlee, Sir Charles MacAndrew and others—but he never knew anyone with greater integrity than Mam. Mam was sound through and through. Although her talents were different from his, she was his model. Perhaps it is better to say that he tested his integrity by hers. She was proud of his achievements but never hesitated to point out what she believed to be his faults. She never allowed him to become too proud.

Bereavement

Just two months after Mam's death, George's younger brother also died. This left him the sole survivor of his family, both his sisters having died some years before, and he felt acutely lonely. As the years went by, he realized more and more how much he owed to Mam. Of course, she could not live for ever and he had had her wisdom and company for a long time. For this he thanked God and saw it as a sign of His grace. When she died he was strengthened by the knowledge that both of them believed in life after death in the presence of their beloved Saviour. None the less they had been together in the lesser beauty of this world so long, that it was hard to part. George wrote of his sorrow in his Memoirs and the edge of bereavement is recalled still in 1985, thirteen years after her death: "When my mother died, the thought of carrying on in the Commons suddenly held no attraction for me. It seemed that my ambition had died with Mam . . . For a short time I even questioned my faith."

George likes telling the story of his appointment as Secretary of State for Wales. He had been told of his promotion a day before the news was to be released on the media. He had asked the Prime Minister if he could give the news to Mam. On being given instructions that no one else but Mam was to know the news before the media announced it to the public, George set off for his bungalow home in Cardiff. Standing before his eighty-seven-year-old mother he recounts that he stated, "Mam, you are looking at the new Secretary of State for Wales. I am to be in the Inner Cabinet, and I am due to go to Windsor Castle on Monday morning to be sworn in as a Privy Councillor." His aged mother smiled with pride, but as she said, "Congratulations, George," she added the sobering words, "You won't lose your head, will you, George? Remember it is only for a while."

Mam had had her own ambitions for George. He recalls how he was once taking her by car over the Brecon Beacons to help his friend, Tudor Watkins, newly elevated to the House of Lords, to choose his new title. Mam's hopes for George were revealed by a chance remark, "Tudor has done well, hasn't he, George?" When George realized what she was thinking he replied, "Yes, he has, Mam, but I can go to the Lords if I want to do so." He was met with the query, "Are you sure, George?" and when he replied that every former cabinet minister could go there when he retired, she asked, "What title would you take, George?" "I will give you one guess," was his instant answer. Mam said, "Tonypandy", and they both laughed, because they shared the same deep love for the place they looked upon as home. With just a twinge of sadness in his voice, George Thomas now says, "I remember clearly the part of the Beacons where that conversation took place, and I never pass it without whispering, 'Now you know that I kept faith with what I told you, Mam.'"

The last six months of Mam's life had been severely testing, as her memory, her hearing and her sight failed her. It seemed like a miracle to George that although her memory had failed in everything else, she remembered the words of all her favourite hymns. Two weeks before her sudden death, whilst being taken for a ride in George's car, she had sung three verses of "What a friend we have in Jesus", and the four verses of "When I survey the wondrous Cross, on which the Prince of Glory died".

Someone leaked to the *Western Mail* that George Thomas would not stand at the next election. That put him on the spot. He must either deny the rumour or, as he put it, "my parliamentary influence as spokesman for the Welsh MPs would melt as snow on a spring day". He issued on indignant denial. The leak, which had featured on the paper's front page, stimulated him to action and was really a great help in his decision-making; it led to many more years of life in the Commons. In denying that he planned to resign at the next election, he began to realize what things he could do as Secretary of State for Wales. He was sure by now that Ted Heath's government could not last long. Industrial disputes which reduced the country to a three-day working week, and imposed discipline even in the use of electricity, left the people dissatisfied. If Heath were to go to the country in the next year or so, he was sure Labour would be back in power. He was right.

The Dream for Wales

It was like a new start. His ambition was stimulated again. The young man of thirty years before who had argued for a status for Wales equal to that of Scotland, recovered his vision. Then he had asked for a Secretary of State, now Wales had a Secretary of State with an efficient Welsh Office. He had argued for the upgrading of Cardiff docks, for better housing, for Cardiff to be recognized as a capital. All this had been achieved, and he was now anxious to get his hands on the levers of power again and to accomplish far more for Wales. Now, he knew where he was going. There was nothing in the world he wanted more than to be Secretary of State for Wales in a strong Labour-controlled United Kingdom. He was moreover an experienced politician and statesman now—no mere dreamer—and his influence was considerable. Harold Wilson listened to him, and many of those who would be in office in a Labour government trusted his judgement, particularly on Welsh affairs. He saw the need to improve transport in Wales, to save as much as was possible of the coal mining industry, to introduce new industries and to encourage investment. Homes fit for human habitation were badly needed and the standard of life in rural and urban Wales was lagging behind that in England. He was opposed to the break up of the United Kingdom for the sake of Wales. He knew that Wales would be harmed by a separate Assembly, but was not blind to the growing strength of Plaid Cymru and its gathering support. But he felt able to deal with that. When prosperity returned to Wales, the people would see the sense of fostering Welsh culture within the United Kingdom. In his optimism he underestimated the strength of Plaid Cymru.

His vision included a revival of chapel influence. He knew that Welsh culture and Welsh strength lay in the rich chapel tradition. He had never ceased to play his part in Methodism, at the Welsh, United Kingdom and international levels. He was honoured throughout the world as a Methodist lay preacher and a supporter of Methodist causes, especially the National Children's Home. His vision for Wales was one of Christian Socialism, and he knew the continuing resources left in the declining chapels, where the true roots of Welsh culture could be found, whether the language was English or Welsh.

Recovery

Within a very short time, he was his old self again in Parliament. On 22nd July 1972, the political columnist, Norman Shrapnel of the *Guardian*, reported the proceedings of the day before with gusto: "The member for Cardiff West, who is also the former (and on this showing, the future) Secretary of State for Wales, was defending the County of Glamorgan from what he regarded as the outrageous assaults of the Government." He made the Tory plans for the county sound like "a mixture of false pretences, mass burglary and rape, with a little looting and malicious damage thrown in". The rather dull discussion on the Local Government Bill had been suddenly brought to life and made to sound like a "kind of one-man Eisteddfod". He described George's manner as like that of an energetic preacher in the pulpit! "He gives his argument the full operatic works, and conducts it with every gesture in the book, from the vibrating single finger to the double-arm sweep. He even clenches his fists and drums his chest with them, a gesture which has scarcely been seen in Parliament since the days of Nye Bevan." There is a hint also in his description of a tolerance the House did not show to many of its members, because they knew that there was never any rancour in George Thomas's bitterest attacks. For example, "When the Government MPs hear Mr Thomas speaking of 'secret, rotten manoeuvres at Tory head-quarters', or accusing them of shoddy, brazen deception of the mean-est and most contemptible kind, they see no special reason to take offence."

Norman Shrapnel was a shrewd observer. He noted the good humour with which the opposition received his near-insults as "just George's way", but warned that he was not harmless: "One day Mr Thomas will roar 'wolf' and a ravenous one will really be there. He sounded convinced of it yesterday, though all the rest of us could see was that other Thomas—the agreeable Peter [Peter Thomas, the Conservative Secretary of State for Wales and chairman of the Party], in whose presence any Glamorgan Red Riding Hood would surely be safe."

It was a long and enjoyable speech, and those who did not take it seriously were very unwise, because George meant what he said and, despite the charm and humour, he was indeed angry. One thing he made very clear: "Whatever unspeakable things the government does to Glamorgan's boundaries now, Labour reserves the right to change them again when it returns to power."

Both the text of this long speech in Hansard and the lively account of it in the *Guardian*, show that George Thomas had recovered from the depression which almost led him to abandon Parliament after Mam's death.

The Fall of the Heath Government

From 1972, Heath was beset with problems. First came the oil crisis, in which he appeared to give in to the pressure of the oil states in the Middle East, and then the coal crisis, which was largely caused by protest against the closure of pits. The effect upon the country was a lack of confidence in the government and, as industrial disputes increased, the Conservatives lost one by-election after another. Even when they retained a safe seat it was with a greatly reduced majority, but Labour did not profit much. It was the Liberals who picked up the disgruntled Tory votes. Labour was seen to be in as much trouble as the Tories and there was a growing fear of the trade unions acquiring too much power. There were many who feared that a Labour government would be a puppet of the unions. The Liberals won the Ripon by-election in this climate. In the autumn of 1973, Heath was punished by the oil states for his support of Israel during the Yom Kippur War. Then the miners voted for a ban on overtime. When this had happened the previous year, Heath had caved in, but he was determined not to do so now. He tried to fight both the oil crisis and the mining disputes at the same time. He imposed a three-day working week to conserve fuel, although he did not impose petrol rationing. It was discovered, however, that he had already printed the coupons for such a contingency. Throughout January 1974, he considered and reconsidered the wisdom of calling an election. His advisers contradicted one another. There was no clear sign that he would win, but Labour seemed also a poor opposition. Eventually he called the election in February. Almost as soon as it was announced, and before polling day, the miners called a full-time strike. That should have worked in Heath's favour. He went to the polls with the slogan, "Who governs the country?" and should have won but did not. He was an unpopular Prime Minister and the people blamed him rather than the miners for their privations during the three-day week. Conservatives polled more votes, but Labour won more seats—four more.

George noted with some concern the growth of the Welsh Nationalist vote; Labour's influence in Wales had weakened, and the Liberals did better than they expected. Although Labour was thirty-four short of an absolute majority, they could count on more support from the Nationalists and Liberals than Conservatives could do, and they did have a slender lead of four seats. Ted Heath tried to persuade the Liberals to support him in government, but after days of wrangling he left Number Ten and Harold Wilson was asked by the Queen to form a government.

By this time, George had a flat in Artillery Mansions, off Victoria Street and very near to the House. On the crucial evening when Heath resigned, George went back to his flat and listened to the news on the radio. Harold Wilson was once again Prime Minister. That meant the realization of his dreams—his return from the sidelines to become Secretary of State for Wales.

Disappointment

George had often known disappointment—it is something a politician has to get used to—but there can have been no moment to compare with his meeting with the Prime Minister that evening. He had waited all day for a call, confident that Harold Wilson would bring him back into his cabinet with the office of Secretary of State for Wales. Of this he had no doubts. At last the call came, at ten minutes to ten, and he caught a cab and was at Number Ten in no time, full of confident excitement. He was there by ten o'clock—he heard Big Ben strike as he arrived. Harold Wilson, Fred Peart, Gerald Kaufman and Peter Shore were already there. They watched the television "News at Ten" as far as Harold Wilson waving on the entrance to Number Ten, and then Wilson called George into the Cabinet Room. "I winked at the others as I went," he recalls. George started the conversation in his usual friendly way, saying it was marvellous to be back where power was. He was not allowed to go on to say what he intended to do in Wales, because Harold Wilson blurted out, "How would you like to be Deputy Speaker, and Chairman of Ways and Means?"

In fact, George Thomas had become an embarrassment to Harold Wilson, and it was not easy for Wilson to tell him that he was not to be in the cabinet after all. The Labour government was moving towards a separate Assembly for Wales, and George was known to be against this.

During the years of opposition, he had written a weekly column in the *Liverpool Daily Post*, and had often annoyed Welsh MPs by his strong resistance to Welsh Nationalism. There had been a delegation of Welsh MPs to Harold Wilson complaining about him. Wilson was loyal to his friend, but warned him of enemies in his own ranks and advised him to be more cautious. George ignored the warning and the advice, and went on as though nothing had happened. He could be a little too sure of himself at times! A journalist on the *Western Mail* told him even before the election that John Morris would be Secretary of State for Wales if Labour won the election. Even this did not perturb George. He was too confident that he knew Harold Wilson. But now the unbelievable was happening. Several senior ministers had impressed on Wilson that devolution was unlikely to succeed if George Thomas was back in the Cabinet—in whatever capacity. The Prime Minister had therefore to find for him something else he wanted, something with sufficient prospects, and a post which did not seem like demotion. He was the only former minister not to go back in the cabinet after the 1974 election. Harold Wilson hated doing it but he felt it was inevitable. He knew how much George wanted one day to be Speaker. He was also aware of George's great experience as a chairman, and knew that he would make an outstanding and fair-minded Speaker. But he did not have that gift in his power. What he could do was put him on the road towards the Speakership, so he asked, "How would you like to be Deputy Speaker and Chairman of Ways and Means?" George was flabbergasted— "Not Secretary of State for Wales?" Wilson knew the shock he had delivered, and to comfort him said, "Before you get agitated, remember how old Selwyn Lloyd is." Selwyn Lloyd had been Speaker since he had succeeded Horace King in 1971. The implication was that George would be Speaker before long.

Harold Wilson at his best was a shrewd judge of people. He knew that he was dangling before George's eyes the equivalent of offering a knight the holy grail. With a shrug of the shoulders, George ceased arguing: "If you think that that is the best way that I can serve, so be it." But for months the disappointment rankled. He had not heeded either the warning of Harold Wilson or that of the *Western Mail* journalist, so in some way he had only himself to blame for this disappointment. But like other people, the last person he blamed was himself. He never again attended a Labour Parliamentary Party meeting, for he had a strong conviction that the Deputy Speaker, like Mr Speaker himself, had to be seen to be completely impartial. Even in the years of his retirement he follows the tradition that Speakers of the Commons never return to the party fray, but sit on the cross benches in the House of Lords. When he answered Harold Wilson's call to Number Ten Downing Street he was not to know that for him the party political strife was over. Thus ended a whole chapter of his life.

But who was to be Secretary of State for Wales? The *Western Mail* journalist was right: John Morris, who was the candidate of the Welsh-speaking part of the Welsh Labour group landed the post. He shared the views of Cledwyn Hughes and the other Welsh-speaking members of the Welsh Parliamentary Party on devolution. It was a little ironic that John Morris was the MP for Port Talbot, where George Thomas had been born and where his father had come to grief! Apart from the great disappointment at not being appointed Secretary of State, George Thomas was surprised that Harold Wilson had so misjudged the power of the Welsh Nationalists. They did not represent the majority of the Welsh people, as a later referendum was to show. Proof of that lay in the future.

Deputy Speaker and Chairman of Ways and Means

George Thomas was not a man to let disappointment turn into bitterness. He looked now to his new job and its prospects. A week after his interview with Harold Wilson the motion went on the order paper for the Rt Hon. George Thomas to be elected Deputy Speaker and Chairman of Ways and Means. Of those two offices, the older and more prestigious is Chairman of Ways and Means, although nowadays it is always combined as a title for the senior of the three Deputy Speakers. Originally, its function was to replace the Speaker when the House was talking about raising money. In those earlier years of Parliament, MPs were afraid that the Speaker would tell the monarch which members had spoken against his requests to raise the taxes!

The Deputy Speaker also works closely with the committees in the House and advises the Speaker on the Panel of Chairmen to supervise the committees. George Thomas took his appointment seriously and resolved to end all connections with party politics. He was not going to let the Labour Party use him as a parliamentary pawn to get their own way:

> My first decision was that I would not attend any party political meetings in the House or in the country, except for the management committee of my constituency, because even Deputy

Speakers have to seek re-election on the party ticket. Every month I gave a speech in the privacy of the Cardiff West Labour Party management committee, but I never once made a party political speech in public.

It was not an easy part to play. George did not cease to be a socialist, but his high respect for the House and for his office made him impartial without being indifferent. The house soon came to respect his integrity. Not all Deputy Speakers have behaved with such scruples before or since. Harold Walker, when he was Deputy Speaker, canvassed for Tony Benn, saying that it was unreasonable for people to expect him to be impartial.

There was one ceremonial change which at first made George feel embarrassed—he had to wear morning dress when in the House; but he later saw that it was a kind of uniform which gave a signal to MPs that he was now linked with the Chair. He soon began to enjoy his freedom—he could sit in the Members' Tea Room with Tories or Liberals, or even Nationalists!

George had always enjoyed friendship with members from other parties than his own, but they were on the basis of a clearly understood stand in his own party. Now, he felt that he must isolate himself from party loyalty in order to retain the respect that goes with true impartiality. He was more conscientious in this than some other Deputy Speakers had been, and was thus occasionally held suspect by his former colleagues. He had the difficult task of persuading his Labour friends that he was still a socialist, as indeed he had to convince his constituents in Cardiff West. At the same time, his office required him to be fair and impartial when presiding over a debate. This would reach a crucial stage later when he became Speaker and had to use his casting vote. But in less dramatic moments also, it was difficult for a person of integrity and strong convictions to hold together convincingly those two roles. His constituency had no doubts. They knew him well, and his relations with them never wavered. Indeed, now he could broaden that relationship and take all Cardiff to his heart. Inevitably, the people of Cardiff wanted to honour their distinguished member.

The Freedom of the City of Cardiff

In 1975, both Jim Callaghan and George Thomas had been for thirty years members for Cardiff. The city decided to honour these two distinguished members, Jim Callaghan was then Foreign Secretary and George Thomas had his new role of Deputy Speaker and Chairman of Ways and Means. The city was proud of them both and wanted to make them Freemen of Cardiff. It was a matter of enormous pride for George Thomas that the city in which he had spent half his life as schoolteacher, MP and Secretary of State, a city which he had campaigned to make the capital of Wales, should honour him with its freedom. The missing person was Mam, whose happiness he recalled when he had received the Freedom of Rhondda in 1970.

The ceremony was influenced by Jim Callaghan's invitation to Henry Kissinger to be his guest of honour. This naturally upstaged George. Kissinger made a speech at the dinner in honour of the two MPs at the City Banqueting Hall, where he courteously praised the British Foreign Secretary. "But", George writes in memory, "both Kissinger and his wife showed a sensitivity to me and the position he was putting me in, which moved me very much." For all the upstaging, George enjoyed the occasion.

The next day every newspaper in Wales had Kissinger in the headlines. But the *South Wales Echo*, on the eve of the event, Wednesday 5th March 1975, carried a double article on the two men about to be honoured. They were compared a little and their careers contrasted. Mike Graham's article on George Thomas was headed, "Deputy Speaker—and even the kids call him George". Derek Hooper's article on James Callaghan was headed, "Sunny Jim—the tough statesman with the big smile". Their very different faces looked out at the reader pleasantly, side by side. At the bottom of the page were the pictures of Mrs Emma Thomas Davies—Mam—and Mrs Audrey Callaghan: "The women behind them".

Mike Graham summarized George's career and concluded that it revealed "a distinct pattern ranging from rebel to mature front bencher". He dealt with two issues that were much talked about— was George on his way to the House of Lords, and what was the influence of Mam upon him? On the first, he quoted George as saying: "If I went to the Lords—I was going to say kicking and screaming—it would be with sorrow at leaving the House of Commons, which to my mind is the greatest Parliamentary institution in the world." On the second, he quoted George's words after his mother died in 1972:

> My mother played an enormous part in every decision I took. I know there is talk of a mother complex, but my Mam and I had a close partnership both politically and socially. There is no doubt that she guided my political life for twenty-seven years, and I am not finding it easy without her ... I keep thinking of her ... I have been nurtured in the belief that we are surrounded by a host of unseen witnesses. I think she knows about the Freedom ceremony and will be sharing my happiness with me.

After that came the great day of 6th March with all the panoply that Cardiff could muster, ending with a glittering dinner to honour the two Freemen of Cardiff, to join the ranks that included Gladstone, Lloyd George and the Queen. Before the dinner, this most solemn and ceremonial occasion brought the silver band out in force, blowing away with patriotic Welsh tunes. The two honoured members stood solemnly and listened to the tribute of the band. George could bear the strain no longer and his impish humour broke out as he turned to Jim Callaghan and said, "Isn't it marvellous, Jim? For thirty years we've had to blow our own trumpet and now they're doing it for us!"

That story gives point to another remark by Graham: "The young rebel MP of thirty years ago surprises himself with the ease in which he can remain silent on provocative issues in the House of Commons today." One questions the use of the word "ease"!

Selwyn Lloyd

George's apprenticeship for Speaker was served under a very kindly but firm man, who was also a fellow Methodist. Selwyn Lloyd kept a tight control on his Deputies. When backbenchers complained that they had not been called, George had the simple answer that he was following the Speaker's list. Selwyn Lloyd made his promises and it was up to him to keep them. When George later became Speaker, he allowed his Deputies more discretion if they felt that the list he had left with them appeared unfair.

Selwyn Lloyd and George got on very well together, though they had totally different backgrounds. Selwyn Lloyd, who like George had entered Parliament in 1945, eventually became Chancellor of the Exchequer under Harold Macmillan, but with five other cabinet ministers fell to the reshuffle which earned the name of "the night of the long knives". Shattered by his sacking, he nevertheless sat quietly on the back benches, showing no public sign of resentment, which earned him great respect. His election as Speaker in 1971 undoubtedly owed much to the dignity with which he had borne disappointment. His grandfather had been a Welsh-speaking Methodist minister and this also helped to endear him to George. They became good friends despite their political differences. George stayed with him twice at the Wirral and preached in his local Methodist church. They could talk naturally about their faith with understanding. It made their co-operation much easier. When, some years later, Selwyn Lloyd died, it was George Thomas who preached the sermon at his memorial service in Westminster Abbey. But in the early days of their acquaintance, when he was still smarting with disappointment, George learned much from the way Selwyn Lloyd had taken his humiliation. "He could only do what the rest of us have to do, forget the disappointment and accept it," was George's heartfelt comment.

The Methodist Preacher

George made much of the importance of an MP giving his whole time to his work. "If I had been a part-time MP, I could not have done . . ." was among his favourite phrases. Mam, also, commended him for the devotion he showed to his work as a Member of Parliament. But it could not be the whole of his life. He had a home life, he had a social life, he knew how to enjoy himself and he was a chapel man. Whenever he could he would preach on Sunday—and wherever he was! Throughout his papers there are hundreds of invitations to speak or preach, or conduct a funeral, not only in great places, or places associated with the great, but in tiny chapels and small Labour Party meetings, or remote associations of teachers. There is no end to the number of times that he was invited to speak at the opening of some hospital, children's home, memorial or some such institution. He rarely declined, and when he had to, it was with sincere regret. There is a warmth about his responses, and genuine appreciation in the letters of thanks afterwards. One of the most telling thank you letters was from the National Federation of Old Age Pensioners, when he preached at the funeral of their Vice-President, usually known by his initials, A.J.; it offered this singular praise: "What a wonderful job you did in putting A.J. away." His speaking and his preaching were of one piece, a seamless robe. Whether he was preaching as a delegate at the International Methodist Conference, or as President of the Brotherhood Movement, as Vice-President of the Methodist Conference of Great Britain, or reopening the Tonypandy Central Hall, his message would vary to suit the occasion but he never trimmed his gospel. At a Methodist Peace Movement or a local Labour Party, as well as a local committee of the NUT, he made it perfectly clear where he stood—for peace, for justice and for Christian principles. His sermons were not always comforting, his speeches were not uncritical, his challenges could not be avoided. Wherever he was or whatever the issues he was invited to address, he spoke as a Methodist with unshakeable Christian and Socialist principles.

For some years he read with care the *Gospel Witness* of Toronto, which published articles and sermons on religious themes. He had a habit of underlining sentences which impressed him, and no doubt used some as quotes in his sermons! In the issue for 3rd May 1973, he underlined the sentence: "The Spirit of God called and still calls for absolute separation from all appearances of evil." A sermon by Eric Gurr of Melbourne Hall, Leicester, in the September issue that year was heavily underlined:

> ... but if God's purpose is not being fulfilled in and through your life, and you are lost to God, Jesus is your friend this morning, and it cost him something to be your friend ...
> If I respond to the gospel, what will it mean?

In reference to the three parables in Luke 15, he underscored "The things that were lost were in no position to help themselves." And further in the same article:

> And the sheep was lost through *aimlessness*. That sheep just took things as they came. It ate grass at its feet. It never gave a thought to tomorrow ... The piece of silver was lost through *carelessness* ... through the carelessness of someone else in the home. That is the word for fathers and that is the word for mothers ... And the son was lost through *wilfulness*. "I am not going to be tied to my mother's apron strings. I am going out into the world. I am going to do things. I am going to see places. I am going to be somebody. I am!"

Whether that sermon helped him in the crisis in February 1974 it is impossible to know, but we may learn something of his preacher's mind in his underlining. There was much straight evangelical preaching of the gospel in George Thomas, but he had also a strong social conscience. He was a true son of John Wesley, who remained his hero.

In his early political and electioneering speeches he often quoted two aphorisms:

> There is no political alchemy by which you can get golden conduct from leaden instincts. (Spencer, *The Man versus the State*)
> Social justice is the foundation of world peace. (Zilliacus)

When he was addressing Methodist ministers in Cardiff in 1966, he tackled the problems of gambling and Sunday observance which were troubling many of them. He expressed his conviction that the reform of the gambling laws was a greater priority than Sunday observance. He said that the Labour Party intended to reform the Gambling and Betting Act which, he added, "has made London the centre of international gambling". But it was the big gambling that he wanted to attack—"a general crack-down on casinos, not bingo and betting shops."

The Sermon

George Thomas preached on so many occasions and over so long a period that it is not easy to find a typical sermon, and yet it is in the sermon that he reveals his innermost thoughts. He almost always took a theme, which could be topical or fundamental, related it to the Bible and spoke eloquently from his own experience. Many of his sermons gain their authority from his reference to something he has participated in himself. In his eighties, he was still using recent experiences, not, like so many old men, drawing upon experiences of long ago! On a visit to Hastings Banda in Malawi as late as 1990, he went to see the refugee camps for those who had fled from the war in Mozambique. He was shocked, and his sermons after his visit referred to those camps. He could illustrate "leadership" to a public school congregation by contrasting the deprivation of the young people in Malawi with their own privileged conditions. This has always been his style.

Although he did not abuse his position in the pulpit to preach party propaganda, he did make political references and exercise a political judgement. Here is a typical example from 1947:

> Fascism breeds on economic depression, unemployment and mass hunger and misery. Only the present regime stands between democratic control in Britain and totalitarianism. Unless the vote of democratic leaders can be made heard above the din of jazz bands and the yells of the dog track, this country will yet be swallowed up in the vortex of Fascism at no distant date.

There were no elections imminent in 1947 and George had the democratic system in mind when he spoke of "the present regime" although he personally believed it was safest in Labour hands.

In 1960, George Thomas was made Vice-President of the Methodist Conference, the first Member of Parliament ever to be so elected. It took him round the country, preaching in Methodist chapels and Central Halls. He preached as a son of John Wesley and a personal disciple of Jesus Christ, but never regarded that as a purely personal affair. It had public consequences and he did not hesitate to put forward the social teaching of the Methodist Conference, which was not in any significant way different from his socialist principles. Few of the sermons lacked social reference, but all called for personal commitment. Some of his sermons were broadcast. On 29th January 1960, for example, he preached from Wesley Methodist Church, Canton, Cardiff. He took his text from both Old and New Testaments: "Remember the Sabbath day to keep it holy" (Exodus 20:8), and "Have I been so long with you, and yet hast thou not known me, Philip? He that hath seen me hath seen the Father; and how sayest thou *then*, Shew us the Father?" (John 14:9). He spoke of Moses and the Ten Commandments with their continuing value, taking as his theme, "Growth in knowledge, but not in moral stature". He spoke of the neglect or disregard of the Ten Commandments with the inevitable consequences of an anaemic moral condition of the country. He spoke of the need for a divine dimension, not unknown, but recognized in the teaching and example of Jesus—"He that hath seen me hath seen the Father." Many of his phrases were memorable —"Christ puts the stamp of value on all men whatever be their social status"; "In this unbalanced world where two out of every three of the human family are tortured by gnawing hunger, by disease that

229

could be avoided and by illiteracy that spoils their living, there is plenty to challenge the Christian social conscience"; "Christian living requires all that is best in every man. It takes no strength of character to reject its discipline and its challenge."

A Touch of Humour

During his preaching tours as Vice-President he travelled with senior staff members from the Methodist headquarters in Westminster Central Hall. There are many stories told of his encounters. Kenneth Greet, one of his companions, tells of a conversation in the hotel where they were staying. George was always ready to talk, but found one of the men staying at the hotel difficult to engage. He was a Yorkshireman and distinctly not talkative. A transcript of the attempt to engage him in conversation will show much of George's humour and humanity:

> *George*: Do you come from Wales?
> *The silent man*: No!
> *George*: Ah! A pity! Where from then?
> *The S.M.*: Hull!
> *George*: Spelt with a "u" or an "e"?
> *The S.M.*: A "u".
> *George*: Are you a Methodist by any chance?
> *The S.M.*: No!
> *George*: Oh! I think you'd better become one then, or else it might be spelt with an "e".

It is not recorded whether that broke the ice. Probably not, but it is vintage George. His sermons too had their flashes of humour on the most serious subjects. The humour and the passionate preaching continued all his life. He has an irrepressible humour and many are the stories told, but the best of them belong to the time when he was Speaker of the House.

Selwyn Lloyd Resigns

One of the most difficult times for humour, and even for preaching, was during the 1975 election. He was not yet Speaker, and therefore had to fight an election against stiff opposition. He survived, but as he commented afterwards, "It was a dangerous task fighting an election as Deputy Speaker in 1975. This was the biggest hurdle I had to surmount."

He knew that his time as Deputy Speaker and Chairman of Ways and Means could be crucial to his future. He was in a sense on trial. There was no guarantee that when Selwyn Lloyd retired, he would be chosen by the House as its Speaker. The choice lay with the House and the leaders of all the parties had a say. The Prime Minister had no more influence than the leader of the Opposition or of the Liberals. The way he behaved as Deputy Speaker would influence the decision more than anything else. One row in the house which he could not contain might ruin his chances. But he was experienced by now. His work in Committees of the House, his chairmanship of the Welsh Grand Committee, his long experience of the ways of the House (more than thirty years a member) all made it much easier for him to win the support he needed. Most of the House saw him as the natural successor to Selwyn Lloyd. But when would Selwyn Lloyd go? It was a tantalizing time. For a full year before he finally resigned Selwyn Lloyd kept saying that he had had enough and was going to retire. He was emphatic in June 1975—"after the summer recess". Came October, and he said, "Certainly at Christmas." In early December, he said he had changed his mind and would not retire after all. At last, he retired from office on 3rd February 1976.

CHAPTER FIFTEEN

◆◆◆

Speaker Thomas

T HE RETIREMENT of Selwyn Lloyd from the Speaker's Chair
was announced to the House of Commons on Friday, 23rd
January 1976, and he fixed the date of his retirement as 3rd February.
Thus for ten days, George Thomas waited—"probably the longest
ten days of my life". He was the prime candidate, but nothing is sure
in politics and nobody had the Speakership in his gift. Each party had
to decide. The first to inform him was the leader of the Scottish
Nationalists, Donald Stewart, accompanied by the party's chief whip.
Other parties followed until he was confident that he would be
elected. On that Tuesday, 3rd February, Selwyn Lloyd would be
praised for his service as Speaker and a new Speaker would
be elected. George followed the procedure to the letter. He wore a
formal morning suit and sat on the third row behind the government
front bench. Jim Callaghan sat beside him with the friendly words,
"We sat next to each other on our first day in this House. This is
your last day on these benches so I will sit next to you again." It was
a gesture of friendship which George appreciated. He was proposed
by George Strauss, the Father of the House, and seconded by Sir
Derek Walker-Smith, the senior Conservative backbencher. The
House was crowded and it was a moment of intense excitement for
George—"I was on fire inside", he recalls—as the proposer and
seconder came to drag him to the Chair. He was supposed to be
reluctant and Jim Callaghan threw his arms around him to prevent
him going. Such play-acting had gone on for centuries when a new
Speaker was elected. George's humour did not desert him as he asked
Jim to let him go: "I want to look reluctant, but not too reluctant." He
went to the Chair and made his acceptance speech with a full heart
because, as he said, "I knew the House and I loved the House. We
had shared a good many laughs there and the House was very kind
to me." It was the happiest moment of his life, the pinnacle of his

ambition. At the moment of the Speaker's election the bells of St Margaret's church pealed out a joyful sound.

That night he gave a private dinner party which included Cledwyn Hughes, Jim Callaghan and John Morris "who had taken my job in Wales". But this was a night for goodwill and George always enjoyed that.

The Speaker's Chair

The office of Speaker is rooted in antiquity and weighed down with dignity. Philip Laundy's masterpiece on *The Office of Speaker* begins his history of the House of Commons premier office by quoting the sixteenth edition of Erskine May's *Parliamentary Practice*: "The Speaker of the House of Commons is so essential a piece of machinery that without him the House has no constitutional existence."

The office came into being because the early Commons, under pressure from the monarch to provide him with ever more supplies, felt the necessity to have a spokesman who would convey their decisions to the king. Because he would speak for them, they resolved to call him the Speaker. As they were also aware of the dire troubles that could beset the purveyor of unwanted news from the Commons to the monarch, it was resolved that the entire House would accompany the Speaker to make sure that he did not dilute the strength of their message. To this very day, whenever the Speaker is called upon to convey a message from the Commons to the Queen, he is invariably accompanied by the leader of each party in the House of Commons. This usually applies nowadays for ceremonial purposes. For example, when Speaker George Thomas had to convey to HM The Queen the congratulations of the Commons on the birth of Prince William, who was in direct line of succession to the throne, he went to Buckingham Palace accompanied by an entourage of leaders of parties in the Commons.

Within the Commons itself, the Speaker is pre-eminent. When he rises, whoever may be addressing the House, sits down. In every way the Speaker is treated with overwhelming courtesy, and his word is accepted as a parliamentary ruling. If a Member of Parliament feels strongly that the Speaker has been in the wrong, his recourse is to table a motion which amounts to an expression of no confidence.

This has either to be given speedy attention through debate in the Chamber, or withdrawn from the order paper. In modern history there is no precedent of a Speaker losing the vote on a motion criticizing his judgement.

The Speaker may get elected after a contest in the House, as did both Speaker Morrison and Speaker Selwyn Lloyd, but once elected to the office, he receives the wholehearted support of every party in the House. Even if the political party to which the Speaker belonged before his election to office is ultimately defeated at the polls, he is hopeful of re-election to the Chair. Once he wears the wig, no one any longer thinks of him as a party protagonist.

For two centuries the Speaker has been drawn from the majority party in the Commons. Thus the first three Speakers under whom George Thomas served as MP were previously Conservative MPs. In 1945, following tradition, the Labour Party re-elected Speaker Clifton-Brown to the Chair. When he retired at the general election in 1951, a Conservative majority voted William Shakespeare Morrison into the Speaker's Chair. Labour were furious because it was felt that it was time for a Labour MP to be elected Speaker, and they had submitted the name of Major Milner for that office. He had given faithful service as Deputy Speaker and Chairman of Ways and Means from 1945 to 1951, but the Tory majority carried the day. When the time came for Speaker Morrison to retire, the Conservatives still had a majority in the Commons, so Conservative Harry Hylton-Foster QC, MP was duly elected.

Speaker Hylton-Foster died in office, when Labour was in power, so Horace King was elected as the first Labour Speaker. Because the Speakership is such a highly coveted office it is natural for the party with sufficient votes in the House to select one of their own MPs to fill the post.

None the less, there is always much discussion between Government and Opposition before any name is submitted for election. Thus at the end of the day whoever gains the majority votes will be acceptable to both sides of the House.

The custom has been that when a member has been elected as Speaker, he is returned to Parliament unopposed at the general election. The Conservative and Liberal parties have unfailingly followed this custom throughout this century, but the Labour Party officially opposed the re-election of Speaker Clifton-Brown in the 1945 general election and that of Speaker Morrison in 1955. Speaker Selwyn Lloyd was officially opposed in 1974.

Speaker Horace King and Speaker George Thomas were more fortunate. Both Liberal and Conservative parties respected the parliamentary convention of not putting candidates into the Speaker's constituency.

The Speaker enjoys autocratic power, and yet is servant of the Commons. He is given immense authority, such as selecting which members may participate in a debate, and also selecting which amendments may be discussed on the Report Stage in the House. He holds serious disciplinary power. He is housed in handsome state rooms and wears the same Speaker's garb as that worn by Mr Speaker Onslow in the eighteenth century. All this is to remind members that although he is of them, he is not with them.

Even the Speaker's Chair is designed and placed so that he is clearly seen to belong to no particular side of the House. It is situated in between the Government and the Opposition benches, and there are four steps for Mr Speaker to climb so that he has a clear commanding view of the entire House of Commons.

What Kind of Man?

When Sergeant Yelverton was elected Speaker in 1597, he attempted an answer: "a man big and comely, stately and well spoken, his voice great, his carriage majestical, his nature haughty—and his purse plentiful." Such a definition would rule out George on many points. In six hundred years the ceremony has changed little, but the kind of man required is very different. The plentiful purse is no longer needed and the estimate of influence has changed. George Thomas is not a big man, although he is comely and well-spoken. A Welsh accent has also helped him. His voice is strong enough, but not used to shout members down by its sheer volume.

He quickly took to the ceremony and his carriage on state occasions is indeed "majestical", but he is not by nature "haughty". He brought other gifts which are not mentioned by Yelverton. The House liked him and he was fair in his dealings. Although he had strong views and no one doubted his loyalty to the Labour and socialist ideal, he had friends across the parties and was popular with many different factions. They had seen him chair Committees of the House and he had replaced the Speaker on Budget days. He had a sense of humour which he liked to use at his own expense, but never to put people down. Fairness and respect were two of his greatest qualities, spiced with a kindly humour, with the joke often against himself.

One of his eminent predecessors, Speaker Onslow, who retired in 1761 after thirty-three years' service, put it in a way that George Thomas would have approved:

> When I began my duties here, I set out with a Resolution, and Promise to the House, to be impartial in every Thing, and to show respect to Every Body. The first I know I have done, it is the only merit I can assume: if I have failed in the other, it was unwillingly, it was inadvertently; and I ask their pardon, most sincerely to whomsoever it may have happened—I can truly say, the giving satisfaction to all has been my constant Aim, my Study and my Pride.

It was this Speaker on whom George Thomas set out to model himself.

"Mr Speaker, do call us by name"

George Thomas was not the first Labour member to become Speaker, but he was the first representative from Cardiff in four hundred years to be chosen for the office and only the second MP selected from a Welsh constituency. The first Speaker to be selected from a Welsh constituency was Sir John Trevor in 1685, and he set a precedent which has been followed ever since. It was to call members by name rather than to point at the member he had selected to speak. The reason in his case was because of a double squint. For three hundred years, the Speaker had pointed at a member who had caught his eye, giving him permission to speak, but Sir John's double squint often made members feel they had been called when he was really calling their neighbour. This happened so often that the Commons became angry and shouted, "Mr Speaker, do call us by name." The practice gave the Speaker the unique right to call members by their names rather than after their constituencies or some other way which might avoid using their name. Members address each other as "The honourable member for Paddington", or "My honourable friend", or, if a serving officer, as "the honourable and gallant member for . . ." or even "the honourable gentleman from the party opposite." So an ability to match the names to the faces was essential. This calls for a prodigious visual memory by the Speaker. George Thomas had a very good visual memory, but even he would spend time every morning looking at photographs and memorizing names and faces. He never forgot that quite early in his time as MP he had been called by the wrong name.

Above all, the Speaker had to keep his cool and make good use of his sense of humour. The oft-repeated story of George's rich lilting accent was told around the table many times. "When a Scottish nationalist Member complained that she had not understood a word spoken by a Labour member because of his thick Liverpool accent there was a roar of protest from other regional Labour MPs. It dissolved into appreciative laughter as the Speaker almost sang the lines, "There are many accents in this House. I only wish I had one myself."

Approved by the Queen

The House had elected him, but before he could function, his appointment had to be approved by the Queen. On the following day, 4th February, the Speaker-elect went to the House of Lords with Black Rod and the Serjeant at Arms who carried the mace in his arms, indicating that George was not yet Speaker. With appropriate courtesies he faced the Lord Chancellor, Lord Elwyn Jones, and history was re-enacted. Both Speaker and Lord Chancellor were of the same age, both Welsh, both Labour, but with very different educational backgrounds. They had entered the House together, but Elwyn Jones had represented Plaistow in the East End of London (later his constituency was changed to West Ham South). He was a barrister and had played a leading part in the Welsh judicial circuit. He had also been part of the prosecuting counsel in the Nuremberg Trials. George's mind, however, was not on Nuremberg as he bowed at the appropriate time and said: "My Lords, I have to inform your Lordships that her Majesty's faithful Commons, in obedience to the Royal Command, and in the exercise of their undoubted rights and privileges, have proceeded to the election of a Speaker, and that their choice has fallen on me. I therefore present myself at your Lordships' bar and submit myself with all humility for Her Majesty's gracious approbation."

Lord Elwyn Jones, as Lord Chancellor replied: "Mr George Thomas, we have it in command from Her Majesty to declare Her Majesty's entire confidence in your talents, diligence and sufficiency to fulfil the important duties of the high office of Speaker of the House of Commons to which you have been chosen by that House; and in obedience to the Commission which has been read, and by virtue of the authority therein contained, we do declare Her Majesty's Royal allowance and confirmation upon you, Sir, as Speaker of the House of Commons."

George Thomas replied: "My Lords, I submit myself with all humility to Her Majesty's Royal will and pleasure, and if, in the discharge of my duties and in the maintenance of the rights and privileges of the Commons House of Parliament, I should inadvertently fall into error, I pray that the blame may be imputed to me alone and not to Her Majesty's faithful Commons."

It thrilled George Thomas that he was now part of a tradition that went back seven hundred years. He marvelled at his inheritance. A miner's son, a schoolmaster from the chapels of Rhondda, a fighter for the just treatment of the poor, the aged and children who were deprived; this man was now to be the voice of the Commons, the Mother of Parliaments. He vowed to himself not to lose his sense of wonder nor his humility before the dignity of his office. He had been raised to great heights, far beyond his dreams, and that was a tribute to a tradition of democracy that had endured. There were many, particularly in his own Labour Party, who were impatient with the ceremony and tradition that enshrined for them the centuries of privilege and oppression. George was as opposed to injustice as any of them, but he accepted humbly and with admiration the traditions which had endured for centuries and he admired a system which could put a man without privileges at the very apex of the Commons.

Several of George's friends on the Labour benches tried to persuade him to refuse to wear the two-centuries-old type of garb that Speakers of the House of Commons wore. But he was a traditionalist to his fingertips and resolutely declined to change the style of Mr Speaker's costume.

Equally he was under pressure not to accept the hitherto lonely role of the Speaker, by which he would neither take his meals in the members' dining room, nor frequent either the members' smoking room or the members' tea room. His left-wing friends wanted him to behave just as any other member of the House.

Two years as Deputy Speaker had convinced him that isolation for the Speaker was one of his greatest assets. He escaped all the pressures of individuals seeking to be called in key debates. He also avoided being caught up in any party intrigues. His personal views on red hot issues could not be sought. The strict impartiality which everyone expected of him required the Speaker's isolation upon which the House of Commons had decided centuries earlier when it provided him with accommodation in Speaker's House.

The Work Begins

The day after his visit to the Lords, he walked in procession as the Speaker for the first time from the Speaker's House to the Chamber of the Commons. The procession was led by the Serjeant at Arms, with the mace now on his shoulder, signifying that now he led the fully approved and accredited Speaker of the House. Now, George Thomas really was Mr Speaker. As he left Speaker's House in robes and full-bottomed wig, to his surprise, he saw the entire length of the library corridor lined on both sides with members who bowed as he passed. It was a genuine welcome to the new Speaker whom they had chosen and George was greatly moved. He entered the central lobby and proceeded to the Speaker's Chair, passing crowds of visitors and members, as nervous as any schoolboy on his first day at a new school. And he was not entirely comfortable at being the centre of such attention. For one thing, you didn't dress up like that in a Methodist chapel, even when you were Vice-President of Conference. His own words convey his feelings best, as he remembered them years later:

> My legs felt as if they had turned to wood and I was terribly self-conscious. I do not think I will ever forget the moment I climbed those three or four steps up into the Chair and realized that the buck stopped there; that it is all right to have ambition, to have that wig put on your head, but there are responsibilities that go with it. I had been a Member of Parliament for thirty-one years but there had been no other moment like the first time I sat in the Chair as Speaker.

Until then, as Deputy Speaker, he had had responsibilities, but there was always a final reference elsewhere. If members complained that they had not been called, he could refer to the list prepared by Selwyn Lloyd. Now, he must stand on his own.

A Man Set Apart

The Speaker is far more than a chairman; he is the embodiment of the House of Commons itself. The Prime Minister and the government of the day represent power, but all—including the Prime Minister—must give way to the Speaker in Parliament. His official dress is that of a judge and there are times when the House of Commons is a judicial court. The superior position of the Speaker is bound to the constitutional doctrine that the legislature must take precedence over the executive.

The Speaker becomes a man apart. He is different from other members. He withdraws from these places where other members meet. He takes up his official residence within the Palace of Westminster in the stately accommodation beneath Big Ben. His dress sets him apart, but it is far more the attitude of other members towards him that creates a sense of restrained awe around him. The Commons have access to the monarch through him.

All that we know of the popularity of George Thomas, his enjoyment of friendly conversation and his warmth of greeting, makes it difficult to believe that such a post was designed for such a man. It must have been a great strain for him to be a man set apart. Yet, he played his role magnificently and became one of the great Speakers of the House.

Trying to Get at the Speaker

It is of considerable importance that the Speaker should be, and should be seen to be, totally impartial. That did not prevent many members from trying to influence him in their favour. He held considerable power, in that he could call upon members who asked to speak, or not call them. He quickly made it clear that he could not be influenced by angry letters, many of which he received from members who had not been called. He also dealt with those who tried to cause an uproar in the House when they were not called, by

The Secretary of State for Wales, descending Nantymoel Pit, 1966

With H.R.H. the Prince of Wales
at the Centenary Dinner of the Western Mail at the Savoy Hotel

Malawi, 1967. Dr. Hastings Banda, Life President, sits in isolation

En route to Caernarvon
Castle for the Investiture
of the Prince of Wales,
2 July 1969

H.M. The Queen
visiting Cardiff

The Wilson Cabinet, 1968

Receiving the Freedom of Rhondda, 1970

Preaching a New Year Sermon in the City of London, 1980

Fund-raising for a Christian charity with Cliff Richard

The first photograph of the new Speaker, 3 February 1976

Prime Minister Harold Wilson at George Thomas' first
reception in Speaker's House, February 1976

The only two Welsh MPs to be elected Speaker – George Thomas
and his seventeenth-century predecessor, Sir John Trevor

George Thomas returns to Parliament following treatment for cancer, 1989

Holding court at his eightieth birthday celebrations, Cardiff City Hall, 1989

"A grandpa for all the children"... birthday greetings in Bridgend

pointing out that such behaviour would disincline him to call them. His skills at maintaining order in the classroom when he was a teacher came in useful! He also kept a register of those who had been called so that he could correct those who complained about never being called. George tells of one member, David Winnick, who demanded to know on what basis the Speaker called members during Question Time. The Speaker does not have to give reasons, but on that afternoon, in a crowded House, it served his interests to do so. He was able to say, with his documents before him: "Everyone who has been called this afternoon has not been called more than once before during Prime Minister's Questions this Session. The honourable member himself has been called four times. I keep a register."

Another problem he faced early was the ugly development of sustained barracking. Selwyn Lloyd had also had to face this. He boasted to George that he had not named or suspended anyone throughout his Speakership. George did not approve of that. For him the dignity of the House was paramount. He spent many hours in his rooms trying to work out ways of dealing with members who disregarded the courtesies of the House. He recognized that sometimes, in the heat of the moment and in a controversial debate, members would say things they regretted, but he would not tolerate behaviour that deliberately disturbed the business of the House. After much thought he decided that he would have to take firm action or the House would spin out of control and parliamentary business become impossible. It was not long before he had to suspend the House in order to save the dignity of Parliament. He also decided that the time would come when, unlike Selwyn Lloyd, he would face the very unpleasant task of having members suspended from the House. He was a firm disciplinarian, but his humour saved him from a grim reputation.

Quite early he discovered that major parties would try to influence his rulings. People from the Opposition as well as from the Government would come to find out what his rulings were likely to be on certain issues and, more than once, he was told that a poor view would be taken if he decided to rule in a certain way. Polite but barely hidden menaces would be hinted at during a friendly conversation in his rooms. George Thomas soon saw that if he took any notice of these he would lose his independence and the integrity of his desired impartiality. He waited for the opportunity to make this clear and it soon came. An influential group from his own party told him in discreet terms what was expected of him in a ruling on which he had reserved judgement. He listened patiently and courteously, but when they had finished, he told them that he was quite prepared to resign if they pressed their hidden threats, but he would then go on to the back benches and from there explain why he had resigned. His words were sharp: "See the door. I do not mind walking out through that door tomorrow, but I will go with my head high. I am not going to be pushed around. And as a backbencher I would tell the House why I had resigned." Within two weeks, he was able to use the same technique and identical language with a group from the Opposition. The result was the same. His comments are: "It is not easy for a Speaker to remain totally impartial and remote from any covert dealings, but if he fails on this, he might as well resign, for his life will not be his own."

Early Troubles

Six weeks after George became Speaker he was invited for tea at Chequers where the Wilson family were celebrating the first birthday of their twin grandchildren. During tea the Prime Minister asked George to stay for dinner because there was something he wished to discuss with him. He gave no indication that it was a major issue, but when the Prime Minister and the Speaker withdrew to the Prime Minister's study, George had one of the greatest shocks of his life.

As they took their seats, the Prime Minister reached into his pocket and took out a sheet of paper. "Read that," he invited George, who felt his colour drain as he realized that he was being shown a statement of the Prime Minister's resignation.

As an immediate reaction he tried to persuade the Prime Minister to change his mind. "Members will fall away from you quicker than the leaves fall in autumn," he blurted out. Harold Wilson was adamant and reminded George that he had told him two years previously that he would retire in 1976, and also that he had renewed this confidential information to George in the previous November. He now said that he had served as Prime Minister for eight years, and that was long enough for anyone in modern conditions. It was time for someone else to take over. He asked George who he thought would win the election to succeed him and received an instant reply, "Jim Callaghan will get it." Harold Wilson agreed, but added that he would remain aloof from the inevitable struggle between the left and right wings of the party. When the Prime Minister emphasized the strict secrecy that must be observed until he informed the cabinet on the following Tuesday morning, George Thomas replied, "I hope and pray that there will be no leak. I shall try to forget the whole thing, but who else knows about it?"

"The Queen," replied Harold Wilson. "You and the Queen are the only ones to know."

"Well," George assured him, "the secret is safe because I know that she will not leak it, and I will certainly not do so."

In the event, it was one of the best kept political secrets of all time. When the bombshell news was released on the Tuesday morning it created a sensation. People were unwilling to believe that it was true. As it became evident that the Prime Minister was indeed going to hand over responsibility to someone else, the universal question was "Why?" No one seemed willing to believe in the simple truth that Harold Wilson had had enough. Investigative journalists frantically sought for some malign reason, but they were defeated.

In the Commons itself, glowing tributes were paid to the outgoing Prime Minister. No one was more magnanimous than Edward Heath, whom Wilson had defeated at the previous general election. Thus Wilson departed with anthems of parliamentary praise in his ears.

As time passed, the miracle of the secret concerning his resignation intention became even greater, for it became known that both Joe Haines, the Prime Minister's media spokesman, and Marcia Williams, his private secretary, had also been in the know. Speculation was rife in the Commons about other leading members of the cabinet having received similar confidential advice as that given to the Speaker. If that were so, it became even more incredible that such a sensational piece of news could be protected from the media.

The change in leadership of the government resulted in the city of Cardiff being the only city in the United Kingdom to have two of its local Members of Parliament holding respectively the office of Prime Minister and the office of Speaker. Inevitably the traditional tension between the government wanting its own way in Parliament, and the Speaker protecting the rights of minority parties, was reflected in the relations between Jim and George, as they were known in Cardiff. Within a short period of Callaghan becoming Prime Minister, the government lost its majority in the Commons due to by-election setbacks. This put the Speaker in greater difficulty than ever. Tied votes in parliamentary divisions became a commonplace and the Speaker was required to use his casting vote. Thanks to Mr Speaker Denison, who had faced a similar situation in the 1860s, there were good precedents to guide the Speaker.

In the event of a tied vote on the Second Reading of a bill, the Speaker would follow Speaker Denison's action in voting with "the Ayes" allowing the bill to proceed for further consideration. On Report Stage the Speaker invariably left his casting vote to keep the bill as it was when it left the Committee Stage. All this the House of Commons understood and accepted, but when it came to the Third and final Reading in the Commons, tension visibly increased when the voting was close.

Knowing that Mr Speaker's personal opinions on the matter under discussion were never allowed to influence his judgement in giving his casting vote, the Chief Whips could fairly ask him well in advance of the debate, "In the event of an equal vote, which way will you exercise your casting vote?" It was George Thomas's custom to answer all such queries frankly and to give the reason why he would so vote. Mr Speaker Denison, faced with the exercise of his critical vote, on the Third Reading of a bill had said, "This is an important Bill and the House has refused to give it a majority. It is not for me, your impartial Speaker, to make up the mind of the House for you. Hon. Members have failed to give the Bill a majority, and therefore my vote is with 'the Noes'. The Noes have it." Thus the bill was defeated.

The closeness of the strength of the Conservative and Labour parties in the House led to other troubles. At the end of April 1976 an angry Opposition demanded equal representation on the Committee of Selection which decided which members should constitute Committees set up to deal with bills not dealt with on the floor of the House.

A parliamentary storm blew up over the membership of a Committee which was given responsibility for investigating the question of private medicine and pay-beds within the National Health Service. Eventually it was resolved that there should be equal representation, which would give a slight advantage to the Government. Members knew that if an amendment had been carried only by the casting vote of the Chairman of the Committee, it would certainly be selected by the Speaker for consideration at the Report Stage of the bill.

The First Mistake

At the end of a stormy Question Time, Nigel Lawson, the Conservative member for Blaby, requested leave under Standing Order No. 9 (application for emergency debate) to move the adjournment of the House to discuss a matter of urgent and specific importance, namely the action of the Selection Committee.

George then made a mistake. He rejected the application. It was a natural reaction to the atmosphere of the House in which George thought that Lawson was trying to involve the Chair in party disputes, of which there had been many that afternoon. Almost as soon as he had rejected the application he realized his mistake, but it was too late. There were, of course, loud protests. On Friday morning, Nigel Lawson came to see him and complained that he was fully within his parliamentary rights to require such an adjournment. George did not need convincing that he was wrong, but he did more than admit that to Nigel Lawson. He decided he must make a statement to the House. On the next day he confessed to the Commons that "as custodian of the unwritten Constitution, I have made a mistake." He further added that any honourable member under similar circumstances would be entitled to make an application under Standing Order No. 9 for the adjournment of the House. He was not simply acting nobly in admitting the mistake, he was putting the record straight. Hansard carried his words of the previous day and these needed correction, not by the altering of Hansard, but by overriding his actions on the next day. As he said, "I felt it would be unwise to leave uncorrected on the record words I myself regret having used." The debate was held and it was agreed that Government and Opposition should have an equal share on Standing Committees.

The Casting Vote

Labour were committed to achieve the nationalization of the ship-building industry. This bill was therefore a fragile thing from the beginning. It had been considered line by line in the Committee stage and reached the Report Stage when it came before the House as the

Aircraft and Shipbuilding Industries Bill, 1976. Robin Maxwell-Hyslop, the Conservative MP for Tiverton, had made himself an expert on House of Commons procedure. He saw a possible weakness in the bill and raised the question of whether it was hybrid. This meant that the bill did not deal fairly and equally with every shipyard, and should be discontinued. This was a complicated problem for the Speaker—the most difficult George had had to deal with so far. Pressure came upon him from Government and Opposition alike. The Conservatives sent a powerful delegation including the Shadow Attorney General, Sir Michael Havers, and the Chief Whip, Humphrey Atkins, with several front bench spokesmen. Labour sent Michael Foot, then leader of the House, Eric Varley, the minister responsible for the bill, Sam Silkin, the Attorney General, and the men who had drafted the bill for the Government. Both sides argued their case passionately. He was not short of advice. This was a crucial decision and George had been Speaker only a few months. He had sympathy with the bill, because it preserved jobs. But he was not in the dusty area of party politics and was bound to judge impartially. He turned to the Clerks of the House for guidance, but the matter was by no means clear. His decision came after Maxwell-Hyslop pointed out to him that the bill read, "For the purposes of this Bill a ship is anything that floats and has a hull." Maxwell-Hyslop then provided a picture of an oil rig which had a hull and floated. Yet oil rigs were not included in the bill, the shipyards which built them were not to be nationalized. There was sufficient evidence to show that the bill was hybrid. Even if there had been doubt, the precedence of Speakers' rulings in the past confirmed that if there was any doubt, the bill should go to the examiners. George fell back again on the precedent of Speaker Denison in the 1860s, but it was a hard decision. If he had been in the government he would have argued passionately for the bill, although perhaps he would have been more careful with its drafting. He knew that the bill would keep many shipwrights and boilermakers in employment. The trades unions wanted it. Eric Heffer came to see him and argued that if he ruled against the government he would make thousands unemployed. This he knew, and it struck at the heart of all his humanitarian instincts, but he had to keep to the rules of the House.

After two days, he gave his ruling as Speaker. The bill was hybrid. He knew that many of his former colleagues would feel betrayed, but

Harold Wilson, passing by the Chair, commented quietly, "The right ruling and a very courageous one." Jim Callaghan was not so generous, but he was Prime Minister, having enough trouble with his small majority, without George Thomas's conscience to worry about. It did not improve the relationship between the two Cardiff members which was already under some strain.

But the Aircraft and Shipbuilding Bill was not finished with yet. Michael Foot was advised by the Clerk of the House that it was possible to bring a motion that, despite the Speaker's ruling, the government could go on and deal with the bill. For a long time George Thomas felt annoyed that his ruling, so carefully and painfully arrived at, was simply ignored. But that was politics, and Michael Foot was within his rights.

So on 27th May, the House of Commons met to decide the fate of the bill. The scent of battle was in the air. Eric Varley proposed the motion to set aside Standing Orders so that the bill could be dealt with. There was a Conservative amendment that the bill should be sent to the examiners. The debate was bad-tempered, even bitter, and tensions were high. There was obviously going to be a close vote and possibly a tie, in which case the Speaker had a casting vote, and George knew that this vote would be the most difficult to exercise. Again he was asked in private how he might use his casting vote if required. Such a situation rarely occurs and George had been Speaker for less than four months. However, it had happened before, and George went back again to Speaker Denison. In answer to those from both sides who came to search his mind, he simply said that he would follow the ruling of Speaker Denison in the 1860s in both the amendment and the motion. This he did. Denison's ruling was clear for a Third Reading tied vote.

After a noisy debate, the voting on the Conservative amendment took place and then the House subsided into silence awaiting the result. It was a tie: 303–303. As George stood up to give the casting vote, Neil Kinnock called out, "Vote Labour, George." The House roared with laughter, but George was not amused. He explained calmly that he would follow the precedent of Speaker Denison. He explained that Denison had said that if the House had not given a majority it should not be carried by the presiding officer. It was of vital importance to George that it should be made clear that he was not voting upon party grounds, but following the custom of the House:

"For this reason my vote has to go with the Noes and I declare that the Noes have it," he stated. This meant that the Conservative amendment had been lost. But it also meant that if there was a tie on the voting for the bill, which was to follow immediately, the bill would also fall.

If the House had been noisy before, it was positively rowdy during the debate on the bill. Michael Foot angrily referred to the damage a vote against the bill would do to the House's reputation: "Nothing could do more injury to the House of Commons than for people outside to hear that the jobs of workers in the shipbuilding and aerospace industries are put in jeopardy by a semi-drunken Tory brawl." He was made to withdraw the offensive remark but his words illustrate the temper of the House.

When the voting was announced, to George's surprise the Government won on one vote—304 to 303. This seemed an impossible result in view of the previous vote. The House broke into pandemonium. Labour members sang "The Red Flag", "We'll keep the red flag flying *here*", with an emphasis on the last word. Michael Heseltine, who had been leading the fight against the bill, was beside himself with anger. While other Conservatives gave the Nazi salute to express their opinion of the Labour Party, he suddenly grabbed the mace and waved it over his head. James Prior wrested it from him and replaced it on the table. A most disorderly House; the Speaker suspended the sitting for twenty minutes. He went to his room and sent for the Clerk. The Leader of the Opposition, Margaret Thatcher, sent a message to say that Michael Heseltine would apologize at once. George showed great discretion and saved a nasty scene. He said he would not receive any apologies that night. He intended to adjourn the sitting until the following day. He knew that if he had received Heseltine's apology with the House in that mood, the Labour side would have demanded that Heseltine be "named", and then a vote on his suspension would have to be taken. The House was very angry and even worse scenes could have followed. In any case, he felt it would have been wrong to "name" Heseltine but not the singers of "The Red Flag".

George Thomas showed great wisdom in allowing tempers in the House to cool. He knew that he could not fairly name only one member. Many had behaved badly. After twenty minutes he returned to the Chamber and remained standing at his Chair. That meant that no one could speak. The crowded House was spoiling for a fight but was rendered dumb by the action of the Speaker, who simply announced that he was suspending the sitting until the following morning because of the scenes of grave disorder.

Next morning, Heseltine took the first opportunity to apologize unreservedly and George would have left it at that, but Eric Heffer rose to say that he hoped the Speaker would make some comment on the incident. In reply George said: "May I tell the House that I gave careful consideration to whether I should make a statement this morning. I have been in the House thirty-one years. I have witnessed many occasions when tempers have become frayed and right honourable and honourable members have said and done things which they regretted afterwards. I hope that the House will remember that any action which undermines the dignity of the House undermines its authority both here and outside."

But for a few grumbles and an attempt to blame the Serjeant at Arms for unseemly language, which George quickly quashed, that was the end of the matter. The House now knew the kind of Speaker they would have to deal with. It was a disgraceful night and George had proved his mettle.

Consequences for Parliament

The unexpected miracle of the 304 to 303 vote led to greater distrust between the parties. George Thomas also suspected that Labour had broken the pairing arrangement they had with the Tories about who should be paired and thus not vote. It looked as if they had smuggled a member into the Division Lobby who had promised a pair with a Conservative who could not be present. Pairing was an old custom of the House and invariably honoured. The Conservatives abandoned the pairing arrangement after the disgraceful night of 27th May. Tempers ran high for the rest of that Parliament and there was a great strain on the Speaker to maintain the fair dealing in the House. This was illustrated over a motion by Margaret Thatcher that the Shipbuilding Bill should be referred to a Select Committee. It was important for the Labour government that there should be a guillotine on the debate. Michael Foot, as leader of the House, came with their chief Whip, Michael Cocks, to enquire how George would vote in the event of a tie, and how he would vote on a guillotine motion. It was the middle of June and George pointed out that only two weeks before he had explained that he cast his vote always according to precedent. Michael Foot was insistent that the guillotine was essential to the government. George consulted the clerks and within half an hour told Michael Foot that in the event of a tie he would vote against Margaret Thatcher's motion, but that he would vote against the government on the guillotine motion. Michael Foot argued but without effect. George would follow the precedent of earlier Speakers, because he was not a party man any more. He was now a servant of the House and of the House alone.

George's comment on this experience of being pressurized by the Labour leader was:

> It became clear to me then that whereas the struggle of my early predecessors had been to protect the rights of the Commons against the monarch, a modern Speaker's struggle is to be independent of the Government. In former days the monarch was the Government, for he was all-powerful. Now the Government is all-powerful and I believe passionately that the Speaker's role is to confine himself to protect the rules of the House and not to take sides in the battle. It was not an easy passage but I resolved to keep my integrity and to vote regardless of any old loyalties.

For his seven years as Speaker, he kept to this, whether the government was Labour or Conservative. And he had experience of both.

In subsequent months there were other pressures from both sides and George soon discovered how lonely the job of Speaker was. He could not yield to pressure and old loyalties tugged at him. But he accepted that, for all its prestige and trappings, the post was a very isolating one. He liked to be liked. It was his nature to please people and he was perhaps over-conscientious. The mixture was an uncomfortable one. The only way to live was to make a decision and then stop worrying. He would worry a great deal before arriving at a decision on vital matters, but then he knew how to relax after he had made up his mind. He also ignored complaints that he was too frequently with his old colleagues. This seemed childish. For example, for twenty-five years he had worked with Cledwyn Hughes, and it was absurd to think he must break off a friendship when he became Speaker. Once he had made it quite clear that he would not bend the rules for his friends, the House put its trust in him and together they faced the storms that were to come. He watched the Callaghan government limp along without an overall majority during his first year of office. It weathered many a storm, and although George was not involved, members from both sides came to Speaker's House to tell him the latest rumours. He was a confidant to many of them as Labour and Liberal made their pact to help Callaghan survive, which he did until 1979, a great deal longer than most expected, including George Thomas.

◆◆◆

CHAPTER SIXTEEN

Mr Speaker Thomas and a Labour Government

T HE SPEAKER of the House of Commons enjoys enormous power within the legislature. For a period of more than two hundred years, he was the First Commoner in the land. He was given this exalted status by William and Mary after the Glorious Revolution of 1688. They felt in need of parliamentary support and exalted the Speaker as the voice of the Commons. This continued until the end of the First World War. Then a change came about because of Speaker Lowther's concern that he should not take precedence over the Prime Minister. David Lloyd George leaped into action when Speaker Lowther expressed his concern in the closing months of his period of office. A Parliamentary Commission of senior Privy Councillors was set up to consider the whole question of precedence. The consequence was that, although the Speaker took precedence over everyone in the House of Commons, outside Parliament the Prime Minister and the Lord President of the Council take precedence over Mr Speaker. In due course, it was Speaker Whitley, Lowther's successor, who experienced the change. After a few months as the First Commoner in the land, he was reduced to a lower status, but only outside Parliament.

In the House of Commons, the Speaker is much more than a Presiding Officer. The dignity of his office is matched by enormous powers over the business of the House. Total authority in the selection of amendments to be discussed in the Report Stage of bills before the House is held in parallel with total responsibility for maintaining order during Question Time and in Debates. Apart from the selected MPs chosen by their parliamentary party to be spokesmen in opening and winding up debates, the Speaker decides which backbenchers are called to participate in the proceedings.

The Speaker's choice of members is watched with care by both sides of the House. Everyone knows that the Speaker wants to be fair, to ensure not only a good balanced debate, but also to persuade backbenchers that they are getting fair play. George made clear that he kept a register of which members he called, how often and how long they spoke. Tension can often reach bursting point when far more members wish to speak in a critical debate than can possibly be called. Some MPs, as they watch the clock ticking remorselessly on, begin to realize that they are unlikely to "catch the Speaker's eye". It is then that interruptions occur, partly out of frustration and partly to get a mention in the media reporting the debate!

When George became Speaker, his former colleagues Oscar Murton and Myer Galpern, who had served as Deputy Chairmen of Ways and Means, remained in his team of Deputy Speakers. They were joined by Bryant Godman Irvine. Subsequently, George also had Paul Dean, Richard Crawshaw and Ernest Armstrong as Deputy Speakers. They were a happy team, who met each day at noon, from Monday to Thursday, when the House was sitting, to discuss the business of the day. Possible pitfalls were discussed and a timetable rota agreed for duty in the Chair. For Committees of the House, a Panel of Chairmen provided support for the Speaker.

George Thomas showed that courtesy and understanding in his dealing with those who came as his guests to Speaker's House. There are two stories he tells of this period which illustrate his courtesy and his sense of humour.

> In my first month I gave a dinner for all the church leaders in the country. They were very distinguished people and had dressed for a state occasion in their various robes and cassocks of different colours. Basil Hume came in, also fairly new to his job, as Cardinal Archbishop of Westminster, wearing a black suit with a black stock and a white collar. He took one quick look around the room and whispered, "George, am I improperly dressed?" When I replied, "Not at all, Basil, you look like a Methodist minister," I think he took it as a great compliment.

The other story concerns the state visit of President Ceausescu of Rumania, who at that time was very much in favour and honoured by the Queen and her government, because of his regular payment of debts. But he was very ill at ease with all the trappings of the state banquets and with the elaborate ceremonies intended to honour him. When he came to Speaker's House, he was still uneasy. George sized up the situation and greeted him with words he did not expect: "You are welcome to the house of the son of a coalminer." When this was translated to him, his face beamed. We did not then know of his brutal treatment of his own people.

"You are invited to Speaker's House"

There are few things George Thomas enjoys more than entertaining. He is the perfect host, whether at the Travellers' Club in London, in the House of Lords or a restaurant in Cardiff. Even when he entertains in a hotel where his guests are staying, he makes them feel that they have been invited to a special place. When he became Speaker, he had the finest house he would ever know for entertaining. There is a long tradition of Speakers' hospitality and George entered into it with enthusiasm. It was his conviction that the House of Commons belongs to the people and that therefore everything connected with the Speaker, who is the official embodiment of the House, should belong to them too. The House has a magnificent dining room and he determined not to use it only for formal official occasions. He delighted also in spreading the table with the Speaker's state silver. There is a story attached to that state silver, which was told by Charles Pannel, MP for West Leeds, in a BBC broadcast beamed to Europe in May 1958:

> Before 1790 the Speaker received part of the fees paid by the promoters of private bills. These, with allowances from the Civil List and other lucrative offices gave him about £3,000 per annum. This was deemed inadequate for the "First Commoner of the Kingdom" and was raised to £6,000. He was also allowed to buy a new service of silverplate up to 4,000 ounces or could take £1,400 in lieu of this and this at every fresh election, whether a new Speaker was involved or the old one carried on. In 1835 the set of plate was bought "to remain the property of the public" and attached to his official residence.

The silver plate was for his own use, but belonged to the people. George Thomas took this seriously and used it when his friends came to dine. It was his house and he invited his friends, and what a lot of friends he had. Stanley Baker, a distinguished film star who was a friend from the Rhondda Valley, came to visit him on the day after his election. George prided himself on the wide range of guests, a great cross-section, he called it: "from the Archbishop of Canterbury to Menachem Begin, from ex-President Nixon to Chairman Hua of China, from Penelope Keith to Sheik Yamani, from policemen to union leaders." They all sat at the great table.

He used these occasions to provide an opportunity for those on opposite sides of controversy to meet in a relaxed and informal way. In his first month of office as Speaker, he decided to take an unprece-dented initiative and to invite each of the party leaders to dine with him in his private apartments rather than in the glittering state rooms. At that time there were eight separate parties in the Commons, which included the various Nationalist parties and the Ulster parties. After issuing the invitations, George began to see the snags and confesses that he had cold feet the night before the dinner party. He suddenly thought how terrible it would be if everyone addressed his conver-sation to him alone and they did not speak to one another. He need not have feared. It turned out to be a thoroughly happy occasion. His own contented remarks after the party were typical: "We live in a wonderful country." "I should have known", he said to himself, "that courtesy and kindness is not the monopoly of any single party." It was a thoroughly convivial evening, during which not a hint of party politics was heard. At the end of the evening, when party leaders were dispersing to enable George to don his wig and gown to do his stint in the Chair, Jeremy Thorpe, then leader of the Liberal Party, said, "We cannot go without telling the Speaker that this has been an historic night; never before have all the party leaders met for dinner with the Speaker alone."

George always looked back on that night as one of the happiest and proudest occasions in his life. That event was a pointer to the way in which Speaker's House would be used during the regime of Speaker Thomas.

It was not long after that David Steel, the Liberal Chief Whip, came almost in tears to say that Jeremy Thorpe had decided to resign. It was to George they went in trouble as well as in entertain-ment.

Another peculiar characteristic of George's time in Speaker's House was the number of children among those who were invited. When he asked a family, he nearly always said, "Bring the children!"

The First Recess

After that stormy night of 27th May, when Labour sang "The Red Flag" and Michael Heseltine waved the mace over his head like a battle-axe, George was very grateful for the short spring recess—only ten days, but badly needed. It also gave him his first taste of foreign travel as Speaker. It was a formal occasion, a response to the visit of a high-level delegation of senators and congressmen to London in celebration of the USA Bicentenary. The British parliamentary delegation, led by Lord Elwyn Jones, then Lord Chancellor, and Speaker Thomas, took with them one of the four original copies of Magna Carta, to be displayed in the Rotunda on Capitol Hill. On his way to Washington, George visited Asbury Methodist College in Kentucky to give the college Commencement address. He received there his first honorary doctorate (Ll.D). He was deeply moved by this award, because Francis Asbury had been one of the two pioneers whom John Wesley had sent out to preach in America. He had also been among the foremost supporters of American Independence among the Methodists in 1776. It was a great distinction that such an institution should award George his first honorary doctorate. Although he was Mr Speaker and would often be honoured as such in later years, in Asbury most people knew little of that. They were honouring a great Methodist preacher who had been Vice-President of the Methodist Conference in England. George was well known to American Methodism. He had preached in every State of the Union except Florida. When asked why he had never preached in Florida, he used to say, "I thought of it as the wealthiest state and that I would not have been welcome there." He added, wryly, "I was wrong on both counts."

It was during the 1976 visit to Washington for the Bicentenary celebrations that George met President Ford in the Oval Office of the White House. George and the whole British delegation were deeply impressed by President Ford and saw no trace of the caricature that the media had invented of a bumbling President always liable to slip up. George found him alert and fully aware of European political issues.

The Commonwealth Speakers' Conference

It was not long after his return from America that George had the pleasure of entertaining Speakers from many Commonwealth countries. In 1976, it was the turn of Westminster to host the Commonwealth Speakers' Conference. He saw it as his good fortune that Westminster's turn fell during his Speakership.

The Fourth Conference of Speakers of Commonwealth Parliaments was held from Tuesday 7th to Friday 10th September. As the majority of the twenty-eight Speakers and Deputy Speakers and nineteen Clerks attending were Presidents (or Chairmen) and Secretaries respectively of their Commonwealth Parliamentary Associations, the conference was a unique occasion. The United Kingdom Branch of the CPA readily accepted responsibility for organizing the conference and George was in his element. The official photograph shows the truly multi-racial nature of the conference.

There was important business and George had his part in this as Speakers shared their problems and developed respect for one another. The Mother of Parliaments was happy with her distinguished offspring and George Thomas felt proud to be the Speaker who, so soon after his initiation, was the host.

On Thursday 9th September, the conference adjourned to enable the overseas guests to spend a day in the country, visiting Penshurst Place, the home of the Rt Hon. Viscount De L'Isle of Dudley, VC, for lunch, proceeding to Chartwell later. There was a state dinner in Speaker's House, when George could indulge his delight at entertaining. The Corporation of London received the conference guests in the crypt of Guildhall, and on the Friday evening at the conclusion of the conference, a dinner-dance was held at the Savoy, with 140 guests.

On the following day, Saturday 11th September, twenty-two Speakers and Clerks with their ladies left London by coach and with a short stop at Queen Elizabeth House in Oxford, reached Stratford-on-Avon for lunch. That night they saw a performance of *Romeo and Juliet* at the Shakespeare Memorial Theatre. On the Sunday, the tour continued with a drive through the farming country of the Cotswolds.

But it was not all entertainment. They were there to do business and the first action of the conference was to elect George Thomas as its Chairman, in his capacity as Speaker of the host Parliament. The experience pleased him and at the conference he formed friendships, some of which he has maintained for the rest of his life. He also learnt a great deal from the subjects discussed. He may have been Speaker of the Mother of Parliaments, but he was not the most experienced Speaker there. A list of the main subjects discussed tells at once how important this conference was for his own education as Speaker:

> Problems of Parliamentary procedure; the Speaker's control of debate; the Speaker as the protector of the rights of Members; Parliament and the Executive; the administrative responsibilities of the Speaker and the provision of services to Members of Parliament; Parliamentary machinery for the redress of public grievances; the experience of various Parliaments in the broadcasting of Parliamentary proceedings by Radio and TV; and the functioning of Parliament in a bi-cameral system.

Of course, many had much more to learn than George. He had the long tradition of the British Parliament behind him and thirty years of working within it as a Member of Parliament and a minister. There were Speakers there whose Parliament was quite young and who had little political experience. For them this conference was invaluable even if they could not always put into practice back home the grand ideas they had talked of in the conference.

There is no doubt that George Thomas grew in stature during this conference. He already had experience of Commonwealth countries and had admired the way in which Parliamentary systems of government had grown up in former British territories. But now he was talking with his colleagues about common problems, which he recalled in subsequent months.

Sir Roy Jack, MP, Speaker of the House of Representatives in New Zealand, could tell of tough problems in controlling debate and also express his views on broadcasting parliamentary proceedings; Speaker Jerome of Canada was able to outline the differences in a bi-lingual Parliament; India's Speaker outlined problems of different languages and cultures; Malawi was clearly totally subordinate to the forthright Life President, Dr Hastings Banda.

The Speakers' Conference served as a morale booster for persons who normally have lonely existences in their own Parliaments. It also provided an opportunity for discussion on problems likely to place any Speaker in great difficulty. A common anxiety, which George noted, in every parliamentary democracy, was where and how the Speaker resists pressure either from Government or Opposition, seeking to influence his rulings.

An Early Attempt to Introduce Devolution

Nothing quite so dramatic as Michael Heseltine's antics in the House occurred during the next session of Parliament, but the Labour government did make it clear that they wanted to introduce devolution for Scotland and Wales. Denis Healey confessed that during a visit to Scotland he began to see the high quality of the Scottish socialists and felt some sympathy with the Scottish Nationalists. His former commanding officer, Brigadier Reggie Fellowes, was an ardent supporter of the Scottish Nationalists. The quality of the Labour Party and trade union leaders in Scotland was very high. Even those who were really Communists were level-headed and dedicated to those they represented. There was a general feeling among the Scots that Scottish affairs were not properly understood in England.

Meanwhile in Wales, Plaid Cymru won its first seat in the general election of 1974. The Labour Party was divided, and an unsuccessful attempt was made by the government to introduce devolution in November 1976. It was a disastrous failure. Some Scottish and Welsh MPs, notably Tam Dalyell and Neil Kinnock, opposed it as the thin end of a wedge which would end by splitting both the Labour Party and the country into fragments. Some of the leaders of the Labour Party in Scotland were opposed to devolution for the same reasons. There were also many Labour MPs in north-east England and Merseyside, who thought that devolution in Scotland and Wales would divert resources from their own regions, and even create a disruptive demand for devolution elsewhere. In December 1976, those Labour MPs opposed to devolution were joined by the Tories to defeat the attempt.

The defeat did not displease George, although he was no longer able to take part in the debate.

Following the Speaker's long tradition of impartiality on issues before the House of Commons, George consciously endeavoured to ensure a fair hearing for the minority of Welsh MPs who were fiercely advocating major devolution of political powers to a Welsh National

Assembly. He was very pleased when both Dafydd Wigley, and Dafydd Ellis-Thomas made known the fact that their former adversary, Speaker Thomas, had given them the opportunity to fight for their cause. They let everyone know that they had received a fair deal from the Speaker.

Emergency Debates

One of the most difficult decisions for any Speaker to make is whether or not to grant an emergency debate. It is usually the Opposition which asks for it, because it gives them a further opportunity to attack the Government on some aspect of its policy or the failure of its action. Requests came with increasing pressure, but George very rarely granted them. In 1977, when Alex Lyon, the Labour MP for York and a former junior minister at the Home Office, asked for an emergency debate, he pointed out that in George's first year as Speaker, he had granted only four such requests and they had all been on the Tory side. On that occasion the issue was settled by Michael Foot, the Leader of the House, in a way that did not increase George's opinion of him. He felt it personally, because, as he said, "If he [Michael Foot] felt that he could escape from any difficulty by planting his responsibilities on me, he never hesitated to do so."

It was a very stormy Parliament and Prime Minister Callaghan was hanging on with a slender majority and a divided party. Only by a pact with the Liberals could he be sure of getting his measures through, and the government began to disintegrate.

The Silver Jubilee

It was said that Harold Wilson's election in 1966 was greatly helped by the fact that England won the World Cup that year. If so, Jim Callaghan might have counted upon the prestige of the Silver Jubilee of the Queen's accession which fell in 1977.

The House of Commons had voted to present a Loyal Address to the Queen and to congratulate her on her twenty-five years on the throne. As Speaker, representing the voice of the Commons, George laboured at putting into words what he thought was the feeling of the House, but that was not his most perilous labour. Both Houses of Parliament were assembled in Westminster Hall on 4th May 1977 and the Speaker read the Loyal Address on behalf of the Commons, while the Lord Chancellor, at that time his friend Elwyn Jones, did so on behalf of the Lords. It was not a private ceremony. Both Houses were there to see and hear what their "voices" said. This meant involving George in a most difficult operation. He had to dress in the Speaker's robes, of course, and they were centuries old, made for a much bigger man. In that heavy uniform, like David in the armour of Saul, he had to kneel and present the Queen with the Loyal Address, then rise and take three steps backwards.

He practised this complicated and dangerous manoeuvre four times and fell every time. A piece would have to be cut out of the state robes. The very thought sent horror into the minds of his staff. He could not do it. On the day of the ceremony, he rose early and said his prayers with deep feeling! He was nervous about the speech, which he rehearsed most carefully, but that was nothing to the precarious movements that he had to make in his oversized robes. He rehearsed with grim determination on a stool in his own apartments, with his train bearer, a former marine, taking the part of the Queen. He still stumbled until he found that he could make the movement without tripping by clutching a great piece of the gown in one hand and throwing it backwards as he rose. He succeeded in getting through the ceremony with perfect decorum and not a stumble in sight, but he thought he noticed that the Queen looked anxious as he proceeded. He wondered if someone had told her about his predicament.

George was told that if he issued an invitation to the Queen to dine with him in Speaker's House, it would not be unacceptable. He issued the invitation through the proper channels and it was accepted. The Queen came to dinner at Speaker's House—the first time a monarch had dined there for 150 years. Every living former Prime Minister who had served in her twenty-five years reign came: Harold Macmillan, Alec Douglas-Home, Ted Heath, Harold Wilson and Jim Callaghan. George's pleasure comes through in his description of the evening:

> The Queen was relaxed and gracious and I believe she thoroughly enjoyed herself. She stayed at least half an hour over the time stipulated for her return. Harold Macmillan who was holding court with Margaret Thatcher and James Molyneaux, was reluctant to go, enjoying telling stories of Churchill as Prime Minister when he, Macmillan, served in his Government. That night was probably the most glittering night in Speaker's House and I was glad it happened in my time.

He then made a comment which illustrates his consistent view of the Speaker and the Speaker's House, as belonging to the people: "I have often thought that the fact that the Queen herself came meant that everybody else realized that Speaker's House belonged to the country."

The Jubilee celebrations continued through the summer, with a spirit of carnival throughout the land. A highlight of the celebrations was the service in St Paul's Cathedral, in June, fully covered by television and relayed to many countries. George rode to the service in the Speaker's coach, given to the Speaker by King William IV, drawn by Shire horses owned by Whitbreads the brewers. Curious as ever, he enquired about the connection. Some 125 years previously, Speaker Shaw-Lefevre had married the daughter of Samuel Whitbread. He also learnt that the coach had not been used since Speaker W. S. Morrison had been driven in it to the coronation twenty-five years before. The coat of arms of Speaker Morrison had been on the door. So now George's coat of arms was there instead of Morrison's.

He had carefully thought about his coat of arms when he became Speaker. It can be seen in many places today, featuring symbols of the two essentials in George's life that he never wanted to forget. Prominent in the centre is an open Bible, while the crest is a miner's lamp.

When the Queen visited Wales in the course of the celebrations, George was delighted to be there. He wanted to appear in his state robes, to let Wales see their MP, their miner's son, as Speaker with state regalia as in St Paul's, but he was instructed by the Lord Chamberlain that state dress should not be worn. He was disappointed, but obeyed. However he put on record his objection: "I readily accept your judgement in this matter, though I would like it placed on record that I believe the Welsh people would like their service to be given the same significance as the service in St Paul's." Of course, there was no small measure of personal pride in the desire to wear his state robes in Wales.

Conduct of Members

Amid the Jubilee festivities, it began to look as if things were getting better for the Callaghan administration. Inflation was down and there was much work, although unemployment was still too high. The trade unions seemed to have come to an understanding with the government.

July 1977 was a tense month for George in Parliament. There were many late night sittings, although he could always hand over to one of his Deputy Speakers, as he frequently did, to divide the long sessions. On 25th July, for example, he was in the Chair for the beginning of the session at 2.30 p.m. He guided the miscellaneous issues of Oral Questions, leading to an important debate on Rhodesia: then came the beginnings of the discussion of amendments to the Finance Bill which the Deputy Speaker took over until "sixteen minutes to four" in the morning! The immense amount of legislation necessitated these late night sessions frequently. It was a tiring job and the Speaker and Deputy Speakers had to keep their wits about them.

There were some debates which he could not hand over to the Deputy Speaker. Such a one occurred on 26th July, when the House had been up late the night before. A tired House is liable to say silly things and George Thomas, as Speaker, was often prepared to pretend not to hear offensive remarks uttered in the heat of the moment.

The afternoon of 26th July opened in routine form—Oral Questions, mostly on education, in which George must often have wanted to join, followed by a statement by Michael Foot on "Devolution to Scotland and Wales". He listened to a discussion on the statement by the government that it intended to hold a referendum to ensure a separate Assembly for Scotland and then Wales. Francis Pym was the principal antagonist. Remembering the occasion later, George commented, "Pym, a forceful speaker, clean and fair, emerged as the winner", but he could make no comment at the time. He admits that he felt frustrated! The Speaker allowed only forty minutes for the discussion of Michael Foot's statement, "because of the business which is on everybody's mind".

This was the question of the conduct of two members: Reginald Maudling and Albert Roberts. Both were involved in a scandal which concerned a hospital contract granted while Reginald Maudling was Home Secretary. The charge was bribery and corruption by the contractor, Mr Poulson, and turned upon the omission of both members to declare a financial interest when the matter was first discussed.

George explained the procedure and promised that he would

remain in the Chair for the greater part of the debate. Members under attack would normally state their defence and then leave the Chamber. The offence was reputed to have been committed five years before and a Select Committee had examined the evidence and reported. Although there were strictures in the report, it was largely favourable. Reginald Maudling defended himself against the charge that he should have declared an interest when the matter was being debated, by saying that he had told the Speaker, Horace Maybray King, who had thought it unnecessary to declare. Albert Roberts, the member for Normanton, had worked for Mr Poulson and he also put forward his defence, answering some of the points raised in the Select Committee report. Both expressed concern that the Select Committee had not called them to answer those points. The Speaker gave some idea of when he was likely to call for a division and warned members that they must be in the House in time for that. On several occasions, members had complained that they were not given time to get to the lobbies—lifts had broken down, or they were too far away. He also explained that while the Select Committee had asked for Privy Councillors to be given opportunity to offer their expert guidance, he felt the need to allow backbenchers an opportunity and might not therefore call all the Privy Councillors who had asked to speak.

George also departed from tradition by permitting the members concerned to return to the Chamber to hear what was being said about them. He added: "Today's debate is a rare occasion and one of particular concern to the whole House. It is not a party occasion. It is a House of Commons occasion." Reginald Maudling and Albert Roberts returned, but when one of them spoke, a member complained that they should be allowed to listen only. George defended Reginald Maudling, whose intervention had caused the complaint, by saying, that they must be allowed their full privileges as members, adding, "We cannot have a second-class honourable and right honourable member in the Chamber." The debate went on with amendments until 10 p.m. as George had indicated. He then took a series of divisions, wearisome to some members, but each amendment had to be dealt with. Ultimately, the House agreed to "take notice" of the Select Committee Report and no further charges were made against the two members. They were not even suspended for a period, as one amendment proposed and received only thirteen votes. It was all over by 10.55. George had seen it through and then the Deputy

Speaker took the Chair for a debate on sound broadcasting. The debate ended at 2.28 a.m., only because there were too few members in the House to pass anything! The question of broadcasting the proceedings of Parliament by radio was left over to the next session.

The Debate on the Select Committee Report gave George a chance to assert his total authority in the House. Against all precedents, he firmly ruled that honourable and right honourable members who were being criticized by a Select Committee Report had every right to stay in the Chamber and to intervene in other MPs' speeches if they felt it essential for their own defence to do so. Hitherto, MPs under criticism had been permitted to make a personal statement only, and were then required to leave the Chamber.

Parliamentary Language and Parliamentary Privilege

As early as November 1976, George had found it necessary to tell the House that he would not rely on his "legendary deafness" when unparliamentary language was used. He declared that he would take a much firmer line than they had been used to previously. There was much more than a touch of the Methodist in this decision, because he was genuinely offended by some of the language that was being used, as tempers frayed. He stated that if necessary he would not hesitate to order guilty members to withdraw from the Chamber for the day. Parliamentary privilege allows members to speak freely in the Chamber without fear of legal proceedings, but George was determined that this privilege should not be abused, nor standards of parliamentary language lowered.

A particular example was a speech by Ian Sproat, Conservative member for Aberdeen. He alleged that certain Labour MPs, whom he named, were agents of a foreign power. Arthur Latham, the member for Paddington and the Chairman of the Tribune Group, one of those named, raised an objection and George gave his ruling that there was a *prima facie* case for breach of privilege. Michael Foot moved that it be referred to the Committee of Privileges. An angry debate followed in which the Speaker had to call for order as members below the gangway hurled abuse at one another. The turmoil went on for an hour and a half. Twice George threatened to suspend the House. It was almost as bad as the scene when Heseltine had lifted the mace. In the midst of it all, Sir Paul Bryan, Conservative member for Howden, raised, as a matter of privilege, a statement issued by the Socialist Democratic Union (a breakaway group of right-wing Labour supporters in London) accusing thirty-three members of the Labour Party of being under alien influence. This time Michael Foot attempted to prevent the intervention, but he could not. Sir Paul Bryan's complaint went to the Committee of Privileges. Arthur Latham had done no good by raising his motion and members of the Labour Party in general were furious with him for being so stupid. It meant that the House had an opportunity to debate whether or not the Labour Party was under Communist control, or at least influence. There was a real danger that unparliamentary language might be used and George's warning hung over their heads. It was a near thing, but no one was suspended.

On another occasion Eric Heffer described Mrs Thatcher as a "stupid woman". George let it pass, pointing out, however, that courteous behaviour was always required in the House, and hurling abuse at one another added nothing to the debate.

He always came down very heavily on members calling each other liars, and ruled that blasphemy was unparliamentary. This last ruling was made after the word "Christ" had been used.

Usually, these matters could be dealt with then and there, without wasting the time of the House, but there were more serious occasions. One morning, Edward du Cann, chairman of the 1922 group of Conservative backbenchers, protested on the telephone to the Speaker about a statement made by Willie Hamilton the previous evening in the House. Hamilton had described the board of Lonrho as a "bunch of crooks who should be locked up in Brixton prison". Edward du Cann was known to be a member of that board. The offending remarks were made when the Deputy Speaker was in the Chair. Unfortunately, he did not intervene at once, as he should have done, so that the matter could have been settled that evening. Instead it dragged over to the next day when George was in the Chair. At the next sitting, George called upon Edward du Cann to raise his point. Courteously, he ruled firmly that it was unparliamentary to cast any reflection on the honour of a member of the House. Hamilton withdrew his words and apologized. Again, on another occasion when the Deputy Speaker was in the Chair, Reg Race, Labour member for Wood Green, used an offensive four-letter word when he was addressing the House. His excuse was that it was in a quotation. Next morning, George was horrified to find the word emblazoned in the newspapers. He had a message sent to Mr Race requesting him to be in his place in the Chamber at the end of Question Time, when the Speaker would make a ruling on the matter. The Speaker's statement then made it clear that "offensive language" would not be tolerated, even if used under the guise of being a quotation. This ruling will stand future Speakers in good stead.

Another illustration of George's effort to maintain standards was provided by Jeff Rooker, the Labour member for Birmingham Perry Bar, who accused a businessman of improper practices. Outside the House he could have been sued for such a libellous statement, but privilege protected him in the House. The businessman had no right of reply or recourse to law. The Conservatives insisted that the member either justify his claims or withdraw them. Mr Rooker was repentant and agreed to withdraw the allegations. George's advice then was: "If you make a withdrawal, do so wholeheartedly. If you make a wholehearted withdrawal, you will get the support of the House. A half-withdrawal could produce a worse position than saying nothing at all, because it could only mean that you wanted the smear to stay."

George recalls his most embarrassing case of misuse of privilege, in connection with an army colonel in the intelligence service who had been referred to in the criminal court, but not by name. The court ruled that the man's name should not be used in the reports of the trial. In April 1979, Jo Richardson, the Labour MP for Barking, asked for a debate on press freedom and at the very end of her question used the colonel's name. George did not know of the court ruling and wondered why a Conservative member shouted out, "Disgraceful". The House was crowded and nobody raised any objection. Later, three other members repeated the colonel's name. No one rose on a point of order. That evening, George received messages from the newspapers, asking whether they were free to publish the colonel's name. Jeff Rooker said he was going to raise the matter in the House when the Speaker returned to the Chair in the evening. Meanwhile, George was informed that the Director of Public Prosecutions had issued a further warning that the ban on publishing still applied. In the House, a group of left-wing MPs, supported by Peter Rees, Conservative member for Dover and himself a QC, wanted the Speaker to summon the Director of Public Prosecutions to the

Bar of the House to explain his action in apparently overruling the House of Commons. George took the line throughout a stormy debate that it was not for the Speaker to rule what was contempt of court. The whole question of parliamentary privilege was raised, and George said that he would give a considered ruling in the morning. The House was not easily pacified and in particular the Tribune group was angry.

Next morning his ruling was quite clear. He reminded the House that it had been in breach of its own rules, which were that where a matter is before the courts, the House of Commons would not discuss it. He then told the House in no uncertain terms: "The proper course for Members who disapprove of the rule is for them to attempt to get it altered but not to flout it or even bend it. I must advise the House that I will not permit any further identification of the officer nor any reference to the criminal case in which he is involved."

Points of Order and Being Called

The Speaker was very vulnerable to a "point of order" in those days. The procedure has since been revised so that at least when a member wishes to question a matter of parliamentary privilege he must put his question in writing to the Speaker. This now gives the Speaker some protection, which George did not have, but he is still vulnerable. When a member rises on a point of order, it is usual for the Speaker to listen. However, it is possible to tell after a sentence or two whether it is a genuine point of order or a device used improperly. George reacted once to a phoney point of order in direct terms: "It is very interesting that whenever the honourable Member has not been called to ask a supplementary question, he gets up on a point of order and that does not help him." Members who were desperately anxious to be called would find all sorts of reasons in an effort to persuade the Speaker that they had a special claim to be called to speak. One experienced old hand in the House one day stood alongside the Speaker's Chair and whispered, "My grandson is in the Gallery, and he is hoping to hear his grandpa speak!" He knew that George could not disappoint a child. Within half an hour, that honourable member was on his feet addressing the House, whilst George scanned the Strangers' Gallery until he saw a little fellow with a beaming face proving that his grandfather had at least one ardent supporter.

Select Committees

In a lecture on "The Changing Face of Parliamentary Democracy", given at the National Museum of Wales in Cardiff on 14th May 1982, George Thomas, by then an experienced Speaker of the House of Commons, described the changes that had taken place in parliamentary life since the war. He argued that the strength of Parliament was due to its ability to change. This he illustrated with details of changes during his time as Speaker. One of the most evident of these was the way in which Parliament dealt with the enormous increase in the business it had to handle: "Thus the House of Commons from time to time had been obliged to vote enormous sums of money for public expenditure without being satisfied that it had adequately debated the sums required." That was obviously unsatisfactory, and as business increased there would be a danger that power could be transferred, imperceptibly but inevitably, from the Commons to the government, which would spell the death of parliamentary democracy. While a government is appointed to govern, it does so by the permission of the House and is answerable to it, and through it to the electorate.

George Thomas greatly approved of the system of Select Committees, which, in his words, was designed "to ensure that both Parliament and the Government are responsive to the wishes of the electorate". He freely admits from his own experience that neither the civil service nor the ministers were very favourable to that system which added so much to their work. But it preserved democracy. Select Committees are able to cross-examine in searching fashion both ministers and their advisers and the chairmen of nationalized industries. This, he maintains, "brought new tracts of the public sector to be accountable to the House of Commons". In the 1977/78 sessions of Parliament, when George Thomas was in his second year as Speaker, a procedure committee was set up which later recommended twelve new committees to cover the activities of all departments, and of all nationalized industries and all Quangos within the responsibility of the departments. He freely gives praise to the Leader of the House, who by that time was Norman St John-Stevas, for this measure. He regards him as "one of the greatest Parliamentary reformers in this century because he fought to bring power back to the Commons through these Select Committees".

Devolution

In the Queen's Speech on 3rd November 1977, she made it clear that her government would seek to establish directly elected Assemblies for Scotland and Wales. Later that month, Michael Foot announced that there would be only a one-day debate on the Scottish and Welsh Devolution Bills, at Second Reading. At the Report stage in February 1978, amendments made it unlikely that the referendums in Scotland or in Wales would succeed. A principal amendment was that a majority in favour would only be valid if 40 per cent of the electorate voted for it. In Scotland, when the referendum was held on 1st March 1979, there was a majority, but the figures were 33 per cent for, 31 per cent against; 36 per cent did not vote. Consequently it failed. In Wales, as George had repeatedly predicted, although now as Speaker he was bound to be silent, the people voted overwhelmingly against a separate Assembly.

In private conversation with colleagues of long standing, George made it clear that he believed that neither Welsh-speaking nor English-speaking Welshmen wanted a mini-Parliament. He had watched from the protection of his own House the fierce campaign being waged in Wales by Leo Abse and Neil Kinnock, who strenuously rejected devolution. His own previous experience as Secretary of State for Wales had convinced him that the issue stirred no deep emotions with the man in the street in Wales.

It appeared to him that the Callaghan administration was seeking relief from internal dissensions by legislating for the referendums both in Scotland and in Wales. To make the most of the sentimental appeal to Welsh electors, it was resolved to hold the ballot on St David's Day. Such a ploy was doomed to failure. Even those counties where Welsh was the first language gave poor support to the government's proposals.

The Collapse of a Government

These referendums were held when the popularity of the government was at an all-time low, following what came to be known as the Winter of Discontent. Callaghan's advisers had urged him to call the election in the autumn of 1978, but also warned that it would result in another hung parliament. "He was sick to death of the continual compromises required for our survival as a minority government: I think he would rather have lost than be condemned to a repetition of the previous three years," writes Denis Healey. And so Callaghan delayed until he could hold out no longer and by then things were much worse and the prospects of a Labour victory at all were very slight.

By November 1978 the Conservatives were already asking, "Who rules the country?" with "The trade unions" as the implied answer. Labour went from one disaster to another. Until that autumn, they had a chance, even though opinion polls gave the Conservatives a slight lead. The polls also changed around October to give Labour a 7 per cent lead and Jim Callaghan was more popular than Margaret Thatcher. The beginning of the end was on 14th November when by the casting vote of the chairman, the TUC rejected a proposal from the Callaghan administration which could be described as "a helpful statement of guidance on pay". Denis Healey assesses this turning point in Labour's fortunes with characteristic definiteness: "The cowardice and irresponsibility of some union leaders in abdicating responsibility at this time guaranteed Mrs Thatcher's election; it left the trades unions with no grounds for complaining about her subsequent actions against them."

The government had recommended a 5 per cent norm in wage increases, which the unions claimed was too low. By December, although half a million workers had already settled within the government's guidelines, most of the other unions were steadily increasing their demands. Just before Christmas, the Ford Motor Company settled for 17 per cent. This put in jeopardy the Labour motion in Parliament to keep wage rises to 5 per cent. In the event, five Labour left-wing MPs voted against it, and with the Tories they defeated the government.

Strikes hit the country as claims as high as 25 per cent were demanded. The city of Liverpool was in chaos, with the dustmen and the grave-diggers on strike. In January 1979 the TUC joined with the government to draft a sensible guide to negotiating procedures, but by then neither government nor TUC had any power over the strikers.

George Thomas had been quite sure that an election would be called earlier. Even in October 1978, when he was attending the Commonwealth Speakers' Conference in Australia, he returned home after a week because he was advised that he would be needed after a dissolution of Parliament until an election, expected on 28th October. But Jim Callaghan, who alone could decide, plodded on into chaos.

As it became clear that Prime Minister Callaghan was increasingly losing touch with the feelings of voters, George began to realize that a general election would prove disastrous for the Labour government, and yet he felt it could not be far away. As the government was slowly dying, Jim Callaghan sent Michael Cocks to him to say that the cabinet was complaining that too much time was being given to the questioning of ministers after they had made statements in the House. George's judgement was that ministers were under such stress that they felt it necessary to engage in long political arguments every time they were asked a question. His response to the request could not have pleased the Prime Minister or the embattled cabinet. He pointed out that it was up to ministers to be more brief and not to provide a wide target for supplementary questions.

It was unfortunate that when the financial crisis was at its worst, Jim Callaghan was attending a Summit Conference in Guadeloupe. The media did not help him by showing pictures of the Prime Minister under a tropical sun while the people of Britain were suffering from trade union action in a cold British winter. It did not help him either when, asked at the airport on his return about the crisis, he was reported as saying, "Crisis? What crisis?" He was unpopular, as any Prime Minister would have been with the country in such a dismal condition. He was also tired and dispirited. In fact, it was a tired government which George watched from his "neutral" Speaker's Chair. He could do nothing to help his ailing Labour Party as Jim Callaghan limped on into 1979 and to the fatal month of March. The year had started with the referendum on devolution which was a fiasco and continued with constant attacks on the government's policy on defence and its handling of the financial crisis.

The Motion of No Confidence

On 28th March 1979, Margaret Thatcher, as leader of the Opposition, tabled a motion of no confidence in the government. It needed no eloquence to show the failure of the government to govern, and the Tories had a field day. George recalls that, as the voting came and the lobbies were crowded, before the result was known, the atmosphere in the House was charged with emotion. Members followed one after another to tell him that, "The Government has a majority of one", others that it was a tied vote. The tension was almost unbearable.

The tradition is that, after a division of this kind the tellers, who have been counting the votes in the lobbies, each hand to the Clerk their papers with the figures for each lobby. He adds them up and hands a paper with the results to the winning side to give to the Speaker, who will announce the result. When the Clerk of the House handed the paper to the Conservative Whip, a thunderous roar of cheers came from the Opposition. Glum disbelief spread over the government benches.

George admits that his voice trembled as he announced the figures to the excited House. The motion of no confidence was carried by 312 votes to 311. George was relieved that he did not have to cast his decisive vote! But the government was finished. When the result was announced, Prime Minister Callaghan said: "Mr Speaker, now that the House of Commons has declared itself, we shall take our case to the country. Tomorrow, I shall propose to Her Majesty that Parliament be dissolved as soon as essential business can be cleared up."

The House adjourned until 4th April and had cleared the essential business by 9th April.

The Tragedy of Airey Neave

George watched the disintegration of his Labour Party from the eye of the storm. For a loyal Labour man it was tragedy; but nothing like so startling as the tragedy of Friday, 30th March, when Airey Neave was murdered by the IRA in the very precincts of Parliament itself. George had been in the Chair that morning and had then left for Cardiff. There he received a telephone call from his secretary to say that a bomb had exploded in a car in the underground car park of Westminster. Later he learnt that it was Airey Neave who had been killed. In George's comments years later you can feel still the sense of horror and loss:

His death was a stunning blow. Not just because of the awful personal tragedy for the Neave family, who had lost a father and a husband, nor even because Airey himself was on the brink of becoming a powerful figure in the country, but for the inescapable realization that even the seat of democracy was vulnerable to the bombers and madmen.

During the period between the dissolution of Parliament and the return of a new one after the general election, the Speaker is in sole charge of the House of Commons. He is the only one left and stays in office until a new person is elected as Speaker. With this authority at his disposal, George decided that Airey Neave's coat of arms should be put up inside the Chamber, to mark the tragic fact that he had been assassinated on the premises. There are few who would have disagreed with his decision and it was never questioned.

The 1979 General Election

George Thomas waited for the results of the election. His own seat was unopposed by Liberals and by Conservatives, though both the Welsh Nationalists and the National Front nominated candidates against him. In his election manifesto to the electors of Cardiff West, George made it clear that as Speaker he could not enter into a political campaign. His election address carried a message from the Conservative, the Liberal and the Labour parties: each of whom urged the people of Cardiff West to send back the Speaker to the House of Commons. During the general election campaign, George had no public meetings, and at the request of the Cardiff West Conservatives, he nominated the minister of his church as his election agent, so that no flavour of party politics was involved. Fred Tyrell, his faithful friend and agent at several previous general elections, magnanimously agreed to supervise all the arrangements for the preparation and issue of the election address, but made no objection to the substitution of another name as official agent for Mr Speaker's election. Both the Conservatives and the Liberals were well aware that George's Labour friends addressed all the envelopes for sending out the election addresses, but honour was satisfied because the name of Labour's stalwart, Fred Tyrell, did not appear as agent.

On election day, George was ill in bed at Speaker's House, Westminster. He received a call from one of his closest friends in Cardiff who had supported him in every general election since 1945. She told him that tears were being shed because he was not there. George's reaction was typical of the man. Despite the angry protests of his secretary, Sir Noel Short, and of his London doctor, he insisted on leaving his bed and travelling to Cardiff. When he unexpectedly arrived at the Speaker's election committee room, George recalls, "there were more tears, but this time they were tears of joy."

CHAPTER SEVENTEEN

◆◆◆

Mr Speaker with a Conservative Government

GEORGE THOMAS frequently commented on the different ways in which Labour and Tory treated their leaders, particularly when they lost. Jim Callaghan continued as leader of the party after losing the 1979 election and even told Denis Healey, without fear of contradiction, that he would continue for about eighteen months— "to take the shine off the ball" for his successor.

Life is not as easy for a Conservative leader who loses an election. Sir Alec Douglas-Home went quietly and with dignity when he lost. George expresses great admiration for him, "enormous respect and one whom I would like to emulate in many ways". Ted Heath departed after his defeat with more fight. He was voted out by the woman he had appointed to his Shadow Cabinet as Shadow Education Minister in place of the "liberal" Edward Boyle. In 1974, she succeeded him as leader of the party. The speed with which the Conservatives reject a failure led Harold Wilson to comment on the difference. He had good reason to do so, because during the life of his own administration he had become seriously unpopular with the Parliamentary Labour Party because of his ambivalence over the European Assembly. When they grumbled about his leadership it seemed that trouble was unavoidable. At that time, George warned him of the dangers and explained that the trouble was linked with his changing posture on Europe. Wilson replied that the party was split from top to bottom over Europe, and that the leader had to pay the price in order to keep the party together. He then commented: "Our boys talk a lot and threaten a lot, but they never do anything to the party leader. The Tories say little, but their leader is out almost before he knows that he is under attack." George recalled these words, spoken in 1968, when more than twenty years later Margaret Thatcher was forced out. But in 1979, this was far from anyone's thoughts. The Conservatives were back in power and Britain had its first woman Prime Minister.

Margaret Thatcher had proved herself while in opposition. Denis Healey claims to have first spotted her quality when she joined Geoffrey Howe as one of the Shadow Chancellor's team and gave Healey a rough time with his Finance Bill! Once she was party leader there was no holding her. George obviously liked her personally and admired her ability.

She won the general election for the Conservatives on 3rd May 1979. The next step was crucial for George Thomas. Would a Conservative government want to put one of its own people in the Speaker's Chair? Their majority was adequate to ensure that their selection would be accepted by the House. Margaret Thatcher, however, saw the value of a Speaker who was truly impartial and upon whom she could rely to be fair and firm. As leader of the Opposition, she had seen him at work and she liked his work and the Speaker personally. She wanted no change and George continued as Speaker. Prime Minister and Speaker developed a good relationship, both personally and in public. She knew exactly where she was going and she brooked no opposition. In an article in the *Observer* even before the 1979 election, Margaret Thatcher had outlined her method quite frankly. Her government would have in it "only the people who want to go in the direction in which the Prime Minister wishes to go. It must be a conviction government. As Prime Minister I could not waste time having any internal arguments." She was very much against any consensus policy. "To me," she wrote, "consensus seems to be the process of abandoning all beliefs, principles, values and policies. So it is something in which no one believes and to which no one objects."

Although, as a lifelong Labour man, George Thomas disagreed with some of her policies, he could not fail to admire the single-minded purpose of a determined leader, who really believed what she said. Besides, she had been brought up a Methodist!

Far closer than that with the Prime Minister was George's relationship with Lord Hailsham, the Lord Chancellor. Their respective offices brought them into frequent contact and much discussion. It was therefore natural that Lord Hailsham should turn to George in moments of great sorrow. One particular crisis was the tragic death of Lord Hailsham's wife. He was shattered by it and, in his bereavement, he found George to be a good counsellor. His letters illustrate this:

> *18th May 1978*: You are a great dear to write. Continue to pray for me for I am in dire distress. I still hold to my Christian Faith but it is as if the Good Lord had hidden his countenance from me. But amid all the tears of this present darkness I do not cease to thank him for thirty-four years of the humorous, loyal, devoted companionship of my darling wife; my one regret, that I did not realise until I lost her how deeply I loved her. Also my children are beyond praise. Bless you dear George. I value your friendship.

George did not content himself with one letter, but continued to pray for Lord Hailsham and two months later he wrote to him again. Lord Hailsham's second letter shows how much he valued this:

> *18th July*: With all your other preoccupations, to write to your stricken friend was a work of kindness. I hope and pray for a joyful reunion with my beloved and acknowledge my duty to my youngest child. But no day now passes without tears. No night goes by without wakeful hours of mental anguish. She was part of me. We were one flesh, and that part now lies deep underground . . . When I first came back from Australia, I could not bear to see the sun shine, the flowers blossom, the grass grow green. I could not bear to hear the birds sing. What business had they to be happy when my darling wife was dead? I am less desperate now. The tears are less frequent, but I remain as miserable. I am too old to be of use to anyone . . . I am an old watch of obsolete pattern, with a broken mainspring, which cannot be replaced. Blessed are they that mourn, we are promised. For they, we are promised, will be comforted. But when? Pray for me.

These two letters tell us of Hailsham's deep bereavement, but equally they say a great deal about the kind of man to whom they could be addressed.

Lord Hailsham clearly recognized that George was a man of faith and spiritually perceptive. Experience had shown that George listened and understood when a person suffered. These qualities are rare enough in public life and Lord Hailsham knew a treasure when he found one. George's greatest bereavement had been the death of his mother and Lord Hailsham saw him live through that with faith, troubled, but unbroken. The foundations of his faith were not shaken and when Lord Hailsham was bereaved, he needed such a rock.

The close friendship continued over the years. Almost three years later, when George had announced that he intended to retire at the end of the life of that Parliament, Lord Hailsham wrote again:

> *7th March 1981*: I am indeed sad to hear of your impending retirement, I will plead with Margaret Thatcher to postpone the next General Election as long as possible. They all tell me that you have been and are a Great Speaker. But I wish you could teach me the art of not being lonely though unmarried.

Of course George had other close friends, and a wide circle of people whom he delighted to entertain. In a period of less than six months from 28th April to 18th November 1976, he entertained 970 people at Speaker's House! The breakdown into categories of this very high figure is most interesting:

Minister and front benchers	213
Backbenchers	348
Public figures outside Parliament	50
Officers of the House and officials	174
Private and constituency friends	185

Not all of these were state dinners, many were simply coffee or tea at Speaker's House, but they show an immense activity of friendly hospitality, which George so thoroughly enjoyed. They eased the sense of isolation to which his office tended to raise him.

George had no wife with whom to share this magnificent home and his entertainment. Much of his extensive activity was undoubtedly a compensation and a cure for loneliness. He had many friends, men and women, who admired him and enjoyed his company. He was and is one of the pleasantest companions. His own family meant much to him, but by now its closest members were dead. He devoted himself to the care of children as though he would have longed for children of his own. But as in so much of his life, he gave himself lavishly to the needs of many. The loneliness remained, but it found its solace if not its cure in his communion with God, who was very real to him. He did not create a God for his comfort, but found in God the comfort that he needed. Those early morning prayers, when he was alone with God, warmed his heart and enabled him to live through the activities of life without the close companionship of marriage. He knew the answer to Lord Hailsham's comment: "I wish you could teach me the art of not being lonely, though unmarried." Such an art cannot be taught, it must be wrestled for with God.

World Travel

During the parliamentary recesses, George took the opportunity of travelling as Speaker. This meant that he could meet Speakers of other Parliaments throughout the world. But it also meant that he could make contact with Welsh and religious organizations and leaders. It gave him the opportunity to preach internationally and he became well known through many parts of the world as a Methodist and a patriotic Welshman.

The first long recess after Parliament adjourned in July 1979 is a good example of this. He travelled with Lord Parry of Neyland to Canada to share in a united American and Canadian Welsh Singing Festival. After the formalities of welcome on their first day, there was at 9 a.m. next morning the Annual General Meeting of the Welsh National *Gymanfa Ganu*, followed immediately by a delightful Welsh Children's Hour (*Awr y Plant*) in the ballroom. That evening, George was guest of honour at a banquet and concert given at the convention centre by the Hamilton Orpheus Male Choir. At breakfast the next day, a Sunday, he met with representatives of the Welsh American youth. A bi-lingual worship service followed at 10.30 a.m. in the convention centre. The rest of the day was spent with various cultural leaders and groups from *Gymanfa Ganu*, which kept him busy until nightfall. On the Monday, they flew to Ottawa to meet the Speaker of the Canadian Parliament and then on to Toronto for a reception by the Speaker of the Ontario Legislature. That night they flew back to Heathrow and a car took him home to Speaker's House, where many messages and requests awaited him. That was typical of the August and September travel. Holidays, in any sense of the word, were usually left to the Christmas break.

The Wally White Memorial Lecture

In July 1979, before that whistle-stop tour in Canada, George was delivering a series of lectures in Louisiana. A Methodist family had lost their small boy in a tragic accident. Wallace Harp (Wally) White was only two years old when he fell into the family's swimming pool. For almost a year he was in a coma and he died on 21st May 1974. In commemoration of his short life, his parents endowed a lecture series each year from 1978. The first series was given by

Bishop J. Kenneth Shamblin: George agreed to do the 1979 series. The theme for the lectures was "Perspective for Living" and the small hall was surrounded by carefully worked banners with notices which showed the Christian basis of these perspectives. The six banners read: "In the beginning God created"; "Happy is the man who finds Wisdom"; "All things come from Thee, O Lord"; "Let everything praise the Lord"; "Thy law is my delight"; "With thee all get understanding".

For his lectures, George chose the theme, "Human Rights and the Aspect of Law". He drew heavily on his own experiences. He spoke of his emotion in Mombasa when he stood on the steps down which captured Africans had been pushed into boats taking them to slavery in the deep south of America. This emotion he linked with his feeling in New England when he stood on the shore where the Pilgrim Fathers had landed. Then his mind had crossed the Atlantic Ocean to the steps he knew so well in Plymouth, England, down which the Pilgrim Fathers had stepped to the *Mayflower*. Freedom and human rights were expressed in New Testament terms, for each of his lectures was orientated to the Christian faith.

It was in these lectures that his indignation at the poverty that walked hand in hand with excessive wealth in some democracies, led him to declaim that the brotherhood of man is not an ideal towards which we strive, but a fact which is continually denied by our political system. Humour was never far from the surface, even when he dealt with solemn issues. He reminded his audience that it was in the USA, in the early 1960s, that he had been confronted for the first time with doors that opened as you approached them, without anyone holding them open for you. His host, who asked about his impressions, enquired with surprise whether such self-opening doors were not in the United Kingdom. He replied that there "we have old school ties that will open any door at any time, and in any place."

The emphasis which George brought to the Louisiana lectures was that neither colour nor race could be grounds for withholding human rights. Quoting the American preacher, Emerson Fosdick, George claimed that we should look at all people in terms of their possibilities once they are given equal opportunity to grow in stature.

As he argued his case in these three lectures he must have felt that he was once more speaking from the floor of the House of Commons rather than from the limitations of the Speaker's Chair.

The one constant theme in his lectures and his preaching was that no human being is ever unimportant. Every baby born is a VIP. The stamp of God Almighty is on those who make a mess of their life, as much as it is on the sheltered people who never seem to go wrong. The love of Christ has a healing power that can change human beings, so that no one is beyond his reach. The sermons and the lectures always call for complete dedication to the service of Christ, which is caring for people in the spirit that Jesus revealed. Conduct and faith are seen as reverse sides of the same coin. His preaching reveals the source of his political convictions. He has consistently maintained that human rights spring from our divine rights as children of God.

After those lectures, there was Canada, but even then it was not the end of his travels. By September, he was in Dallas, Texas, speaking and preaching. He was not back in Britain until 7th October. Among the many engagements that followed, one was in Edinburgh preaching to the students at the beginning of term. The title of his sermon was, "From the Questioning mind to the Healing touch". "I believe in miracles," he said, "miracles of lives changed and the world, God's world, changed." Although phrased differently and with an approach suited to his audience, it was the same message— "human rights based upon the divine inheritance, children of the King". When he addressed students, he began with their enquiring and questioning minds. They were not to be deceived by magic, but he talked of another kind of miracle, lives changed because, by the healing touch of Jesus, they became aware of their status as children of God.

Even while the House was sitting, he was travelling at weekends and evenings, opening homes for children or old people, encouraging, and appealing for good works, many for children. And on Sundays he was usually to be found in some pulpit, often near or in Cardiff.

The Silence of the Speaker

Mike Graham, in the article written for the *South Wales Echo* on the eve of the ceremony of Freedom of the City of Cardiff in 1975, when George Thomas was Deputy Speaker, records that George surprised himself by the ease with which he could remain silent on provocative issues in the House. Remembering the rebel of thirty years before, that was indeed surprising. But at that time there was a Labour government. The question needed to be asked again after 1979 when Margaret Thatcher was leading a rejuvenated Conservative government. At times, it must have seemed as though she was dismantling the Welfare State for which George and his colleagues had fought a good fight in 1945 and the years that followed. As Speaker he could not join in the attacks by his colleagues upon this policy. But how did he feel? Was he at ease as he remained silent? We have seen that he had a good personal relationship with Margaret Thatcher and that he admired her firm principled approach, although he was still the candidate adopted by the Cardiff West Labour Party and he was now Mr Speaker. Yet he was still a Labour MP. It appears that he sat more easily than he could have done thirty years before. The times had changed and the mood of the country had changed too. George shared in the general reaction against the permissiveness of the 1960s. He regretted the break-up of families and the loss of "family values", which used to provide a moral framework for personal behaviour.

To this day he regrets that one of the unanticipated side effects of the Welfare State was the disappearance of granny and grandpa from the family hearth into the old people's homes. Instead of these homes being a last resort, intended for old people who had lost their partner or those who could no longer care for themselves, George saw families disowning responsibility for their old people in their own home life. Sadly he comments, "The day when grandpa or grandma could make a quiet contribution to family issues seems to have been diminished by the Welfare State." The young MPs of 1945 were already questioning the Welfare State when they were thirty years older, and George was among them.

Margaret Thatcher did not invent "Thatcherism", it was already in the air and she gave political muscle to it. Her insistence that "Victorian values", no longer to be sneered at, would reverse the trend of violence and disorder in society, was a flawed outlook but in those early days, there was a spirit of optimism in the House.

There was also a widespread desire to reduce the role of government in economic and social affairs. There was pressure for people to be self-reliant, less dependent on state assistance. Too many people were thought to be scroungers on the Welfare State and there was a growing dissatisfaction with what was thought to be inefficiency and over-manning in nationalized industries. George did not go along with all this, but he was influenced by the mood of the times.

The National Health Service, adequate pensions, much that Beveridge had written about education, the importance of keeping unemployment low, and many other elements of the Welfare State, continued to have his support. But there were side effects of many measures taken to care for people which caused him concern as they did many others in the Labour Party. At first Mrs Thatcher did not seem to be dismembering the Welfare State. Her appeal for self-reliance, efficiency, hard work, law and order, seemed right. George was not too troubled, and he concentrated on being a good —some were saying great—Speaker.

His wit often broke the silence to encourage a better atmosphere in the House and his winsome authority allowed debate to proceed more sensibly. When, one Question Time, he asked for brevity, his comment was "Yesterday, both questions and answers were inordinately long, and in this place brevity is not only the soul of wit but a mark of wisdom and compassion."

Commonwealth Speakers

At his first Commonwealth Conference in Westminster in 1976, George realized the importance of these consultations which were regularly conducted in different parts of the Commonwealth. He was a member of the Standing Committee of Commonwealth Speakers and Presiding Officers when it met in Nicosia on 4th February 1980. The meeting lasted only a day, but he took the opportunity to stay in Cyprus after the meeting. The Speakers or Presiding Officers at that meeting were from Australia, Cyprus, Great Britain, Zambia, India, Trinidad and Tobago, and Canada. Most of them were accompanied by their clerks, and minutes of the meeting were taken by a remarkable man, Philips Laundy, Director of the Research Branch of the Library of Parliament in Canada. It had been the custom for minutes to be taken by the host country, but after his excellent work in Canada he was soon made more or less permanent minute-taker. Canada was showing a particular interest in strengthening Commonwealth links. She was ever aware of her giant neighbour, the USA, and needed another context of her own. It was at this Standing Committee in Nicosia that it was decided to hold the next Speakers' Conference in Ottawa in April 1981. George's whistle-stop tour of Canada and the stopover in Ottawa no doubt had something to do with this. George was a key person in this Standing Committee and he was building up a network of friends throughout the Commonwealth.

Rumours of Retirement

Despite keeping up his punishing programme, and perhaps because of it, there were signs of weakening health. George had to cancel some engagements and shorten some visits. Rumours began to circulate about his health and imminent retirement. George himself had made no mention of this. On his birthday, 29th January 1980, he acknowledged the birthday greetings of the House and said that he wanted to make a personal statement. He was not asking for more birthday greetings, he said, but he had to speak in reference to an article in the *Times*, to the effect that at the age of seventy-one, Mr Speaker was considering retirement. His words were:

> In view of the article in the *Times* today, it is in the interest of the House for me to make a brief statement to end speculation about my intention for the future. It is but eight months since this House did me the honour of electing me Mr Speaker for the life of this Parliament. That is a trust that I hope to fulfil. I do not want to tempt providence, but I am feeling as fit as when I assumed the Chair. Therefore, it is my intention to continue to serve the House for this Parliament, as it invited me to do eight months ago.

Honourable Members cheered him at this news.

Asserting the Authority of the Speaker

Certainly no physical loss of energy manifested itself while George occupied the Speaker's Chair. With his high sense of the dignity of the House, he insisted upon the ceremonial surrounding the office of Speaker. According to custom, as the procession of the Speaker enters the Chamber, he stands at the Bar of the House and bows. He then walks forward with the Serjeant at Arms at his side and bows to the Chair from the table. When he is at the steps leading to the Chair he bows again before kneeling for prayer. There were some Members who felt that it was medieval to bow to the Chair. They criticized George for submitting to this humiliating process. "Is all this bowing and scraping necessary?" his colleagues asked him, and George explained: "I bow to the Chair three times a day and I do not think I lose any dignity by it. I believe that I am bowing to the authority of the House and the greater authority that lies behind it."

This towering sense of propriety and respect enabled him to maintain and strengthen his own authority as Speaker in times of noisy debate. A good illustration of this is his dealing with Dennis Skinner, the Labour MP for Bolsover. He was one of the noisiest members in the House and the newspapers soon named him "the Beast of Bolsover", a term which George ruled as "unparliamentary" when Norman Tebbit used it in the House. George had quite an affection for Dennis Skinner and saw his strong points: "Dennis Skinner himself is a very able man with a good brain and a forthright style in debating." He was skilful in heckling, but usually knew when to stop. George had many a jousting with him from his first days as Speaker. Dennis Skinner frequently tried his luck and pushed to see how much he could get away with. "He knew exactly how far to go," George writes, "and so for a long time kept out of trouble, often only by half an inch." All restraint went out of the window on one memorable parliamentary day in 1980 when he interrupted James Prior, then Employment Minister, and shouted abuse at Mrs Thatcher. George stood up and called "Order!", very firmly. Skinner was in full throttle and too excited to listen, despite attempts to calm him. The Speaker remained standing and though the custom of the House requires that in such a situation members must sit down, Skinner continued on his feet, still shouting. George repeated "Order!" and then added, "The honourable gentleman will resume his seat at once." Skinner ignored him and George suspended him for the rest of the day. The battle was then joined. Dennis Skinner folded his arms and said, "That's what you think." George tried again to get him to obey the order of the Chair, without effect. Finally George called upon the Serjeant at Arms to conduct him out of the Chamber. The Members could not believe their eyes or ears. It was the first time the Serjeant had been called to do this for a hundred years. George was anxious. He could not permit a scene or scuffle in the House if Skinner refused to go. He determined that if that happened he would suspend the sitting. It was a battle of nerves. The House waited in barely controlled silence, knowing that they were watching high drama. Skinner had really challenged the authority of the Chair and a failure in performance would have meant a failure of George's authority. George's own words are needed for the description of that tense scene:

> On this occasion, the Serjeant at Arms stood up and walked up the floor of the House. You could feel the electricity in the air with everyone holding their breath wondering what would happen. Skinner was pale but not saying a word. He was shaken and looked around at the Serjeant at Arms, Colonel Sir Peter Thorne, a slim fellow, and said, "What him? Get back in your chair." I was tempted to laugh, but naturally did not because I knew there was a great issue on for me and for him. One of us was going to be broken that day and it was not going to be me. The Serjeant at Arms was within one yard when Skinner's nerve cracked and he stood up and walked out docilely.

George knew this to be a very important turning point. Dennis Skinner and the House knew the kind of Speaker with whom they had to deal.

No Hard Feelings

George had won a clear victory and he held nothing against Skinner for challenging him. In a roundabout way he was thankful. Dennis Skinner had enabled him to show the House that they had a Speaker who would defend their dignity and authority against anyone who challenged it, whether it were a backbencher or a Prime Minister.

Some time later, George had a telephone call from Dennis Skinner who was in his home recovering from an accident. George was pleased to talk with him. To his surprise, he learnt that Dennis Skinner wanted a ticket for his son to visit the House of Commons. George readily agreed—and assured Skinner, despite argumentative protests, that he would not only give him a ticket, but would invite him to tea at Speaker's House. The boy came and when he entered the Speaker's room, George teased him and said, "Oh no, not another Skinner!" He laughed and said, "My old man's given you a lot of trouble." George's reply was typical: "Yes, and I've given him some trouble too."

The Speaker's Chaplain

Almost within the precincts of Parliament are two churches. The one, Westminster Abbey, is the church of kings and those whom the nation delights to honour after their death. It is a national church, a record of the nation's history, used by the nation for great events, and there the monarch is crowned. The other, St Margaret's Westminster, is the church of Parliament. By tradition, its Rector is normally made the Speaker's Chaplain. The Revd Dr David Edwards was Speaker's Chaplain when George succeeded Selwyn Lloyd in the Chair. When David Edwards left to become Dean of Norwich, he was succeeded by John Baker, who later became Bishop of Salisbury. The question arose about his successor. John Baker had greatly valued the office of Chaplain to the House, although the duties were largely ceremonial. He led prayers at the opening of each new session and appeared on state occasions to accompany the Speaker. But, in view of George's deep appreciation of the value of the Christian tradition in Parliament, he probably had more to do than most previous Speaker's Chaplains.

There were, however, times when, according to the correspondence, George acted more as John Baker's chaplain. He even consulted George on one occasion when his "daily help" was worried about her husband who would not give up smoking! But George Thomas was that kind of man. Whether he was Speaker or simply MP, a schoolteacher or just a neighbour, people came to him with their problems. He listened, and it may have been in this listening to the everyday concerns of ordinary people that he served his apprenticeship as Speaker. Certainly, his chaplain looked upon him as a helpful friend and fellow-Christian. John Baker was reluctant to leave and said so in fulsome terms, but George did not urge him to neglect his career for the sake of loyalty. Canon Baker decided to accept the invitation to Salisbury.

The nominee for St Margaret's was the Revd Trevor Beeson, an experienced journalist—he had been Editor of the *New Christian*, a radical journal which could not ultimately be sustained—and an extremely good preacher and pastor. He was an excellent choice for St Margaret's. But was he a suitable man to be the Speaker's Chaplain? St Margaret's decided that they must take into account the Speaker's views when appointing a Rector, and if the proposed Rector was unacceptable to the Speaker, they would not appoint him. George was not opposed to Trevor Beeson. In a semi-humorous conversation with him, he pointed out that he would have trouble because Trevor was of the same political persuasion as he was and he might be accused of smuggling Labour policy into the Speaker's Office! But they liked each other. Both were miner's sons and both were Christians who believed that politics—if not party politics—had a place in the Christian message to society.

The Royal Wedding

On 29 July 1981, the heir to the throne, Prince Charles, was married with great celebrations to Lady Diana Spencer in St Paul's Cathedral. Since his Investiture as Prince of Wales, when George Thomas was Secretary of State for Wales, Prince Charles had watched his career. As Speaker, George had no official duties at the wedding, but he was asked to read the Lesson. This was in response to a request by the Prince of Wales to have Wales and the Nonconformists represented at his wedding. The ceremony was on television and the nation watched in admiration. Many Nonconformists and many Welsh people were proud that a Methodist layman and fellow-countryman was to read at the Crown Prince's wedding.

He read 1 Corinthians 13 and read it wonderfully, not as an actor, but as one who really believed what he read. It was that rich Welsh accent, that careful declamation of the great poem of love and the deep sincerity of a believer that combined to make his reading a high point in the service. Among the Tonypandy papers in the National Library of Wales in Aberystwyth, there are three bulging files of letters of appreciation. Many come from Wales and from chapel people, proud that their man was there. Many more came from people who had never heard that beautiful chapter read like that before. One writer, a Methodist, even thanked George for his wonderful "speech" at the wedding. So completely had he made it his own that that writer thought it was more than a reading of the Bible, but rather his own thoughts passed on to the young couple: "What a wonderful speech you gave at the wedding of the Prince and Princess of Wales. Methodism thrilled that a Methodist was to take part—and it was the lynchpin of the service."

It was undoubtedly a high point of the service, for which St Paul must be given some credit! Edward Barrett, a publisher, was so impressed by the reading that he had a hundred copies of the chapter printed on artistic paper as a commemoration of the event. It was described as a "tribute", no doubt to the Prince and Princess of Wales, but also to an outstanding rendering. Malcolm Muggeridge went a little far when he wrote to George about the wedding that he had watched on a neighbour's television set: "To tell the truth it all struck me as a bit tawdry—no particular reflection on those concerned—until suddenly came your reading of the wonderful 13th chapter of the Epistle to the Corinthians, which lifted everything right up to the sky."

A Household Figure

The Speaker of the House of Commons is not by his office a popular national figure. His kingdom is confined to the House, whose custodian he is. But George believed that the House was the custodian also of the people's freedom. Several opportunities on radio and television pushed him forward in a way that previous Speakers had not experienced. Shortly after he was elected Speaker, a television programme, arranged before his appointment, presented the work and lifestyle of the Speaker. It was also during his time, from 3rd April 1978, that the proceedings of the House of Commons were first broadcast by radio. This did not follow the practice of other countries, broadcasting live, but recorded extracts were taken for a popular programme called *The Day in Parliament*. The producer decided to open this programme each evening with a recording of the Speaker bringing the House to order, with his familiar call, "Order! Order!" Those two words were to make George a radio star. His Welsh intonation and his way of insinuating the authority of the Speaker into the atmosphere of the House made it a perfect opening. There was never any irritation in the way he spoke those words.

And so, already known on television and popular on radio, his reading at the Royal Wedding put him high up in the "charts". He was soon besieged with requests to read at weddings. He was frequently in demand on both radio and television. When he recovered from an illness or when he retired, the media would be after him, so that he appeared in every conceivable programme. And he enjoyed it. There is, of course, a proper modesty about George, but he makes no secret of the fact that he likes being praised—and he had plenty of praise for his superb reading.

In later years, commenting on Sir John Templeton—donor of the

"Nobel Prize" for religion which bears his name, the Templeton Award—he illustrated the unpretentious nature of that very successful investor and benefactor, by saying that when he and his wife walked down the Strand, no one noticed anything about them. They were passed by as ordinary people. George would not like that! He loves to be recognized by everybody and he responds with great warmth to expressions of affection for him, of which there are many. There is both a touch of vanity and a sad remembrance of a lonely boy in Tonypandy, an unnoticed student in Southampton, and even of the first time he was called in Parliament, by the wrong name. When people recognize him, he responds warmly; when they do not, he is disappointed. A trivial incident in a taxi illustrates this. As always, he talked to the taxi driver, who persistently showed himself unimpressed. He had never heard of George Thomas, who was just another fare. George was not pleased.

Security and Tragedy

George had not forgotten the murder of Airey Neave, and every indication of a breach in security of the House disturbed him. On 9th July 1981, he reported to the House: "Just after 3 p.m., a man scaled the perimeter at Black Rod's garden. He gained entry to the Precincts of Parliament. He was carrying a knife." On 17th July: "Two intruders gained entry into the Palace of Westminster."

Between those two incidents, another tragic murder of an MP occurred—on 14th July, the Revd Robert Bradford, Unionist MP, was killed by the IRA while conducting a constituency clinic. He was shot through the head. By December there were bomb alerts and the Speaker outlined procedure in such cases. The Metropolitan Police reported that in the year ending 31st December 1981, there had been twenty-five hoax bomb calls and 199 suspect parcels. Although nothing came of these, it was necessary to be on the alert. Neither Parliament nor the Metropolitan Police could afford to ignore any warning. This problem was particularly acute after the murder of Robert Bradford.

George was not able to act after Robert Bradford's death as he had after Airey Neave's. Then he was the sole embodiment of the House, because it was in dissolution. Now, when a suggestion was made that

a similar plaque be erected in memory of Robert Bradford, he passed
the decision to the House. He drafted the following statement for
22nd December 1981:

> During the dissolution period in April 1979, I authorized on my
> own responsibility the erection in our Chamber of a commemor-
> ative plaque to the late Airey Neave, displaying his coat of arms.
> As the House knows, this is positioned over the door leading to
> the Members' Lobby. It has recently been suggested to me that
> a similar plaque might be erected in memory of the late Reverend
> Robert Bradford. In my view this is now a matter for the House,
> since I do not think that it would be right for me in present
> circumstances to exercise responsibilities which were appropriate
> only when the House was in dissolution and the Speaker was
> the sole embodiment of its administrative authority.

The House was sympathetic, but Robert Bradford, unlike Airey
Neave, had not been killed within the precincts of Parliament and no
plaque was approved. There was a growing anxiety about IRA attacks
and Parliament was feeling vulnerable.

The year 1982 opened with further bomb threats and a fear that
the IRA might celebrate the anniversary of what they call "Bloody
Sunday" on 30th January, with an escalation of their bombing campaign on the mainland. George had to announce special precautions
which were to be taken from 25th January to 12th February.

The Calm before the Storm

Apart from bomb scares and IRA threats, 1982 began like every
other year. George returned from a holiday and issued details of
special precautions which had to be taken for security reasons. The
session proceeded as usual.

There were noisy scenes in the House when the figure of three
million unemployed was announced. A leak that said President
Reagan had been invited to address both Houses of Parliament led
to a row over whether the Prime Minister had the right to invite him
without prior permission of the House. There was trouble with Ian
Paisley, when Enoch Powell protested about him being called on a
sensitive issue, expressing himself very strongly: "The House has
only itself to blame if a bully and braggart treats it in this way." On
23rd March, George met his new Chaplain, Trevor Beeson and on

1st April, Cranley Onslow proposed that an artist be allowed to paint the House in session for George Thomas' portrait. All part of the routine life of the Speaker of the House of Commons. On 2nd April the storm broke.

CHAPTER EIGHTEEN

◆◆◆

The Falklands War

ON FRIDAY 2ND APRIL 1982, George Thomas, like most members of Parliament, was unaware of the events taking place in the South Atlantic. He was relaxed enough to go to the Polytechnic of Wales in Treforest, to receive an Honorary Fellowship. He had been given permission to be absent from the House and few thought that history would be made that day. He reached the college at 10 a.m. and within half an hour, there was a telephone call from his secretary to say that it was believed that the Falkland Islands had been invaded by Argentina. Throughout the day the information was confused. George was interrupted three times that day by telephone calls from his secretary as news became a little firmer. Michael Cocks, Opposition Chief Whip, John Silkin, Shadow Defence Minister, and Francis Pym, Leader of the House, also telephoned. They were anxious for the Speaker to authorize a special sitting of Parliament on Saturday, 3rd April. George returned to Westminster on the Friday night in order to preside over a debate on the following day.

The Saturday Debate

The day began badly for the government. Humphrey Atkins, Lord Privy Seal and deputy to Lord Carrington at the Foreign Office, asked the Speaker's permission to make a personal statement. He was very agitated as he explained to George that he had to correct something he had said yesterday. With permission, he told the House: "Following my statement at eleven o'clock yesterday, when I said that we had been in touch with the Governor of the Falkland Islands half an hour before, I must now say that that was inaccurate. We had in fact been in touch earlier, at 8.30 a.m. our time. No invasion had then taken place, and when I made my statement I had no knowledge of any change in the situation."

The atmosphere was foreboding. George saw that this was going to be one of the most dramatic debates in recent times. One indication of this was that the House was crowded for Prayers. Usually most members would rush in as soon as Prayers were over, but on 3rd April 1982 they could not risk losing a good seat!

From his position in the Chair, George could see Ian Gow, Margaret Thatcher's Private Secretary, talking to Ray Whitney, a former diplomat of considerable experience. George concluded that Mrs Thatcher wanted him to speak. When he did, he carefully outlined the progress of negotiations with Argentina and advised a cautious, unemotional approach to the present situation. He pointed out the danger of any military action. This did not please the House. Michael Foot was in full spate against Argentina's General Galtieri and made a magnificent speech calling for "deeds, not words". Privately, George recalled the Suez debate in 1956, and Eden's ill-fated escapade. At that time Gaitskell, who had supported Eden at first, backtracked later. It seemed to George that the scene was going to be run again. The Labour opposition was now urging the government to take action which later they would renounce.

Assembling the Task Force

Neither the Conservatives nor Labour were, however, unanimous. One of the main Labour opponents of the use of military force after the invasion was Denis Healey, and he was away in Rhodes at a conference. He later said that he believed the invasion could have been prevented if Britain had made it quite clear earlier that she intended to take firm action and if she had prepared the Falklands to resist. As it turned out, the Falklands were almost defenceless. The possibility of an invasion had been apparent for months and yet there were only two officers and sixty fighting men on the islands when the Argentinians landed—and these men were without weapons. The Governor of the Falklands was not warned until sixteen hours before the invasion took place, although Britain had been assembling her task force secretly for three days.

Some of this was known to some members and George describes the House on that Saturday as "anxious and even rather frightened at what might happen". There were six Falklands debates, and Labour swung over gradually to a more conciliatory approach. They pressed for further negotiations at the United Nations rather than continuing with military action.

The task force was assembled and brilliantly managed. It seemed an impossible task to retake those islands so far away. But once the fighting had started, the country was behind the government. Britain was swept by a tide of patriotic feeling, and the personal popularity of the Prime Minister soared. The tabloid press cashed in on this and fanned the flames into crude jingoism. Apart from this, there was a genuine spirit of patriotism in the country which arose unexpectedly among the young. An article published in the *Guardian* on St George's Day, 1982, observed,

> Working class and lower middle class youngsters, who are pretty disgruntled with Mrs Thatcher's Britain, are nevertheless ready to fight for it. While their notions of patriotism are confused, they strongly support the hardline policy towards Argentina and, if the worst came to the worst, would favour a military call-up to win a war against it.

George Thomas was never nearer to the grass roots of Britain than during this period of the Falklands War. He understood those young people better than the writers of that article did. His assessment of the young was clear:

> The whole exercise showed that British youth, who never thought they would have to do that sort of thing again, could respond magnificently to the challenge. The Falklands affair reinforced my belief that the British character has not really changed, despite all the troubles that we face with violence and sometimes appallingly selfish behaviour. We are still a tough little race, and now the world knows it.

Shadows over Victory

The loss of life was comparatively small—it was a small war—but a few shadows troubled Britain's victory when it came. The loss of the destroyer *Sheffield* and damage to other ships with loss of lives caused alarm and criticism. The sinking of the Argentinian warship *Belgrano* became a source of criticism also—it was sunk outside our declared exclusion zone and many people were outraged by this. The unnecessary loss of life at Bluff Cove also troubled many, including Mrs Thatcher. George recalls how at the state banquet for President

Reagan, she showed signs of strain, knowing the news, that had not then been released, of the heavy losses in Bluff Cove as Welsh Guards were being landed. It was the only time he had seen her showing real tension during the whole Falklands campaign.

When war was over in May, George wrote to her to congratulate her on the victory. He had been glad of the revived patriotism and the devoted service and skill of the armed forces. He did not mention the *Belgrano*, but showed his concern for her and the strain she had endured. He was of the opinion that "had a man been Prime Minister, he would probably have lost his nerve long before". Later he enlarged on this by adding, "Any man would have gone back to the United Nations to make sure he was not going to be ostracized by the world community." George disapproved strongly of the behaviour of the Opposition, who put themselves in the clear in case things went wrong by urging a return to the United Nations. He was convinced that had Mrs Thatcher done this, Argentina would never have left the Falklands. All this went into the letter of congratulation. Certainly Margaret Thatcher established herself as an international figure, the "Iron Lady" who knew her own mind and made Britain count in world affairs. She was delighted by George's letter:

> Thank you for your wonderful letter about the Falklands victory. The news was marvellous and somehow the end came more quickly than we had expected. We never doubted that we would win—we knew we had the best fighting men in the world and that they would overcome all the difficulties. Our real worry was about the lives we would lose, and I am so thankful that the numbers were not higher. The best thing of all was the way our people recognized what was *right* and supported it the whole way *because* it was right. This was a triumph for the invincibility of the human spirit. If only we could have the same virtues harnessed to the battle of peace.

Looking back, it is difficult to realize how near Britain came to losing the war. Denis Healey pointed out that "eleven of the twenty-five bombs which hit our ships failed to explode because the Argentine pilots flew in so low," and he added, "otherwise we might have lost the war."

Although both sides of the House were divided between military action and United Nations diplomacy, the Labour Party was seen most clearly to have swung around in favour of negotiation, and this, in the exaltation of victory, spoiled its chances of regaining power in the general election of 1983. Margaret Thatcher was also quick to assert the unity of her policy. What had proved successful in the crisis of war, was good for the country at peace. The virtues which won the Battle of the Falklands could win the battles of peace.

The Speaker Criticized

The use of the Speaker's authority to choose who should speak in the House inevitably led to criticisms, impugning his fairness. George felt that he did his best to ensure that he was not too much influenced by the extroverts who clamoured to speak often, and that the steady, solid members got their share of being called, both at Question Time and in debate. Certain members, like Dennis Skinner, would jump up on a point of order and others would give a black look if they were not called. Andrew Foulds, Labour member for Warley East, was highly critical of the Speaker who called him less frequently than he thought he deserved. He tried every method of being heard, including a point of order which turned out to be a question, or an opportunity to be heard. George's rule of thumb judgement was that if a member was called for two questions in the same week he had not done badly. After all, there were 535 members eligible to ask questions—the other hundred being members of the government who had to answer them!

Tempers were obviously more frayed during the six Falklands debates, particularly when Labour began to move away from their original position of support for the government in the war. During the third Falklands debate on 14th April, Andrew Foulds jumped up shouting that he had not yet been called to speak in any of the three debates. George recalls that he was most abusive. His criticism of the Speaker was very severe: that he had a coterie of favourites whom he always called; that he intervened with one of his quips instead of hearing out a point of order; that he placed arbitrary limits of time on questions, before he could assess the extent of a member's feelings as the question developed.

Although George explained that at least one hundred members had been standing without being called, he continued to shout and George ordered him to leave the Chamber for the rest of the day's sitting. The House was crowded and the proceedings were being broadcast. Andrew Foulds was aware of this and used his opportunity to be at the centre of a drama on stage. He walked down the centre of the floor of the House, turned and started to wave his arms and shout at the Speaker. George named him, but that was not the end of it. Michael Foot advised the Opposition not to support the naming. For the first time in his Speakership, George had to put the suspension to a vote of the House. It carried easily because many Labour members abstained.

This unique incident caused George to ponder the value of broadcasting the proceedings of Parliament which he had previously supported. He still thought it was a good thing, but cautioned:

> I think that some members of the House of Commons too often forget the responsibility they have to maintain the deservedly high reputation of the House, built up over the centuries, which could be lost by a few selfish words or a bout of stupidity that is heard on the radio (including the BBC World Service). To prevent a point of view from being heard just because you personally do not agree with it is undermining the basis of parliamentary democracy.

The First Hansard Society Lecture

The Hansard Society was founded in 1944 by Stephen King-Hall, as a non-party organization. Its purpose was to spread information about the working of the British Parliament. It broadened its interests by promoting discussion of key issues of the day, with a view to educating public opinion. This was done in the form of lectures, meetings and conferences. It publishes a quarterly journal, *Parliamentary Affairs*, which covers all aspects of government and politics. In 1982, it sponsored the first Hansard Society Lecture, which was intended to offer a prominent parliamentarian a platform to educate a wider public in some aspect of political life, and the Rt Hon. George Thomas, Speaker of the House of Commons, was invited to give it. He decided to deliver the lecture in Cardiff's National Museum of Wales on 14th May, before an audience principally of sixth-form students. This was in keeping with the objects of the Hansard Society, which were mainly educational. He took the theme, "The Changing Face of Parliamentary Democracy". It is an excellent guide to George's thinking on the eve of his retirement as Speaker, a lucid description of the changes as he had seen them from the Speaker's Chair.

Britain's membership of the European Community since 1973 gave him his first example of Parliament's ability to change, since it "meant that we have to adapt our work in order to keep in step with that development". He saw the reason for the changes that had to take place in the greatly enlarged world, as well as "the very substantial increase in Parliament's responsibilities". It was in this context that he saw the value of the Select Committees. Their setting up, he maintained, "proved to be a giant step forward in bringing back to the Commons a power and an authority that it had lost". He dealt at length with their timeliness and their success: "Our generation has seen a monumental increase in investigative journalism: the Commons has more than matched this by an increase in investigative Select Committees."

After that he turned to the broadcasting of parliamentary proceedings. By 1982, Parliamentary proceedings had been broadcast for four years and generally he approved of this. It had conveyed the very spirit of Parliament to the nation. The noise may have shocked listeners, but even on that point the proceedings were quieter than they used to be and members were more aware that what they said was heard throughout the land. With a special reference to the Falklands War, during which proceedings were often broadcast live in their entirety, as on 3rd April 1982, he said,

> Our recent debates on the Falkland Islands crisis have had an enormous audience throughout the land. There are millions of our fellow citizens who are better informed on that crisis because our proceedings have been broadcast than they would otherwise have been, while the knowledge that our proceedings have been broadcast has a substantial effect in the Commons itself.

As for televising Parliament, that was under discussion and George could not express an opinion, but it was clear from what he said that he expected it to happen.

He described how Parliament was taking every possible step to educate the nation and explain what was happening. This included the establishment of a Public Information Office, which although only recently set up, had already dealt with 50,000 enquiries in a year. A Parliamentary Education Officer had also been appointed to keep in touch with the schools. These changes were all part of a growing concern to inform the public about what happened in Parliament, "to ensure that there is nothing secret about our proceedings".

George emphasized that all those changes were signs of vitality and that as a result the public were far more interested in Parliament than ever before.

At the end of the lecture, he turned to the theme of the next annual conference of the Hansard Society: "Is Parliament failing the Nation?" He emphasized the fact that Parliament is a mirror of the nation. One of his duties as Speaker was to see that the opinions of the members were fairly expressed—even the most unpopular ones. The parliamentary democracy which we cherish is safe if members are representative of their constituencies, not answerable to a caucus, and "responsible above all to their consciences". He saw the dangers to democracy, particularly from those who denied the right to freedom of speech, the authoritarians: "They are like weevils in the woodwork: if ignored they can cause enormous damage to things we value most of all." But with constant vigilance, he was convinced that Parliament would not fail the nation, nor would democracy be lost: "The greatest heritage we have is the heritage of a parliamentary democracy with freedom of speech, freedom of worship, freedom of movement, independence of spirit."

The Conference of European Speakers

This same high view of parliamentary democracy led George to place importance on conference with other Speakers. First, in the Commonwealth, where Britain played a key role; but also in Europe, where many countries had democratic systems close to that of Britain. In 1975, the Speakers from several European parliaments met in Paris and formed a Conference of European Speakers. That year, it held its first meeting in Rome, and then subsequently in Bonn, Vienna, The Hague and Madrid. At first it met every year and then from 1978 every other year. It was invited to London in 1982, in June. George was relieved that the Falklands war was over! The Queen received the delegates in Buckingham Palace on 3rd June and the conference was officially opened by George Thomas and Lord Hailsham on the following day.

It was becoming a very heavy year for George and the strain was beginning to show. Several private letters to him expressed anxiety about his health. But he did not let up. He accepted chairmanships, received the usual visitors, including the Tunisian Ambassador, wrote the "Langham Diary" in the *Listener*, and when the House was in recess went to America to lecture in Louisiana and Texas, visiting Washington on official business. His friends began to advise him about the need for rest. He took the opportunity of the Christmas recess to visit Gibraltar and Tangiers. It was a pleasant holiday without official duties. He spent Christmas at the Rock Hotel in Gibraltar and New Year at the famous Minzah Hotel in Tangiers. He enjoyed them both.

Looking Back

Mrs Thatcher called a general election on 9th May 1983. The campaign began with everything in her favour and eventually she won. For George, there was no campaign. He had said that he would retire at the end of the life of this Parliament, and his political career in the House of Commons would therefore close when the next government was elected. Then he would be neither MP nor Speaker. He would lose much—particularly Speaker's House—but he would also gain a great deal. It was a time to look back and assess his achievements. His Hansard Lecture had listed some of his reforms and he recalled many others, including the printing of the Speaker's "rulings" so that they would be clearer to the whole House and not depend upon the memory of some. He had worked for clarity, fairness, openness and a supreme respect for the dignity of the House.

But what had he done specifically as a Christian? He would say that every act of clarity and truth, of freedom of speech and fairness, of open dealing and access to information, as well as respect for the authority of the House and parliamentary democracy, was a Christian witness.

But what had he done more specifically in the religious field? He was proud of the fact that he had agreed to the formation of a group for Christian wives of MPs. It proved a great strength to wives who faced tensions of insecurity with their husbands' involvement in politics. Late hours and excessive travel had wrecked many marriages. He invited the Christian Wives' Fellowship to meet in Speaker's House and was amazed at how many came. When they had a distinguished speaker, such as the Archbishop of Canterbury, they would invite their husbands and as many as 120 would have dinner: "The wives would all make special dishes for these meetings—never was so much food seen in the Speaker's House." The only request that George made to his successor was that he would allow the Christian Wives' Fellowship to continue to meet in Speaker's House. He did.

There was also in the House of Commons a Prayer Group which met for breakfast once a month. It was a branch of the International Christian Leadership Movement, which had its greatest strength in America. When he had first met it as a member, George had feared that it might be one more of those movements linked to the CIA which fostered anti-communist propaganda. He was eventually persuaded that it was a genuine Christian movement and, as soon as he became Speaker, he invited this group also to meet in Speaker's House.

But his most dramatic religious act was in 1978, when he gave permission for the Roman Catholics to celebrate mass in the crypt of the House of Commons. Kevin McNamara, a Roman Catholic and Labour MP for Hull, approached him first, although such a precedent needed also the approval of the Lord Chancellor and the Lord Great Chamberlain. George was known to be a Methodist and if he agreed, the other two were unlikely to object. They supported the action of the Speaker. The occasion was the 500th anniversary of the death of Sir Thomas More. George had fought for the right of Nonconformists to use the crypt for religious services and he struck a blow for religious freedom when he agreed to this the first Roman Catholic mass in the crypt since the Reformation. The Cardinal Archbishop of Westminster, Basil Hume, was to celebrate. Much publicity was given to this and the Protestants of Northern Ireland predictably rose up in disagreement.

The Revd Ian Paisley came to see George and registered his protest, indicating that he would speak out at the service. He based his objection upon his belief that the mass was blasphemous and should not therefore be allowed in the precincts of the House. He declared his intention to protest at the most sacred moment in the mass, the elevation of the host. This moment is specially sacred to Roman Catholics and a protest at that point would have caused great distress. George persuaded him to make his protest at the very beginning of the service and then walk out. He warned Basil Hume and suggested that it would be wiser to make no response to Dr Paisley. This happened and the service was not unduly disturbed, while the protest was made and honour satisfied.

George was invited and agreed to read the lesson. He stepped forward humbly recalling with a sense of history that Sir Thomas More also had been Speaker, briefly, before he became Lord Chancellor. He remembered this as he recalled the words, "We are surrounded by a cloud of unseen witnesses." Looking back he wrote:

> It was more than 500 years since Catholics had been allowed to worship God, according to their beliefs, in that crypt, and I found the service most moving. I believe that God used me on this occasion to provide another step forward in religious freedom in Britain; the bigotry of 500 years ago should not decide the way we behave today.

CHAPTER NINETEEN

◆◆◆

Retirement

THE GERMAN PHRASE for "retirement" means literally, "to go into a state of rest"; when a bishop retires, he is henceforth called an "old" bishop. Neither of these attempts to describe the new state of one who is retired would adequately cover the rest of George Thomas' life. The flurry of invitations that came to him as soon as it was known that he intended to retire ensured that he would have a very active "retirement", and by no means go into "a state of rest". Almost a decade after his retirement, he cannot be described as "old", either, despite the onset of cancer twice, from which he recovered.

But Hansard labels 12th May 1983 as "Mr Speaker (Retirement)". It was a great day in the House of Commons. At the end of Prayers, George repeated the Grace. He then proceeded for an hour to preside over Oral Questions as though it were any other Thursday.

Then at 3.30 p.m., following an attack on the Prime Minister by Tam Dalyell about her attitude to the Falklands, the Argentinian dead and the sinking of the *Belgrano*, the Speaker closed the session and made a personal statement "of a valedictory nature".

Mr Speaker Gives Thanks

On this, his last day as Speaker, it was appropriate that he should thank "those who serve in various Departments of the House". This he did graciously, adding his thanks to the Deputy Speakers, the Lobby and the Press Gallery, his three chaplains and a very special word for "the personal staff in Speaker's House, where I have been protected and cared for in a most wonderful way". He wistfully added, "Indeed, they have been my family." He duly acknowledged others who were leaving the House and wished them well.

Then came the most personal part of his valedictory statement:

I want to express to the House the humble pride that I shall always have in the knowledge that for seven years I have been trusted by the House with the high and honourable office of Speaker of this House of Commons at Westminster. One of the great joys of my life has been to forge friendships in all parties in the House. My office has also led to friendship with Speakers throughout our Commonwealth, in Europe and in other parts of the world. I am proud that the House is still held by other Parliaments in affectionate respect and referred to as the Mother of Parliaments.

Throughout my thirty-eight years' membership of the House I have always felt deep affection and respect for the traditions. Traditions which have survived the test of time should not lightly be discarded. There is a meaning and a strength behind the traditions which we observe and I rejoice to know that the House still guards them. I rejoice in the place the House has in our national life. Despite all our human frailties, the House is still Britain's bastion for democracy. It is here in this Chamber and in Parliament as a whole that the liberties of our people must be protected. We are a great parliamentary democracy and I trust that the House will ever protect the values that brought greatness to our history.

My heart will be with you, and I shall never forget the steadfast support and friendship that I have received from both sides of the House and which is reflected in the early-day motion on the Order Paper today, for which I express deep gratitude.

God bless you all. God bless this House and our country that we may always cherish the heritage of freedom handed to us by our fathers. Thank you for the privilege of serving as your Speaker.

The "early-day motion" to which he refers was from the Prime Minister: "*Resolved*, That the thanks of this House be given to Mr Speaker for what he has said this day to the House; and that the same be entered in the Journals of this House." With that George could not resist a last flash of humour as he said, "I would have taken a poor view had the motion not been resolved."

Tributes to a Great Speaker

The tributes that followed over the next hour were more than formal courtesy. They were heartfelt and frank.

The Prime Minister began with a motion:

That the thanks of this House be given to the Right Honourable George Thomas for the great distinction with which he has upheld the traditions of the Speakership during the past seven years; that he be assured that his unfailing fairness, personal kindness and dedication to the House has earned him its respect and affection; and that all Members unite in wishing him every happiness in his retirement.

Margaret Thatcher had a special relationship with George Thomas as a friend. He respected her, and in her tribute she showed how great an affection she had for him. As she recounted his achievements, not only as Speaker, but as "a minister, as a member of the cabinet [not hers], as the first Chairman of the Welsh Grand Committee and then as Chairman of Ways and Means", it was clear that she was expressing her gratitude to a senior member of the House from whom she had learnt much. Her tribute shows how well she knew and admired him: "You have upheld with a special combination of impartiality and authority the dignity of your office and of this House. You have been not only our Speaker but our friend." She recalled how, in moments of tension and drama, he had displayed "a characteristically Celtic humour that has delighted us all". After speaking for the House in gratitude for his service and good wishes for his retirement, she ended with, "We say farewell to one of our greatest Speakers."

A Generous Tribute from the Leader of the Opposition

George had not always seen eye to eye with the leader of his own party in the House, but on this occasion it was time for generosity and Michael Foot did not fail, nor did he lose his sense of history. He followed the Prime Minister with acknowledgements to her, made a side swipe at the introduction of broadcasting into the House— "not necessarily an unmitigated boon"—and continued:

Only a few weeks ago, Mr Speaker, I paid a visit to your home town of Tonypandy to commemorate the services given to the House by the former right hon. Member for Rhondda, Alec Jones. I am sure that if he were present he would be one of the first and most eager of hon. members to join in the tributes to you. He had special knowledge of your service to the House, and also of how much your election as Speaker of the House meant to the people of Tonypandy. I recall that some time ago I went to Cardiff, where your Speakership was also celebrated.

It celebrated the special combination of qualities that you have brought to the office—qualities of wit, humour, practical experience, Welsh courtesy and Welsh guile, all in their special quantities. I assure you that they have all been appreciated.

I had a special opportunity of seeing some of those qualities in action as I attended some meetings or functions when my right hon. friend the Member for Cardiff South-East [Mr Callaghan] was Prime Minister and you were Speaker. They gave to me, a naive politician from the valleys, an insight into the way in which Cardiff politics are conducted, which I have never forgotten and never betrayed.

The most famous of all speeches ever made by any of your distinguished predecessors was that made by Speaker Lenthall on the most famous of occasions when the rights of the House were protected. All right hon. and hon. Members know the speech. Speaker Lenthall said:

> "May it please your Majesty, I have neither eyes to see, nor tongue to speak in this place, but as the House is pleased to direct me, whose servant I am here."

That I am sure is what you, Mr Speaker, would have said on that occasion if you had been in charge. It is a good lesson for all subsequent Speakers. I shall not press the comparison too strongly because Speaker Lenthall, despite his great service to the House and country on that occasion, was subsequently involved in financial dealings that led to an investigation. He wavered in his party allegiance, although I am not sure in which direction. He ended up in Oliver Cromwell's House of Lords. I do not know whether any such fate is to befall you, Mr Speaker.

You, Mr Speaker, have always followed the tradition of Speaker Lenthall in defending and sustaining the rights of the House with a peculiar grace and charm that nobody else could have matched. There is a Methodism in your magnificence. It will be extremely difficult for anybody to follow in your footsteps. I pity your successor, for you have followed, which is not always possible to achieve, a straight and narrow path to a destination of universal acclaim. Some right hon. and hon. Members wish that we could do the same.

Michael Foot added his wishes for a continuing active life in politics: "We consider that you still have a great contribution to make to the political life of this country."

Roy Jenkins

Representing the Alliance of Liberal and Social Democratic parties, Roy Jenkins added his tribute. He compared the first year of George Thomas' Speakership with the last (the only two years Roy Jenkins had been a member under him) with characteristic style: "At the beginning you were in gentle command and at the end you were supreme but still gentle." He recalled that when he was Home Secretary and George Thomas a humble Under Secretary of State in the Home Office, it was a tradition in the office that whenever they were in more trouble in the House than usual the cry went up, "Let George do it. He will disarm." His tribute to the Speaker as Speaker was also generous:

> There have been six Speakers since the war. Few of us have served under all of them. None of them has been bad, most have been good, but without question you have enhanced the standard during your seven years of office. Reference has already been made to the introduction of broadcasting. There is clearly room for differing views about its impact on the public consciousness of the House, but there is no doubt that it has enhanced the public impact of the Speaker and that popular respect for both the office and the man has greatly increased.
>
> To add even temporary lustre to an office that has existed for more than 600 years is a difficult feat. To add a little that will last is almost impossible, yet I believe that you have achieved that. More domestically, we in the Social Democratic Party and the Liberal Party—not in parliamentary terms, one of the juggernauts of our jousting politics—are grateful to you for your courtesy and fairness.

Roy Jenkins was followed by Sir Derek Walker-Smith, of whom George once said, "The Rt Hon. and learned Member for Hertfordshire East has now proposed or seconded the re-election of the Speaker more often than I have preached Methodist sermons." Walker-Smith paid a generous tribute, reaffirming what he had said when he seconded the initial election of George Thomas in 1976:

> He is richly endowed with those qualities that make a good parliamentarian and a much loved colleague—not only eloquence and judgement, although he has both in good measure, but courtesy and consideration, affability and sensibility, kindli-

ness and good humour, and a wit that often scores but never wounds.

He added that this judgement had been confirmed by the years: "What was then aspiration is now present certainty, based upon the solid foundation of past performance."

Jim Callaghan

One man George Thomas wanted to hear that day stood up just before four o'clock and paid his tribute. James Callaghan, Member for Cardiff South East, one-time Prime Minister. Their relationship had suffered over the years. What did Jim really think of him? The tribute repays careful study:

> You and I, Mr Speaker, have been parliamentary neighbours for thirty-eight years. We have been close personal friends for more than forty years, and I suppose that there has never been a parliamentary partnership as long-standing as ours. We fought our first campaign together when we were young men. When we first entered the House, rather nervously on that first proud day, when we sat side by side, I do not think that I then saw in you the qualities that have distinguished you since as Speaker. I do not think that I recognized that cool judicial approach. What is more I am certain that you did not think that I would ever make a Prime Minister. We were very proud of ourselves on that day. You and I were proud to enter the House together. We have been proud to serve it ever since.
>
> Perhaps I am in a unique position as Mr Speaker's parliamentary neighbour. I shall take a few minutes to speak of the deep respect and affection in which he is held in his constituency and throughout Cardiff by political supporters, political opponents and by members of all parties and of none. Mr Speaker is referred to as "Our George", which in itself is sufficient testimony of the deep love that people have for him.
>
> If friendship is one of the most rewarding gifts, Mr Speaker is the wealthiest man alive. He gives himself so spontaneously and so generously that all he meets find him quite irresistible. He is a living example of the old truth that it is better to give than to receive. His generosity of spirit has come back to him and brought him very great happiness. Although he has maintained a strictly judicial approach to his duties as Speaker, those of us who know him best are only too aware of the passionate nature

that lurks behind that wig and robes and that occasionally he fails to conceal.

I know, as most of us know, Mr Speaker, that your strong moral convictions are derived from the Christian Socialist precepts that were instilled into you by your beloved mother. They have guided you throughout your life. Those who have known you only as Speaker will not have seen what a passionate controversialist you can be, as you showed in your long and successful fight for leasehold enfranchisement for the people of South Wales.

Most of us know of Mr Speaker's infectious good humour. We know that he seldom, if ever, uses his famous wit at the expense of hon. Members. In eloquence, Mr Speaker is of the self-mocking type. Despite his great achievements, he has always been unduly modest about his own very considerable ability. By general consent, he has been an outstanding Speaker. By his conduct in the Chair and with the aid of broadcasting, he has transformed what always has been an important but nevertheless relatively obscure, office into one that is known and respected throughout the length and breadth of Britain.

In doing that, Mr Speaker, you have elevated Parliament and made it the rightful focus and centre of the nation's attention. No one could leave behind a more valuable testimony than that to the democratic traditions that you hold so dear.

Although you are leaving the House, Mr Speaker, I can assure you that your influence will remain. Your concept of the way in which Mr Speaker's responsibilities and powers should be exercised is stamped upon our practices. Knowing your ardent spirit, I do not expect that you will fade into silence. Indeed I trust that you will continue to remain a force in our public life. For me the House will never be quite the same again. I cannot even be sure that I shall be called to speak. As one old friend to another, thank you and God bless you.

A Shamrock Tribute from Ian Paisley

Tributes followed from James Molyneaux, with special reference to George's sympathy and understanding for the people of Ulster; Edward du Cann, for the backbenchers; Jack Dormand, originally from Durham, as a personal friend; A. J. Beith, as a young Liberal in the House: Robin Maxwell-Hyslop, expressing particular thanks for his decision that "private rulings by Mr Speaker which might be regarded as precedents are to be published".

Then Ian Paisley gave him a "Shamrock Tribute":

> I shall probably be the only Member to speak on this motion who has run foul of your rulings on two occasions—one on the floor of the House and once in the Gallery. I wish to make it clear that I am not here today as a penitent, but that with great gladness I join other Members in paying to you the eulogy you deserve. Coming from that part of Ireland where Patrick first evangelized, perhaps I might say that I am presenting you with a shamrock tribute. There is nothing sham about it, and it is not like the eulogies that most politicians in Ulster receive—a literal rain of stones. The rock is solid and we wish you well.
>
> I call the attention of the House to one thing that happened in the House today which I think illustrates your character and your convictions. It was so nice that, at the end of Prayers, you repeated the Grace. Acting perhaps in another capacity, I would simply say to you, as a staunch Calvinist to a staunch Arminian and Methodist, "May the grace of the Lord Jesus Christ, and the love of God, and the fellowship of the Holy Spirit be with you for ever." Thank you.

There were lighter moments and John Page, MP for Harrow West, provided a poem:

> If I may cause our proceedings slight delay,
> To thank you for the things you do
> In helping out the IPU
> When outward delegations went
> To Lima, Cairo or Tashkent,
> You never failed to take the Chair,
> Adjudging with the greatest care
> Which members from those who applied
> Should go or should be set aside.
> Disappointed chaps were cowed
> To know by whom they weren't allowed.
> When inward delegations came
> They were invited in your name
> And said the part they liked the most
> Was dining with you as their host.
> In Speaker's House they grandly sit,
> Responding to your charm and wit.
> And when at last they travelled from us
> Like us they praise our Speaker Thomas.

The tributes ended with John Parker, the member for Dagenham, who was the Father of the House.

The motion was carried *nem. con.* and Speaker Thomas contented himself with saying "Thank you." But he was deeply moved.

It was Jim Callaghan's tribute that he most commented upon. Years later he could say, "He never said I was a good Speaker!"

"Mr Speaker makes a dignified exit"

This was the title of an article by William Foster in the July 1983 issue of *Choice* magazine, described as "the magazine for leisure and retirement planning". It was based upon an interview in Speaker's House on the day after George Thomas had made his last procession as Speaker from his House to the House of Commons. William Foster watched that last procession and was overwhelmingly impressed. Even more was he overwhelmed by the "gilded splendour of the Speaker's House". He wondered how George Thomas could ever be an ordinary mortal again. George admitted it would be a wrench to give it all up, but "the calendar has caught up with me", he said. Then he launched into a peroration about the place he loved:

> I love this House, the Palace of Westminster, Parliament and all it stands for . . . And isn't it a wonderful country that can send me, a Welsh miner's son, from Tonypandy, without wealth or powerful friends, to a place like this to be given the trust of the House and the country's leaders.

It never ceased to astonish him. But why did he retire just then, and how would he adjust to a bungalow in Cardiff after all this? George answered directly and honestly: "There's no retirement age in this job and some of my predecessors went on very much longer. But I want to retire while they still want me to stay. That's the secret, I think." He pointed out that Selwyn Lloyd, his immediate predecessor, had said, "Five years is long enough in this job", and George had done seven. But he was feeling the loss as he continued:

> In a way this House and the people who work here are my family and my home after all these years. I'm a bachelor, so you can understand that. But when I'm finished with it, I shall go back to where I am happiest, a bungalow just outside my Cardiff constituency. I had to adjust upwards to the luxury of all this when I arrived, so going back to my roots won't be difficult.

Then he added wistfully, "Do you know that everyone, even the children, call me George!"

It sounded like a nice cosy retirement. George, with lots of friends, especially children, would bask in his idle leisure and tell his stories, exchanging the silver-buckled shoes of the Speaker for comfortable carpet clippers by the fireside. But the interviewer was not fooled. He had read up on George and knew the necessary activity for such a man. What he did not know was that already a cancer was forming that would in a few months' time cause his friends great anxiety. Instead, he saw a very active retirement based upon what he was already doing: "He is a lay preacher twice on Sundays and plays a big part in Methodist affairs. Invitations to do lecture trips, hand out prizes and talk to delegations will descend in shoals on that modest bungalow. 'There'll be a welcome in the hillside'."

He was right, of course, as he was with another obvious prediction: "If George Thomas finishes up in the Lords, I told myself, he won't even be giving up Westminster anyway." William Foster had rightly assessed his man. It all happened, and far more than anyone could have imagined. *Choice* magazine, in which this article appeared, has a note on its cover, "Incorporating *Life begins at Fifty*". George was about to show them that life begins at seventy-four. It was truly a new life.

George's own comment on retirement was, "However carefully one prepares for it, it is always a shock when the time comes to pack up and walk towards the sunset. Although I was seventy-four years of age, the thought of stopping activity never occurred to me."

Well, of course, he didn't stop activity. Charities poured in their requests for him to become active on their behalf. He agreed to become Chairman of the Methodist National Children's Home, President of the British Heart Foundation, Council Member of the National Asthma Research Council, Chairman of the National Benevolent Fund for the Aged, and many other good causes. "When I accepted these offices," he comments, "I thought that I was going to help the respective charities, but in the event I was to discover that constructive activity gives new energy to older people." His tireless good works were also therapeutic for him. He needed them as much as they needed him.

The Coat of Arms

As Speaker, George Thomas had to have a coat of arms. His friends in Tonypandy, who had laughed at his plus fours, would have laughed even louder in those early days at the idea of George Thomas as a knight with a coat of arms. There was no ancestry to bequeath him one, although in more recent years his genealogy on his mother's side has been traced back to 1602.

But faced with the problem of designing a coat of arms when he became Speaker, he gave the designer all the necessary elements and the motto. The three elements are daffodils for Wales, a miner's lamp for his family and friends in Tonypandy, and an open Bible for his Methodism. The motto is in Welsh, *"Bid ben bid bont"* (He who would be a leader must be a bridge). He explained that motto as "a bridge between the poor and the well-to-do, the fortunate and the unfortunate". He had been a leader in the trade union movement, in Parliament and in the Methodist Church. As Speaker, he was in an exalted position. No one doubted that he had aspired to lead men and women in the ways of righteousness. His motto reminded him that he must continue to be a bridge. Although he took no part in party politics as Speaker, he never ceased to be a socialist. Like the Labour Party, he has changed much since he ventured into Greece and championed the cause of the Communist guerrillas. He has changed, but he still bridges the gap whenever he can between the poor and the well-to-do, the fortunate and the unfortunate.

A Memorable June

After they had said all those nice things about him in Parliament, the members, whether lowly or exalted, went to the hustings to fight an election, which his friend Margaret Thatcher won again, while his party lost. He had no election to face. Instead, requests and honours poured in to that "modest bungalow". As Speaker he had received many honorary doctorates and had been honoured in other ways. On 22nd June, he received what was refused to the triumphant Mrs Thatcher—a doctorate from Oxford. It was a Doctor of Civil Law and a much coveted honour. Together with him was Alfred Brendel, the very distinguished pianist. Oxford honoured two great men that day—both communicators in different ways. George was delighted.

But next day, there was more. Parliament had reassembled without him, but they had not forgotten him. On 23rd June, the following Motion was put to the House by Margaret Thatcher, leading her second government as Prime Minister:

> that an humble address be presented to Her Majesty, praying Her Majesty that she will be most graciously pleased to confer some signal mark of her Royal Favour upon the Right Honourable George Thomas for his eminent service during the important period in which with such distinguished ability and dignity he presided in the Chair of this House.

Her Majesty was most graciously pleased and George Thomas became the Viscount Tonypandy. This meant that his political career could continue in the "other place". Honours were not always in favour among Labour Members of Parliament. Many objected to a non-elected upper Chamber. Principal among them was his old friend and colleague, fellow-warrior in early days against the H-bomb and in many other fights, the Rt Hon. Anthony Wedgewood-Benn, who had renounced his own hereditary title in order to serve in an elected Chamber. For all his objection to honours conferred, he recognized the difference with George. This honour was not included in some privileged list, but asked for by the elected House of Commons. George Thomas went to the House of Lords at the request of the House of Commons. Tony Benn made this distinction quite clear when George interviewed him after his elevation—in fact when he had been a Member of the House of Lords for only a week.

In subsequent months, George took his position seriously and the voice of Viscount Tonypandy could be heard defending his principles —from Sunday observance to the responsibility of the state to prosecute alleged Nazi murderers, who were responsible for deaths in concentration camps, however long after the events.

A Grave Illness

Television was not slow, especially in Wales, to see the value of George as a natural broadcaster. Harlech TV invited him to interview a series of people he had known well in the political arena. The programmes were broadcast at 10.30 p.m. each Monday from 19th September 1983. Those interviewed were Margaret Thatcher, Neil

Kinnock, David Owen, Tony Benn, Lord Hailsham, and Gwynfor Evans of Plaid Cymru.

It was quite a scoop for Harlech TV. The interviews were not of the formal kind in which the interviewer is often in confrontation with his interviewee. George was not that kind of person. He had a conversation with each of these who were his friends. He had been long away from the arena of party politics. In the programmes, he shared opinions, asked about points of view and often put his own. With Tony Benn, for example, he defended the authority of Parliament against Benn's insistence on the authority of the people. George had an immense respect for the long traditions of British democracy which he defended against Tony Benn's reminder that for most of our history only a privileged minority had elected members to Parliament!

In the course of this particular exchange, it was clear that George was having trouble with his voice. The rich tones of "Order! Order!" which had subdued Parliament and delighted the nation on radio, were distorted. He took little notice of this and continued to accept invitations to lecture, preach, travel and accept presidencies which would involve heavy work and an overcrowded diary. However, it became clear that he was ill, and eventually on 6th April 1984, he was admitted to hospital with a "serious throat infection". It was a cancer of the throat. The treatment was severe, but the doctors and consultants gave their skill and many offered their prayers. God is the healer, always, and George acknowledged this, but no less did he acknowledge the skill of the physicians who were God's instruments. He recovered, but not before he had given a fright to many of his friends.

It had been a fright for him too, and a warning. He had to look at the possibility of death, consider what he thought he had still to do and assess priorities. The cure took some time and enabled him to consider and reconsider the things most important to him. The House of Lords meant much to him and his illness silenced him there for a year. His preaching depended much on the quality of his voice. Perhaps he would have to thin out his diary. Spiritually, he was prepared for death and his faith assured him of his meeting again with Mam. But there was work to do and he needed time to do it.

In Aberystwyth there are bulging files of get-well letters. Most of them came at the end of the holiday period, in early September, when people first heard the news. Something of their opinion of George comes out in the messages sent to him. Many were, like Jeremy Thorpe, very distressed and assured him of their prayers. More typical letters were those that said, "You will survive this hurdle"; "It is good to know that you are fighting your illness both physically and spiritually"; "Your faith will surely help you through this difficult period"; ". . . must be serious to cancel a visit to Texas"; and so many reveal what they thought of George. These letters came after an announcement on television that George had started a two-month treatment for cancer. He survived with gratitude to God and to the hospital. He had many years of service yet in the House of Lords, with charities, especially the National Children's Home, with preaching, lecturing and advising many charitable organizations.

He had achieved much in the past and the period of convalescence was a time to look back and forward. He recalled the years of struggle, the support of his family, especially Mam, the changes that had come over his country, his party and himself. He knew that when he returned to the House of Lords he would have to select the important issues to comment upon and he determined to make that part of his life the centre of all his activities. There was, of course, the temptation to feel that there was not much time, and therefore to overcrowd his diary. He never quite cured himself of that temptation.

CHAPTER TWENTY

Viscount Tonypandy

O N 19TH JULY 1983, the Right Honourable Thomas George
Thomas, now the Viscount Tonypandy, of Rhondda in the
county of Mid-Glamorgan, was introduced into the House of Lords
by the Viscount Sidmouth and the Viscount De L'Isle, flanking him
on either side. George was no stranger to ceremony or to robes. As
Speaker, he had shown great respect for ceremony and saw it as a
symbolic reminder of the great tradition of Parliament, although he
had asserted his own personality beneath the wig. It found expression
too in his use of Speaker's House and in his irrepressible humour
when presiding over the House. The years, of course, had taught him
much, but it was the same man under the robes of a Viscount as
the schoolteacher who had paid for the milk of a poor boy at school.
When he thought back to those days in Tonypandy, Dagenham, Cardiff and, as a Member of Parliament, angry at the unjust treatment
of the Greek rebels, he knew that he had changed. When he noticed
a tendency to be pulled away from his roots, he tried to restore his
links with the past which he loved. He continued to live in Cardiff,
and although he had close relations with the highest in the land, he
was pleased that the man or woman in the street in Cardiff or Tonypandy recognized him and spoke to him and cared about his health.
However endangered were his attachment to his roots, they were
never quite pulled up.

A New Political Role

The journalist, William Foster, who had interviewed George on his
retirement from the Speaker's Chair, had written, "If George
Thomas finishes in the Lords, he won't even be giving up Westminster." And here he was now, in the Lords, and he saw his role
there as one of importance. It was no nominal title for him, no spare-

time activity. Once in the Lords, he determined to fulfil his function with integrity and industry.

He not only took his seat on the cross benches, but made clear to his colleagues who were Labour peers, that his impartiality as Mr Speaker had not been merely skin-deep. He intended to remain his own man and they could not always count upon his support. In this he followed the tradition that ex-Speakers always sit on the cross benches. This meant that like every one of his predecessors in the Chair of the House of Commons, he could never return to active party politics. The tradition of continuing impartiality even after retirement has evolved because of Parliament's resolve to protect the current occupant of the Speaker's Chair from any charge that as soon as he leaves the Chair, he will become a party political activist again.

George was now entering the third stage in his political career and, although he was no longer young, he carried his seventy-four years well. He was still capable of strenuous work, as his diary shows, and he brought a great deal of valuable experience to the House of Lords.

He had been made an hereditary peer, which was thought by some of his Labour colleagues to be reactionary. The question was theoretical for him, because he had no one to inherit his peerage, but he did express the opinion that the custom of hereditary peerages brings new blood into an ageing House. Although he felt that we could do without the House of Lords, his experience as Speaker of the House of Commons convinced him that there was a need for a second chamber. Unlike his friend Tony Benn, he considered that it would be a terrible gamble to abolish the House of Lords, and replace it by an elected "House of the People". He saw that our second-chamber system worked. He had not been long in the House of Lords when he summed up his considered opinion, based largely upon his observations from the Speaker's Chair:

> Our second-chamber system . . . gives the Government and even the Opposition the chance for second thoughts. It prevents legislation being pushed through without proper consideration and it also prevents any administration prolonging its own life.

His conclusion was that the House of Commons needed the restraint imposed by the second chamber.

Early Days in the House of Lords

There is a consistency about George's political attitude, which found different expressions in his three roles in Parliament. He was and remained a Christian socialist, taking his inspiration from John Wesley and the New Testament rather than from Karl Marx and *Das Kapital*. He had entered Parliament in 1945 as a Labour MP supported by the National Union of Teachers, on the left wing of the Labour Party. He supported the Welfare State because of its provision of justice for all. He wished no one to suffer as his mother had suffered. He wished to be a leader and he had leadership potential, but he never wavered from his motto, "If you want to be a leader, you must be a bridge." He never pulled up the drawbridge. All those elements have remained with him all his life. As a socialist MP he fought for social justice, condemned nuclear weapons and hovered on the edge of pacifism.

These attitudes did not change when he became Speaker of the House of Commons. Yet he needed to express them differently. There, he had to be totally impartial. He defended the dignity of the House in the interests of parliamentary democracy. He saw his role as the defender of the House of Commons, not so much from the monarch now, as from the government, whether it was Tory or Labour.

Now he was in the House of Lords and the next stage of his political career was starting. He was very different from the eager new MP, feeling eight feet tall, who entered the precincts of Parliament in 1945. Then you could hardly find a Question Time when he was not on his feet. Now, he waited and watched.

After his introduction to the House of Lords, there was not much time before the summer recess. Once Parliament reassembled in October he listened and made his first speech on Cyprus on 16th November. Apart from a brief intervention about the Severn Bridge, he was not heard again until February, and then only once, on the Welsh Plant-Breeding Station. On 21st March 1984, he spoke on the European Council Brussels Meeting; then twice in April on matters that deeply concerned him. He had been admitted to hospital on 6th April with a serious throat infection, but twice on 27th he spoke to the Video Recordings Bill, against what were commonly called at the time "video nasties"; and in reference to the proposed closure of coal mines. His last speech before the throat cancer put him temporarily out of action was on 28th June on the plight of redundant miners.

The illness was not evident except in a certain restriction of his voice, and he completed the session without knowing how serious his condition was. In fact, as late as July 1984, there is a photograph of three friends, Sheik Yamani, Sir Julian Hodge, and George looking well and happy, at a reunion in Cardiff. He would not again speak in the House of Lords until June 1985, but during this silence, he assessed its quality:

> My short experience in the House of Lords has convinced me that there is not the slightest doubt that the debating level in the Lords is much higher than that in the Commons, and bills are examined with much more care. There is not the same vested party interest, with people looking for votes. There is an independence of mind and considerable scholarship that serves the nation well.

He added, with the memory of interruptions in the Commons and even of members being shouted down, that in the Lords, people listened politely to speeches even if they disagreed strongly with them, and waited their turn to make a directly opposing speech, which was also listened to politely. He could see no reason why that should not happen in the Commons, and indeed he had tried to bring about that state of affairs there.

As a Labour MP, he had often spoken against the House of Lords in the past, but he saw its value now. In the Commons, he had observed that the use of the guillotine could be applied to a bill in such a way as to result in rather scrappy legislation. If it were not for the Lords, it would end up on the statute book in that condition. The Lords could scrutinize such poorly drafted legislation. He began to see now that a government with a big majority could force through any measure it wanted without proper debate. The House of Lords prevented that happening.

He also began to look again at his long-held opposition to the hereditary system. His comments on this about this time (1984) are worth quoting in full:

> There is a great deal wrong with the hereditary system but I have been very impressed by the number and quality of young men in the House of Lords who may be there only because a distant ancestor was rewarded many years ago, but who take

their roles in the parliamentary machine very seriously indeed. I hope some way can be found to keep them if the hereditary principle in government is finally abolished. There are, of course, many more who do nothing, save enjoy the privileges of rank, and these people should certainly not be allowed to take part in the process of government.

Proposals for the Second Chamber

Viscount Tonypandy, one-time labour MP for Cardiff, Speaker of the House of Commons, now seated in the House of Lords, began to look at what reforms would give to the House of Lords a greater usefulness to the nation. He opposed the then current proposals for a single-chamber government: "The continuance of a second chamber is essential for the maintenance of democracy in these islands." But what reforms are needed?

George was convinced that it should not be an elected chamber. He had observed America and Australia, each with both chambers elected, plunging the country into crisis when they disagreed. He did not seek greater power for the second chamber, but increased support for its role as a revising chamber to tidy up legislation. He thought it should be appointed in proportion to the strengths in the House of Commons and made up of people from a cross-section of the community, who had proved their ability. "People from the trade unions, business, the universities, the professions, public life, even retired politicians, all could play a part." This meant that while they had real power in the House, their appointments would be limited to the life of one parliament. They would not behave recklessly, because they would wish to be appointed by the next parliament, but they would show sufficient independence and have value in making the House of Commons look again at its legislation. He admitted that the existing House of Lords worked smoothly, but it needed reform.

Cyprus

It was hardly surprising that Viscount Tonypandy's first speech in the House of Lords was about Cyprus. At the 1976 Commonwealth Speakers' Conference in Westminster he had met many Speakers with whom he formed friendships which lasted well into his retire-

323

ment. One of his closest friends was Alecos Michaeliades of Cyprus, whom he met at such a conference in Australia in 1978. After many years of close association and visits to Cyprus, usually at Christmas, he described him as "probably the ablest of Cyprus' post-Independence politicians". Alecos Michaeliades had been a highly successful businessman, matching his ability with an unquestioned integrity. He was a good public speaker and George admired his eloquence. There was no doubt that he saw him as one of the pre-eminent figures in public life in Cyprus. To this day, George, who was made a Freeman of the city of Paphos, finds a second home in Cyprus.

On 16th November 1984, Viscount Tonypandy spoke for the first time in the House of Lords and it was on behalf of Cyprus. This was during one of the short debates drawn by Lord Spens, coincidentally on the day following the declaration of independence by the Turkish Cypriots. George gave notice that he intended to make his "maiden speech" in the House of Lords on that day. Lord Spens, who opened the debate, made reference to it at the beginning, welcoming Viscount Tonypandy and inviting him to speak freely after so long a discipline of virtual silence, other than the famous "Order, Order".

Lord Spens had a special interest in Cyprus, and his visit to North Cyprus in June had already made clear to him what was likely to happen. His speech was a masterly summary of Turkish/Greek relations in Cyprus as he had seen it. He established the setting for the debate, albeit with a strong bias in favour of the Turkish Cypriots. He blamed the British Foreign Office for negligence and justified the Turkish action.

Lord Cledwyn of Penrhos took the side of the Greek Cypriots, accusing Turkey of breaching a treaty made in 1974 and reminding the House that the United Nations Assembly had called for all occupying forces to withdraw from Cyprus. He praised the strenuous efforts of Perez de Cuellar, the UN Secretary General, who tried to reach a settlement with Mr Denktash of Turkey and President Kyprianou of Greece. Viscount Tonypandy then spoke. He was noticeably moved and the whole House was ready to listen with pleasure and courtesy to this maiden speech—as is the custom of the House. He was conciliatory, but undoubtedly pro-Greek. His fear was that the island might be divided. He argued strongly against that, ending with an appeal:

I conclude by making a plea to Mr Denktash and to his Excellency President Kyprianou. They both hold power in their respective areas and with regard to their respective peoples. But it is in the greatest interest of Cyprus that both of them should realize that this is not a time for pride, that it is not a time for bigotry, and that the future—which does not belong to them, but to the young—cannot afford the partition of that small island. I pray that the endeavours of Her Majesty's Government will be successful in ensuring that the federal state, to which President Kyprianou had already agreed and which, as the statement by Mr Denktash indicated, is possible, will come about, and that we shall be able to work on that. We dare not let the situation slide so that Cyprus can suffer the agonies that we suffer in a part of the United Kingdom.

The speakers who followed were all kind but many went further than the required congratulations. The House seemed glad to have him among them. Lord Kennet, for example, spoke of his familiar and authoritative voice, his long career in the House of Commons, his integrity, his political gifts, his sparkling personality which had brought warmth and assurance to all who have known him. "He was a fine Speaker in the House of Commons and we have heard a fine maiden speech in this House."

George did not speak again in the debate, but listened and admired the way in which such debates are conducted in the House of Lords.

Paphos

George was deeply influenced by Greece and in particular Paphos, once one of the largest cities of the Eastern Mediterranean. There he had established firm ties with the Greek Orthodox Church, impressed by the fact that it could trace its origins back to a missionary visit from the Apostle Paul and the conversion of the proconsul Sergius Paulus. Both the Bishop of Paphos and His Beatitude the Archbishop of Cyprus became George's close friends. His visits to Paphos were frequent, and he regularly stayed there with his friend Alecos Michaeliades. But he soon cultivated many more friends there. He became a regular visitor to the mountain monasteries, where abbots and monks alike welcomed him to their ancient abodes. Because of his outspoken criticism of the Turkish invasion and occupation of Northern Cyprus, George Thomas became a household

name throughout the island. When in 1989, he became the first ever
Freeman of the city of Paphos, President Vassiliou wrote to the Mayor
of Paphos, congratulating him and declaring that George Thomas
should be looked upon as a Freeman of Cyprus.

The Freedom ceremony, conducted in the ancient Roman amphi-
theatre in Paphos, moved him deeply. All his old love of history, his
Celtic sensitivity and his love of Greece imbued this ceremony with
a profound symbolic significance. But there was another element. He
had been brought up on the Bible and particularly the New Testament. The landscape and history of the Holy Land and the areas
which St Paul's missionary journeys had covered were as familiar to
him as the landscape and history of Wales. He might have been
standing, he said, on the very place that Paul stood. The strength of
this emotion was similar to what he had felt in Israel where he trod
the path that Jesus trod. The knowledge that he was in the same place
where Jesus had reached out to the suffering, and where our Lord
himself had been crucified, dead and buried and risen again, never
failed to stir his emotions. Paphos had something of the same effect.

George's Continuing Interventions

Viscount Tonypandy could not forget his deep concern, nor his desire
to apply Christian morality to the public life of Britain. He spoke
whenever Wales was threatened or Christian morality tossed too easily
aside. He spoke again when there was a question of access to the
Severn Bridge and he saw the steps being taken as harmful to the
industry of South Wales. He spoke in April about the need to control
pornographic videos, in particular against an amendment which
exempted such videos,

> if taken as a whole they were designed to inform, educate or
> instruct;
> if they were concerned with sport, religion, music etc;
> if they were video games.

George rose in anger—"What! No restraint of any sort? Are we to
allow the filth of the gutter to be available to our children?" He argued
strongly that if that amendment went through, they might as well drop
the bill altogether, and he carried his point.

On that same day, 27th April 1984, only a few weeks after the first worry about his throat infection, he reacted strongly when coal mine closures were being discussed and each side was counting up who had closed the most pits. He intervened effectively:

> My Lords, is the Minister aware that the mining communities are closely linked and that they are good, loyal, patriotic people? Would we not be very wise at this time to say nothing, but to leave those who are responsible to try and reach an agreement? My father was a miner; my brother was a miner; all my teenage friends were miners. And I hate to see one being set against another. I hope that in this House, at least, we shall not try to score off each other.

When, at the end of June, the issue of alternative employment for redundant miners was discussed he urged action and urgent action to give hope:

> My Lords, is the Minister aware that it is quite wrong for any community in this land to be left without hope, and that unless there is a greater urgency shown in telling these mining communities that they are on the conscience of this House and of the government, then we can continue to expect trouble? But if hope is held out, that there is greater action along the lines that the noble Lord, Lord Chelwood, asked for, then we can expect a decent response from these good, loyal communities.

That was the last speech he made before his illness. Anxious months followed, but eventually he emerged cured. His voice was not heard in debate in the House of Lords for a year.

From June 1984 to June 1985, George had one of those periods in his life which drove him in upon himself. He could consider his life and ask how faithfully he had lived out his Christian principles in public. There were incidents which he regretted, times when he wished he had had more courage, issues on which he had not spoken clearly enough. All these need time and leisure to offer them to God and seek forgiveness. But he could not fail to thank God for what he had achieved. There is little false modesty in George. He knows when he has done wrong, but he also knows when he has done "rather well", as he would say. And he has much to be pleased with as he looks back. This book is already full of such achievements.

But was this the end of the story? Was it now to be a real retirement? As he passed his seventy-fifth birthday there were many indications that he might be approaching his end, but he was not prepared to believe it. He had much work yet to do and he had only just started to enjoy the House of Lords and feel comfortable as a member of that House. His determination to live, as well as his faith and the excellent treatment he received, carried him through.

Sunday Trading

On 7th June 1985, Viscount Tonypandy rose during a debate on Sunday trading. He was then content to say, "My Lords, is the Minister aware that if the Government persists in wanting to change our Sunday, they will be asking for trouble?"

His real speech on Sunday opening came later, during the long debate on the Second Reading of the *Shops Bill* on 2nd December 1985. This was one of his great speeches in the House of Lords and it needs to be read at length:

> My Lords, it is a very great privilege to follow the noble Lord, Lord Sainsbury, who speaks with great authority on the retail industry. I noticed that in his concern for the employment protection of people he passed by the fact that, immediately the Act becomes law, anyone employed afterwards has no protection. People have to agree to work on Sunday or the chances are they will not be employed . . .
>
> When Speakers have come to this House they have always stayed outside the party battle. But I feel that I am entitled to speak to you today, because I do not regard Sunday as a party matter . . .
>
> The protection of Sunday was certainly not mentioned at the last election and, with respect, I say to those who sit on the Government Front Bench that if they had campaigned on the promise that they would make a Sunday like Saturday they would not be on that Bench at all. I believe that Her Majesty's Government, far from having a mandate, are indifferent to the reaction and feeling of their own natural supporters in the country as well as of those on the opposite side. They are indifferent to millions of people to whom Sunday is something very precious indeed. It is a reminder that our heritage in the land is a Christian heritage. That is its main symbolism. It is a reminder that we are a people who owe our heritage to our Christian fathers.
>
> I was deeply moved by the sparkling speech of the noble Lord, Lord Mishcon, because I believe humanity is in debt to the

Jewish people. I believe, as it happens, that God spoke to the world through the Jewish people. I believe it and I would be a coward if I did not say it here. But my Lords, the proposal to end all trading restrictions removes any distinction between Saturday and Sunday. Who would have believed that the Government would put as their top priority . . . their idea to end all the distinctions that separate Sunday . . . from Saturday as though it does not matter any longer? Those who are seeking to maintain the old values that guided our fathers in these islands are facing great difficulties. The removal of Sunday, the end of a special day which is a reminder of our heritage, is bound to undermine those who are seeking, in the words of the noble Lord, Lord Mishcon, to maintain the best values in this land.

Why is Sunday so important to us? Why should we feel so deeply, as I certainly do, about finding a Government bringing a Whip, a Government from whom I never expected it? I know it will not come from the opposite side—there are too many chapel people over there. Dare I say that this is much more than a legalistic matter. I did not want to spend any time discussing how we catch people who break the law on Sundays. I am talking of that day being different from any other day—Monday, Tuesday, Wednesday, Thursday, Friday and Saturday. Is Sunday to be the same? In introducing the Bill this afternoon, the Minister, for whom I have a very high regard, reminded us that for 500 years Sunday has survived in this land. Is this to be the generation that will end Sunday, that will take all restrictions away and let it be like any other day of the week? Sunday has a symbolism that cannot easily be defined. Even people who have no link with the Church value Sunday as a day of rest. It is a day for the family. People can laugh as much as they like, but it is the day when the family can get together. A million married women are engaged in the retail industry. I do not know how many of them are mothers because I do not have the statistics, but two out of every three of the shop assistants in the retail industry are married women. Are they to be told, "Never mind the family, work on Sunday?" . . . No formula can measure the intangible, unseen but very real blessings that our quiet Sunday has brought for us. In every town and village of this land today Sunday is different. This Bill will change everything. It will open the floodgates and will sweep away that to which we are accustomed. The Right Reverend Prelate reminded us that we are not alone in legislating in a special way as far as Sunday is concerned. Austria, Belgium, Denmark, Finland, West Germany, Greece, Ireland, the Netherlands, Norway and Switzerland all prohibit or carefully regulate Sunday trading. We are invited, with no substantial reason given, to throw away this priceless heritage.

During this past decade, as the noble Lord, Lord Mishcon, reminded us, we have experienced a serious weakening in family ties. There are many diverse reasons and pressures that have caused this, but this Bill will accelerate the pace of breakdown. Many important signposts which guided us and those who went before us in this land have been demolished in recent years. In my judgement, to remove this symbol from our national life will further deteriorate family life. We cannot afford to do that. This seems to be the age of the iconoclast, of the tearer down, of the destroyer of what other people built and what has endured for 500 years, according to the Minister. The time has come for us to call a halt to the wanton destruction of the things that are best in our heritage. This House can begin that process today, I believe, by giving a substantial vote, an overwhelming vote, to the amendment of the Right Reverend Prelate. To destroy our traditional Sunday merely because there are anomalies would be a criminal betrayal of the heritage we received from our fathers.

There is no public clamour for it. The first indication of a great movement of public opinion in this land is in the postbag of Members of the House of Commons. They have not been receiving letters. I have been making inquiries. The letters only started when the Government's proposals were known. There was no public demand. People were not saying, "Whatever happens, we must change our Sunday."

In recent years your Lordships' House has assumed a new significance in the estimation of the people of these islands. Time and again this House has voted to guard liberties and traditions. Regardless of the pressures put on by the party Whips on this occasion, I hope and I believe that we shall give a message to the people of these islands. Sunday is not for sale. Sunday is too precious a part of our way of life. I trust that this House will prove so today.

It was an effective speech and shows something of his best speaking style during his first few years in the House of Lords. He was certainly gaining confidence. The debate went on for some time and an amendment by the Bishop of Birmingham, Hugh Montefiore, which George supported, seemed to make sense and reflect the feeling of the House. It was to add to the bill: "but that this House considers that the law should be amended so as to rationalize restrictions on trading hours without such extensive deregulation as the Bill proposes." The Whips and government pressure defeated the amendment by 141 votes to 85.

As George had indicated, the amendment might have saved the government a lot of trouble and the bill had a difficult passage through the House of Commons.

Preaching

Once he was free from the responsibilities of office, George was able to give his mind to preaching, which now became an ever greater part of his activities. This was both in the United Kingdom and the United States of America, where he renewed contacts he had made many years before. In 1988, he returned to Seattle, to the First Methodist Church, exactly thirty years after he had preached there earlier. On that tour, he preached his way round the States—Dallas, Houston, Oklahoma, Arizona, Los Angeles—securing his claim that he had preached in every state of the Union.

Back in the United Kingdom, he went north for his second visit to Loretto School in Edinburgh, which eventually he visited five times. He was profoundly moved by the decision of the headmasters and governors of Loretto to establish in perpetuity "The Viscount Tonypandy Award for Service to the School and also to the Community". Later he developed a deep affection for Fettes, which was the school that his predecessor as Speaker, Selwyn Lloyd, had attended as a boy. While he was still Speaker, George had preached the University Sermon in St Giles, Edinburgh. Now he did not confine his preaching to the capital of Scotland, but branched out to Arbroath and Peterhead Methodist Churches. His Scottish visits confirmed his deep and strong affinity with his fellow Celts.

In his native Wales, his friend Sir Julian Hodge established "The George Thomas Centre for Hospice Care", which received widespread public support and still flourishes today. At the same time, George became President of the South Wales Men's Choir, which consisted of three hundred men from all walks of life.

The First Cancer

These strenuous activities had a temporary halt when cancer put him out of action only a year after leaving the Speaker's Chair. Radium treatment at the Royal Marsden Hospital in Chelsea was to restore him to good health, but George readily speaks both of the day that he was told that he had cancer, and of his experience in the out-patients department. On being told of his condition, his first and natural reaction was to pray that his own faith would remain strong in the testing days ahead.

He remembered that his most lonely moments were when the nursing technicians had arranged him in a lying down position so that the radium ray would hit the cancerous spot in his throat, and then they all withdrew quickly, closing the door tightly behind them, so that the danger of radium rays would not reach them. He felt alone and frightened, but immediately a great assurance came over him. Although the technicians left him, he was not alone. He could still pray with confidence. After treatment in the Royal Marsden Hospital his voice gradually returned.

There was a confidence in George which kept him from total despair. His faith was strong. He had no reason to fear death. Yet there was that dilemma in him, which is so aptly expressed by the Apostle Paul:

> To me, to live is Christ and to die is gain. If I am to go on living in the body, this will mean fruitful labour for me. Yet, what shall I choose? I do not know! I desire to depart to be with Christ, which is better by far, but it is more necessary for you that I remain in the body. Convinced of this, I know that I will remain, and I will continue with all of you for your progress and joy in the faith.
> (Philippians 1:21–25)

Soon he was again preaching, speaking and much involved in charitable work. Nor was it long before he returned to the House of Lords, where he was soon defending the special character of Sunday.

The Bank of Wales

Throughout his retirement years, George had one appointment which was unlike all the others; he was a director of the Bank of Wales. All his life, there had been a tendency for him to move towards the chair! He must be one of the most experienced chairmen in the world. It was no surprise, therefore, that after his recovery and the return of his unusual energy, he was invited in 1986 to become Chairman of the Bank. This was work he enjoyed. It was based in his beloved Wales and it gave him prestigious work in Cardiff. The bank's Welshness was threatened, however, when the Bank of Scotland acquired control of the Bank of Wales by purchasing shares of the Bank of Chicago and of Sir Julian Hodge, a good friend of George's. It might have been natural for the Bank of Scotland to bring in its own chairman, but, like Margaret Thatcher in 1979, they knew a good chair man when they saw one, and they had no intention of changing the Welsh character of the Bank of Wales. George was asked to continue as Chairman. It was not only this sensitive choice which led George to speak with affection of the Scots with whom he worked. "Being fellow Celts," he wrote, "they understood how sensitive an issue of national feelings could be, and they leaned over backwards to show respect for all things Welsh. But it was the integrity of the Scottish bankers that shone out for mc." His explanation was typical, and from a Methodist quite generous: "They have the stamp of Calvin on them." He continued for nearly five years as Chairman and it was only on his eighty-second birthday (29th January 1991) that he resolved to hand over responsibility to someone else.

The NCH George Thomas Society

The National Children's Home had been his love for many years. In 1989, when George was celebrating his eightieth birthday, it was decided to form the George Thomas Society within the NCH and by means of it to raise in excess of one million pounds. By that time the NCH was caring for 11,000 needy children and their families each year. As Viscount Tonypandy, he could draw upon very distinguished Founding Fellows of the Society named after him, who gave generously large donations to the work. Those Founding Fellows would attract others to join. There were more than a hundred of them, including the Prince of Wales, the Prime Minister, George's successor as Speaker of the House of Commons, the President of the Methodist Conference, Sheik Yamani, Sir John Templeton, Alecos Michaeliades, Sir Julian Hodge, Sir Sigmund Sternberg, several Lords and many leaders of industry. The list reads like a survey of George's distinguished career. Even the Bank of Wales is not left out. With these distinguished Founding Fellows, George could appeal to others to join them. The condition was a minimum donation of

£1,000. George's style can be detected in the appeal, adding, ". . . but hopefully much more", and then that warm welcome, as so many knew: "Our Founding Fellows would be delighted if you could join them." Not wishing to leave anyone out, the appeal continued, "If you feel that this is too great a commitment then we hope that you will become a Member of the Society upon payment of a minimum annual gift of £150." And again George's hand is acknowledged in the final note: "In order that those with limited means should not feel excluded from the Society, it was the express wish of Viscount Tonypandy that there should be a far wider Associate Membership on payment of an annual gift of £10 or more." The money, "in excess of £1 million", was to increase and improve the services of the National Children's Home, "which are so urgently needed for children involved in physical and sexual abuse which could leave them damaged for life."

For this occasion of the launching of the NCH George Thomas Society, a new portrait was painted by June Mendoza, with George looking like an elder statesman, unusually serious and thoughtful, with Oxford academic gown and hood—The Rt Hon. Dr George Thomas, Viscount Tonypandy. A copy of this portrait was sent to every grade of member in one form or another. The appeal was a great success and continues with an annual dinner and lecture. George supports many charities, but none has his heart so completely as the National Children's Home, which has the added attraction of being Methodist in its foundation.

The NCH George Thomas Society was launched on 3rd May 1989, at an inaugural banquet in the Guildhall, hosted by Lord Ramsey (one of the Founding Fellows) and attended by HRH Princess Alexandra, the Lord Mayor of London and other notable personalities. It was a media event and many saw part of the celebration on television. There we also saw Viscount Tonypandy, weak and obviously seriously ill. Earlier that year, he had felt the weakness that comes with lymphoma, and despite positive tests at St Thomas's Hospital, he continued to keep his appointments until he collapsed.

The whole nation saw it happen on television. There was a stoop in that dignified straight stand to which we had all grown accustomed in Viscount Tonypandy. He looked pale and hesitant in the ceremonies of the occasion. He was the Guest of Honour and the camera was often on him. We could all see that he was in pain and as he processed, he stumbled. Margaret Thatcher caught his arm and gently supported him with dignity along the course of the procession. Viewers had not forgotten the cancer of a few years before and George looked very ill. The BBC announced that night that he had collapsed and was taken to St Thomas's Hospital. No one would have been surprised if the announcement of his death had come next morning.

The Second Cancer

This time it was a cancer of the lymphatic system, the treatment for which was chemotherapy and radiotherapy. If it is caught in the early stages, it is usually curable, but delay is dangerous. Both the disease and the cure are debilitating. Symptoms are described as "a general feeling of illness, with fever, loss of appetite, weight loss and night sweats". The immune system is affected. George was in fact very seriously ill. After the chemotherapy, his hair fell out and his weight dropped below seven stone.

Throughout his illness he was deluged with letters from every part of the United Kingdom, assuring him of prayers for his recovery. The inner peace which these prayers gave him, he acknowledges, was a major contribution to his gradual return to good health, but he corrected those who sought to hold him up as a miracle of healing worked by faith alone. He insisted upon pointing out that while God is always the healer, he works through the doctors, nurses and technicians. He was, of course, interviewed on radio and television in every kind of programme. His lively spirit came over as he discussed his long and eventful life, but when the question turned to his cure, he was most careful and very serious in making two points: first, that his type of cancer was one that could yield to medical treatment and be cured, it was not a terminal cancer; second, while he gave thanks to God, the instrument had been the medical skills found in the hospital, among doctors, consultants, nursing staff and the whole professional team that is geared to cure.

He did not realize how weak he was until he came out of hospital and tried to walk with the aid of a walking stick. Each day he tried to walk a few yards further than the day before. He was determined to get strong again. But he was eighty years old, plus a few months by now. Gradually, his hair and his ability to walk came back. His disarming spirit came back too. When we complimented him on his returning hair he complained that he had ordered "curly and chestnut brown" and was not really satisfied with the delivery.

The House of Lords

After his second serious illness, George began to look at some things that could be cut from his overcrowded diary, but he recognized the primary importance of his place in the House of Lords. This was to be his first priority from now on. It now became his practice once again to organize his life around the sittings of the House. When he is not world travelling or preaching, you can be sure of finding him in one of three places: the House of Lords, the Travellers' Club or in Cardiff, at home in his bungalow, dealing with his post, preparing his sermons or reading his newspaper. He takes his place in the Lords most seriously and stays in London, at the Travellers' Club, during the week when the House is sitting. George's speeches in the Upper House have always adhered to the tradition of impartiality, confined to matters outside the strictly partisan and never consciously supporting one party against another. Whenever he has had to speak on some matter that was either opposed to the Government line or to the Opposition, he has pointed out why he was speaking. He cannot be indifferent to matters deeply concerning Wales, for example, or those involving moral issues. Thus when he opposed the Sunday Trading Bill, he prefaced his remarks by explaining that he was not speaking for or against any party, but defending the moral basis of the nation's life. The question of keeping Sunday different from any other day of the week had been a top priority for him throughout his membership of the House of Commons. He had no intention of changing that priority when he took his seat in the House of Lords. Whenever opportunity arises he raises his voice against the commercialization of the one day of the week Christian believers seek as a reminder that Christian values are the foundation of our way of life. This view is not popular in the House of Lords, but this has never deterred Tonypandy from proclaiming his personal convictions.

The Jewish Question

Another somewhat unexpected issue on which George has fought with passion is the prosecution of alleged Nazi war criminals where evidence of their crime is strong. Whenever issues concerning Jewish people are raised his voice is heard loud and clear.

When George is asked why his feelings are so strong on these matters, he has two answers. First, he tells of his visit to Germany as an MP and his experience at Auschwitz; then he emphasizes the debt Christianity owes to the Jewish people. The Christian faith was born in Judaism, Jesus was reared in a Jewish home. All His disciples were Jews. George's attitude did not differ from that of Martin Luther, the great Reformer who wrote in 1523:

> If the Apostles, who also were Jews, had dealt with us Gentiles as we Gentiles deal with the Jews, there would have been no Christians among the Gentiles. But seeing that they have acted in such a brotherly way towards us, we in turn should act in a brotherly way towards the Jews . . . For we ourselves are not yet fully their equals, much less their superiors.

George often quotes St Luke's reference to the fact that Jesus went to synagogue regularly on the Sabbath Day and that the Scriptures he read were the Old Testament. George avers that he feels a kinship with the Jewish people whom God chose to prepare the world for the coming of the Messiah. But he has made friends with Jews and Arabs alike although, in Israel, his sympathies are usually with the Jews rather than the Palestinians.

During his second serious illness, when he was weakened by chemotherapy and radium treatment, he received a letter from Prime Minister Shamir expressing sympathy and informing him that prayers for his recovery were being said in the Holy City, Jerusalem. George cherished this knowledge. Shamir is not the first Prime Minister of Israel to be a friend to George. When he was still Mr Speaker, during a visit to Israel, Prime Minister Begin invited him to speak to members of the Knesset. Nor are his Jewish friends confined to Israel or those in high places. When his mother died in 1972, the Jewish ladies in Cardiff collected more than £10,000 in her memory and presented it to a school for handicapped children in Israel. George visited the school later and saw his mother's name in a place of honour on a classroom wall. On that same visit he went to a laboratory in the Weitzman Institute, which was named after him. "Of course, I feel close to the people of Israel," he says.

In 1991, as anti-Semitism began to reassert itself in Europe, George became President of the Inter-Parliamentary Association against Anti-Semitism.

Nazi War Criminals

George's sympathy with Israel comes out very clearly in his speeches in the House of Lords. On 8th November 1989, when the House was discussing the closure of the Universities of the West Bank, he defended the Israeli action as necessary to preserve law and order:

> It is much easier in the quiet of this Chamber to give advice to Israelis on how to deal with what is a very difficult situation and there ought to be a little more sympathy for those who are trying to bring law and order into that part of the world.

A few months later, when the Israelis had taken some action, he pointed out that patience and time were needed:

> as all the schools were reopened in July 1989 [he is speaking on the 6th March 1990] and as the further education colleges were opened in January of this year, would it not be helpful if those who have influence in the Arab world tried to stop the universities being used as centres of terrorism in order that Israel might reopen the universities as well, as it is eager to do?

But his sympathies for the Jews were expressed even more strongly in the debates about war criminals who are still at large and living in the United Kingdom. The issue concerned the law. Those who were not United Kingdom citizens when they committed the atrocities, could not now legally be charged, because their crimes had been committed in Germany or German occupied territories. The Nuremberg trials had set a time limit to such proceedings. On 4th December 1989, there was a lively debate on the Report of an Inquiry into the matter of prosecuting Nazi war criminals still at large. The Motion was, "that the House take notice of this Report". The Report had asked that legislation should be introduced to make it possible for persons in the United Kingdom to be prosecuted for atrocities which they are alleged to have committed during the war when they were not resident in the United Kingdom.

The debate began about 3 p.m. and the issue turned on the problem of retrospective legislation on the one hand and justice to be done on the other. George was on the side of justice and pointed out

338

that no new crime was involved in this retrospective legislation. He did not speak until after 7 p.m. He began with a criticism of Lord Macaulay who had preceded him: "He ended up in the same state as the Government—not knowing what to do and seeking the advice of the House." George pointed out that everybody agreed that what had been done was horrible. He referred to the shattering effect upon him of his visit to Auschwitz in 1945 when he was so sickened by the sight of hair shaved from the heads of victims, false teeth in heaps and mountains of children's shoes. That and Nuremberg left indelible marks on his mind. "By chance," he said, "I am the first Gentile to speak in favour of the Motion." Against the amendment that "there being no reasonable assumption of a fair trial", he pointed out that all the House was being asked to do was "when there is sufficient evidence, to ensure that there is a prosecution". He tried to persuade the House that the courts were competent to decide whether there was sufficient evidence and maintained that they would ensure a fair trial. The House agreed to take note of the Report.

Six months later, on 4th June 1990, the War Crimes Bill came to the House of Lords for its Second Reading. This time the Government backed a Motion, "that the courts in this country should have jurisdiction to try offences of murder (and other atrocities) which were committed, as war crimes in Germany or German occupied territory, during the period of the Second World War." A negative Amendment, "there being no reasonable assumption of a fair trial" was proposed by Lord Campbell of Alloway and it was carried after many hours of debate into the midnight hours, by 207 votes to 74. The numbers tell how well attended the debate was. Passions were roused on both sides and it was a powerful debate. Viscount Tonypandy spoke against the amendment with skill and persuasion. His kinship to the Jews was clear that night.

Against those who argued that, in the words of the *Times* editorial that morning, "the Bill would breach the principle hallowed by common law, that no man may be punished retrospectively for an offence for which he could not justly have been tried at the time", he argued convincingly and with righteous anger:

> The truth is that these people could have been tried at the time, and would have been if they had been British citizens. However, they hid by crawling into the mother of democracies and hiding their identities successfully for forty years. It is now claimed that

we should overlook the dramatic story told us by the noble Lord, Lord Kagan, who was in one of the camps.

I am sometimes asked about forgiveness . . . It is not we who are asked to forgive; the people who should forgive are not here. It is those whose children had their brains battered out before them, those who saw their own mothers led to the gas chambers. They are not here to forgive. What an impertinence for anyone here, for a non-elected person, to say, "We forgive on behalf of those people." It is offensive even to suggest that somehow that is our right. If it were, then forgiveness applies to every offence committed within the realm. We should disband our law courts; we should say, "Forgive."

A just society requires law. All that this Bill does is to ensure that the laws that apply to the rest of us shall apply to them since they asked to be British. They wanted to come here. Was it because they liked our way of life, or was it to escape the prosecution to which they knew they were properly liable?

To those who argued that evidence would be so uncertain, because no one could recognize an offender after forty years, he said:

I am satisfied that anyone who saw their persecutor in a concentration camp would, as the noble Lord, Lord Kagan reminded us, remember all right. What is more, those who did these things —and the courts will decide who did them—know and would remember."

The House was deeply moved by this impassioned appeal for the victims of the Holocaust and the desire to see justice done for them.

The Constitutional Argument

Viscount Tonypandy, now a seasoned member of the House of Lords, was also concerned that the Upper House should not go beyond its role as a revising Chamber—"During the seven years that I have been in this House we have been a revising Chamber." He saw danger in the House of Lords acting in a way which exceeded its powers and privileges. The House of Commons has passed a bill with a large majority and the House of Lords may revise it, but it is not its function to reject it:

I love being in this House. I enjoy it here. I like the fellowship and the courtesies. However, I have never deluded myself that we can have a parliamentary democracy where real power is in the hands of non-elected people. I have never believed that. I wish that my noble friend Lord Callaghan of Cardiff were here; we used to sing the same song together in the old days. However, I disagree with him tonight. I must confess that if during his administration this House had said that it knew better than the Commons, there would not have been the same speech from him that we heard tonight.

George was in fighting form and he even suggested that if the House of Lords defied the Commons it would be digging its own grave. He ended with this as the main constitutional argument:

> Let us remember that the Bill is a government Bill; it is not a Private Members' Bill. If tonight this Chamber defeats the Government, noble Lords on the Opposition benches will know what to expect. I hope they will stay and vote against the amendment. The only way to protect our unwritten constitution is to ensure that we keep our power to be a revising Chamber and not take the ultimate step of throwing the Bill out.

Tolerance and Respect

On many occasions throughout his life, from the Rhondda Valley to the House of Lords, George has learnt to respect people of integrity. He has his prejudices as much as anyone else, but they are never carried over into personal relations. When he meets a person of sincerity or an unpopular cause, he can act contrary to his own prejudices. A good example was the agreement to allow the Roman Catholics to celebrate mass in the crypt of the Palace of Westminster. Much earlier, despite his dislike of Communists, he could resent the injustice with which they were treated. In his long career he has met many people who held quite different views from his and were of different religious persuasions. His close connection with the Jews did not change his faith in Jesus Christ his Saviour. And his preference for Israel in the conflict with Palestinians did not prevent him from recognizing a man of faith and integrity in Sheik Ahmed Yaki Yamani. Writing of him during his retirement, George says:

> Through my friendship with Sir Julian Hodge, I came to know Sheik Yamani, the oil minister of Saudi Arabia, who became a frequent visitor to Speaker's House. He is my idea of a sheik, very cultured, courteous and possessed of great natural dignity.

He is a deeply religious man but not in the fanatical, cruel sense of Ayatollah Khomeini, and like me he is a firm believer in the golden rule: Do unto others as you would have them do unto you.

It was Sheik Yamani's utter dedication to his Muslim faith that inspired George to admire him so much. A man of faith can understand a man of faith because there is a wellspring of devotion to God which is deeper than all the divisions in our theology. Apart from the respect for a sincere faith, George found that Yamani's world vision appealed to his own political attitude and his respect for other peoples' faith. Neither Yamani nor George are proselytizers: mutual respect for each other's trust in God binds their friendship.

George Thomas at Eighty-three

It is in the Rhondda that he looks his best. There he is happy and relaxed. You would take him for a man of seventy, a Welshman, even before he speaks, and then that accent brings out the warmth of the Welsh valleys and his smile has the appearance of one who knows that he is loved. You would think he could sit back now, basking in the honours pouring in upon him, the affection so widely expressed and the knowledge that he has had a fruitful life. The poverty of his childhood, remembered in the autumnal years, loses its pain, and memory retains the joys to be recalled and lived again. Ever a willing and compulsive storyteller, there are no stories he tells with greater enjoyment, both to himself and his listeners, than those of his early years. But he has not yet retired. He inherited a good constitution—from his grandfather, John Tilbury, and from his mother. They both lived to a good age and he shows no sign of decline. He has always believed that activity enables elderly people to retain their liveliness of mind and there is no doubt that he is a shining example of this. His diary would pale the face of many a young man.

His preaching continues unabated, as he is aware that his presence as preacher for the day would give a boost to any congregation. Although he speaks in famous churches with large congregations, he has a special delight in preaching in small churches, where his name draws unusually large crowds. To one chapel in the Welsh village of Llangwm, his advertised name drew a large congregation from a wide area. Consequently cars lined the narrow streets. His humour, which has never deserted him, gave him a good opening: "I knew Llangwm," he said, "but I had no idea of your traffic problem!" It is in these small chapels that he is most courteously welcomed, and courtesy means much to him. He likes things done decently and in order. There is a touch of vanity in all this, which he frankly admits, but he is also sensitive to the right way of doing things. He has always been so, but seven years as Mr Speaker taught him the abiding value of maintaining, with ceremonies that are right, the dignity of the occasion and the place.

He continues the activities of his public life through the years of retirement as though no change has occurred and taking very little account of his age, except sometimes to say to his friends who are anxious about him, "Yes, I think perhaps I have been doing too much." But he goes on still doing too much—opening hospitals, preaching, entertaining, debating, launching charity appeals, making celebrity appearances on stage, radio and screen, accepting awards. One of these awards pleased him very much—he was named, "After-dinner Speaker of the Year". He loves speaking, and prepares even his shortest speech with great care. Like a good communicator, he thinks in terms of the listener and not of the speaker. A clever remark is examined to see if it might offend someone or be misunderstood. If it would, then it is out.

Looking back, George can give thanks that he was brought up in the Rhondda, among real people. He can also chart his life as it has been enriched by friendships, to which he freely refers in his speeches in the House of Lords. His debt to his family is considerable, and has been acknowledged many times. His mother, of course, was the dominant influence, through her care, her encouragement and her correction.

Above all he has kept his wonder that a boy from a mining family could attain such heights. It has given him pride in himself, but also in his country, that such a thing has been possible.

And so it goes on . . .

One of the results of the decline of religion in modern society has been the inability of many people to contemplate death as a triumph. We are all affected by this deficiency, even believers, and George among them. Yet, basically, there is in him an assurance that, even if

343

he may regret the prospect of leaving a life as full and enjoyable as his has been, the future is far greater. That is not sentiment, but faith.

As the years mount up, it is faith that both inspires and sustains him. The hymns of the Wesleys and of Isaac Watts give him strength to continue his Christian witness. This is well expressed in a hymn, translated by John Wesley, from Zinzendorf's hymn book by Johann Andreas Rotha:

> Now I have found the ground wherein
> Sure my soul's anchor may remain.

The imagery of the anchor holding fast continues:

> This anchor shall my soul sustain,
> When earth's foundations pass away;
> Mercy's full power I then shall prove,
> Loved with an everlasting love.

BIBLIOGRAPHY

Clement Attlee, *As It Happened*, William Heinemann 1954.

Hugh Dalton, *High Tide and After: A Book of Memoirs 1945–1960*, Muller 1962.

Julius Goebel and J. C. J. Metford, *The Struggle for the Falklands*, New Haven 1982.

J. E. D. Hall, *Labour's First Year*, Penguin 1947.

Kenneth Harris, *Attlee*, Weidenfeld and Nicholson 1982.

Adrian Hastings, *A History of English Christianity 1920–1985*, Collins 1986.

Dennis Healey, *The Time of My Life*, Michael Joseph 1989.

Philip Laundy, *The Office of Speaker*, Cassells 1964.

Parliamentary Reports, Hansard, House of Commons.

Charles Preece, *Woman of the Valleys: The Story of Mother Shepherd*, Mother Shepherd Project, Neath 1988.

George Thomas, "The Changing Face of Parliamentary Democracy" in *Parliamentary Affairs*, Autumn 1982. (The First Hansard Society Lecture.)

Malcolm Thomson, *David Lloyd George*, London 1948.

The Times "House of Commons", 1945, 1950 and 1951.

Viscount Tonypandy, *George Thomas, Mr Speaker*, Century Publishing Co. Ltd 1985. (Memoirs.)

INDEX

Index